THE VISION BOOK OF
FOOTBALL RECORDS 2011

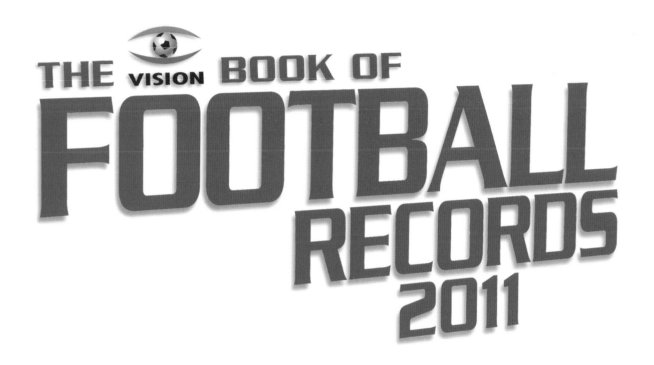

BY CLIVE BATTY

VSP

Published by Vision Sports Publishing in 2010

Vision Sports Publishing
19-23 High Street
Kingston upon Thames
Surrey
KT1 1LL

www.visionsp.co.uk

ISBN: 978-1905326-99-0

Editor: Jim Drewett
Design: Neal Cobourne
Kit images: David Moor, www.historicalkits.co.uk
All pictures: Getty Images, except Didier Drogba cover picture (Press Association)

gettyimages®

Printed and bound in Slovakia by Neografia
A CIP catalogue record for this book is available from the British Library

INTRODUCTION

Welcome to the 2011 edition of the *Vision Book of Football Records*. Much has changed in the football world since the first edition hit the shelves last year, sparking scenes of excitement outside bookshops not seen since the publication of the last Harry Potter novel (OK, that may be a slight exaggeration...oh, alright, it's a big fat porky).

Anyway, as I was saying, the football map has altered considerably in the last 12 months.

As just about everyone on the planet must know, Spain are the new world champions; incredibly, little Blackpool are now a Premier League club (even the Seasiders' own manager, Ian Holloway, sometimes sounds like he can't quite believe it!); and, in the wake of England's gruesome World Cup campaign, Fabio Capello's reputation has plummeted from 'crack coach' to 'clueless chump'. Apart from Paul, the amazing psychic octopus, who would have predicted these unlikely developments a year ago?

Whether unexpected or not, all the changes that have occurred in the sport over the past season are reflected in the pages of this revised edition. As well as updating all the facts, figures, stats and records, numerous new entries have been added for players, managers and clubs who have upped their game over the last season. So it's a big Vision welcome to, among many others, England starlet James Milner, Spanish World Cup hero Andres Iniesta, Liverpool supremo Roy Hodgson and, of course, new Football League clubs Oxford United and Stevenage. To any players flicking through this book who are disappointed to find they have not been included, there is a simple message: score more goals or make more saves and you too may be rewarded with your very own personal entry next year!

Despite all the revisions, the basic core of the book has remained as before. So, within these pages you'll find essential facts about all 92 English league clubs (plus Conference side AFC Wimbledon who, let it not be forgotten, won the FA Cup in fairly recent memory in their previous incarnation) and all the SPL clubs (plus Queen's Park, the dominant force in the early years of the game in Scotland). In addition, there are entries for the most famous and successful teams from continental Europe and South America.

There are also mini-profiles of the top Premiership stars and the world's greatest internationals, not forgetting many of the legendary players from years gone by (from Carlos Alberto to Dino Zoff). Add in a load of managers, pundits, administrators and club owners and you can pretty much take it for granted that if someone is an important figure in the compelling drama that is modern football they will feature somewhere in this book.

Nor is that all. You'll find lots, too, on the top soccer nations (it's tempting to add here 'plus England, Scotland, Wales and Northern Ireland'...but that would be a bit below the belt), the leading domestic and international competitions and the most prestigious individual awards. There are also a host of 'wild card' entries on a range of different subjects such as 'animals' (including our previously mentioned eight-armed friend Paul... although, obviously, he already knew he'd made the cut), 'Pop Songs' (did you know that the England squad have had two number one hits?) and 'Superstitions' (discover which Premier League goalkeeper keeps a vial of Holy Water in his net).

So, all in all, there's more than enough here to keep you occupied when you're not watching footy, improving your keepy-uppy record, or honing your skills on the vuvuzela.

CLIVE BATTY

All statistics in the *Vision Book of Records 2011* are correct up until the start of the 2010/11 season

ABANDONED MATCHES

In British football, a match which has to be abandoned for whatever reason before its completion is generally replayed in full at a later date, although individual competition rules may allow for the result to stand. In the early years of the game in England, until a rule change in 1899, only the time lost was played later.

• Only three England internationals have been abandoned. The first, against Argentina in Buenos Aires on 17th May 1953, was called off after 21 minutes when torrential rain made the pitch unplayable. The second, against Czechoslovakia in Bratislava on 29th October 1975, was abandoned after 16 minutes due to fog but was played in full the following evening with the home side winning 2-1. Then, on 15th March 1995, crowd trouble brought England's match against Ireland in Dublin to a premature halt after 27 minutes.

• The shortest English game ever took place in 1894, when a raging blizzard caused the match between Stoke and Wolves at the Victoria Ground to be called off after just three minutes. Only 400 hardy fans had braved the elements and even they must have been secretly relieved when referee Mr Helme decided the atrocious conditions made any further play impossible.

• A bomb scare led to the match between Real Madrid and Real Sociedad at the Bernabeu stadium being abandoned on 12th December 2004. Amid chaotic scenes, hundreds of fans streamed across the pitch on their way to the exits. England captain David Beckham ended up wandering around in the streets outside while still wearing his boots and kit. Under Spanish FA rules, only the two remaining minutes were played when

IS THAT A FACT?
Bulgarian sides Balkan Belogradchik and Gigant Belene played the shortest match ever on 28th March 2010. Gigant started four players short but when one of their number limped off after a minute the ref had to abandon the match, as the rules state that teams must field at least seven players.

Amazingly this Bundesliga match was not abandoned!

the sides met again three weeks later – just enough time, as it turned out, for Zinedine Zidane to score the winner from the penalty spot for Real in their 2-1 victory.

• Fighting between players has led to numerous matches being abandoned, especially in South America (it's something to do with the Latin temperament, apparently). On 19th April 1990, for instance, a cup match between Uruguayan giants Nacional and Penarol Chile was called off after the referee sent off 20 players following a mass brawl in the centre of the pitch.

• The match between Hamilton and Clyde on 9th September 2006 also failed to go the distance after fighting broke out – although this time it was the coaching staff rather than the players who were trading punches. Tempers flared on the touchline in the 75th minute after an accidental clash between Hamilton defender Ross McCabe and Clyde striker Dougie Imrie, leading the referee to abandon the game.

ABERDEEN

Year founded: 1903
Ground: Pittodrie Stadium (22,199)
Nickname: The Dons
Biggest win: 13-0 v Peterhead (1923)
Heaviest defeat: 0-8 v Celtic (1965)
Colours: Red shirts, red shorts, red socks

Aberdeen were founded in 1903, following the amalgamation of three city clubs, Aberdeen, Orion and Victoria United. The following year the club joined the Scottish Second Division and in 1905 the Dons were elected to an expanded First Division. Aberdeen have remained in the top flight ever since, a record shared with just Rangers and Celtic.

• The club was originally known as the Whites and later as the Wasps or the Black and Golds after their early strips, but in 1913 became known as the Dons. This nickname is sometimes said to derive from the involvement of professors at Aberdeen University in the foundation of the club, but is more likely to be a contraction of the word 'Aberdonians', the term used to describe people from Aberdeen.

• Aberdeen first won the Scottish title in 1955, before enjoying a trio of championship successes in the 1980s under manager Alex Ferguson. Before he moved on to even greater triumphs at Old Trafford, Fergie also led the Dons to four victories in five years in the Scottish Cup, confirming Aberdeen's status as the best Scottish team of the period.

• The club's finest hour, though, came in 1983 when the Dons became only the second Scottish club (after Rangers in 1972) to win the European Cup-Winners' Cup, beating Real Madrid 2-1 in the final. Later that year Aberdeen defeated Hamburg over two legs to claim the European Super Club, and remain the only Scottish side to win two European trophies.

• In 1984 Aberdeen became the first club outside the Old Firm to win the Double, after finishing seven points clear at the top of the league and beating Celtic 2-1 in the Scottish Cup final.

• Since those glory days, however, the club's fortunes have nosedived. Trophyless since the 1995/96 season, Aberdeen's lowest ebb was reached in 2000 when, after finishing rock bottom of the SPL, the Dons were only saved from relegation because Falkirk's ground did not meet league requirements.

• Scottish international defender Willie Miller has made more appearances for the club than any other player, an impressive 556 games between 1973-90. Hotshot striker Joe Harper is the Dons' record goalscorer, with 205 during two spells at Pittodrie (1969-72 and 1976-81).

• Aberdeen's most capped player is Miller's long-time defensive partner and current Birmingham boss Alex McLeish, who made 77 appearances for Scotland between 1977-90.

• Famed as one of the coldest grounds in Britain, Pittodrie Stadium can claim two historic 'firsts'. In the 1920s it became the first ground to have dug-outs installed, following a request by innovative team coach Donald Coleman. Then, in 1978, Pittodrie became Britain's first ever all-seater stadium.

HONOURS
Division 1 champions 1955
Premier Division champions 1980, 1984, 1985
Scottish Cup 1947, 1970, 1982, 1983, 1984, 1986, 1990
League Cup 1956, 1977, 1986, 1990, 1996
European Cup Winners' Cup 1983
European Super Cup 1983

ROMAN ABRAMOVICH

Born: Saratov, Russia, 24th October 1966

Chelsea owner Roman Abramovich has a fortune estimated at £7 billion and, since buying the Blues from previous owner Ken Bates in July 2003, he has invested hundreds of millions in the club in an attempt to establish the west Londoners as a dominant force in the English and European game.

• Abramovich's massive spending spree has been rewarded with three league titles and five domestic cups, including

TOP 10

RICHEST PREMIER LEAGUE SHAREHOLDERS

1.	Sheikh Mansour, Manchester City	Net wealth, £17 billion
2.	Roman Abramovich, Chelsea	£7 billion
3.	Joe Lewis, Tottenham	£2 billion
4.	Alisher Usmanov, Arsenal	£1.5 billion
5.	Lord Grantchester, Everton	£1.2 billion
6.	Mike Ashley, Newcastle United	£700 million
7.	Mohamed Al-Fayed, Fulham	£650 million
8.	Peter Coates, Stoke City	£400 million
9.	The Walker family, Blackburn Rovers	£400 million
10.	The Warburton family, Bolton	£330 million

the Double in 2010, but his burning ambition to see Chelsea win the Champions League has still to be realised. The Blues' failure to capture the biggest prize of all has led Abramovich to part company with former managers Claudio Ranieri, Jose Mourinho, Avram Grant and Luiz Felipe Scolari.

• After starting out selling retread car tyres, Abramovich's business career took off when he began trading oil products out of Russia's largest refinery in western Siberia. He gradually acquired a controlling interest in Sibneft, the country's main oil company, before selling his share to the Russian government controlled Gazprom for an eye-watering £7.4 billion in 2005.

• Abramovich enjoys a lifestyle befitting his billionaire status, owning a number of luxury homes, three yachts and a private Boeing 737 jet.

AC MILAN

Year founded: 1899
Ground: San Siro (82,955)
Nickname: Rossoneri
Colours: Red-and-black striped shirts, white shorts, black socks

One of the giants of European football, the club was founded by British expatriates as the Milan Cricket and Football Club in 1899. Apart from a period during the fascist dictatorship of Benito Mussolini, the club has always been known as 'Milan' rather than the Italian 'Milano'.

• Milan were the first Italian side to win the European Cup, beating Benfica in the final at Wembley in 1963, and have gone on to win the trophy seven times – a record surpassed only by Real Madrid, with nine victories.

• In 1986 the club was acquired by the businessman and future Italian President Silvio Berlusconi, who invested in star players like Marco van Basten, Ruud Gullit and Frank Rijkaard. Milan went on

David Beckham felt the part at Milan!

to enjoy a golden era under coaches Arrigo Sacchi and Fabio Capello, winning three European Cups and four Serie A titles between 1988-94. Incredibly, the club were undefeated for 58 games between 1991-93, the longest such run in Italian football history.

• **Milan's San Siro stadium, which they share with city rivals Inter, is the largest in Italy, with a capacity of over 80,000. As well as football, the stadium has hosted many pop concerts and in November 2009 was the venue for a rugby international between Italy and the All Blacks which attracted a crowd of 81,018 – a record for Italian rugby.**

• Milan's links with Britain have continued into the modern era with a number of stars from these shores, including Jimmy Greaves, Ray Wilkins and David Beckham, having spells with the Italian titans.

> HONOURS
> **Serie A champions** 1901, 1906, 1907, 1951, 1955, 1957, 1959, 1962, 1968, 1979, 1988, 1992, 1993, 1994, 1996, 1999, 2004
> **Italian Cup** 1967, 1972, 1973, 1977, 2003
> **European Cup/Champions League** 1963, 1969, 1989, 1990, 1994, 2003, 2007
> **European Cup Winners' Cup** 1968, 1973
> **European Super Cup** 1989, 1990, 1994, 2003, 2007
> **Intercontinental Cup** 1969, 1989, 1990
> **Club World Cup** 2007

ACCRINGTON STANLEY

> **Year founded:** 1968
> **Ground:** Fraser Eagle Stadium (5,057)
> **Nickname:** The Stans
> **Biggest win:** 10-1 v Lincoln United (1999)
> **Heaviest defeat:** 2-8 v Peterborough (2008)
> **Colours:** Red shirts, red shorts, red socks

Accrington Stanley were founded at a meeting in a working men's club in Accrington in 1968, as a successor to the former Football League club of the same name which had folded two years earlier.

• **Conference champions in 2006, Stanley were promoted to the Football League in place of relegated Oxford United. Ironically, when a financial crisis forced the old Accrington Stanley to resign from the League in March 1962 the club that replaced them the following season was Oxford!**

• In 2010 Stanley reached the fourth round of the FA Cup for only the fourth time in their history. However, their hopes of making a first ever appearance in the fifth round were dashed by Fulham, who won the tie 3-1.

• **With a capacity of just 5,057, the club's tiny Crown Ground is the smallest in the Football League.**

> HONOURS
> **Conference champions** 2006

TONY ADAMS

> **Born:** Romford, 10th October 1966
> **Position:** Defender
> **Club career:**
> 1983-2002 Arsenal 504 (32)
> **International record:**
> 1987-2000 England 66 (5)

Arsenal legend Tony Adams is the only player in English football history to have skippered a title-winning side in three different decades. 'Mr Arsenal', as he is sometimes called, led the Gunners to the championship in 1989, 1991, 1998 and 2002, while his glittering career also saw him land silverware in the FA Cup (1993, 1998 and 2002), the League Cup (1987 and 1993) and the European Cup-Winners' Cup (1994).

• A one-club man as a player, Adams made his debut for the Gunners in 1983 and his impressive displays at centre half soon ensured he was a first-team regular. He won his first England cap in 1987 aged just 21 and went on to represent his country 66 times, captaining the Three Lions at Euro '96.

• **Adams's total of 668 games for Arsenal in all competitions puts him second in the Gunners' list of all-time appearance-makers behind David O'Leary. The longevity of his career, though, is all the more remarkable given that for much of it he was a self-confessed alcoholic. In 1990**

Adams's excessive drinking led to a conviction for drink-driving and he served two months in prison. He eventually sought treatment for his condition in 1996 and, encouraged by new Arsenal manager Arsene Wenger, put his boozing days behind him.

• In 2003 Adams became manager of Wycombe Wanderers, but left the club the following year citing personal reasons. In 2006 he was appointed assistant manager of Portsmouth, becoming manager in 2008 when Harry Redknapp moved to Tottenham. However, after Pompey picked up just ten points in 16 games while Adams was in charge, he was sacked in February 2009. The following year he returned to management with Azerbaijan club FC Gabala.

EMMANUEL ADEBAYOR

> **Born:** Lome, Togo, 26th February 1984
> **Position:** Striker
> **Club career:**
> 2001-03 Metz 44 (15)
> 2003-06 Monaco 78 (18)
> 2006-09 Arsenal 105 (46)
> 2009- Manchester City 26 (14)
> **International record:**
> 2000-10 Togo 38 (16)

In July 2009 Emmanuel Adebayor became the most expensive African player ever when he moved from Arsenal to cash-rich Manchester City for a staggering £25 million. He enjoyed a decent first season at Eastlands, scoring 14 league goals and helping City to finish in fifth place, their best ever showing in the Premier League.

• **Adebayor signed for Arsenal from Monaco for a bargain £3 million in January 2006, having previously played for Metz. In 2004 he helped Monaco reach the Champions League final, but was an unused substitute for the French side's defeat by Porto. He also missed out on Arsenal's Champions League final defeat by Barcelona two years later, being cup-tied after playing for Monaco in an earlier round.**

• Nicknamed 'Baby Kanu' for his striking resemblance to former Arsenal star Nwankwo Kanu, Adebayor scored an impressive 30 goals in the 2007/08 campaign. Less happily, he made the headlines for the wrong reasons that

same season after an on-pitch clash with Gunners team-mate Nicklas Bendtner.

• In January 2010, four years after helping his country reach the World Cup finals for the first time, Adebayor was travelling on the Togo team bus to the Africa Cup of Nations finals in Angola when it came under machine gun attack. Although Adebayor was physically unscathed in the incident the emotional scars remained and he later announced his retirement from international football.

AFC WIMBLEDON

Year founded: 2002
Ground: The Fans' Stadium, Kingsmeadow (4,722)
Nickname: The Dons
Biggest win: 9-0 v Chessington United (2004) and v Slough Town (2007)
Heaviest defeat: 0-5 v York City (2010)
Colours: Blue shirts with yellow trim, blue shorts, blue socks

AFC Wimbledon were founded in 2002 by supporters of the former Premiership club Wimbledon, who opposed the decision of the FA to sanction the 'franchising' of their club when they allowed it to move 56 miles north from their south London base to Milton Keynes in Buckinghamshire (the club later becoming the MK Dons).

• In October 2006 an agreement was reached with the MK Dons that the honours won by the old Wimbledon would return to the London Borough of Merton. This was an important victory for the fans of AFC, who view their club as the true successors to Wimbledon FC.

• In their former incarnation, Wimbledon won the FA Cup in 1988, beating hot favourites Liverpool 1-0 at Wembley. Incredibly, the Dons had only been elected to the Football League just 12 years earlier, but enjoyed a remarkable rise through the divisions, winning promotion to the top flight in 1986. Dubbed the 'Crazy Gang' for their physical approach on the pitch and madcap antics off it, Wimbledon remained in the Premiership until 2000.

• Between February 2003 and December 2004 AFC went an amazing 78 league games without defeat, a record for senior football in the UK. They are now in the Conference, just one promotion away from a return to the Football League.

> HONOURS
> *Division 4 champions 1983 (As Wimbledon FC)*
> *FA Cup 1988 (As Wimbledon FC)*

AFRICA CUP OF NATIONS

The Africa Cup of Nations was founded in 1957. The first tournament was a decidedly small affair consisting of just three competing teams (Egypt, Ethiopia and hosts Sudan) after South Africa's invitation was withdrawn when they refused to send a multi-racial squad to the finals. Egypt were the first winners, beating Ethiopia 4-0 in the final in Khartoum.

• With seven victories, current holders Egypt are the most successful side in the history of the competition. After triumphing in Angola in 2010 following a 1-0 victory over Ghana in the final the north Africans claimed a record three consecutive trophies. However, Ghana were the first country to win the tournament three times and, following their third success in 1978, were allowed to keep the original Abdel Abdullah Salem Trophy, named after the first president of the Confederation of African Football.

• The final has been decided on penalties on six occasions, with Ivory Coast winning the longest shoot-out 11-10 against Ghana in 1992.

• The top scorer in the history of the competition is Cameroon striker Samuel Eto'o, who has hit a total of 18 goals in the tournament to date. Mulamba Ndaye of Zaire holds the record for the most goals in a single tournament, with nine in 1974.

"Now you're Ghana believe us..."

Stanley Matthews literally hangs up his boots, aged 50

AGE

Wing legend Sir Stanley Matthews is the oldest player to appear in the top flight of English football. 'The Ageless Wonder' had celebrated his 50th birthday five days before playing his last match for Stoke against Fulham in February 1965.

• Matthews, though, was something of a spring chicken compared to Neil McBain, the New Brighton manager, who had to go in goal for his side's Division Three (North) match against Hartlepool during an injury crisis in 1947. He was 51 and 120 days at the time, the oldest player in the history of English football.

IS THAT A FACT?
The youngest player to appear for a professional team anywhere in the world is Mauricio Baldivieso, who was three days short of his 13th birthday when he came on as a sub in the Bolivian first division for Aurora FC on 19th July 2009. "I am the happiest man in the world," he said after his nine-minute cameo against La Paz FC.

• Manchester City goalkeeper John Burridge became the oldest player in the Premiership when he came off the bench at half-time in City's match against Newcastle in April 1995, aged 43. The youngest player is Fulham's Matthew Briggs, who was aged 16 and 65 days when he made his debut for the Cottagers against Middlesbrough in May 2007.

• The oldest international in British football was Wales's Billy Meredith, who played against England in 1920 at the age of 45. England's youngest international is Arsenal winger Theo Walcott, who was 17 and 75 days when he played as a sub in the 3-1 victory over Hungary at Old Trafford in May 2006.

• The youngest player to appear in the Football League is Barnsley striker Reuben Noble-Lazarus, who was 15 years and 45 days old when he faced Ipswich Town in September 2008. Afterwards Barnsley boss Simon Davey joked Noble-Lazarus would be rewarded with a pizza as he was too young to be paid!

AIR CRASHES

On 6th February 1958 eight members of the Manchester United 'Busby Babes' team, including England internationals Roger Byrne, Duncan Edwards and Tommy Taylor, were killed in the Munich Air Disaster. Their plane crashed while attempting to take off in a snowstorm at Munich Airport, where it had stopped to refuel after a European Cup tie in Belgrade. In total, 23 people died in the crash, although manager Matt Busby and Bobby Charlton were among the survivors. Incredibly, United still managed to reach the FA Cup final that year, but lost at Wembley to Bolton Wanderers.

• The entire first team of Torino, the strongest Italian club at the time, were wiped out in an air disaster on 4th May 1949. Returning from a testimonial match in Portugal, the team's plane crashed into the Basilica of Superga outside Turin. Among the 31 dead were ten members of the Italian national side and the club's English manager, Leslie Lieveseley. Torino fielded their youth team in their four remaining fixtures and, with their opponents doing the same as a mark of respect, won a fifth consecutive league title at the end of the season.

• On 28th April 1993 a plane crash off the coast of Gabon claimed the lives of 18 members of the Zambia team. The squad was on its way to Senegal to play a World Cup qualifier.

AJAX

Year founded: 1900
Ground: Ajax ArenA (51,628)
Nickname: The Jews
Colours: White shirts with a broad red stripe, white shorts, white socks

Founded in 1900 in Amsterdam, Ajax are named after the Greek mythological hero. The club is the most successful in Holland, having won the league a record 29 times and the Dutch Cup a record 18 times.

• Ajax's white shirts with a broad vertical red stripe are among the most iconic in world football. However, the club's original kit was very different – an all-black outfit with a red sash tied around the players' waists.

• The Dutch side's most glorious decade

was in the 1970s when, with a team featuring legends like Johan Cruyff, Johan Neeskens and Ruud Krol, Ajax won the European Cup three times on the trot playing a fluid system known as 'Total Football'. In 1995 a young Ajax team won the trophy for a fourth time, Patrick Kluivert scoring the winner in the final against AC Milan.

• **When Ajax beat Torino in the final of the UEFA Cup in 1992 they became only the second team, after Juventus, to win all three major European trophies.**

• In 1996 Ajax moved into a brand new all-seater stadium, the Amsterdam ArenA. With a capacity in excess of 50,000 it is the largest football stadium in Holland.

HONOURS
***Dutch League champions** 1918, 1919, 1931, 1932, 1934, 1937, 1939, 1947, 1957, 1960, 1966, 1967, 1968, 1970, 1972, 1973, 1977, 1979, 1980, 1982, 1983, 1985, 1990, 1994, 1995, 1996, 1998, 2002, 2004*
***Dutch Cup** 1917, 1943, 1961, 1967, 1970, 1971, 1972, 1979, 1983, 1986, 1987, 1993, 1998, 1999, 2002, 2006, 2007, 2010*
***European Cup/Champions League** 1971, 1972, 1973, 1995*
***European Cup Winners' Cup** 1987*
***UEFA Cup** 1992*
***European Super Cup** 1973, 1995*
***Intercontinental Cup** 1972, 1995*

Ajax are the most famous club in the Netherlands

CARLOS ALBERTO

Born: Brazil, 17th July 1944
Position: Defender
Club career:
1963-66 Fluminese
1966-74 Santos
1974-77 Fluminese
1977 Flamengo
1977-80 New York Cosmos 80 (6)
1981 California Surf 19 (2)
1982 New York Cosmos 20 (0)
International record:
1964-77 Brazil 53 (8)

Carlos Alberto captained the great Brazil team which won the World Cup in Mexico in 1970. After his side's thrilling 4-1 victory over Italy in the final, he was the last skipper ever to be presented with the Jules Rimet trophy as Brazil were given the prize permanently in recognition of their record three wins.

• Carlos Alberto's goal in the final, scored with a low shot on the run after a flowing end-to-end move, remains one of the best

and most famous in the history of football. In 2002 it was voted one of the top ten World Cup goals of all-time in a poll on FIFA's website.

• A defender who loved to overlap down the right wing, Carlos Alberto is a legend in South America and the wider football world. In 1998 he was voted into the World Team of the 20th Century by a panel of 250 football journalists, alongside fellow Brazilians Nilton Santos, Garrincha and Pele.

• After managing clubs in Brazil, Colombia and Mexico, Carlos Alberto became the boss of Azerbaijan in 2004. During his year in charge of the Azeris he bizarrely accused England striker Michael Owen of being "a midget who should be cleaning David Beckham's boots". He resigned from the post after running onto the pitch to launch a verbal attack on the referee during a World Cup qualifier against Poland.

TOP 10

BEST WORLD CUP GOALS*
1. Diego Maradona,
Argentina v England, 1986
2. Michael Owen,
England v Argentina, 1998
3. Pele,
Brazil v Sweden, 1958
4. Diego Maradona,
Argentina v Belgium, 1986
5. Gheorghe Hagi,
Romania v Colombia, 1994
6. Saeed Owairan,
Saudi Arabia v Belgium, 1994
7. Roberto Baggio,
Italy v Czechoslovakia, 1990
8. Carlos Alberto,
Brazil v Italy, 1970
9. Lothar Matthaeus,
West Germany v Yugoslavia, 1990
10. Vincenzo Scifo,
Belgium v Uruguay, 1990

* As voted in a 2002 poll on www.fifa.com

ALDERSHOT TOWN

Year founded: 1992
Ground: The Recreation Ground (7,100)
Nickname: The Shots
Biggest win: 4-0 v Canvey Island (2004) and v Haverhill Rangers (2006)
Heaviest defeat: 2-6 v Brighton (2000)
Colours: Red shirts with blue trim, red shorts, red socks

Aldershot Town were founded in the spring of 1992 as successors to Aldershot FC, who had been forced to resign from the Football League for financial reasons just weeks earlier. The newly-formed Shots began life in the Isthmian League Division Three, five tiers below the Football League.

• **Remarkably, the club rose through the divisions to finally clinch a place in League Two in 2008 by winning the Conference with a record tally of 101 points.**

• Although most of their short existence has been as a non-league club, a number of famous names have turned out for the Shots, including former Manchester United and England midfielder Neil Webb and Marcus Gayle, previously a battling striker with Wimbledon during the Dons'

Premiership heyday.

• **Left-back Jason Chewins made a record 489 appearances for Aldershot between 1994-2004. Stuart Udal, brother of England cricketer Shaun, is one of just four other players to play more than 200 games for the club.**

HONOURS
Conference champions 2008

JOHN ALDRIDGE

Born: Liverpool, 18th September 1958
Position: Striker
Club career:
1979-84 Newport County 170 (69)
1984-87 Oxford United 114 (72)
1987-89 Liverpool 83 (50)
1989-91 Real Sociedad 63 (33)
1992-98 Tranmere Rovers 242 (138)
International record:
1986-96 Republic of Ireland 69 (19)

Republic of Ireland international John Aldridge is the leading scorer in post-war English football, with an incredible total of 476 goals in 889 career appearances.

• **His most prolific campaign was with Oxford United in 1984/85, when his 30 goals in 42 matches helped the Us win the Second Division title and set a club record. The following season he was a member of the Oxford side that won** the League Cup, the club's only major honour.

• Aldridge won the league title with Liverpool in 1988, but in the same year set an unwanted record when he became the first player to miss a penalty in the FA Cup final at Wembley. His boob proved costly, as the Reds lost 1-0 to underdogs Wimbledon. However, the next year Aldridge scored after just four minutes in the final against Everton, a match Liverpool eventually won 3-2.

• **In 1989 Aldridge became the first non-Basque player to appear for Spanish side Real Sociedad, following a £1 million move from Anfield. He later returned to English football with Tranmere, managing the club for five years from 1996-2001.**

SAM ALLARDYCE

Born: Dudley, 19th October 1954
Managerial career:
1991-92 Limerick
1994-96 Blackpool
1997-99 Notts County
1999-2007 Bolton Wanderers
2007-08 Newcastle United
2008- Blackburn Rovers

One of the most experienced managers in the Premier League, Blackburn boss Sam Allardyce has overseen steady progress at

John Aldridge becomes the first person to miss an FA Cup final penalty, v Wimbledon in 1988

the Lancashire club since replacing Paul Ince in the Ewood Park hotseat in December 2008.

• **Big Sam, as he is known, had previously made his managerial name at Bolton. During his eight-year spell in charge, he led the Trotters back into the Premiership in 2001, to the Carling Cup final in 2004 and into the UEFA Cup for the first time in the club's history the following year.**

• In 2007 Allardyce left the Reebok stadium, saying: "I want silverware. I'm determined to get it before my days are over." He was soon appointed manager of Newcastle but only lasted half a season in the job before leaving by mutual agreement.

• **A no-nonsense central defender in his playing days, Allardyce won the Second Division title with Bolton in 1978 and captained Preston to promotion from the Third Division in 1987.**

CARLO ANCELOTTI

Born: Reggiolo, 18th September 1958
Managerial career:
1995-96 Reggiana
1996-98 Parma
1999-2001 Juventus
2001-09 AC Milan
2009- Chelsea

Chelsea boss Carlo Ancelotti enjoyed a tremendous first season at Stamford Bridge in 2009/10, guiding the Blues to the Premier League title and the FA Cup, following a 1-0 win over Portsmouth in the final at Wembley. The Double was the first in Chelsea's history, making Ancelotti an instant club legend.

• **The former Italian international made his name as a manager with his previous club, AC Milan, where he was in charge for eight years from 2001. During his time at the San Siro Ancelotti led the Italian giants to two triumphs in the Champions League, against Juventus in 2003 and Liverpool in 2007, as well as winning the Serie A title in 2004.**

• Ancelotti was manager of AC Milan for a total of 413 games, a record only surpassed by the legendary Nereo Rocco in three spells at the club between 1961-77. Prior to his appointment at the San Siro, Ancelotti had spells with Juventus and Parma, after starting his managerial

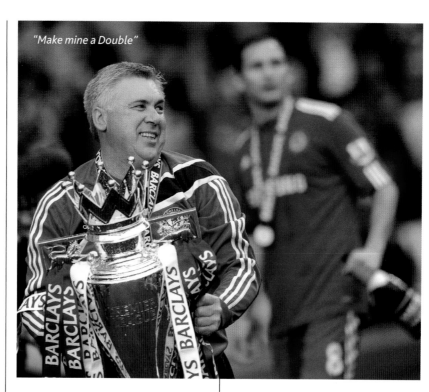

"Make mine a Double"

career at Reggiana, who he led to promotion from Serie B in 1996.

• **A talented and hard-working midfielder in his playing days, Ancelotti started his career with Parma before moving to Roma where he won the Coppa Italia four times and the Serie A title in 1983 before leaving the Italian capital to join AC Milan in 1987. In total he scored 35 goals in 338 league appearances.**

• In five years with Milan Ancelotti enjoyed further success, playing alongside stars such as Marco van Basten, Ruud Gullit and Paolo Maldini. A key member of the team, he helped Milan win the European Cup in both 1989 and 1990 and the Serie A title in 1988 and 1992.

NICOLAS ANELKA

Born: Versailles, France, 14th March 1979
Position: Striker
Club career:
1995-97 Paris St Germain 10 (1)
1997-99 Arsenal 65 (23)
1999-2000 Real Madrid 19 (2)
2000-02 Paris St Germain 39 (10)
2001-02 Liverpool (loan) 20 (4)
2002-05 Manchester City 89 (35)
2005-06 Fenerbahce 39 (14)
2006-08 Bolton Wanderers 53 (21)
2008- Chelsea 84 (31)
International record:
1998- France 69 (14)

Much-travelled striker Nicolas Anelka is one of the most expensive players in football history, his various moves having commanded more than £85 million in transfer fees since he first emerged as an exciting teenager in the mid 1990s with French club Paris St Germain.

• **Anelka joined Arsenal for a bargain £500,000 fee in 1997 and, the following year, helped the Gunners win the Double for a second time in the club's history. With the league already sewn up, Anelka scored in the FA Cup final against Newcastle at Wembley to wrap up a 2-0 victory. The next year, 1999, he was voted Young Player of the Year by his peers in the PFA.**

• In 1999 Anelka moved from Arsenal to Real Madrid in a £22.3 million deal. He won the Champions League with the Spanish giants the following year, but his time in Madrid was not altogether happy – after refusing to train, Anelka was dubbed 'Le Sulk' by the local media –

IS THAT A FACT?
Carlo Ancelotti is one of just six men to win the European Cup/ Champions League as both a player and manager. Real Madrid coach Miguel Munoz was the first man to achieve this feat in 1960, having previously won the European Cup as a player with the Spanish giants in 1956 and 1957.

and he was soon packing his bags again, returning to PSG.

• After spells with Liverpool, Manchester City, Fenerbahce and Bolton, Anelka joined Chelsea in January 2008. However, his first months at Stamford Bridge proved disappointing – summed up, perhaps, by his missed penalty in the 2008 Champions League final shoot-out which gifted the trophy to Manchester United. The next season, though, he was the top scorer in the Premiership with 19 goals. Then, in 2009/10, he helped the Blues win the Double to become the first man (along with team-mate Ashley Cole) to achieve this feat with two different clubs.

• Anelka, who converted to Islam in 2007 and changed his name to Abdul-Salam Bilal, has played nearly 70 times for France but didn't feature at the World Cup until the 2010 finals in South Africa. It proved to be a miserable tournament for the striker, who was sent home in disgrace and later banned for 18 internationals after swearing at coach Raymond Domenech during half-time of France's 2-0 defeat by Mexico.

Weymouth-born octopus Paul was England's most consistent performer at the 2010 World Cup!

ANIMALS

Strange though it sounds, a variety of different animals have influenced the course of football matches around the world.

• During a match between Brazilian sides Botafogo and Gremio in 2002, a giant lapwing bird swooped from the sky and deflected a goalbound shot from Botafogo striker Fabio away from the line. Gremio fans celebrated their team's lucky escape by chanting 'lapwing, lapwing' and the game ended in a draw.

• In a 1985 Staffordshire Sunday Cup match a dog scored a goal for Knave of Clubs against Newcastle Town. A shot from a Knave striker was heading harmlessly wide until the pooch ran onto the pitch and bundled the ball over the line. The referee awarded the goal, although the dog's effort couldn't prevent Knave going down to a 3-2 defeat.

• On the final day of the 1986/87 season a police dog inadvertently played a part in saving Torquay from relegation from the Football League. With minutes to go, the Gulls were losing 2-1 at home to Crewe when the dog, named Bryn, ran onto the pitch and bit Torquay player Jim McNichol. In the time added on for treatment to his injury, Torquay launched a desperate last attack and scored an equaliser which sent Lincoln down instead. McNichol may not have appreciated the gesture, but Bryn's contribution to Torquay's escape was recognised by chairman Lew Pope who gave the dog a juicy steak.

• During a match between Santacruzense and Oeste Paulista in Brazil in February 2008, the home side's left back, Marcus Paulo, was attacked by a colony of ferocious red ants after he was tackled and fell to the ground. "My body was numb," he said afterwards. "I thought I was having a stroke or something when I realised my shirt was full of ants." To the bewilderment of the other players and the crowd, who had no idea what was going on, Paulo tore off his shirt before running into the dressing room to take a shower.

• The most famous dog in football, Pickles, never appeared on the pitch but, to the relief of fans around the globe, discovered the World Cup trophy which was stolen while on display at an exhibition in Central Hall, Westminster, on 20th March 1966. A black and white mongrel, Pickles found the trophy under a bush while out for a walk on Beulah Hill in south London with his owner. He was hailed as a national hero but, sadly, later that same year he was strangled by his lead while chasing after a cat.

• The World Cup also made an international celebrity of Paul, an octopus based at the Sea Life Aquarium in Oberhausen, Germany. During the 2010 finals in South Africa, the two-year-old cephalopod correctly predicted the result of all seven of Germany's games by choosing his favourite food, mussels, from one of two boxes marked with the national flag of the competing teams. Before the final between Holland and Spain, Paul's choice of breakfast snack suggested that the trophy would be heading to Madrid rather than Amsterdam... and, yet again, the amazing 'psychic' octopus was spot on!

APPEARANCES

Goalkeeping legend Peter Shilton holds the record for the most League appearances, playing in 1,005 games between 1966-97. His total was made up as follows: Leicester City (286 games), Stoke City (110), Nottingham Forest (202), Southampton (188), Derby County (175), Plymouth (34), Bolton (1) and Orient (9).

• England goalkeeper David James holds the Premier League appearance record, making 573 appearances for Liverpool, West Ham, Manchester City and Portsmouth between 1992-2010.

• The record for most League games with one club is held by Swindon Town's stalwart defender John Trollope, who appeared 770 times for the Robins between 1960-80.

• On 24th April 2010 Linfield defender Noel Bailie played his 1,000th game for the Northern Irish club. No other player in the world has made as many competitive appearances for the same team.

ARGENTINA

First international: Uruguay 2 Argentina 3, 1901

Most capped player: Javier Zanetti, 134 caps (1994-present)

Leading goalscorer: Gabriel Batistuta, 56 goals (1991-2002)

First World Cup appearance: Argentina 1 France 0, 1930

Biggest win: 12-0 v Ecuador, 1942

Heaviest defeat: 1-6 v Czechoslovakia, 1958

Colours: Sky blue-and-white striped shirts, black shorts, white socks

Outside Britain, Argentina is the oldest football nation on the planet. The roots of the game in this football-obsessed country go back to 1865, when the Buenos Aires Football Club was founded by British residents in the Argentine capital. Six clubs formed the first league in 1891, making it the oldest anywhere in the world outside Britain.

• **Losing finalists in the first World Cup final in 1930, Argentina had to wait until 1978 before winning the competition for the first time, defeating Holland 3-1 on home soil. Another success, inspired by brilliant captain Diego Maradona,**

TOP 10

MOST LEAGUE APPEARANCES

1. Peter Shilton (1966-97) 1005 apps
2. Tony Ford (1975-2001) 931 apps
3. Terry Paine (1957-77) 824 apps
4. Tommy Hutchinson (1968-91) 794 apps
5. Neil Redfearn (1982-2004) 790 apps
6. Robbie James (1973-93) 781 apps
7. Alan Oakes (1958-76) 776 apps
8. Dave Beasant (1980-2003) 773 apps
9. John Trollope (1960-80) 770 apps
10. Jimmy Dickinson (1946-65) 764 apps

---

followed in 1986 and Argentina came close to retaining their trophy four years later, losing in the final to West Germany. Argentina have also won the Copa America 14 times, a record only matched by Uruguay.

• Argentina's oldest rivals are neighbours Uruguay. The two countries first met in 1901, in the first official international to be played outside Britain, with Argentina winning 3-2 in Montevideo. In the ensuing years the two sides have played each other 160 times, making the Argentina-Uruguay fixture the most played in the history of international football.

Argentina's Diego Maradona has been accused of being big-headed and two faced...

• With an impressive 56 goals in 78 matches, former Fiorentina striker Gabriel Batistuta is Argentina's highest ever goalscorer. 'Batigol' is followed by another pair of legendary South Americans, Hernan Crespo (35 goals) and Diego Maradona (34 goals). Just three Argentinean players have won more than 100 caps for their country: Javier Zanetti (136, 1994-present), Roberto Ayala (115, 1994-2007) and Diego Simeone (106, 1988-2002).

HONOURS
World Cup 1978, 1986
Copa America 1921, 1925, 1927, 1929, 1937, 1941, 1945, 1946, 1947, 1955, 1957, 1959, 1991, 1993
World Cup record
1930 Runners-up
1934 Round 1
1938 Did not enter
1950 Did not enter
1954 Did not enter
1958 Round 1
1962 Round 1
1966 Quarter-finals
1970 Did not qualify
1974 Round 2
1978 Winners
1982 Round 2
1986 Winners
1990 Runners-up
1994 Round 2
1998 Quarter-finals 2010 Quarter-finals 2002 Round 1
2006 Quarter-finals
2010 Quarter-finals

Arsenal's Andre Arshavin gets stuck in

ARSENAL

Year founded: 1886
Ground: Emirates Stadium (60,355)
Previous name: Dial Square, Royal Arsenal, Woolwich Arsenal
Nickname: The Gunners
Biggest win: 12-0 v Ashford United (1893) and Loughborough Town (1900)
Heaviest defeat: 0-8 v Loughborough Town (1896)
Colours: Red shirts with white sleeves, white shorts, white socks

Founded as Dial Square in 1886 by workers at the Royal Arsenal in Woolwich, the club was renamed Royal Arsenal soon afterwards. Another name change, to Woolwich Arsenal, followed in 1891 when the club turned professional. Then, a year after moving north of the river to the Arsenal Stadium in 1913, the club became simply 'Arsenal'.

• **One of the most successful clubs in the history of English football, Arsenal** enjoyed a first golden period in the 1930s under innovative manager Herbert Chapman. The Gunners won the FA Cup for the first time in 1930 and later in the decade became only the second club to win three league titles on the trot. The first was the club Chapman managed in the 1920s, Huddersfield Town.

• When Arsenal won the title for the first time in 1931 they did so in fine style, finishing seven points clear of runners-up Aston Villa and scoring an incredible 60 goals in 21 away matches – an all-time record for the Football League.

• **More recently, Arsenal have experienced enormous success under French manager Arsene Wenger. In 1998, just two years after Wenger arrived in England, the Gunners won the Double, a feat they repeated in 2002. The club had previously won the league and FA Cup in the same season for the first time in 1971, and their total of three Doubles is only matched by Manchester United.**

• Wenger's greatest triumph, though, came in the 2003/04 season when his team were crowned Premier League champions after going through the entire campaign undefeated. Only Preston North End had previously matched this feat, way back in 1888/89, but they had only played 22 league games compared to the 38 of Wenger's 'Invincibles'.

• **The following season Arsenal extended their unbeaten run to 49 matches – setting an English league record in the process – before crashing to a bad-tempered 2-0 defeat against Manchester United at Old Trafford on 24th October 2004.**

• One of the stars of that great Arsenal side was striker Thierry Henry, who is the Gunners' all-time leading scorer with 226 goals in all competitions between 1999-2007. The former fans' favourite is also the most-capped Arsenal player, appearing 81 times for France during his time with the club.

• **In 1989 Arsenal won the closest ever title race by beating Liverpool 2-0 at Anfield in the final match of the season to pip the Reds to the championship on goals scored (the two sides had the same goal difference). But for a last-minute goal by Gunners midfielder Michael Thomas the title would have stayed on Merseyside.**

• Irish international defender David O'Leary made a club record 722 first-team appearances for Arsenal between 1975-93.

• **Arsenal endured a nightmare season in 1912/13, finishing rock bottom of Division One and winning just one home game throughout the campaign – an all-time record. However, the Gunners returned to the top flight in 1919 and have stayed there ever since – the longest ever unbroken run in the top tier.**

• Arsenal tube station on the Piccadilly Line is the only train station in Britain to be named after a football club. It used to be called Gillespie Road, until Herbert Chapman successfully lobbied for the name change in 1932.

• **Three years later, on 14th December 1935, Arsenal thrashed Aston Villa 7-1 at Villa Park. Incredibly, centre forward Ted Drake grabbed all seven of the Gunners' goals to set a top-flight record that still stands to this day.**

• Arsenal spent 93 years at their old ground, Highbury, before moving to the state-of-the-art Emirates Stadium in 2006. With a capacity of 60,355, the Emirates is the second biggest club stadium in England after Old Trafford.

• **Arsenal won the Fairs Cup in 1970 (beating Anderlecht 4-3 on aggregate) and the Cup-Winners' Cup in 1994 (a 1-0 victory over Parma). The Gunners** almost made it a clean sweep of European trophies in 2006, but narrowly lost 2-1 to Barcelona in the Champions League final in Paris.

• Previously famed for being a rather dull team who specialised in 1-0 victories, Arsenal have become the great entertainers in the Wenger era. Proof of the Gunners' attacking prowess came when they established an English league record by scoring in 55 consecutive matches between 2001-02.

• Arsenal's most expensive signing is Spanish winger Jose Antonio Reyes who cost £20.5 million when he joined from Sevilla in 2004. The club's record sale is Emmanuel Adebayor, who raised a staggering £25 million for the Highbury coffers when he signed for Man City in 2009.

• The Gunners have a host of celebrity supporters, including snooker star Ronnie O'Sullivan, Sex Pistols singer John Lydon and *Britain's Got Talent* judge Piers Morgan. Prince Harry is also a fan as, apparently, is his grandmother. In 2007 a Buckingham Palace spokesman surprised the football world by revealing that, "Her Majesty has been fond of Arsenal for over 50 years."

HONOURS
Division 1 champions 1931, 1933, 1934, 1935, 1948, 1953, 1971, 1989, 1991
Premier League champions 1998, 2002, 2004
FA Cup 1930, 1936, 1950, 1971, 1979, 1993, 1998, 2002, 2005
League Cup 1987, 1993
Double 1971, 1998, 2002
Fairs Cup 1970
European Cup Winners' Cup 1994

ANDREI ARSHAVIN

Born: St Petersburg, Russia, 29th May 1981
Position: Striker
Club career:
2000-09 Zenit St Petersburg 238 (52)
2009- Arsenal 42 (16)
International record:
2002- Russia 51(16)

Russian striker Andrei Arshavin moved to Arsenal from Zenit St Petersburg for an undisclosed fee in February 2009.

• He made an immediate impact, scoring a stunning goal against Blackburn and then hitting four in an amazing 4-4 draw against Liverpool, making him the first away player to score four goals at Anfield since Dennis Westcott for Wolves in 1946. He also became only the sixth player to score four away goals in the history of the Premier League.

• The Russian player of the Year in 2006, Arshavin – nicknamed Shava – was Man of the Match in Zenit's 2008 UEFA Cup triumph against Rangers and then starred at Euro 2008 as Russia reached the semi-finals playing some breathtaking football.

• The son of a top amateur footballer, Arshavin's talents were spotted early when he was enrolled in the Zenit St Petersburg academy at the age of seven. He survived a near-fatal road accident as a child to become one of the most promising players in Russia while also studying for a diploma in fashion design. He later admitted that he chose that particular college course because "I knew there would be lots of girls on it."

ARTIFICIAL PITCHES

The first artificial pitch was installed in the Houston Astrodrome in Texas in 1965. The new surface, called Astroturf, took its name from the stadium.

• In 1976 the first World Cup match to be played on an artificial pitch, a qualifier between Canada and the USA, took place in Vancouver.

• At the start of the 1981/82 season QPR became the first English club to replace their grass with an artificial surface, Omniturf. Opposition players and managers, however, were generally unimpressed, claiming the ball bounced unnaturally high and that players who fell over risked getting carpet burns.

• Despite these reservations, Oldham Athletic, Luton Town, Preston North End and Stirling Albion all followed QPR's lead in the 1980s. By 1994, however, Preston were the last club still playing on 'plastic' and at the start of the 1994/95 season the Football League banned all artificial pitches on the grounds that they gave home clubs an unfair advantage. North of the border, though, Dunfermline were allowed to play on an artificial pitch between 2003-05, before complaints from other clubs led the Scottish Premier League to order the Pars to return to grass.

• By 2005 UEFA was sufficiently impressed by the 'new generation' of artificial pitches, which played much like

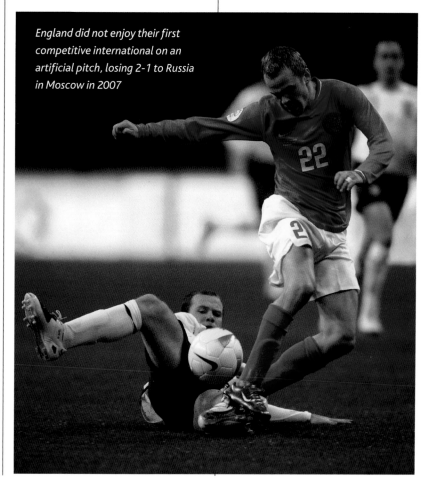
England did not enjoy their first competitive international on an artificial pitch, losing 2-1 to Russia in Moscow in 2007

grass, to allow teams to use them in their competitions. Russia took advantage of this ruling in October 2007 to play a vital European Championship qualifier against England in Moscow on an artificial pitch, winning the match 2-1. However, UEFA ruled that the 2008 Champions League final at the same stadium could not be played on artificial turf, so a temporary natural grass pitch was installed for the clash between Chelsea and Manchester United.

ASTON VILLA

Year founded: 1874
Ground: Villa Park (42,640)
Nickname: The Villans
Biggest win: 13-0 v Wednesbury Old Athletic (1886)
Heaviest defeat: 1-8 v Blackburn Rovers (1889)
Colours: Claret and sky blue shirts, white shorts, sky blue socks

One of England's most famous and distinguished clubs, Aston Villa were founded in 1874 by members of the Villa Cross Wesleyan Chapel in Aston, Birmingham. The club were founder members of the Football League in 1888, winning their first title six years later.

• **The most successful team of the Victorian era, Villa became only the second club to win the League and FA Cup Double in 1897 (Preston North End were the first in 1889). Villa's manager at the time was the legendary George Ramsay, who went on to guide the Villans to six league titles and six FA Cups – a trophy haul which has only been surpassed by Liverpool's Bob Paisley and, more recently, Manchester United boss Sir Alex Ferguson.**

• Ramsay is also the second longest-serving manager in the history of English football, taking charge of the Villans for an incredible 42 years between 1884 and 1926. Only West Brom's Fred Everiss has managed a club for longer, racking up 46 years' service at the Hawthorns.

• **Although they slipped as low as the old Third Division in the early 1970s, Villa have spent more time in the top flight than any other club apart from Everton (100 seasons compared to the Toffees' 108). The two clubs have played each other 190 times to date, making Aston**

Villa v Everton the most played fixture in the history of league football.

• Villa won the last of their seven league titles in 1980/81, when manager Ron Saunders used just 14 players throughout the whole campaign. The following season Villa became only the fourth English club to win the European Cup when they beat Bayern Munich 1-0 in the final.

• **In 1961 Villa won the League Cup in the competition's inaugural season, beating Rotherham 3-2 in a two-legged final. The Villans are the second most successful side in the tournament behind Liverpool with five triumphs, the last of which came thanks to a 3-0 win over Leeds in the 1996 final.**

• Aston Villa have provided more full internationals for England than any other club. At the last count a total of 69 Villans had pulled on the three lions shirt, including Gabriel Agbonlahor, James Milner and Ashley Young.

• **Stalwart defender Charlie Aitken made more appearances for the club than any other player, turning out in 657 games between 1959-76. Villa's all-time top goalscorer is Billy Walker, who found the back of the net an incredible 244 times between 1919-33.**

• Walker helped Villa bang in 128 league goals in the 1930/31 season, a record for the top flight which is unlikely ever to be broken. In the same campaign Tom 'Pongo Waring' scored a club record 49 league goals.

• **Before FA Cup semi-finals moved to Wembley, Villa Park staged a record 55 of these fixtures. The stadium has also hosted 16 England internationals and was the first venue to be used by the national team in three different centuries.**

• Villa's biggest league win came back in 1892 when they thrashed Accrington Stanley 12-2 in Division One – no side has scored more goals in a top flight fixture. Six years earlier, though, the club recorded their biggest ever victory in the FA Cup, humiliating Wednesbury Old Athletic 13-0. In total Villa have scored 817 goals in the cup, a record unmatched by any other club.

• **More recently, in 1990, Villa became the first top-flight club to appoint a foreign manager when Jozef Venglos took over from new England boss Graham Taylor. However, the Czech failed to make much of an impression,**

Aston Villa's greatest moment came when they won the European Cup in 1982

Brazil and Uruguay play in front of the biggest crowd ever to witness a football match, the final game of the 1950 World Cup

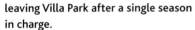

leaving Villa Park after a single season in charge.

• Famous Villa fans include punk violinist Nigel Kennedy, Prince William and David Cameron, who is a nephew of former club chairman Sir William Dugdale.

> **HONOURS**
> *Division 1 champions 1894, 1896, 1897, 1899, 1900, 1910, 1981*
> *Division 2 champions 1938, 1960*
> *Division 3 champions 1972*
> *FA Cup 1887, 1895, 1897, 1905, 1913, 1920, 1957,*
> *Double 1897*
> *League Cup 1961, 1975, 1977, 1994, 1996*
> *European Cup 1982*
> *European Super Cup 1982*

ATTENDANCES

The Maracana stadium in Rio de Janeiro holds the world record for a football match attendance, 199,589 spectators having watched the final match of the 1950 World Cup between Brazil and Uruguay. Most of the fans, though, went home in tears after Uruguay came from

behind to win 2-1.

• The biggest crowd at a match in Britain was for the first ever FA Cup final at Wembley in 1923. The official attendance for the match between Bolton and West Ham was 126,047 although, with thousands more fans gaining entry without paying, the actual crowd was estimated at 150,000-200,000. The record official attendance for a match in Britain is 149,547, set in 1937 for Scotland's 3-1 victory over England in the Home International Championship at Hampden Park.

• In 1948 a crowd of 83,260 watched Manchester United entertain Arsenal at Maine Road (United's temporary home in the post-war years after Old Trafford suffered bomb damage during the conflict), a record for the Football League. Not including games played behind closed doors, the lowest attendance for a Football League game is 450, a record set in 1974 for the Division Three match between Rochdale and Cambridge United. There was some excuse for the pitiful showing by the two groups of fans, however – the match was played on a

Tuesday afternoon because a miners' strike had led to power cuts and a ban on floodlit games.

• The highest attendance at a Premier League match is 76,097 for the game between Manchester United and Blackburn Rovers on 31st March 2007. At the other end of the scale, just 3,039 fans turned out for Wimbledon's home game against Everton at Selhurst Park on 26th January 1993.

TOP 10

AVERAGE PREMIERSHIP ATTENDANCE 2009/10

1.	Manchester United	74,864
2.	Arsenal	59,927
3.	Manchester City	45,512
4.	Liverpool	42,863
5.	Chelsea	41,422
6.	Sunderland	40,355
7.	Aston Villa	38,573
8.	Everton	36,725
9.	Tottenham Hotspur	35,794
10.	West Ham United	33,683

ROBERTO BAGGIO

Born: Caldogno, Italy,
18th February 1967
Position: Striker
Club career:
1982-85 Vicenza 46 (15)
1985-90 Fiorentina 135 (55)
1990-95 Juventus 201 (115)
1995-97 AC Milan 67 (19)
1997-98 Bologna 33 (23)
1998-2000 Inter Milan 62 (18)
2000-04 Brescia 100 (46)
International record:
1988-2004 Italy 56 (27)

Despite being a wonderfully gifted player, Roberto Baggio is probably best remembered for the penalty he skied over the bar in the 1994 World Cup final shoot-out between Italy and Brazil. Baggio had been his country's outstanding individual at the finals, scoring five goals in the competition, but his uncharacteristic miss condemned Italy to a heartbreaking defeat.

• However, 'The Divine Ponytail', as he was nicknamed, remains a legendary figure for Italian football fans. The only player from his country to score at three World Cups (in 1990, 1994 and 1998), Baggio notched nine goals in total at the finals of the tournament – a figure only matched by two other Italian greats, Paolo Rossi and Christian Vieri.

• A devout Buddhist, Baggio began his career with Vicenza, before moving to Fiorentina. He was so popular in Florence that his transfer to Juventus in 1990 for a then world record £7.7 million sparked riots in the city. The move proved a good one for Baggio, though, as he won the UEFA Cup with Juve in 1993 and in the same year was voted European and World Footballer of the Year. Then, in 1995, Baggio helped Juve win the Serie A title for the first time in five years.

• After spells with AC Milan (where he won another Serie A title in 1996 but was often controversially left on the subs' bench by manager Fabio Capello), Bologna, Inter Milan and Brescia, Baggio retired in 2004. His career total of 318 goals is unparalleled in the modern era in Italy and only surpassed by two legends from the past, Silvo Piola (364) and Giuseppe Meazza (338). 76 of Baggio's goals came from the penalty spot – an all-time record in Italian football.

GARETH BALE

Born: Cardiff, 16th July 1989
Position: Midfielder
Club career:
2006-07 Southampton 40 (5)
2007- Tottenham Hotspur 47 (5)
International record:
2006- Wales 24 (2)

Tottenham's fleet-footed left-sided midfielder Gareth Bale is the youngest player to appear for Wales, making his debut against Trinidad and Tobago on 27th May 2006 when he was aged 16 years and 315 days. Later that year he scored his first international goal, in a 5-1 home defeat by Slovakia, to become his country's youngest ever scorer.

• Bale began his career at Southampton, where he was the second youngest player to debut for the club (behind Theo Walcott) when he appeared in a 2-0 win against Millwall in April 2006. The following season his outstanding displays for the Saints helped him claim the Football League Young Player of the Year award.

• In the summer of 2007 Bale joined Tottenham for an initial fee of £5 million. Incredibly, he failed to feature on the winning side for Spurs in his first 24 league games – a Premier League record – but once he had buried that jinx his form rapidly improved, and he was soon being hailed as one of the most exciting talents in the game.

ALAN BALL

Born: Farnworth, 12th May 1945
Died: 25th April 2007
Position: Midfielder
Club career:
1962-66 Blackpool 116 (40)
1966-71 Everton 208 (66)
1971-76 Arsenal 177 (45)
1976-78 Southampton 132 (9)
1978-79 Philadelphia Fury 34 (5)
1979-80 Vancouver Whitecaps 38 (10)
1980-81 Blackpool 30 (5)
1981-82 Southampton 63 (2)
1983-84 Bristol Rovers 17 (2)
International record:
1965-75 England 72 (8)

The youngest member of England's 1966 World Cup team, Alan Ball was just 21 when his tireless performance in midfield in the final against West Germany was rewarded with a winners' medal. In all he played 72 times for his country, captaining England on six occasions.

• Ball's long career spanned 22 years, during which he appeared in an incredible 975 competitive games. Having initially been rejected by Bolton for being too small, he was signed up by Blackpool and spent five years with the Seasiders before joining Everton for a record £110,000 in 1966. He won the league championship with the Toffees in 1970, but the following year moved on to Arsenal for another record fee, £220,000. After five years at Highbury he continued travelling south, signing for Southampton.

• Strangely, when Ball joined Everton, Arsenal and Southampton all three clubs were reigning FA Cup holders. Yet, despite playing in two finals in 1968 and 1972, Ball never won the cup and he also finished on the losing side in the League Cup final with Southampton in 1979.

• Back in the early 1970s Ball was one of the first players to wear coloured boots, sporting a distinctive white pair after signing a £2,000 sponsorship deal with boot manufacturers Hummel.

• Ball later managed a number of clubs, including Portsmouth, Southampton and Manchester City, but without notable success. By the time of his final post, a second stint with Pompey in the late 1990s, he was the last remaining member of the 1966 team to be involved in management. Awarded the MBE for services to football in 2000, Ball died of a heart attack in 2007 while attempting to put out a fire in his garden.

MICHAEL BALLACK

Born: Gorlitz, Germany, 26th September 1976
Position: Midfielder
Club career:
1995-97 Chemnitz 49 (10)
1997-99 Kaiserlautern 46 (4)
1999-2002 Bayer Leverkusen 79 (27)
2002-06 Bayern Munich 107 (44)
2006-10 Chelsea 105 (17)
2010- Bayer Leverkusen
International record:
1999- Germany 98 (42)

Germany captain Michael Ballack became an influential figure in Chelsea's midfield after arriving at Stamford Bridge on a free transfer from Bayern Munich in May 2006.

• **Following spells with local side Chemnitz and Kaiserlautern, Ballack rose to prominence with Bayer Leverkusen. After finishing as a runner-up with Bayer in the Bundesliga, the German Cup and the Champions League in 2002 – a series of near misses dubbed the 'Treble Horror' by the German media – Ballack moved to Bayern Munich that same summer.**

• Ballack enjoyed better fortune with Bayern, winning three Bundesliga and German Cup doubles in four seasons. He was also voted German Footballer of the Year in 2003 and 2005, an award he had previously won with Bayer in 2002.

• **An attacking midfielder with an excellent goalscoring record, Ballack was made Germany captain in 2004. In 2008 he led his country to the European Championship final but had to be satisfied with a runners-up medal after Germany lost 1-0 to Spain in Vienna.**

• Ballack helped Chelsea win the Carling Cup in 2007 and the FA Cup in 2009. The following year he was a key member of the Blues side that won the Double, but he limped off in the FA Cup final against Portsmouth with an ankle injury that later ruled him out of the World Cup in South Africa.

• **In the summer of 2010 he rejoined Bayer Leverkusen on a free transfer.**

BALL BOYS

Ball boys developed from a gimmick employed by Chelsea in the 1905/06 season. To emphasise the extraordinary bulk of the team's 23-stone goalkeeper, William 'Fatty' Foulke, two young boys would stand behind his goal. They soon proved themselves useful in retrieving the ball when it went out of play and so the concept of the ball boy was born.

• **Amazingly, a ball boy scored a goal in a match between Santacruzense and Atletico Sorocaba in Brazil in 2006. Santacruzense were trailing 1-0 when one of their players fired wide in the last minute. Instead of handing the ball back to the Atletico goalkeeper, the ball boy kicked it into the net and the goal was awarded by the female referee despite the angry protests of the Atletico players.**

• Almost as bizarrely, a ball boy was credited with an 'assist' during an Israeli second division match between Hapoel Haifa and Bnei Lod in 2009. After the visitors' goalkeeper raced out of his area to head clear, 12-year-old Ofek Mizrachi quickly threw the ball he was carrying to a Haifa player whose equally rapid thrown-in was smashed into an empty net by striker Eran Levi.

BALLS

The laws of football specify that the ball must be an air-filled sphere with a circumference of 68-70cm and a weight before the start of the game of 410-450g. Before the first plastic footballs appeared in the 1950s, balls were made from leather and in wet conditions would become progressively heavier, sometimes

IS THAT A FACT?
In a Copa Libertadores match between Brazilian team Flamengo and Uruguayan side Nacional on 6th March 2008 a player was sent off for pushing a ball boy. Flamengo midfielder Toro was shown the red card by the referee after an altercation with the 13-year-old. To complete a bad night for his team they slumped to a 3-0 defeat.

actually doubling in weight.

• **Most modern footballs are made in Pakistan, especially in the city of Sialkot, and are usually stitched from 32 panels of waterproofed leather or plastic. In the past child labour was often used in the production of the balls but, following pressure from UNICEF and the International Labour Organisation, manufacturers agreed in 1997 not to employ underage workers.**

• Adidas have supplied the official ball for the World Cup since 1970. Before the start of the 2010 tournament in South Africa a number of top goalkeepers, including Italy's Gianluigi Buffon and Brazil's Julio Cesar, criticised the World Cup ball, the Jabulani, for being too unpredictable in its trajectory.

• **The record for juggling a football in the air without the use of hands ('keepy uppy') is held by England's Dan Magness, who clocked up 24 hours in Covent Garden on 1st May 2009. The following year Magness set another record when he juggled a ball 30 miles**

"Like this Rob!" Colombian singer Shakira appears to have no difficulty handling the controversial World Cup ball

across London, visiting every Premier League ground in the capital along the way.

• Remarkably, the ball burst during both the 1946 and 1947 FA Cup finals at Wembley – an unlikely coincidence which was probably caused by the poor quality of leather available after the World War II.

• Before the 1930 World Cup Final in Montevideo neither of the two competing teams – hosts Uruguay and their arch rivals Argentina – could agree on whose ball to use. Following a coin toss the Argentinian ball was used in the first half (at the end of which Argentina led 2-1) before it was replaced by the Uruguayan ball at half-time. The change certainly suited Uruguay, who recovered to win 4-2.

• Sunderland's Darren Bent scored the most bizarre goal in the history of the Premier League against Liverpool in October 2009 when his shot deflected past Reds' keeper Pepe Reina off a stray red beach ball, which the wind had blown into the six-yard box. Callum Campbell, the 16-year-old Liverpool fan who had thrown the beach ball onto the pitch later said: "It's bad enough when Liverpool lose, like in a normal way, but this was just one big disaster."

GORDON BANKS

Born: Sheffield, 30th December 1937
Position: Goalkeeper
Club career:
1955-59 Chesterfield 23
1959-67 Leicester City 293
1967-72 Stoke City 194
1977 St Patrick's 1
1977-78 Fort Lauderdale Strikers 39
International record:
1963-72 England 73

One of the finest goalkeepers ever, Gordon Banks will always be remembered for his part in England's 1966 World Cup success. Dubbed 'Banks of England' (because he had "the safest hands in the country"), he lived up to his nickname by keeping four straight clean sheets at the start of the tournament – part of an England record run of 718 minutes without conceding a goal.

• His finest single moment, though, came at the 1970 World Cup in Mexico

when he produced a save which is widely considered to be the best in the history of the game. A powerful downward header by the great Brazilian striker Pele seemed destined for the bottom corner of the goal, but somehow Banks managed to rush across his line before diving slightly backwards to turn the ball over the bar.

• The tournament ended badly for Banks, though, as a stomach upset kept him out of England's quarter-final defeat by West Germany. England manager Sir Alf Ramsey believed that the result might have been very different if Banks had played, wistfully saying, "Of all the players to lose, we had to lose him."

• In club football, Banks won the League Cup with Leicester in 1964 and Stoke in 1972 and was a beaten FA Cup finalist with the Foxes in 1961 and 1969. He was awarded the OBE in 1970 and was Footballer of the Year in 1972.

• Aged 34, Banks' career in England was ended in 1972 when he lost the sight in his right eye in a car crash, although he later played for Irish club St Patrick's and in the North American Soccer League with Fort Lauderdale Strikers.

BARCELONA

Year founded: 1899
Ground: Nou Camp (98,772)
Nickname: Barca
Colours: Red-and-blue shirts, red shorts, red/blue socks

One of the most famous and popular clubs in the world, Barcelona were founded in 1899 by bank worker Joan Gamper, a former captain of Swiss club Basel. The club were founder members and first winners of the Spanish championship, La Liga, in 1928 and have remained in the top flight of Spanish football ever since.

• For the people of Catalonia, Barcelona is more like a national team than a mere club. As former manager Bobby Robson once succinctly put it, "Catalonia is a country and FC Barcelona is their army."

• Along with Ajax, Juventus and Bayern Munich, Barcelona are one of just four clubs to have won three different European trophies: the European Cup/ Champions League, the European Cup-Winners' Cup (a record four times) and the Fairs Cup (Barça being the first winners of the competition in 1958).

• With a capacity of 98,772, Barcelona's Nou Camp stadium is the largest in Europe. Among the stadium's many facilities are a museum which attracts over one million visitors a year, mini training pitches and a chapel for the players.

• For many years Barcelona played second fiddle to bitter rivals Real Madrid. Finally, in the 1990s, under former player turned coach Johan Cruyff, Barca turned the tables on the team from the Spanish capital, winning four La Liga titles on the trot between 1991-94. Cruyff also led the Catalans to a first taste of glory in the

Barcelona - more than just a football club

European Cup, Barcelona beating Sampdoria at Wembley in 1992. The club have since won the Champions League on two more occasions, beating Arsenal 2-1 in the 2006 final and Manchester United 2-0 in 2009.

• With 25 victories to their name, Barcelona have won the Copa del Rey (the Spanish version of the FA Cup) more times than any other club.

> **HONOURS**
> *Spanish League* 1929, 1945, 1948, 1949, 1952, 1953, 1959, 1960, 1974, 1985, 1991, 1992, 1993, 1994, 1998, 1999, 2005, 2006, 2009, 2010
> *Spanish Cup* 1910, 1912, 1913, 1920, 1922, 1925, 1926, 1928, 1942, 1951, 1952, 1953, 1957, 1959, 1963, 1968, 1971, 1978, 1981, 1983, 1988, 1990, 1997, 1998, 2009
> *European Cup/Champions League* 1992, 2006, 2009
> *European Cup Winners' Cup* 1979, 1982, 1989, 1997
> *Fairs Cup* 1958, 1960, 1966
> *European Super Cup* 1992, 1997, 2009
> *World Club Cup* 2009

BARNET

Year founded: 1888
Ground: Underhill Stadium (6,200)
Previous name: Barnet Alston FC
Nickname: The Bees
Biggest win: 7-0 v Blackpool (2000)
Heaviest defeat: 1-9 v Peterborough United (1998)
Colours: Amber shirts with black sleeves, black shorts and black socks

Founded in 1888, Barnet spent more than a hundred years in non-league football before finally gaining promotion from the Conference to the Fourth Division in 1991. The Bees (the nickname derives from their distinctive amber-and-black striped shirts) certainly made up for lost time – their first two games in the 1991/92 season, against Crewe (lost 4-7) and Brentford (drew 5-5), produced an incredible total of 21 goals!

• Barnet may be London's smallest league club, but some famous names have been associated with the Bees over the years. Legendary England goalpoacher Jimmy Greaves turned out for Barnet at the end of his career in the late 1970s, while fellow internationals Ray Clemence, Alan Mullery and Tony Cottee have all managed the club at some point.

• Despite their lowly status, Barnet have some of the best training facilities in the lower leagues. Opened by Fabio Capello in December 2009, the Bees' £11 million 'Hive' complex was used by the visiting Egyptian national team the following year before their friendly with England at Wembley.

• In October 1946, the first live televised football match was broadcast by the BBC from Barnet's tiny Underhill Stadium. Around 75 minutes of the Bees' encounter with Wealdstone were screened before it got too dark for the broadcast to continue.

> **HONOURS**
> *Conference champions* 1991, 2005
> *FA Amateur Cup* 1946

BARNSLEY

Year founded: 1887
Ground: Oakwell (23,009)
Previous name: Barnsley St Peter's
Nickname: The Tykes
Biggest win: 9-0 v Loughborough United (1899)
Heaviest defeat: 0-9 v Notts County (1927)
Colours: Red shirts, white shorts, red socks

Founded as the church team Barnsley St Peter's in 1887 by the Rev Tiverton Preedy, the club changed to their present name a year after joining the Football League in 1898.

• The Tykes have spent more seasons (67) in the second tier of English football than any other club and had to wait until 1997 before they had their first taste of life in the top flight.

• The Yorkshiremen's finest hour came in 1912 when they won the FA Cup, beating West Bromwich Albion 1-0 in a replay. The club were nicknamed 'Battling Barnsley' that season as they played no fewer than 12 games during their cup run, including six 0-0 draws, before finally getting their hands on the trophy. Barnsley came close to repeating this feat in 2008, but were beaten in the semi-finals by fellow Championship side Cardiff City after they had sensationally knocked out Liverpool and cup holders Chelsea.

• When Barnsley sold prolific striker Tommy Taylor to Manchester United in 1953 it was for a then world record fee of £29,999. United manager Matt Busby insisted on a pound change as he didn't want Taylor saddled with the label of the first £30,000 footballer. Taylor went on to play 19 times for England before his life was tragically cut short by the Munich air crash in 1958.

• Barnsleys record buy is Macedonian international striker Gorgi Hristov, who signed from Partizan Belgrade for £1.5 million in 1997. An expensive flop in his three years at Oakwell, Hristov didn't exactly endear himself to Tykes fans when he complained that, "The local girls are far uglier than the ones in Belgrade. Our women are far prettier and they don't drink as much beer."

> **HONOURS**
> *Division Three (N) champions* 1934, 1939, 1955
> *FA Cup* 1912

Barnsley celebrate promotion to the Championship in 2007

GARETH BARRY

Gareth Barry and England found the sloping pitches in South Africa very hard to deal with!

GARETH BARRY

Born: Hastings, 23rd February 1981
Position: Midfielder
Club career:
1997- Aston Villa 365 (41)
2009- Manchester City 34 (2)
International record:
2000- England 40 (2)

One of the most consistent performers in the Premier League, Gareth Barry joined Manchester City from Aston Villa in the summer of 2009 in a £12 million deal.

• Although still only 29, Barry is immensely experienced. In October 2007 he became the youngest player (aged 26 and 247 days) to appear in 300 Premier League games, beating the previous record held by Frank Lampard. To date, though, he only has an FA Cup runners-up medal, which he collected in 2000, to show for all his efforts. His lack of success with the Midlanders prompted Barry to seek a move to Liverpool in the summer of 2008 but, after lengthy negotiations, the two clubs failed to agree a fee.

• A versatile player who is an equally capable performer in defence or midfield, Barry has played under six England managers since making his debut against Ukraine in May 2000. However, he was largely overlooked by Sven-Göran Eriksson and only became a regular name on the teamsheet under the Swede's successor, Steve McClaren.

• Barry scored his first goal for England in a 3-0 friendly win away to Trinidad and Tobago in June 2008, a match in which he also captained his country for the first time in the second half.

The following year he scored his first competitive goal for England, opening the scoring with a header in a 4-0 win away to Kazakhstan in a World Cup qualifier. He recovered from an ankle injury to play in the finals but, like many of his team-mates, failed to show his best form in South Africa.

BAYERN MUNICH

Year founded: 1900
Ground: Allianz Arena (69,901)
Nickname: The Bavarians
Colours: Red-and-white striped shirts, red shorts and red socks

The biggest and most successful club in Germany, Bayern Munich were founded in 1900 by members of a Munich gymnastics club. Incredibly, when the Bundesliga was formed in 1963, Bayern's form was so poor they were not invited to become founder members of the league. But, thanks to the emergence in the mid 1960s of legendary players like goalkeeper Sepp Maier, sweeper Franz Beckenbauer and prolific goalscorer Gerd Muller, Bayern rapidly became the dominant force in German football. The club won the Bundesliga for the first time in 1969 and now have a record 21 German championships to their name.

• In 1974 Bayern became the first German club to win the European Cup, defeating Atletico Madrid 4-0 in the only final to go to a replay. Skippered by the imperious Beckenbauer, the club went on to complete a hat-trick of victories in the competition. However, Bayern had to wait another 25 years before winning the trophy again, beating Valencia on penalties in the Champions League final in 2001. More recently, Bayern reached the final again in 2010, but lost 2-0 to Inter Milan in Madrid.

• Bayern are one of just four clubs to have won three different European trophies, having also been triumphant in the Cup-Winners' Cup in 1967 and the UEFA Cup in 1996.

• With 140,000 registered fans, Bayern have the third largest membership of any club in the world after Benfica and Barcelona.

• In 2005, following complaints from their fans that the pitch was too far away from the stands at their old Olympic Stadium ground, Bayern moved to the Allianz Arena in northern Munich. The first player to score at the new venue, in a match against Borussia Monchengladbach, was then Bayern player Owen Hargreaves.

HONOURS
German championship 1932, *1969, 1972, 1973, 1974, 1980, 1981, 1985, 1986, 1987, 1989, 1990, 1994, 1997, 1999, 2000, 2001,2003, 2005, 2006, 2010*
German Cup 1957, 1966, 1967, *1969, 1971, 1982, 1984, 1986, 1998, 2000, 2003, 2005, 2006, 2008, 2010*
European Cup/Champions League 1974, 1975, 1976, 2001
Cup Winners' Cup 1967
UEFA Cup 1996

FRANZ BECKENBAUER

Born: Munich, Germany, 11th September 1945
Position: Defender
Club career:
1964-77 Bayern Munich 427 (60)
1977-80 New York Cosmos 105 (19)
1980-82 Hamburg 28 (0)
1983 New York Cosmos 29 (2)
International record:
1965-77 West Germany 103 (14)

Germany's greatest ever player, Franz Beckenbauer's elegant playing style

TOP 10

BUNDESLIGA CHAMPIONS

1. Bayern Munich 21 titles
2. Borussia Monchengladbach 5 titles
3. Werder Bremen 4 titles
4. Borussia Dortmund 3 titles
   Hamburg 3 titles
   Stuttgart 3 titles
7. FC Cologne 2 titles
   Kaiserlautern 2 titles
9. Munich 1860 1 title
   Eintracht Braunschweig 1 title
   FC Nuremberg 1 title
   Wolfsburg 1 title

and outstanding leadership qualities earned him the nickname 'Der Kaiser' ('The Emperor'). Having started out as a midfielder, Beckenbauer created and defined the role of the offensive 'sweeper' in the late 1960s, turning defence into attack with surging runs from the back.

• Beckenbauer enjoyed huge success at both club and international level. He captained Bayern Munich to three consecutive victories in the European Cup between 1974-76, matching Ajax's treble earlier in the decade. As skipper of West Germany Beckenbauer led his country to victory in the 1972 European Championships and two years later he cemented his reputation as a national icon by collecting the World Cup trophy after a 2-1 defeat of Holland in the 1974 final in Munich.

• His consistent performances won him the European Footballer of the Year award in 1972 and 1976 – the first German player to win the award twice. He was also voted German Footballer of the

IS THAT A FACT?

David Beckham is the only England player to have been sent off twice, receiving his marching orders at France 98 against Argentina and in a World Cup qualifier against Austria at Old Trafford in 2005.

Year a record four times.

• More success followed for Beckenbauer in the late 1970s after he accepted a lucrative offer to play in America, his New York Cosmos side winning the NASL Soccer Bowl in 1977, 1978 and 1980.

• Beckenbauer was appointed manager of West Germany in 1986 and when, four years later, his country triumphed at Italia 90 'Der Kaiser' became the first man to both captain and coach a World Cup-winning team. Later, in 1996, he led Bayern Munich to glory in the UEFA Cup, before becoming the driving force behind Germany's successful bid to host the 2006 World Cup.

DAVID BECKHAM

Born: Leytonstone, 2nd May 1975
Position: Midfielder
Club career:
1993-2003 Manchester United 265 (62)
1995 Preston North End (loan) 5 (2)
2003-07 Real Madrid 116 (13)
2007- LA Galaxy 41 (7)
2009 AC Milan (loan) 18 (2)
2010 AC Milan (loan) 11 (0)
International record:
1996-2009 England 115 (17)

One of the most famous names on the planet, David Beckham's fame extends far beyond the world of football. Yet, for all the interest in his marriage to Spice Girl Victoria Beckham, his fashion sense, his numerous haircuts and tattoos, it shouldn't be forgotten that his celebrity status stems primarily from his remarkable ability on the ball.

• A superb crosser of the ball and free-kick expert, at his peak Beckham was probably the best right-sided midfielder in the world. He twice came close to winning the World Player of the Year award, finishing as runner-up in 1999 and 2001.

• Beckham enjoyed huge success with his first club Manchester United, winning six Premiership titles, two FA Cups and, as the final leg of 'the Treble', the Champions League in 1999. However, his glamorous lifestyle began to irritate United boss Sir Alex Ferguson and the deteriorating relationship

David Beckham - England's most capped outfield player!

between the pair led to Beckham's departure to Spanish giants Real Madrid in 2003.

• As one of Real's 'galacticos', Beckham was part of a team which was much hyped but frequently failed to deliver. He eventually won the Spanish title with Real in 2007, shortly before making a lucrative move to Major League Soccer in the USA with LA Galaxy. In 2009 he joined AC Milan on loan and performed so well that the Italians were delighted to welcome him back to the San Siro in a similar deal the following year.

• One of just five players to win more than 100 caps for his country and the only England player to have scored at three different World Cups, Beckham captained his country from 2000-06. After being sent off against Argentina at the 1998 World Cup he was made the scapegoat for England's elimination from the competition, but famously bounced back to score the winning goal from the penalty spot

against the same opposition at the 2002 tournament in Japan and Korea.

• Beckham's England career appeared to be over when he was dropped from the squad by new manager Steve McClaren in 2006. However, he was recalled the following year and was rewarded with his 100th cap by McClaren's successor, his former Real boss Fabio Capello, against France in 2008. The following year he became England's most-capped outfield player, beating the old record set by the great Bobby Moore, when he won his 109th cap against Slovakia. Sadly for Beckham, injury ruled him out of the 2010 World Cup.

CRAIG BELLAMY

Born: Cardiff, 13th July 1979
Position: Striker
Club career:
1996-2000 Norwich City 84 (32)
2000-01 Coventry City 34 (6)
2001-05 Newcastle United 93 (28)
2005   Celtic (loan) 12 (7)
2005-06 Blackburn Rovers 27 (13)
2006-07 Liverpool 27 (7)
2007-09 West Ham United 24 (7)
2009- Manchester City 40 (12)
2010- Cardiff City (loan)
International record:
1998- Wales 59 (18)

A much-travelled striker whose various moves have totalled more than £45 million in transfer fees, Craig Bellamy is one of just five players to have scored for six different Premier League clubs.

• Bellamy began his career at Norwich, before moving to Coventry in 2000 for £6.5 million. Following the Sky Blues' relegation the following year, he was snapped up by Newcastle where he won the PFA Young Player of the Year award in 2002. After falling out with Toon boss Graeme Souness, Bellamy went on loan to Celtic, with whom he won the Scottish Cup in 2005. Spells with Blackburn, Liverpool and West Ham followed before he joined Manchester City in January 2009 in a £14 million deal.

• Once described by former Newcastle boss Sir Bobby Robson as "a great player wrapped round an unusual and volatile character", Bellamy has been involved in numerous controversial incidents. Perhaps the most notorious was during his time at Liverpool, when he allegedly hit team-mate John Arne Riise with a golf club, earning the nickname 'The Nutter with the Putter'.

• First capped in 1998, Bellamy has scored 18 goals for Wales – a total only surpassed by four other players. In 2007 he was appointed captain of his country by Wales manager John Toshack.

BENFICA

Year founded: 1904
Ground: Estadio Da Luz, Lisbon (65,400)
Nickname: The Eagles
Colours: Red shirts, white shorts, red socks

Portugal's most successful club, Benfica were founded in 1904 at a meeting of 24 football enthusiasts in south Lisbon. The club were founder members of the Portuguese league in 1933, and have since won the title a record 32 times.

• With over 175,000 registered members, Benfica is officially the biggest club in the world, ahead of Manchester United and Barcelona.

• Inspired by legendary striker Eusebio, Benfica enjoyed a golden era in the 1960s when the club won eight domestic championships. In 1961 Benfica became the first team to break Real Madrid's dominance in the European Cup when they beat Barcelona 3-2 in the final in Berne. The following year, the trophy stayed in Lisbon after 'the Eagles' sensationally beat Real 5-3 in the final in Amsterdam.

• In 1972/73 Benfica went the whole season undefeated – the first Portuguese team to achieve this feat – winning a staggering 28 and drawing just two of their 30 league matches. The great Eusebio struck 40 goals that season to top the European scoring charts as Benfica were crowned champions once again.

• Among the big names to have managed Benfica are Sven Goran Eriksson (1989-92), Graeme Souness (1997-99) and Jose Mourinho (a brief spell in 2000). Despite these high profile appointments, the club slipped behind deadly rivals Sporting Lisbon and Porto before landing only their second title in 16 years in 2010.

HONOURS
Portuguese championship 1936, 1937, 1938, 1942, 1943, 1945, 1950, 1955, 1957, 1960, 1961, 1963, 1964, 1965, 1967, 1968, 1969, 1971, 1972, 1973, 1975, 1976, 1977, 1981, 1983, 1984, 1987, 1989, 1991, 1994, 2005, 2010
Portuguese Cup 1930, 1931, 1935, 1940, 1943, 1944, 1949, 1951, 1952, 1953, 1955, 1957, 1959, 1962, 1964, 1969, 1970, 1972, 1980, 1981, 1983, 1985, 1986, 1987, 1993, 1996, 2004
European Cup 1961, 1962

Benfica - officially the biggest club in the world

DENNIS BERGKAMP

RAFA BENITEZ

Born: Madrid, 16th April 1960
Managerial career:
1995-96 Valladolid
1996-97 Osasuna
1997-99 Extremadura
2000-01 Tenerife
2001-04 Valencia
2004-10 Liverpool
2010- Inter Milan

Rafa Benitez became the top flight's first ever Spanish manager when he joined Liverpool from Valencia in the summer of 2004. In his first season at Anfield he guided Liverpool to victory in the Champions League, and the following year his side won the FA Cup - both triumphs achieved following nerve-jangling penalty shoot-outs.
• In just three years at Valencia, **Benitez won the Spanish league twice and the UEFA Cup in 2004, making him the most successful manager in the club's history. Along with Bob Paisley (Liverpool) and Jose Mourinho (Porto) he is one of just three managers to win the UEFA Cup and the European Cup/Champions League in consecutive seasons.**
• Despite bringing some of the world's top players to Anfield, including Spanish striker Fernando Torres and Argentinian midfielder Javier Mascherano, Benitez was criticised for failing to mount a serious challenge for the Premiership title. After a bitterly disappointing final campaign, which saw Liverpool finish seventh in the Premier League and fail to reach the knock-out stages of the Champions League, he left the club by mutual consent in June 2010. A week after leaving Anfield he was appointed manager of Italian champions Inter Milan.

DIMITAR BERBATOV

Born: Blagoevgrad, Bulgaria, 30th January 1981
Position: Striker
Club career:
1999-2001 CSKA Sofia 50 (25)
2001-06 Bayer Leverkusen 152 (68)
2006-08 Tottenham Hotspur 70 (27)
2008- Manchester United 64 (21)
International record:
1999-2010 Bulgaria 77 (48)

Sublimely skilled striker Dimitar Berbatov signed for Manchester United from Tottenham for a near British record £30.75 million in August 2008, having rejected the chance to move to United's moneybags neighbours, Manchester City. In his first season at Old Trafford Berbatov became the first Bulgarian ever to win the Premiership title.
• **Berbatov began his career with CSKA Sofia, with whom he won the Bulgarian Cup in 1999, before moving to Bayer Leverkusen in 2002. The following year he played in the Champions League final for Bayer, although they were narrowly defeated by Real Madrid in Glasgow. He joined Tottenham in 2006 and two years later scored a vital goal from the penalty spot to help Spurs beat Chelsea in the Carling Cup final at Wembley.**
• Bulgarian Footballer of the Year on a record six occasions, Berbatov is the highest ever scorer for Bulgaria. He will not be adding to his tally of 48 goals, though, as he announced his retirement from international football in 2010.
• **As a teenager, Berbatov was a big fan of Newcastle striker Alan Shearer and even used to go to bed wearing a 'Shearer' shirt bought for him by his parents as a birthday present. "He even thinks this shirt may have been a sign he was meant to play in England," said his mother, Margarita.**

DENNIS BERGKAMP

Born: Amsterdam. Holland, 10th May 1969
Position: Striker
Club career:
1986-93 Ajax 185 (103)
1993-95 Inter Milan 52 (11)
1995-2006 Arsenal 315 (87)
International record:
1990-2000 Holland 79 (37)

One of the most talented overseas players to grace the English game, Dennis Bergkamp spent more than a decade with Arsenal after signing from Inter Milan in 1995. His highly successful striking partnerships with Ian Wright and, later, Thierry Henry helped the Gunners win an armful of honours, including two Doubles in 1998 and 2002.
• **Named after Scottish striker Denis Law by his football-mad parents,** Bergkamp began his career with Ajax, with whom he won the European Cup Winners' Cup in 1987, the Dutch league in 1990 and the UEFA Cup in 1992. He was also named Dutch Footballer of the Year on two occasions before moving to Inter in 1993 for £12 million, making him the second most expensive player in the world at the time. His time in Italy was altogether less successful, although he did win the UEFA Cup again in 1994.
• After an indifferent start to his Arsenal career, Bergkamp's excellent ball control and visionary passing soon marked him out as one of the Premiership's top performers. Although not a prolific scorer many of his goals were spectacular, and in September 1997 he became the first player to come first, second and third in *Match of the Day's* Goal of the Month competition. The following year Bergkamp won the programme's Goal of the Season award, a feat he repeated in

Arsenal hero Dennis Bergkamp was named after Scotland legend Denis Law

2002 to become only the second player (after Liverpool's John Aldridge) to win the award twice. Bergkamp was voted Footballer of the Year by both his fellow pros and the football writers in 1998, having previously twice finished third in the World Player of the Year poll.

• Bergkamp's total of 37 international goals made him Holland's all-time leading scorer for a short time, until his tally was beaten by Patrick Kluivert. Dogged by a crippling fear of flying – a phobia which inevitably earned him the nickname 'The non-flying Dutchman' – Bergkamp retired from international football in 2000, as he knew he wouldn't be able to travel to the 2002 World Cup in Japan and Korea.

• When he eventually retired from club football in 2006 Bergkamp was awarded a testimonial by Arsenal in the first ever match played at the club's new Emirates Stadium.

GEORGE BEST

Born: Belfast, 22nd May 1946
Died: 25th November 2005
Position: Winger
Club career:
1963-74 Manchester United
361 (138)
1975 Stockport County 3 (2)
1975-76 Cork Celtic 3 (0)
1976-77 Fulham 33 (7)
1977-78 Los Angeles Aztecs 55 (27)
1978-79 Fort Lauderdale 26 (6)
1979-80 Hibernian 22 (3)
1980-81 San Jose Earthquakes 56 (28)
1983 Bournemouth 4 (0)
International record:
1964-78 Northern Ireland 37 (9)

Possibly the greatest natural talent in the history of the British game, George Best was a football genius who thrilled fans everywhere with his dazzling dribbling skills, superb ball control and goalscoring ability.

• **Best left his native Northern Ireland as a youngster to play for Manchester United, making his debut at Old Trafford in 1963 when aged just 17. His most memorable achievements were all packed into the next five years as he helped fire United to two league titles in 1965 and 1967 and to glory in the European Cup in 1968, Best scoring the vital second goal**

TOP 10

DUTCH PLAYERS AT ENGLISH CLUBS

1. Dennis Bergkamp, Arsenal (1995-2006)
2. Ruud van Nistelrooy, Manchester United (2001-06)
3. Edwin van der Sar, Fulham & Manchester United (2001-)
4. Arnold Muhren, Ipswich Town & Manchester United (1978-85)
5. Ruud Gullit, Chelsea (1995-98)
6. Jimmy Floyd Hasselbaink, Leeds United, Chelsea, Middlesbrough, Charlton & Cardiff City (1997-2008)
7. Jaap Stam, Manchester United (1998-2001)
8. Arjen Robben, Chelsea (2004-07)
9. Frans Thijssen, Ipswich Town & Nottingham Forest (1979-83)
10. Robin van Persie, Arsenal (2004-)

against Benfica at Wembley. In 1968 he was also named Footballer of the Year and European Footballer of the Year.

• Dubbed 'The Fifth Beatle' for his long hair and good looks, Best was the first footballer to become famous outside the game. He cashed in on his celebrity status by opening a chain of boutiques, appearing in a number of TV ads and dating a seemingly never-ending series of Miss World winners.

• **In 1970 Best scored six goals to set a still unbeaten United record as the Red Devils thrashed Northampton 8-2 in an FA Cup fifth round tie at the Cobblers' old County Ground. "I was so embarrassed that I played the last 20 minutes at left-back," he said years later.**

• There appeared to be no limit to what he might achieve, but Best's career nosedived in the 1970s as his hard-drinking, glamorous lifestyle inevitably took its toll. Sacked by Manchester United for repeatedly missing training sessions, Best played for a succession of lesser clubs in Britain and the USA, only occasionally showing

George Best, one of the greatest players ever

flashes of his old brilliance.

• **Easily the finest player ever to represent Northern Ireland, Best never appeared in the final stages of the World Cup or European Championships.** Yet he remains idolised in his home country, his standing summed up by the popular Belfast saying: "Maradona good, Pele better, George Best".

• After a long battle with alcoholism, Best died in November 2005. His passing was marked by a minute's applause at grounds up and down the country – the first British player to receive this continental-style tribute.

BIRMINGHAM CITY

Year founded: 1875
Ground: St Andrew's (30,009)
Previous names: Small Heath Alliance, Small Heath, Birmingham
Nickname: The Blues
Biggest win: 12-0 v Nottingham Forest (1899), Walsall Town Swifts (1892) and Doncaster Rovers (1903)
Heaviest defeat: 1-9 v Blackburn Rovers (1895) and Sheffield Wednesday (1930)
Colours: Blue shirts with white trim, white shorts and blue socks

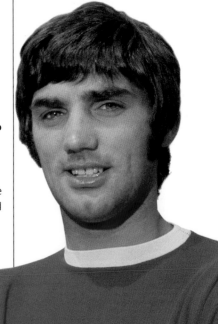

Birmingham's only major trophy was the League Cup in 1963... but they did beat Villa!

BLACKBURN ROVERS

Year founded: 1875
Ground: Ewood Park (31,367)
Nickname: Rovers
Biggest win: 11-0 v Rossendale United (1884)
Heaviest defeat: 0-8 v Arsenal (1933)
Colours: Blue-and-white halved shirts, white shorts, white socks

Founded in 1875 as Small Heath Alliance, the club were founder members and the first champions of the Second Division in 1892. Unfortunately, Small Heath were undone at the 'test match' stage (a nineteenth century version of the play-offs) and failed to gain promotion to the top flight.

• That proved to be the first of many disappointments for a club which has only rarely emerged from the shadows to rival Aston Villa as the second city's biggest outfit. In their long history, Birmingham have managed to win just one major trophy – the League Cup in 1963, although pleasingly for their long-suffering fans this success came at the expense of Villa, who were beaten 3-1 on aggregate in the final.

• On 15th May 1955 Birmingham became the first English club to compete in Europe when they drew 0-0 away to Inter Milan in the inaugural competition of the Fairs Cup. In 1960 the Blues went all the way to the final of the same tournament to set another first for English clubs in Europe, but lost 4-1 on aggregate to Barcelona. The following year Birmingham were runners-up in the Fairs Cup again, this time going down 4-2 on aggregate to Roma.

• Between December 1892 and September 1894 Birmingham went 43 consecutive league matches without a single draw – easily a record for any Football League club.

• The Blues are the only club to have hit double figures in a league fixture on five separate occasions, although they haven't managed the feat since 1915 when they trounced Glossop North End 11-1 in a Second Division fixture.

• When Birmingham won promotion to the Premier League under manager Alex McLeish in 2009 it was the 11th time in their history that had gone up to the top flight, equalling a record set by Leicester City.

• England goalkeeper Gil Merrick played in a record 551 games for Birmingham in all competitions between 1946-59. The club's record goalscorer is inter-war striker Joe Bradford with 249 league goals in the 1920s and 1930s.

• Birmingham's most famous fan is comedian Jasper Carrott, who once summed up the often depressing experience of following the club with the wry remark: "You lose some, you draw some." The Blues' lack of success over the years has been blamed on a 100-year curse put on St Andrew's by discontented gypsies who were evicted from the site when the club moved there in 1906. Various managers attempted to exorcise the curse before it ended in 2006, including 80s boss Ron Saunders who had crucifixes attached to the stadium's floodlight pylons.

HONOURS
Division 2 champions 1893, 1921, 1948, 1955
Second Division champions 1995
League Cup 1963
Football League Trophy 1991, 1995

Founded in 1875 by a group of wealthy local residents and ex-public school boys, Blackburn Rovers joined the Football League as founder members in 1888. Two years later the club moved to a permanent home at Ewood Park, where they have remained ever since.

• Blackburn were a force to be reckoned with from the start, winning the FA Cup five times in the 1880s and 1890s. Of all current league clubs Rovers were the first to win the trophy, beating Scottish side Queen's Park 2-1 in the final at Kennington Oval in 1884. The Lancashire side went on to win the cup in the two following years as well, setting a record which still stands by remaining undefeated in 24 consecutive games in the competition between 1884-86.

• Rovers won the cup again in 1890, 1891 and 1928 to make a total of six triumphs in the competition. In the first of these victories they thrashed Sheffield Wednesday 6-1 in the final, with left-winger William Townley scoring three times to become the first player to hit a hat-trick in the final.

• The club have won the league title three times: in 1912, 1914 and, most memorably, in 1995 when, funded by the millions of local steel magnate Jack Walker and powered by the deadly 'SAS' strikeforce of Alan Shearer and Chris Sutton, Rovers pipped reigning champions Manchester United to the Premiership title. The team soon broke up, though, and Rovers were relegated from the top tier just four years later.

• Derek Fazackerley made the most appearances for Blackburn, turning out in 596 games between 1970-86. The club's all-time leading scorer is Simon Garner, with 168 league goals between 1978-92, although Alan Shearer's incredible record of 122 goals in just 138 games for the club is arguably more impressive.

• **In 1891 Blackburn featured in one of the most bizarre matches in the history of the game against bitter local rivals Burnley. After two mass brawls, all the Rovers team except goalkeeper Herby Arthur decided they'd had enough and left the field. Facing the entire Burnley side on his own, Arthur successfully appealed for offside and then refused to take the free kick because he had no one to pass to, forcing the referee to abandon the game.**

• Blackburn won the League Cup for the first and only time to date in 2002, beating Tottenham 2-1 in the final at the Millennium Stadium in Cardiff. A year earlier the club had returned to the Premiership after a two-season absence.

• **During the 1990s the club twice broke the British transfer record, signing Alan Shearer from Southampton for £3.5 million in 1992 and Chris Sutton from Norwich City two years later for £5 million. The club's record purchase, however, is Andrew Cole, who cost Rovers £8 million when they bought him from Manchester United in 2001. Paraguayan striker Roque Santa Cruz is the most expensive player to leave Ewood Park, Manchester City paying £18 million for his services in 2009.**

> **HONOURS**
> *Premier League champions* 1995
> *Division 1 champions* 1912, 1914
> *Division 2 champions* 1939
> *Division 3 champions* 1975
> *FA Cup* 1884, 1885, 1886, 1890, 1891, 1928
> *League Cup* 2002

BLACKPOOL

> **Year founded:** 1887
> **Ground:** Bloomfield Road (12,555)
> **Nickname:** The Seasiders
> **Biggest win:** 10-0 v Lanerossi Vincenza (1972)
> **Heaviest defeat:** 1-10 v Small Heath (1901)
> **Colours:** Tangerine shirts, white shorts, tangerine socks

Founded in 1887 by old boys of St John's School, Blackpool joined the Second

Division of the Football League in 1896. The club merged with South Shore in 1899, the same year in which Blackpool lost their league status for a single season.

• **Blackpool's heyday was in the late 1940s and early 1950s when the club reached three FA Cup finals in five years. The Seasiders lost in the finals of 1948 and 1951 but lifted the cup in 1953 after defeating Lancashire rivals Bolton 4-3 in one of the most exciting Wembley matches ever. Although centre forward Stan Mortensen scored a hat-trick, the match was dubbed 'the Matthews final' after veteran winger Stanley Matthews, who finally won a winners' medal at the grand old age of 38.**

• An apprentice at the time of the Matthews Final, long-serving right-back Jimmy Armfield holds the record for league appearances for Blackpool, with 569 between 1952-71. Now a match summariser for BBC Radio Five Live, Armfield is also Blackpool's most capped player, having played for England 43 times. His name is honoured at Bloomfield Road in the form of the Jimmy Armfield South Stand, which opened in 2010.

• **The club's record scorer is Jimmy Hampson who hit 248 league goals between 1927-38, including a season best 45 in the 1929/30 Second Division championship-winning campaign.**

• The club first began wearing their famous tangerine shirts in 1923, following a recommendation by referee Albert Hargreaves, who had officiated at a match between Holland and Belgium and had been impressed by the Dutchmen's bold colours.

• **Blackpool's local derby at home to Bolton on 10th September 1960 was the first league game ever to**

be televised. The match didn't make great viewing for the Seasiders' fans, however, as their team slumped to a 1-0 defeat.

• Blackpool are the only club to have gained promotion from three different divisions via the play-offs, most recently rising from the Championship to the Premier League in 2010 after a thrilling 3-2 win over Cardiff City at Wembley. More than 30,000 ecstatic tangerine-clad fans celebrated the club's return to the top flight for the first time since 1971 by bringing the town's famous Golden Mile to a virtual standstill.

• **The Seasiders are arguably the smallest club to have ever hosted Premier League football. Certainly, their ramshackle Bloomfield Road ground has the lowest capacity (just 12,555) in the league's history, while the club's budget and transfer kitty are equally miniscule.**

> **HONOURS**
> *Division 2 champions* 1930
> *FA Cup* 1953
> *Football League Trophy* 2002, 2004

IS THAT A FACT?
Blackburn Rovers spent a total of £615 on players' wages in the 1885/86 campaign, the first season that FA regulations allowed professional players in English football.

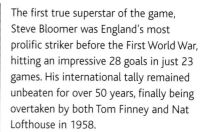

DANNY BLANCHFLOWER

Born: Belfast, 10th February 1926
Died: 9th December 1993
Position: Midfielder
Club career:
1945-49 Glentoran
1949-51 Barnsley 68 (2)
1951-54 Aston Villa 148 (10)
1954-64 Tottenham Hotspur 337 (15)
International record:
1949-63 Northern Ireland 56 (2)

An inspirational leader and cunning midfield playmaker, Danny Blanchflower was Tottenham's captain in 1961 when the club became the first in the 20th century to win the League and FA Cup Double. In the same year Blanchflower won the Footballer of the Year award for the second time, having previously been honoured in 1958. He also won the FA Cup with Spurs in 1962 and the European Cup-Winners' Cup the following year.

• Often playing alongside his brother, Jackie, Blanchflower won 56 caps for Northern Ireland. In 1958, at the World Cup in Sweden, he skippered his country to the quarter-finals of the competition for the first time before a 4-0 thrashing by France ended Northern Ireland's hopes.

• Famously, Blanchflower was the first celebrity to refuse to appear on the popular TV show *This Is Your Life*. Approached by presenter Eamonn Andrews, he walked away live on air saying, "I consider this programme to be an invasion of privacy."

• Blanchflower was a great believer in positive, attacking football and despised the win-at-all-costs mentality espoused by some managers. "The game is about glory," he once said, "it is about doing things in style and with a flourish, about going out and beating the other lot, not waiting for them to die of boredom." However, as a manager with Northern Ireland and Chelsea, who he led to relegation from the top flight in 1979, Blanchflower struggled to turn his football philosophy into practice.

STEVE BLOOMER

Born: Cradley Heath, 20th January 1874
Died: 16th April 1938
Position: Forward
Club career:
1892-1906 Derby County 375 (238)
1906-10 Middlesbrough 125 (61)
1910-14 Derby County 98 (53)
International record:
1895-1907 England 23 (28)

The first true superstar of the game, Steve Bloomer was England's most prolific striker before the First World War, hitting an impressive 28 goals in just 23 games. His international tally remained unbeaten for over 50 years, finally being overtaken by both Tom Finney and Nat Lofthouse in 1958.

• Despite being slightly-built, Bloomer was a phenomenal player, possessing a powerful shot with both feet. His career total of 317 goals in the top flight with Derby County and Middlesbrough has only been bettered by two players since, Dixie Dean and Jimmy Greaves.

• With 291 league goals, Bloomer is Derby's leading scorer of all time. He remains a legend at Pride Park where the club anthem, *Steve Bloomer's Watchin'*, is played before all home games.

• A useful all-round sportsman, Bloomer also played baseball for Derby County Baseball Club, helping them to become British champions on three occasions in the 1890s.

• After retiring as a player, Bloomer went to Germany in July 1914 to coach in Berlin. A few weeks after his arrival World War I broke out and Bloomer was interned for the duration of the conflict in a civilian detention centre.

BOCA JUNIORS

Year founded: 1905
Ground: La Bombonera (57,395)
Nickname: Los Xeneizes ('The Genoese')
Colours: Blue shirts with a yellow hoop, blue shorts, blue socks

Boca Juniors were founded in 1905 by a group of Italian immigrants in the colourful La Boca neighbourhood of Buenos Aires and, along with city rivals River Plate, are the most famous club in Argentina. Winners of the Copa Libertadores (the South American equivalent of the Champions League) six times, Boca have also won the World Club Cup (formerly the Intercontinental Cup) on three occasions.

• According to legend, the club's distinctive blue shirts with a broad

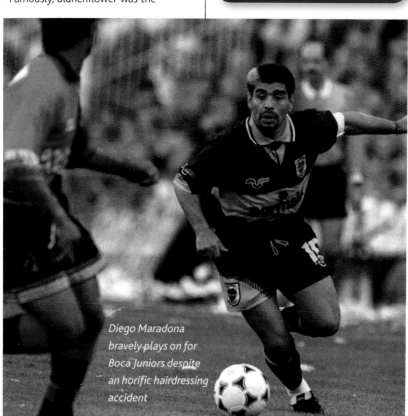

Diego Maradona bravely plays on for Boca Juniors despite an horific hairdressing accident

yellow hoop were chosen completely by chance in 1906 after it was agreed that Boca's colours would be based on the flag of the next ship to sail into the local port. As it turned out, the ship happened to be flying the blue-and-yellow flag of Sweden.

• The club's most celebrated player is Diego Maradona, who initially left Boca for Barcelona in 1982 for a world record £4.2 million. A devoted fan of the club, he returned 13 years later sporting a bizarre blue-and-yellow haircut.

• **In 1971 Boca Juniors were involved in one of the most notorious matches in the history of the game in the Copa Libertadores against Sporting Cristal of Peru. A bad tackle sparked a mass punch-up which resulted in 19 players being sent off. The brawlers were all later jailed for 30 days, apart from three who were so badly injured they had to stay in hospital. Needless to say, the match was abandoned.**

• Between May 1998 and June 1999 Boca set an Argentine record when they were undefeated for 40 consecutive games.

• **As well as running basketball and volleyball teams, the club is involved in numerous commercial activities. These include a fleet of Boca taxis, Boca wine and even a Boca-themed cemetery for deceased fans of the club!**

HONOURS
Argentine champions: 1919, 1920, 1923, 1924, 1926, 1930, 1931, 1934, 1935, 1940, 1943, 1944, 1954, 1962, 1964, 1965, 1976, 1981, 1993, 1998, 1999, 2000, 2003, 2005, 2006, 2008
Copa Libertadores: 1977, 1978, 2000, 2001, 2003, 2007
Intercontinental Cup: 1977, 2000, 2003

TOP 10

ARGENTINIAN LEAGUE WINNERS

1. River Plate 33 titles
2. Boca Juniors 23 titles
3. Independiente 14 titles
4. San Lorenzo 10 titles
5. Velez Sarsfield 7 titles
   Racing 7 titles
7. Newell's Old Boys 5 titles
8. Rosario Central 4 titles
   Estudiantes de la Plata 4 titles
10. Ferro Carril Oeste 2 titles
    Argentinos Juniors 2 titles

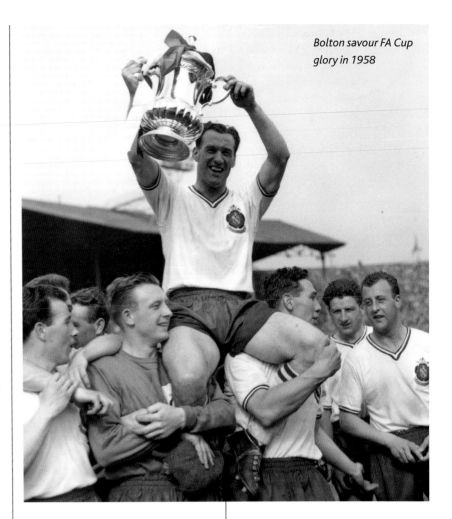

Bolton savour FA Cup glory in 1958

BOLTON WANDERERS

Year founded: 1874
Ground: The Reebok Stadium (28,723)
Previous name: Christ Church
Nickname: The Trotters
Biggest win: 13-0 v Sheffield United (1890)
Heaviest defeat: 1-9 v Preston North End (1887)
Colours: White shirts, navy blue shorts, white socks

The club was founded in 1874 as Christ Church, but three years later broke away from the church after a disagreement with the vicar and adopted their present name (the 'Wanderers' part stemmed from the fact that the club had no permanent home until moving to their former stadium Burnden Park in 1895).

• **Bolton were founder members of the Football League in 1888, finishing fifth at the end of the campaign. The Trotters have since gone on to play more seasons in the top flight without ever winning the title, 70, than any other club.**

• The club, though, have had better luck in the FA Cup. After defeats in the final in 1894 and 1904, Bolton won the cup for the first time in 1923 after beating West Ham 2-0 in the first Wembley final. In the same match Bolton centre forward David Jack enjoyed the distinction of becoming the first player to score a goal at the new stadium. The Trotters went on to win the competition again in 1926 and 1929.

• **In 1953 Bolton became the first, and so far only, team to score three goals in normal time in the FA Cup final yet finish as losers, going down 4-3 to a Stanley Matthews-inspired**

IS THAT A FACT?

In 1993 Bolton became the last club from outside the top two flights to knock out the reigning FA Cup holders when they beat Liverpool 2-0 at Anfield in a third round replay. The following season Wanderers, by then in the second tier, accounted for the holders again, beating Arsenal 3-1 in a fourth round replay at Highbury.

Blackpool. In 1958 Bolton won the cup for a fourth time, beating Manchester United 2-0 in the final at Wembley. Since then major honours have eluded the club, although the Trotters were runners-up in the League Cup in 1995 and 2004.

• The lowest moment in the club's history came at the end of the 1986/87 season when Bolton were relegated to the old Fourth Division for the first time. However, a remarkable recovery saw them reach the Premiership for the first time in 1995. Despite twice being relegated from the top flight in the late 1990s, Bolton bounced back again and under former manager Sam Allardyce established themselves as Premier League regulars.

• During Allardyce's eight-year reign at the Reebok, Bolton qualified for Europe for the first time after finishing sixth in the Premiership in 2005. The following season the Trotters reached the last 32 of the UEFA Cup before losing to Marseille. Three years later they reached the same stage of the UEFA Cup before bowing out to Sporting Lisbon.

• Bolton's old Burnden Park stadium was the scene of one of the worst disasters in the history of English football in 1946 when 33 people were killed after two barriers collapsed during a cup tie with Stoke. Amazingly, the match was played to a conclusion on the advice of the police.

• The club's top scorer is legendary centre forward Nat Lofthouse, who notched 285 goals in all competitions between 1946-60. Lofthouse is also Bolton's most capped international, making 33 appearances for England. The Trotters' appearance record is held by another England international of the same era, goalkeeper Eddie Hopkinson, who turned out 578 times for the club between 1952-70.

• In June 2008 Bolton splashed out a club record £8.2 million to bring Toulouse striker Johan Elmander to the Reebok. The club's record sale was made a few months earlier when Nicolas Anelka joined Chelsea for £15 million.

Michael Own tries on Peter Crouch's boots

BONUSES

Incentive payments above a player's salary to encourage good performance were first allowed by the Football Association in 1910. In the same year, Morton players were given a lamb by a local butcher for every goal they scored. One of the animals was made the team mascot, a role in which it served the club for some years before it drowned in the players' bath.

• **The England World Cup-winning squad of 1966 received a bonus of just £1,000 per man from the Football Association – and had to go through a lengthy court case to win exemption from the £300 tax which would otherwise have been deducted.**

• Unusual bonuses, particularly of food or drink, are especially common in Spain. For instance, Atletico Madrid's first scorer of the season can expect to receive his weight in wine while, in 2009, Osasuna's players were given a suckling pig each after a vital relegation-avoiding victory.

• **Among the most extravagant bonuses were the gifts of Cadillacs, villas, gold watches and speedboats showered on the Kuwait players by the Crown Prince when the country qualified for the 1982 World Cup in Spain.**

• Contrastingly, Iraqi players were regularly punished for defeats with beatings and imprisonment during the bloody reign of dictator Saddam Hussein. On some occasions the players were even threatened with having their legs cut off if they lost, although this brutal punishment was never carried out.

BOOTS

The first record of a pair of football boots goes back to 1526 when Henry VIII, then aged 35, ordered "45 velvet pairs and one leather pair for football" from the Great Wardrobe. Whether he actually donned the boots for a Royal kick-around in Hampton Court or Windsor Castle is not known.

• **Early leather boots were very different to the synthetic ones worn by modern players, having hard toe-caps and protection around the ankles. Studs were originally prohibited, but were sanctioned after a change in the rules in 1891. Lighter boots without ankle protection were first worn in South America, but did not become the norm in Britain until the 1950s, following the example of England international Stanley Matthews who had a lightweight pair of boots made for him by a Yorkshire company.**

• Herbert Chapman, later Arsenal's manager, is believed to be the first player to wear coloured boots, sporting a yellow pair in the 1900s. White boots first

BOURNEMOUTH

became fashionable in the 1970s when they were worn by the likes of Alan Ball (Everton), Terry Cooper (Leeds) and Marvin Hinton (Derby County). In 1996, Liverpool's John Barnes was the first player to wear white boots in an FA Cup final.

• **Boots, or rather the lack of them, became a major issue at the 1950 World Cup. After qualifying for the tournament for the first time, India pulled out of the finals after their players were refused permission to play barefoot!**

• Today's top players all have individual boot sponsorship deals with the major manufacturers. Current stars linked with the various boot companies include Cristiano Ronaldo (Nike), Kaka (Adidas) and John Terry (Umbro). In a patriotic gesture at the 2006 World Cup, all the Germany players wore boots made by the nation's leading boots manufacturer, Adidas.

BOURNEMOUTH

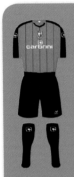

Year founded: 1899
Ground: Dean Court (11,933)
Previous names: Boscombe, Bournemouth and Boscombe Athletic
Nickname: The Cherries
Biggest win: 11-0 v Margate (1970)
Heaviest defeat: 0-9 v Lincoln City (1982)
Colours: Red-and-black shirts, black shorts and black socks

The Cherries were founded as Boscombe FC in 1899, having their origins in the Boscombe St John's club, which was formed in 1890. The club's name changed to Bournemouth and Boscombe FC in 1923 and then to AFC Bournemouth in 1971, when the team's colours were altered to red-and-black stripes in imitation of AC Milan.

• **However, any similarities with the Serie A giants end there, as much of Bournemouth's existence has been spent in the lower divisions struggling with financial difficulties. The club, though, enjoyed a glorious campaign in 2009/10 when they gained promotion to League One under rookie manager Eddie Howe, then the youngest boss in the Football League at just 32.**

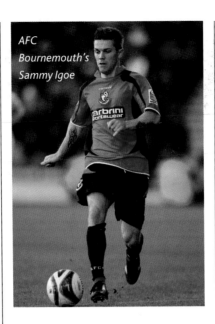

AFC Bournemouth's Sammy Igoe

• Bournemouth recorded their biggest ever win in the FA Cup, smashing fellow seasiders Margate 11-0 at Dean Court in 1970. Cherries striker Ted MacDougall scored nine of the goals, an all-time record for an individual player in the competition.

• **Bournemouth were the first ever winners of the Football League Trophy (then known as the Associate Members' Cup) in 1984, beating Hull City 2-1 in the final at Boothferry Park.**

• Famous names associated with the club include Harry Redknapp (manager, 1983-92), comedian Jim Davidson (a onetime director) and former Manchester United superstar George Best, who ended his playing career at Dean Court in 1983.

HONOURS
Division 3 champions 1987
Football League Trophy 1984

BRADFORD CITY

Year founded: 1903
Ground: Valley Parade (25,136)
Nickname: The Bantams
Biggest win: 11-1 v Rotherham United (1928)
Heaviest defeat: 1-9 v Colchester United (1961)
Colours: Claret-and-amber shirts, claret shorts and claret socks

Bradford City were founded in 1903 when a local rugby league side, Manningham FC, decided to switch codes. The club was elected to Division Two in the same year

before they had played a single match – a swift ascent into the Football League which is only matched by Chelsea.

• **City's finest hour was in 1911 when they won the FA Cup for the only time in the club's history, beating Newcastle 1-0 in a replayed final at Old Trafford. There were more celebrations in Bradford in 1929 when City won the Third Division (North) scoring 128 goals in the process – a record for the third tier.**

• Sadly, City will forever be associated with the fire that broke out in the club's main stand on 11th May 1985 and killed 56 supporters. The official inquiry into the tragedy found that the inferno had probably been caused by a discarded cigarette butt which set fire to litter under the stand.

• **West Indian full back Cec Podd holds Bradford's appearance record, turning out for the club in 502 league games between 1970-84. Northern Ireland international Bobby Campbell is the club's top scorer with 121 league goals in two spells at Valley parade in the 1980s.**

• Bradford City's coffers have been unexpectedly boosted in recent years by Harry Potter fans who have bought thousands of the club's amber and claret scarves as they are identical to Harry's house scarf at Hogwarts School!

HONOURS
Division 2 champions 1908
Division 3 (N) champions 1929
Division 3 champions 1985
FA Cup 1911

LIAM BRADY

Born: Dublin, 13th February 1956
Position: Midfielder
Club career:
1973-80 Arsenal 235 (43)
1980-82 Juventus 76 (15)
1982-84 Sampdoria 57 (6)
1984-86 Inter Milan 58 (5)
1986-87 Ascoli 17 (0)
1987-90 West Ham 89 (9)
International record:
1974-90 Republic of Ireland 72 (9)

One of the most naturally talented players of his generation, Liam Brady was the creative hub of the Arsenal side which won the FA Cup in 1979 and reached two other finals in the

Liam Brady, Arsenal legend fuelled by fish and chips

years immediately before and after that triumph. He was dubbed 'Chippy' by his Gunners team-mates, a nickname which stemmed from his fondness for fish and chips rather than his ability to dink the ball with his favoured left foot.

• Brady's visionary passing earned him the PFA Player of the Year award in 1979, while he was also Arsenal's Player of the Year three times in the 1970s.

• After impressing against Juventus in a European Cup-Winners' Cup tie in 1980, Brady was signed by the Italian titans soon afterwards in a £514,000 deal. He won the Serie A title with Juve, scoring the winning goal from the penalty spot that clinched the team's second success in 1982.

• One of four brothers who all played for English or Irish clubs, Brady won 72 caps for the Republic of Ireland. However, he never played at a major tournament, missing out on the 1988 European Championship in Germany through suspension.

• After stints with Sampdoria, Inter Milan

and Ascoli, Brady returned to England to play for West Ham. He retired in 1990 and later had unsuccessful managerial spells with Celtic and Brighton. He is now the head of youth development at Arsenal.

BRAZIL

First international: Argentina 3 Brazil 0, 1914
Most capped player: Cafu, 156 caps (1990-2006)
Leading goalscorer: Pele, 77 goals (1957-71)
First World Cup appearance: Brazil 1 Yugoslavia 2, 1930
Biggest win: Brazil 14 Nicaragua 0, 1975
Heaviest defeat: Uruguay 6 Brazil 0, 1920
Colours: Yellow shirts with green trim, blue shorts, white socks

The most successful country in the history of international football, Brazil are renowned for an exciting, flamboyant style of play which delights both their legions of drum-beating fans and neutrals alike.

• Brazil is the only country to have won the World Cup five times. The South Americans first lifted the trophy in 1958 (beating hosts Sweden 5-2 in the final) and retained the prize four years later in Chile. In 1970, a great Brazilian side featuring legends such as Pele, Jairzinho, Gerson and Rivelino thrashed Italy 4-1 to win the Jules Rimet trophy for a third time. Further triumphs followed in 1994 (3-2 on penalties against Italy after a dour 0-0 draw) and in 2002 (after beating Germany 2-0 in the final).

• Brazil is the only country to have appeared at every World Cup (a total of 19) since the tournament began in 1930. The South Americans have also scored the most goals (210) and recorded the most wins (67) at the finals.

• Brazil have worn their famous kit of yellow shirts, blue shorts and white socks since 1954 when a newspaper ran a competition for readers to design a new outfit for the national team based around the colours of the Brazilian flag. Originally their shirts were white!

• With eight wins to their name, Brazil are the third most successful side in the history of the Copa America (behind Argentina and Uruguay, who have both won the trophy 14 times). Brazil last won the tournament in Venezuela in 2007, beating neighbours Argentina 3-0 in the final.

• In 1970, after Brazil won the World Cup for a third time, they

were allowed to keep the Jules Rimet trophy. Unfortunately it was stolen from the Brazilian Football Confederation offices in Rio de Janeiro 13 years later and has never been seen since.

HONOURS
World Cup 1958, 1962, 1970, 1994, 2002
Copa America 1919, 1922, 1949, 1989, 1997, 1999, 2004, 2007
Confederations Cup 1997, 2005
World Cup record
1930 Round 1
1934 Round 1
1938 Semi-finals
1950 Runners-up
1954 Quarter-finals
1958 Winners
1962 Winners
1966 Round 1
1970 Winners
1974 Fourth place
1978 Third place
1982 Round 2
1986 Quarter-finals
1990 Round 2
1994 Winners
1998 Runners-up
2002 Winners
2006 Quarter-finals
2010 Quarter-finals

BILLY BREMNER

Born: Stirling, 9th December 1942
Died: 7th December 1997
Position: Midfielder
Club career:
1960-76 Leeds United 587 (90)
1976-79 Hull City 61 (6)
1979-81 Doncaster Rovers 5 (0)
International record
1965-75 Scotland 54 (3)

An inspirational captain for Leeds and Scotland, Billy Bremner was a busy, clever midfielder with a fiercely competitive temperament. As an influential part of the greatest ever Leeds side he won an impressive array of honours including the league championship (1969 and 1974), the FA Cup (1972), the League Cup (1968) and the Fairs Cup (1968 and 1971).

• **Bremner skippered Scotland at the 1974 World Cup in West Germany, earning rave reviews for his energetic, committed performances, but suffered the heartache of seeing his country eliminated at the group stage despite remaining undefeated in their three matches.**

• In the same year Bremner and Liverpool's Kevin Keegan were the first British players to be sent off at Wembley when they were dismissed for fighting during the Charity Shield. Both players tore off their shirts as they headed towards the tunnel, an angry gesture which later earned the pair five-week bans from the game.

• **Footballer of the Year in 1970, Bremner later managed Doncaster (twice) and his beloved Leeds (1985-88). Following his death from a heart attack, just two days before his 55th birthday, a statue of Bremner in celebratory pose was erected outside Elland Road.**

BRENTFORD

Year founded: 1889
Ground: Griffin Park (12,763)
Nickname: The Bees
Biggest win: 9-0 v Wrexham (1963)
Heaviest defeat: 0-7 v Swansea Town (1926), v Walsall (1957) and v Peterborough (2007)
Colours: Red-and-white striped shirts, black shorts, red socks

Brentford were founded in 1889 by members of a local rowing club. After playing at a number of different grounds,

Brazil have won the World Cup a record five times

These Brentford players appear to have recently visited all four of the pubs at each corner of Griffin Park!

BRIGHTON AND HOVE ALBION

Year founded: 1900
Ground: Withdean Stadium (8,850)
Previous name: Brighton and Hove Rangers
Nickname: The Seagulls
Biggest win: 10-1 v Wisbech (1965)
Heaviest defeat: 0-9 v Middlesbrough (1958)
Colours: Blue-and-white striped shirts, blue shorts and blue socks

Founded originally as Brighton and Hove Rangers in 1900, the club changed to its present name the following year. In 1920 Brighton joined Division Three as founder members, but had to wait another 38 years before gaining promotion to a higher level.

• **Brighton reached the top flight in 1979 but were relegated in 1983, the same year that they were beaten in the FA Cup final by Manchester United. Since then the club have yo-yoed between the two lower divisions, occasionally reaching the second tier, while fighting a long-running battle with the local council to get planning permission for a new stadium in Falmer, which is finally due to open in 2011. The low watermark came in 1997 when the Seagulls only avoided relegation to the Conference with a last-day victory over Doncaster Rovers, before consecutive promotions in 2001 and 2002 put a smile back on the fans' faces.**

• Brighton's record scorer is 1920s striker Tommy Cook, with 114 league goals. Cult hero Peter Ward, though, enjoyed the most prolific season in front of goal for the club, notching 32 times as the Seagulls gained promotion from the old Third Division in 1976/77.

• **Currently managed by former Chelsea and Spurs star Gus Poyet, the club's fans include TV presenters Des Lynam and Jamie Theakston and DJ Norman Cook.**

the club settled at Griffin Park in 1904.
• **The club enjoyed its heyday in the decade prior to World War II. In 1929/30 Brentford won all 21 of their home games in the Third Division (South) to set a record which remains to this day. Promoted to the First Division in 1935, the Bees finished in the top six in the next three seasons before being relegated in the first post-war campaign.**
• Despite winning the League Two Championship in 2008/09, Brentford have achieved little of note since those glory days. Supporters, though, have ample opportunity to drown their sorrows as the club's ground, Griffin Park, uniquely has a pub on all four corners.
• **Club legend Ken Coote is Brentford's leading appearance maker, playing in** 514 league games between 1949-64. The Bees' top scorer is Jim Towers, who hit 153 goals for the club in the 1950s.
• Singer Rod Stewart had trials at Brentford in 1961 before concentrating on his music career. Other famous names associated with the club are former BBC director general Greg Dyke, who is currently Brentford's chairman, and Hollywood actress Cameron Diaz, a keen fan of the Bees.

HONOURS
Division 2 champions 1935
Division 3 (S) champions 1933
Division 4 champions 1963
Third Division champions 1999
League Two champions 2009

HONOURS
Division 3 (S) champions 1958
Second Division champions 2002
Division 4 champions 1965
Third Division champions 2001

BRISTOL CITY

Year founded: 1894
Ground: Ashton Gate
(21,497)
Previous name:
Bristol South End
Nickname: The Robins
Biggest win: 11-0 v
Chichester City (1960)
Heaviest defeat: 0-9
v Coventry City (1934)
Colours: Red shirts, white shorts,
red socks

Founded as Bristol South End in 1894, the club took its present name when it turned professional three years later. In 1900 City merged with Bedminster, whose ground at Ashton Gate became the club's permanent home in 1904.

• **The Robins enjoyed a golden decade in the 1900s, winning promotion to the top flight for the first time in 1906** after a campaign in which they won a joint record 14 consecutive games. The following season City finished second behind champions Newcastle then, in 1909, they reached the FA Cup final for the first and only time in their history, losing 1-0 to Manchester United at Crystal Palace.

• Since then the followers of Bristol's biggest club have had to endure more downs than ups. The Robins returned to the top flight after a 65-year absence in 1976 but financial difficulties led to three consecutive relegations in the early 1980s (City being the first club ever to suffer this ghastly fate).

• **With 314 goals in 597 league games for the club between 1951-66, England international striker John Atyeo is both the Robins' top scorer and record appearance maker. Following his death in 1993, a stand at Ashton Gate was named after him.**

• Between October 1932 and December 1933 Bristol City conceded at least one goal in 49 consecutive Division Three (South) fixtures – a record for any division.

• **Bristol City are the only club to have won both the Welsh Cup (1934) and the Anglo-Scottish Cup (1978). Famous fans of the club include comedy genius John Cleese, *Time Team* presenter Tony Robinson and excitable BBC football commentator Jonathan Pearce.**

IS THAT A FACT?
Bristol Rovers legend Ronnie Dix is the youngest player ever to score in the Football League, getting off the mark in a 3-0 win against Norwich City in 1928 when he was aged just 15 and 180 days.

HONOURS
Division 2 champions *1906*
Division 3 (S) champions *1923,*
1927, 1955
Football League Trophy *1986*
Welsh Cup *1934*

BRISTOL ROVERS

Year founded: 1883
Ground: Memorial
Stadium (11,724)
Previous name: Black
Arabs, Eastville Rovers,
Bristol Eastville Rovers
Nickname: The Pirates
Biggest win: 15-1
v Weymouth (1900)
Heaviest defeat: 0-12
v Luton Town (1936)
Colours: Blue-and-white quartered
shirts, blue shorts, blue socks

Bristol Rovers can trace their history back to 1883 when the Black Arabs club was founded at the Eastville Restaurant in Bristol. The club was renamed Eastville Rovers the following year in an attempt to attract more support from the local area, later adding 'Bristol' to their name before finally settling on plain old 'Bristol Rovers' in 1898.

• **Rovers have lived up to their name by playing at no fewer than nine**

Derby day in Bristol is a quiet, gentle affair!

different grounds. Having spent much of their history at Eastville Stadium, they are currently based at the Memorial Stadium which they share with Bristol Rugby Club.

• The only Rovers player to have appeared for England while with The Pirates, Geoff Bradford is the club's record scorer, netting 242 times in the league between 1949-64. The club's record appearance maker is Stuart Taylor, who turned out in 546 league games between 1966-80.

• **Rovers were the first league club to play a match behind bars, taking the field against a team of prisoners at Erlestone Prison in Wiltshire in 1982.**

> HONOURS
> *Division 3 (South) champions* 1953
> *Division 3 champions* 1990

STEVE BRUCE

> **Born:** Corbridge, 31st December 1960
> **Managerial career:**
> 1998-99 Sheffield United
> 1999-2000 Huddersfield Town
> 2001 Wigan Athletic
> 2001 Crystal Palace
> 2001-07 Birmingham City
> 2007-09 Wigan Athletic
> 2009- Sunderland

Much-travelled Sunderland manager Steve Bruce enjoyed a decent start to his tenure at the Stadium of Light in 2009/10, guiding the Black Cats to mid-table respectability.

• **After starting his managerial career at Sheffield United, Steve Bruce had brief spells in charge of Huddersfield, Wigan and Crystal Palace before eventually joining Birmingham in 2001. In six years at St Andrew's he guided the Brummies to two promotions to the Premiership, before leaving to rejoin Wigan in 2007.**

• Often described as one of the best defenders never to win an England cap, Bruce became the first Englishman in the 20th century to captain a Double-winning side when he led Manchester United to league and cup glory in 1994. In a nine-year career with United, after signing from Norwich in 1987, Bruce also won two other Premier League titles, the FA Cup in 1990, the Cup-Winners' Cup in 1991 and the League Cup in 1992.

• Bruce has published three novels featuring the exploits of fictional football manager Steve Barnes. One of the trilogy was described by a reviewer as "surprisingly punchy and pacey, although the plot is essentially ludicrous."

GIANLUIGI BUFFON

> **Born:** Carrara, Italy, 28th January 1978
> **Position:** Goalkeeper
> **Club career:**
> 1995-2001 Parma 168
> 2001- Juventus 273
> **International record:**
> 1997- Italy 102

Gianluigi Buffon became the world's most expensive goalkeeper when he moved from Parma to Juventus in 2001 for a staggering £52 million. He soon proved his worth, though, helping Juve win consecutive titles in his first two seasons with the Turin club, having previously lifted the UEFA Cup with Parma in 1999.

• **Since making his international debut against Russia in 1997, Buffon has been a fixture between the posts for Italy. In 2006 he won a World Cup winners' medal with the azzurri, after Italy beat France in a penalty**

Buffon: more than 100 caps for Italy

shoot-out in the final in Berlin. Buffon's outstanding form – he conceded just two goals in the entire tournament – earned him the Yashin Award for the best goalkeeper in the competition. At the end of the year he was runner-up to Italian team-mate Fabio Cannavaro in the European Footballer of the Year poll, the first goalkeeper to be ranked so highly since Italian legend Dino Zoff also came second in 1973.

• Buffon would have had two more Serie A titles to his name had Juventus not been stripped of their 2005 and 2006 championship victories for their part in a match-fixing scandal. The club was also punished with relegation to Serie B in 2006 but, to the surprise of many, Buffon decided to stay put and help Juve win promotion the following year.

• **Serie A Goalkeeper of the Year on a record nine occasions and the fourth-highest capped Italian international ever, Buffon is married to Czech model and former Miss World contestant Alena Seredova.**

BURNLEY

Year founded: 1882
Ground: Turf Moor (22,546)
Nickname: The Clarets
Biggest win: 9-0 v Darwen (1892), v New Brighton (1957) and v Penrith (1984)
Heaviest defeat: 0-11 v Darwen (1885)
Colours: Claret shirts with sky blue sleeves, white shorts, claret and blue socks

One of England's most famous old clubs, Burnley were founded in 1882 when the Burnley Rovers rugby team decided to switch to the round ball game. The club was a founder member of the Football League in 1888 and has since won all four divisions of the league – a feat matched only by Preston and Wolves.

• **Burnley have twice won the league championship, in 1921 and 1960. The first of these triumphs saw the Clarets go on a 30-match unbeaten run, the longest in a single season until Arsenal** went through the whole of 2003/04 undefeated. In its own way, Burnley's 1960 title win was just as remarkable, as the Clarets only ever topped the league on the last day of the season.

• The club's only FA Cup triumph came in 1914 when they defeated Liverpool 1-0 in the last final at Crystal Palace. After the final whistle Burnley's captain Tommy Boyle became the first man to receive the cup from a reigning monarch, King George V.

• **Less gloriously, Burnley were the victims of one of the biggest ever FA Cup shocks when, as a First Division club, they lost 1-0 at home to Southern League Wimbledon in 1975. The club were relegated to the Second Division the following year, and their slide continued until 1987 when only a last-day victory saved them from relegation to the Conference.**

HONOURS
Division 1 champions 1921, 1960
Division 2 champions 1898, 1973
Division 3 champions 1982
Division 4 champions 1992
FA Cup 1914

BURTON ALBION

Year founded: 1950
Ground: Pirelli Stadium (6,200)
Nickname: The Brewers
Biggest win: 12-1 v Coalville Town (1954)
Heaviest defeat: 0-10 v Barnet (1970)
Colours: Yellow shirts, black shorts, black socks

Burton Albion were founded at a public meeting at the Town Hall in 1950. The town had previously supported two Football League clubs, Burton Swifts and Burton Wanderers, who merged to form Burton United in 1901 before folding nine years later.

• **The Brewers gained promotion to the Football League for the first time in 2009. Their inaugural season in the league was satisfying rather than spectacular, boss Paul Peschisolido leading them to a position halfway up the table.**

• Famous names to manage the club include Crystal Palace boss Neil Warnock,

Burnley triumph in the 2009/10 'shout the loudest' competition

former England international Ian Storey-Moore, Peter Taylor, Brian Clough's assistant at Derby and Nottingham Forest in the 1970s, and Clough's son, Nigel.

• Burton have reached the third round of the FA Cup on three occasions, most recently in 2006 when they held mighty Manchester United to a 0-0 draw at home. A record visiting contingent at Old Trafford of 11,000 Brewers fans attended the replay, but they had little to cheer about as United strolled to an emphatic 5-0 victory.

HONOURS
Conference champions 2009

BURY

Year founded: 1885
Ground: Gigg Lane (11,669)
Nickname: The Shakers
Biggest win: 12-1 v Stockton (1897)
Heaviest defeat: 0-10 v Blackburn Rovers (1887) and West Ham (1982)
Colours: White shirts, blue shorts, blue socks

The club with the shortest name in the Football League, Bury were founded in 1885 at a meeting at the Old White Horse Hotel in Bury, as successors to two other teams in the town, the Bury Unitarians and the Bury Wesleyans. Bury were founder members of the Lancashire League in 1889, joining the Second Division of the Football League five years later.

• Bury have won the FA Cup on two occasions, in 1900 and 1903. In the second of these triumphs, The Shakers thrashed Derby County 6-0 at Crystal Palace to record the biggest ever victory in an FA Cup final.

• On 27th August 2005 Bury became the first club to score 1,000 goals in all four tiers of the Football League. The landmark was reached when Brian Barry-Murphy scored the first of the Shakers' goals in their 2-2 home draw with Wrexham in a League Two fixture.

• The following year Bury set a less happy record, when they became the first club to be thrown out of the FA Cup for fielding an ineligible player – Stephen Turnbull, a loan signing from Hartlepool United.

HONOURS
Division 2 champions 1895
Division 3 champions 1961
Second Division champions 1997
FA Cup 1900, 1903

SIR MATT BUSBY

Born: Orbiston, North Lanarkshire, 26th May 1909
Died: 20th January 1994
Managerial career:
1945-69 Manchester United
1970-71 Manchester United
1958 Scotland

The longest-serving post-war manager in English football, Manchester United legend Sir Matt Busby was in charge at Old Trafford for a total of 25 years until he retired in 1971. In that time he won five League championships (1952, 1956, 1957, 1965 and 1967) and the FA Cup in 1948 and 1963.

• Busby was also the first manager to win the European Cup with an English club, United defeating Benfica 4-1 at Wembley in 1968. Shortly after this triumph, Busby was knighted.

• It had long been Busby's dream to win club football's greatest prize and it was one he might have fulfilled much earlier but for the Munich air crash of 1958, in which eight members of his brilliant United side (nicknamed the 'Busby Babes' because they were so young)

TOP 10

BIGGEST FA CUP FINAL VICTORIES

1. **1903** Bury 6 Derby County 0
2. **1890** Blackburn Rovers 6 The Wednesday 1
3. **1900** Bury 4 Southampton 0
   1983 Manchester United 4 Brighton 0
   1994 Manchester United 4 Chelsea 0
6. **1894** Notts County 4 Bolton Wanderers 1
   1899 Sheffield United 4 Derby County 1
   1939 Portsmouth 4 Wolverhampton Wanderers 1
   1946 Derby County 4 Charlton Athletic 1

were killed. Busby himself suffered multiple injuries in the crash and spent two months in hospital before returning to Old Trafford to rebuild his shattered team.

• Ironically, Busby's playing career was spent with United's two great rivals, Liverpool and Manchester City (with whom he won the FA Cup in 1934). A defensive midfielder, he won one cap for Scotland against Wales in 1933. Some 25 years later he briefly managed the Scots on a part-time basis, during which time he gave an international debut to future United star Denis Law.

Matt Busby (far right) takes the FA Cup back to Manchester in 1953

Eric Cantona only failed to win the league title in one of his six seasons in English football

ERIC CANTONA

Born: Paris, France, 24th May 1966
Position: Striker
Club career:
1983-88 Auxerre 81 (23)
1985-86 Martigues (loan) 15 (4)
1988-91 Marseille 40 (13)
1988-89 Bordeaux (loan) 11 (6)
1989-90 Montpellier (loan) 33 (10)
1991-92 Nimes 17 (2)
1992 Leeds United 28 (9)
1992-97 Manchester United 144 (64)
International record:
1987-95 France 45 (20)

Maverick Frenchman Eric Cantona is one of the most successful foreign players in Premiership history, winning the league championship in five of his six seasons in English football and landing the Double twice.

• In 1993, Cantona became the first ever player to win back-to-back league titles with two different clubs when he fired Manchester United to the championship just 12 months after helping Leeds do the same. Amazingly for such an influential figure, Cantona's switch across the Pennines cost the Old Trafford side just £1.2 million in November 1992.

• The signing of the inspirational Cantona proved to be the catalyst for a decade of dominance by United in the 1990s. In 1994 the former Marseille star was voted PFA Player of the Year as United won the Double for the first time in their history, Cantona coolly slotting home two penalties in his side's 4-0 thrashing of Chelsea in the FA Cup final. Two years later, United won the Double for a second time and again Cantona was their match-winner in the FA Cup final, scoring the only goal of the game against Liverpool. Another PFA Player of the Year award duly followed.

• However, the period in between these triumphs saw Cantona serve an eight-month ban after he launched a 'kung fu' kick at an abusive Crystal Palace fan in a match at Selhurst Park in January 1995. The hot-headed Frenchman was also fined £10,000 by the FA and ordered to complete 120 hours of community service after being found guilty of assault.

• Since his retirement from the game in 1997 when he was aged just 30, Cantona has pursued a successful career as an actor, starring as himself in the 2009 film *Looking for Eric*.

FABIO CAPELLO

Born: Pieris, Italy, 18th June 1946
Managerial career:
1991-96 AC Milan
1996-97 Real Madrid
1997-98 AC Milan
1999-2004 Roma
2004-06 Juventus
2006-07 Real Madrid
2008- England

Legendary Italian manager Fabio Capello has enjoyed mixed fortunes since being

appointed England boss in January 2008. He led the Three Lions to their best ever start to a World Cup qualifying campaign, with seven straight victories, but at the finals in South Africa saw his team thrashed 4-1 by Germany in the first knock-out round — England's worst ever World Cup defeat.

• A strict disciplinarian and astute tactician, Capello has a hugely impressive managerial CV. With AC Milan in the early 1990s he won the league title in four out of five seasons, and also led the rossoneri to a stunning Champions League final victory over Barcelona in 1994. Further titles followed at Real Madrid in 1997, Roma in 2001 and Juventus in 2005 and 2006 (although the club was later stripped of these honours for their involvement in a match-fixing scandal). In 2006 Capello returned to Madrid and guided the Spanish giants to another title on the last day of the season, but his cautious tactical approach was not appreciated by Real president Ramon Calderon and he was sacked.

• During his playing days, Capello won three Serie A titles with Juventus in the 1970s. He also played for Roma and AC Milan and represented Italy on 32 occasions. Capello scored the only goal of the game when Italy won at Wembley for the first time in 1973.

• Capello has a keen interest in fine art, with a collection estimated to be worth around £17 million.

CAPS

Legendary goalkeeper Peter Shilton has won more international caps than any other British player. 'Shilts' played for England 125 times between 1970-90 and would have won many more caps if he had not faced stiff competition for the No. 1 shirt from his great rival Ray Clemence, who won 61 caps during the same period. Along with Billy Wright, Sir Bobby Charlton, Bobby Moore and David Beckham, Shilton is one of just five players to have won over 100 caps for England.

• The first international caps were awarded by England in 1886, following a proposal put forward by the founder of the Corinthians, NL Jackson. To this day players actually receive a handmade 'cap' to mark the achievement of playing for their country. England caps are made by a Bedworth-based company called Toye, Kenning & Spencer, who also provide regalia for the freemasons.

Fabio Capello oversaw England's worst ever World Cup defeat, 4-1 to Germany

• A handful of players have won caps for more than one country, including the great Real Madrid striker Alfredo di Stefano who represented Spain and Colombia as well as his native Argentina.

CARDIFF CITY

Year founded: 1899
Ground: Cardiff City Stadium (26,828)
Previous name: Riverside
Nickname: The Bluebirds
Biggest win: 8-0 v Enfield (1931)
Heaviest defeat: 2-11 v Sheffield United (1926)
Colours: Blue shirts, white shorts, white socks

Founded as the football branch of the Riverside Cricket Club, the club changed to its present name in 1908, three years after Cardiff was awarded city status.

• Cardiff are the only non-English club to have won any of the three main English honours, lifting the FA Cup in 1927 after a 1-0 victory over Arsenal at Wembley. The Bluebirds came close to repeating that feat in 2008, but were beaten 1-0 by Portsmouth in only the second FA Cup final staged at the new Wembley.

• In 1924 Cardiff were pipped to the league title by Herbert Chapman's Huddersfield on goal average, after being held to a 0-0 draw by Birmingham in their final match. If striker Len Davies hadn't missed a penalty in that game the title would have gone to Wales for the first and only time.

• Cardiff, who missed out on promotion to the Premier League in 2010 after losing to Blackpool in the play-off final, have won the Welsh Cup 22 times, just one short of Wrexham's record. The Bluebirds' domination of the tournament in the 1960s and 1970s earned them regular qualification for the European Cup-Winners' Cup and in 1968 they reached the semi-finals of the competition before losing 4-3 on aggregate to Hamburg.

• Cardiff's record appearance maker is Phil Dwyer, who turned out 471 times for the club between 1972-1985. The Bluebirds' record scorer is Len Davies, who banged in 128 league goals in the 1920s.

> **HONOURS**
> *Division 3 (S) champions* 1947
> *Third Division champions* 1993
> *FA Cup* 1927
> *Welsh Cup* 1912, 1920, 1922, 1923, 1927, 1928, 1930, 1956, 1959, 1964, 1965, 1967, 1968, 1969, 1970, 1971, 1973, 1974, 1976, 1988, 1992, 1993

CARLISLE UNITED

Year founded: 1903
Ground: Brunton Park (16,651)
Nickname: The Blues
Biggest win: 8-0 v Hartlepool (1928) and v Scunthorpe (1952)
Heaviest defeat: 1-11 v Hull City (1939)
Colours: Blue shirts, white shorts, white socks

Carlisle United were formed in 1903 following the merger of two local clubs, Shaddongate United and Carlisle Red Rose. The Blues joined the Third Division (North) in 1928 and were long-term residents of the bottom two divisions until 1965, when they won promotion to the second tier for the first time.

• Although the club have enjoyed consecutive promotions from the Conference to League One in recent years, Carlisle's finest moment came in 1974 when, in their one season in the top flight, they sat on top of the old First Division after three games. Sadly, the Cumbrians were soon knocked off their lofty perch and finished the campaign rock bottom.

• A long period of decline meant that by 1999 Carlisle were facing relegation from the Football League. However, needing a win against Plymouth on the last day of the season to stay up, United were saved when on-loan goalkeeper Jimmy Glass went up for a corner and scored a dramatic last-gasp winner.

• In 1946 Carlisle appointed 23-year-old Ivor Broadis as their player/manager, the youngest man ever to take on the role with any club. Three years later Broadis transferred himself to Sunderland for £18,000 but he returned to Carlisle as player/coach in 1955.

• Carlisle have reached the final of the Football League Trophy on a record five occasions, but only managed to lift the cup on one of those occasions, against Colchester in 1997.

> **HONOURS**
> *Division 3 champions* 1965
> *Third Division champions* 1995
> *League Two champions* 2006
> *Football League Trophy* 1997

JAMIE CARRAGHER

> **Born:** Bootle, 28th January 1978
> **Position:** Defender
> **Club career:**
> 1996- Liverpool 435 (4)
> **International record:**
> 1999-2010 England 38 (0)

The rock at the heart of Liverpool's defence for many years, Jamie Carragher is the Reds' vice-captain and the longest-serving player at the club. After making his debut in 1996 Carragher had to wait until 2001 before winning his first silverware, when he was a member of the Liverpool side which won the 'treble' of FA Cup, League Cup and UEFA Cup.

• Carragher's greatest triumph, though, came in 2005 when, despite being afflicted with cramp, he helped Liverpool win the Champions League after a dramatic penalty shoot-out victory over AC Milan in Istanbul. Two years later he was a member of the Reds side that reached the final again, this time losing to Milan in Athens.

• An excellent man-marker and reader of the game who can operate equally effectively in central defence or at right back, Carragher has made more appearances in Europe than any other player in Liverpool's history, becoming the first Red to reach three figures in 2008.

• Carragher was one of three England players to miss from the penalty spot in the quarter-final shoot-out against Portugal at the 2006 World Cup. The following year, frustrated at not holding down a regular place in the England team, he announced his retirement from international football but Fabio Capello persuaded him to come back to the fold for the 2010 World Cup, where he made two appearances in the group stage.

IKER CASILLAS

> **Born:** Madrid, 20th May 1981
> **Position:** Goalkeeper
> **Club career:**
> 1999- Real Madrid 385
> **International record:**
> 2000- Spain 112

Spain captain Iker Casillas is the only goalkeeper to have skippered his country to success in both the European Championships and the World Cup. The Real Madrid star pulled off the first leg of this double when Spain beat Germany in the Euro 2008 final in Vienna, before landing the biggest prize of all two years later after Spain's 1-0 defeat of Holland in the 2010 World Cup final in Johannesburg.

• In 2000 Casillas became the youngest goalkeeper to play in the Champions League final, appearing in Real's 3-0 victory over Valencia just four days after his 19th birthday. He won the competition again two years later, after coming on as a sub in Real's 2-1 defeat of Bayer Leverkusen in the final in Glasgow.

• Casillas is the second-highest capped international in Spanish football history, but still has a little way to go to beat fellow goalkeeper Andoni Zubizarreta's record of 126 games for Spain, set between 1983-96.

• A superb shot-stopper, Casillas made a crucial penalty save in Spain's 1-0 quarter-final win against Paraguay at the 2010 World Cup. Perhaps, though, the most important save of his career came in the final against Holland when he blocked a close-range shot

Iker Casillas is well on his way to becoming Spain's mopst capped player ever

TOP 10

PLAYERS NAMED AFTER COUNTRIES

1. Petr Cech (Czech Republic, 2002-)
2. Mike England (Wales, 1962-75)
3. Joe Jordan (Scotland, 1973-82)
4. Matt Holland (Republic of Ireland, 199-2006)
5. Alan Brazil (Scotland, 1980-83
6. Stephen Ireland (Republic of Ireland, 2006-07)
7. Jason Scotland (Trinidad & Tobago, 2000-)
8. Ryan France (Sheffield United)
9. Gary Wales (ex-Kilmarnock)
10. Lee Poland (ex-Northwich Victoria)

CELTIC

Year founded: 1888
Ground: Celtic Park (60,832)
Nickname: The Bhoys
Biggest win: 11-0 v Dundee (1895)
Heaviest defeat: 0-8 v Motherwell (1937)
Colours: Green-and-white hooped shirts, white shorts, green and white socks

by Arjen Robben with his feet. Casillas had previously twice saved two penalties in high-profile shoot-outs, against Italy in a Euro 2008 quarter-final and against the Republic of Ireland at the 2002 World Cup.

PETR CECH

Born: Plzen, Czech Republic, 20th May 1982
Position: Goalkeeper
Club career:
1999-2001 Chmel Blsany 27
2001-02 Sparta Prague 27
2002-04 Rennes 70
2004- Chelsea 184
International record:
2002- Czech Republic 70

A brilliant shot-stopper who dominates his penalty area with his imposing physique, Cech joined the Londoners from French club Rennes for £10 million in 2004. During Chelsea's title-winning season in 2004/05, Cech set two Premiership records by keeping 25 clean sheets and going 1,025 minutes without conceding a goal (the second record has since been beaten by Edwin van der Sar).

• **He had previously set a similar national record in his native Czech Republic, clocking up 855 minutes without conceding in the 2001/02 season while with Sparta Prague.**

• Cech was a member of the Czech Republic side which reached the semi-finals of Euro 2004 before losing to eventual winners Greece. He also played at Euro 2008, but a rare mistake in a 3-2 defeat against Turkey cost his team a place in the knock-out stages.

• **In October 2006 Cech suffered a depressed fracture of the skull following a challenge by Reading's Stephen Hunt. He returned to action after three months out of the game wearing a rugby-style headguard for protection, and later added a chin guard after being accidentally kicked in the face by Chelsea team-mate Ben Tal Haim during a training session.**

The first British team to win the European Cup, Celtic were founded by an Irish priest in 1887 with the aim of raising funds for poor children in Glasgow's East End slums. The club were founder members of the Scottish League in 1890, winning their first title three years later.

• **Celtic have won the Scottish Cup more times than any other club, with 34 victories in the final. The Bhoys first won the cup in 1892, beating Queen's Park 5-1 in a replay.**

• Under legendary manager Jock Stein Celtic won the Scottish league for nine consecutive seasons in the 1960s and 1970s, with a side featuring great names like Billy McNeill, Jimmy Johnstone, Bobby Lennox and Tommy Gemmell. This extraordinary run of success equalled a world record established by MTK Budapest of Hungary in the 1920s but, painfully for Celtic fans, was later matched by bitter rivals Rangers in the 1990s.

Celtic fans welcome Rangers to Parkhead in the traditional manner!

• The greatest ever Celtic side, managed by Stein and dubbed the 'Lisbon Lions', became the first British club to win the European Cup when they beat Inter Milan 2-1 in the Portuguese capital in 1967. Stein was central to the team's triumph, scoring an early point by sitting in Inter manager Helenio Herrera's seat and refusing to budge and then urging his players forward after they went a goal down to the defensive-minded Italians. Sticking to their attacking game plan, Celtic fought back with goals by Gemmell and Steve Chalmers to spark jubilant celebrations at the end among the travelling Celtic fans. Remarkably, all the 'Lisbon Lions' were born and bred within a 30 mile radius of Celtic Park.

• That 1966/67 season was the most successful in the club's history as they won every competition they entered: the Scottish League, Scottish Cup and Scottish League Cup, as well as the European Cup. To this day, no other British side has won a similar 'Quadruple'.

• The skipper of the Lisbon Lions was Billy McNeill, who went on to play in a record 790 games for Celtic in all competitions between 1957-75. He later managed the club, leading Celtic to the Double in their centenary season in 1987/88. The club's most capped player is goalkeeper Pat Bonner, who made 80 appearances for the Republic of Ireland between 1981-96.

• Jimmy McGrory, who played for the club between 1922-38, scored a staggering 397 goals for Celtic – a British record by a player for a single club. His most prolific season for the Bhoys was in 1935/36 when he hit a club record 50 league goals.

• In 1957 Celtic won the Scottish League Cup for the first time, demolishing Rangers 7-1 in the final at Hampden Park. The victory stands as the biggest by either side in an Old Firm match and is also a record for a major Scottish cup final. Celtic went on to enjoy more success in the League Cup, appearing in a record 14 consecutive finals (winning six)

between 1965-78.

• Celtic hold the record for the longest unbeaten run in Scottish football, with 62 matches undefeated (49 wins, 13 draws) from 13th November 1915 until 21st April 1917 when Kilmarnock finally beat the men from Glasgow 2-0. The club also holds the record for the most points in a single league season, racking up 103 when winning the SPL in 2002.

• **Two years later, during the 2003/04 season, Celtic won an incredible 25 SPL games on the trot. The run was a Scottish record and has only ever been bettered by three clubs worldwide.**

• Celtic's fans are known throughout the world for their passionate and devoted support. In 2003, 80,000 of them pitched up in Seville for the UEFA Cup final defeat by Porto, the largest away following to travel abroad for a match in the history of the game.

HONOURS
Division 1 champions *1893, 1884, 1896, 1898, 1905, 1906, 1907, 1908, 1909, 1910, 1914, 1915, 1916, 1917, 1919, 1922, 1926, 1936, 1938, 1954, 1966, 1967, 1968, 1969, 1970, 1971, 1972, 1973, 1974*
Premier Division champions *1977, 1979, 1981, 1982, 1986, 1988, 1998, 2001, 2002, 2004, 2006, 2007, 2008*
Scottish Cup *1892, 1899, 1900, 1904, 1907, 1908, 1911, 1912, 1914, 1923, 1925, 1927, 1931, 1933, 1937, 1951, 1954, 1965, 1967, 1969, 1971, 1972, 1974, 1975, 1977, 1980, 1985, 1988, 1989, 1995, 2001, 2004, 2005, 2007*
League Cup *1957, 1958, 1966, 1967, 1968, 1969, 1970, 1975, 1983, 1998, 2000, 2001, 2006*
European Cup *1967*

CHAMPIONS LEAGUE

The most prestigious competition in club football, the Champions League replaced the old European Cup in 1992. Previously a competition for domestic league champions only, runners-up from the main European nations were first admitted in 1997 and the tournament has subsequently expanded to include up to four entrants per country.

• **Spanish giants Real Madrid won the first European Cup in 1956, defeating French side Reims 4-3 in the final in Paris. Real went on to win the competition in the next four years as well, thanks largely to the brilliance of their star players Alfredo Di Stefano,**

Inter lift the Champions League trophy in 2010

Ferenc Puskas and Francisco Gento. With six wins in the European Cup and three in the Champions League, Real have won the competition a record nine times.

• The first British club to win the European Cup were Celtic, who famously beat Inter Milan in the final in Lisbon in 1967. The following year Manchester United became the first English club to triumph, beating Benfica 4-1 at Wembley. The most successful British club in the tournament, though, are Liverpool, with five wins in 1977, 1978, 1981, 1984 and 2005 followed by Manchester United with three (1968, 1999 and 2008). Two other English clubs, Nottingham Forest (in 1979 and 1980) and Aston Villa (in 1982), have also won the tournament.

• Real's former striker Raul is the leading scorer in the competition, with an incredible 66 goals. Paulo Maldini of AC Milan holds the record for the most appearances, having played in 163 games in the European Cup and Champions League.

• Dutch midfielder Clarence Seedorf is the only player to have won the Champions League with three different clubs, winning the trophy with Ajax in 1995, Real Madrid in 1998 and AC Milan in 2003 and 2007.

• Between March 2005 and May 2006 Arsenal went a record 995 minutes without conceding a goal in the Champions League. The Gunners' defence was eventually breached by Barcelona, who beat the north

Londoners in the 2006 final in Paris.

• Manchester United were unbeaten in a record 25 games in the Champions League between 2007-09. This impressive run finally came to an end when they lost 2-0 to Barcelona in the 2009 final in Rome.

• Feyenoord recorded the biggest win in the competition in 1969 when they thrashed KR Reykjavik 12-2 in the first round. Benfica hold the record for the biggest aggregate victory with an 18-0 first round humiliation of Luxembourg no-hopers Stade Dudelange in 1965.

CHAMPIONS LEAGUE FINALS
1993 Marseille 1 AC Milan 0
1994 AC Milan 4 Barcelona 0
1995 Ajax 1 AC Milan 0
1996 Juventus 1* Ajax 1
1997 Borussia Dortmund 3 Juventus 1
1998 Real Madrid 1 Juventus 0
1999 Man United 2 Bayern Munich 1
2000 Real Madrid 3 Valencia 0
2001 Bayern Munich 1* Valencia 1
2002 Real Madrid 2
Bayer Leverkusen 1
2003 AC Milan 0* Juventus 0
2004 Porto 3 Monaco 0
2005 Liverpool 3* AC Milan 3
2006 Barcelona 2 Arsenal 1
2007 AC Milan 2 Liverpool 1
2008 Man United 1* Chelsea 1
2009 Barcelona 2 Man United 0
2010 Inter Milan 2 Bayern Munich 0
* Won on penalties

CHANTS

A survey by Sky Sports during the 2008/09 season found that Stoke City fans were the loudest in the Premier League, their chants averaging an impressive 101.8 decibels. They were followed by fans of Tottenham and Liverpool, while Sunderland supporters were the quietest.

• In 2004, in a competition sponsored by Barclaycard, Birmingham fan Jonny Hurst was chosen as England's first 'Chant Laureate' by a judging panel chaired by Poet Laureate Andrew Motion. Bizarrely, Hurst's winning entry, set to the tune of the Barry Manilow song Copacabana, was about Colombian striker Juan Pablo Angel – who, at the time, was playing for Brum's arch rivals Aston Villa!

• Possibly the oldest football chant is 'Who ate all the pies?', which researchers at Oxford University have discovered dates back to 1894 when it was playfully directed by Sheffield United fans at their 22-stone goalkeeper William 'Fatty' Foulke. The chant stemmed from an incident when the tubby custodian got up early at the team hotel, sneaked down into the dining room and munched his way through all the pies that were laid out for the players' breakfast.

HERBERT CHAPMAN

Born: Kiveton Park, Yorkshire, 19th January 1878
Died: 6th January 1934
Managerial career:
1907-12 Northampton Town
1912-19 Leeds City
1921-25 Huddersfield Town
1925-34 Arsenal

Herbert Chapman rivals Arsene Wenger as Arsenal's greatest ever manager. Previously trophyless, the Gunners won two league titles and the FA Cup during Chapman's nine years at the club and went on to dominate English football in the years after his sudden death from pneumonia in January 1934.

• One of the game's first modernisers, Chapman introduced new tactics and training methods, as well as championing floodlights, shirt numbers and a Europe-wide football competition years before they all became an accepted part of the game. He is also credited with adding white

sleeves to Arsenal's previously all-red shirts after admiring the outfit of a staff member in the Arsenal club offices who came to work sporting a white shirt with a red tank top.

• Before he joined Arsenal in 1925, Chapman managed Northampton, Leeds City and Huddersfield Town. His four-year spell with Huddersfield was easily the most successful in the club's history, the Terriers winning the FA Cup and two league titles under his management, with a third following the season after he left. While he was at Arsenal, Chapman also took charge of two England games in 1933.

• In recognition of his achievements with the Gunners, a bronze bust of Chapman stands inside the Emirates Stadium.

JOHN CHARLES

Born: Swansea, 27th December 1931
Died: 21st February 2004
Position: Striker/Defender
Club career
1949-57 Leeds United 297 (150)
1957-62 Juventus 150 (93)
1962 Leeds United 11 (3)
1962-63 Roma 10 (4)
1963-66 Cardiff City 69 (18)
International record:
1950-65 Wales 38 (15)

Until his record was beaten by Ryan Giggs, John Charles was the youngest player to appear for Wales, winning his first cap against Northern Ireland in March 1950 aged 18 and 71 days. Eight years later Charles was the star of the greatest Wales side ever, which reached the quarter-finals of the World Cup in Sweden before going down 1-0 to eventual winners Brazil.

• Charles began his career at Leeds, where he averaged a goal every other game in almost 300 appearances for the club. In 1957 he became one of the first British players to move abroad, joining Italian giants Juventus for £65,000, a British transfer record at the time. Equally comfortable at centre forward or centre-half, the barrel-chested Charles was a sensation in Turin, helping Juve to win three Scudettos and two Italian Cups in his five years with the club.

• Dubbed 'the Gentle Giant' in Italy, Charles was never booked or sent off in

The incredible John Charles in action for Juventus

an 18-year professional career. In 1997 he was voted the best ever foreign player in the history of Serie A and, following his death in 2004, a stand was named after him at Elland Road.

CHARLTON ATHLETIC

Year founded: 1905
Ground: The Valley (27,111)
Nickname: The Addicks
Biggest win: 8-1 v Middlesbrough (1953)
Heaviest defeat: 1-11 v Aston Villa (1959)
Colours: Red shirts, white shorts, red socks

Charlton Athletic were founded in 1905 when a number of youth clubs in the south-east London area, including East Street Mission and Blundell Mission, decided to merge. The club, whose nickname 'the Addicks' stemmed from the haddock served by a local chippy, graduated from minor leagues to join the Third Division (South) in 1921.

• Charlton's heyday was shortly before and just after World War II. In 1937 the Addicks finished runners-up, just three points behind League champions Manchester City, and followed that with fourth and third-place finishes in the two subsequent seasons. After losing in the 1946 FA Cup final to Derby County, Charlton returned to Wembley the following year and this time lifted the cup thanks to a 1-0 victory over Burnley in the final.

• Charlton's home ground, The Valley, used to be one of the biggest in English football. In 1938 a then record crowd of 75,031 squeezed into the stadium to see the Addicks take on Aston Villa in a fifth round FA Cup tie. In 1985, though, financial problems forced Charlton to leave the Valley and the Addicks spent seven years as tenants of West Ham and Crystal Palace before making an emotional return to their ancestral home in 1992.

• When the play-offs were introduced in season 1986/87, Charlton figured among the first finalists, beating Leeds to preserve their First Division status. In 1998, during the long managerial reign of Alan Curbishley, the Addicks triumphed in possibly the most gripping Wembley play-off final, beating Sunderland 7-6 on penalties after a 4-4 draw to earn promotion to the Premiership.

• Sam Bartram, who was known as 'the finest keeper England never had' played a record 623 games for the club between 1934-56. Bearded striker Derek Hales is Charlton's record goalscorer, notching 168 in two spells at the club in the 1970s and 1980s.

> **HONOURS**
> **First Division champions** 2000
> **Division 3 (S) champions** 1929, 1935
> **FA Cup** 1947

SIR BOBBY CHARLTON

> **Born:** Ashington, 11th October 1937
> **Position:** Midfielder
> **Club career:**
> 1956-73 Manchester United 606 (199)
> 1973-74 Preston North End 38 (8)
> 1975 Waterford 31 (18)
> **International record:**
> 1958-70 England 106 (49)

The Charlton brothers (Jack left and Bobby right) discuss whose turn it is to buy a new ball!

One of English football's greatest ever players, Sir Bobby Charlton had a magnificent career with Manchester United and England. He remains the highest scorer for both club and country, with 249 goals in all competitions for the Reds and 49 goals in 106 international appearances.

• **Charlton broke into the United first team in 1956, scoring twice on his debut against Charlton Athletic. Two years later he was one of the few United players to survive the Munich Air Crash, after being hauled from the burning wreckage by goalkeeper Harry Gregg.**

• During the 1960s Charlton won everything the game had to offer, winning the league title twice (1965 and 1967), the FA Cup (1963), the European Cup (scoring twice in the final against Benfica at Wembley in 1968) and the World Cup with England in 1966. Probably his best performance for his country came in the semi-final against Portugal at Wembley, when he scored both goals (including a trademark piledriver) in a 2-1 victory.

• **European Footballer of the Year in 1966, Charlton eventually left United in 1973 to become player-manager of Preston. He returned to Old Trafford as a director in 1984 and was knighted a decade later.**

JACK CHARLTON

> **Born:** Ashington, 8th May 1935
> **Position:** Defender
> **Club career:**
> 1953-73 Leeds United 629 (71)
> **International record:**
> 1965-70 England 35 (6)

A towering centre-half, Jack 'The Giraffe' Charlton made a record 629 League appearances for Leeds United, his only club. While at Elland Road, Charlton won a host of honours including the League championship (1969), the FA Cup (1972) and the Fairs Cup (1968 and 1971). He was also voted Footballer of the Year in 1967.

• **Playing alongside his younger brother Bobby, Charlton was a key figure in England's 1966 World Cup triumph. Despite not making his international debut until he was nearly 30, Charlton went on to play 35 times for his country.**

• Charlton moved into management in 1973 and, following spells with Middlesbrough, Sheffield Wednesday and Newcastle, became boss of the Republic of Ireland in 1986. Two years later, he guided his adopted country to their first major tournament, the 1988 European Championships.

• **His greatest managerial achievement, though, came in 1990 when he led the Republic of Ireland to the quarter-finals of the World Cup in Italy. In 1994 the Republic made the finals again, but the limitations of Charlton's favoured long ball game were exposed in the heat of the USA and he resigned as manager the following year.**

TOP 10

ENGLAND GOALSCORERS

1.	Bobby Charlton (1958-70)	49
2.	Gary Lineker (1984-92)	48
3.	Jimmy Greaves (1959-67)	44
4.	Michael Owen (1998-2008)	40
5.	Tom Finney (1946-58)	30
	Nat Lofthouse (1950-58)	30
	Alan Shearer (1992-2000)	30
8.	Vivian Woodward (1903-11)	29
9.	Steve Bloomer (1895-1907)	28
10.	David Platt (1989-96)	27

CHEATING

The most famous instance of on-pitch cheating occurred at the 1986 World Cup in Mexico when Argentina's Diego Maradona punched the ball into the net to open the scoring in his side's quarter-final victory over England. Maradona was unrepentant afterwards, claiming the goal was scored by "the hand of God, and the head of Diego".

• In a similar incident in 2009 France captain Thierry Henry clearly handled the ball before crossing for William Gallas to score the decisive goal in a World Cup play-off against Ireland. "I will be honest, it was a handball – but I'm not the ref," a sheepish Henry admitted after the match.

• In a 1989 World Cup qualifier Brazil were leading Chile 1-0 when a firecracker landed near Chilean goalkeeper Roberto Rojas. He fell to the ground, blood pouring from his head and, when his team-mates insisted it was unsafe to continue playing, the referee abandoned the match. Video evidence, however, revealed that Rojas had cut his own head with a razor blade hidden inside his glove. FIFA awarded Brazil a 2-0 victory which knocked Chile out of the 1990 World Cup and they were also excluded from the 1994 tournament. Rojas, who had hoped his self-inflicted injury would produce a rematch at a neutral venue, was banned from football for life.

• At the 2002 World Cup Turkey's Hakan Unsal kicked the ball at Brazilian star Rivaldo after Brazil won a corner in the final minutes. Rivaldo fell to the ground clutching his face and Unsal was shown the red card. TV replays of the incident, though, clearly showed that the ball struck Rivaldo on the knee and he was subsequently fined £5,180 by FIFA for 'simulation'.

• Italian football has been thrown into turmoil by allegations of cheating on a fairly regular basis, most recently by the 'Calciopoli' scandal in 2006. A number of leading clubs were found guilty of putting pressure on referees to favour them and were subsequently punished with point deductions. The worst offenders, Juventus, were also stripped of their 2005 and 2006 Serie A titles and demoted to Serie B.

CHELSEA

Year founded: 1905
Ground: Stamford Bridge (42,055)
Nickname: The Blues
Biggest win: 13-0 v Jeunesse Hautcharage (1971)
Heaviest defeat: 1-8 v Wolves (1953)
Colours: Blue shirts, blue shorts, white socks

Oops! Chelsea's Double-winning celebrations get a bit messy!

Founded in 1905 by local businessmen Gus and Joseph Mears, Chelsea were elected to the Football League in that very same year. At the time of their election, the club had not played a single match – only Bradford City can claim a similarly swift ascent into league football.

• Thanks to the staggering wealth of their Russian owner, Roman Abramovich, Chelsea are now one of the richest clubs in the world. Since taking over the Londoners in 2003, Abramovich has pumped hundreds of millions into the club and has been rewarded with back-to-back Premiership titles in 2005 and 2006, the FA Cup in 2007 and 2009, the Carling Cup in 2005 and 2007 and, in Carlo Ancelotti's first season as manager, the league and cup Double in 2010.

• Chelsea clinched the title in 2010 with an 8-0 thrashing of Wigan, a resounding victory that meant the Blues finished the season with a Premier League record 103 goals and a top flight best ever goal difference of 71.

• The Blues' current success is in marked contrast to their early history. For the first 50 years of their existence Chelsea won precisely nothing, finally breaking their duck by winning the league championship in 1955. After a succession of near misses, the club won the FA Cup for the first time in 1970, beating Leeds 2-1 at Old Trafford in the first post-war final to go to a replay. Flamboyant striker Peter Osgood scored in every round of the cup run, and remains the last player to achieve this feat.

• The following year, the Blues won the European Cup-Winners' Cup, beating Real Madrid in Athens after another replay. In 1998 club legend Gianfranco Zola scored the only goal of the final against Stuttgart as the Blues became the only British side to lift the Cup-Winners' Cup on two occasions.

• The club's fortunes declined sharply in the late 1970s and 1980s, the Blues spending much of the period in the Second Division while saddled with large debts. However, an influx of veteran foreign stars in the mid-1990s, including Zola, Ruud Gullit and Gianluca Vialli, sparked an exciting revival capped when the Blues won the FA Cup in 1997, their first major trophy for 26 years.

• In the final against Middlesbrough,

Italian midfielder Roberto di Matteo scored with a long-range shot after just 43 seconds – at the time the fastest ever goal in a Wembley final. Further silverware followed in the League Cup in 1998 and the FA Cup in 2000, in the last final played at the old Wembley.

• Chelsea's arrival as one of England's top clubs was finally confirmed when charismatic manager Jose Mourinho led the Blues to the Premiership title in 2005. The club's tally of 95 points set a record for the competition, while goalkeeper Petr Cech went a then record 1,025 minutes during the season without conceding a goal. A second Premiership title followed in 2006, before Mourinho was sensationally sacked a year later. When the club first won the championship way back in 1955, they did so with a record low of just 52 points.

• In 2007 Chelsea won the first ever FA Cup final at the new Wembley, Ivorian striker Didier Drogba scoring the only goal against Manchester United. In the same year the Blues won the Carling Cup, making them just the third English team after Arsenal (1993) and Liverpool (2001) to claim a domestic cup double. The Blues also won the FA Cup in 2009 and 2010, making them the first team to retain the trophy at the new Wembley.

• Hardman defender Ron 'Chopper' Harris is Chelsea's record appearance maker, turning out an incredible 795 times for the club in all competitions between 1962-80. Harris' team-mate Bobby Tambling is the Blues' top scorer, with 202 goals between 1958-70. Legendary striker Jimmy Greaves scored the most goals in a single season, with 41 in 1960/61.

• Between 2004-08 the Blues were unbeaten in 86 consecutive home league matches, a record for both the Premiership and the Football League. The impressive run was eventually ended by Liverpool, who won 1-0 at Stamford Bridge on 26th October 2008.

• The club's record signing is expensive flop Andriy Shevchenko who cost a staggering £30.8 million when he moved to west London in 2006. The Blues made their record sale the following year, when Dutch winger Arjen Robben moved to Real Madrid for £24 million.

• Among the many celebrities who support the Blues are England cricketer Kevin Pieterson, Blur frontman Damon

Albarn, broadcaster Tim Lovejoy, actor Phil Daniels and veteran film director Richard Attenborough, who is the club's Life Vice-President.

HONOURS
Premier League champions 2005, 2006, 2010
Division 1 champions 1955
Division 2 champions 1984, 1989
FA Cup 1970, 1997, 2000, 2007, 2009, 2010
Double 2010
League Cup 1965, 1998, 2005, 2007
European Cup Winners' Cup 1971, 1998
European Super Cup 1998

CHELTENHAM TOWN

Year founded: 1892
Ground: Whaddon Road (7,300)
Nickname: The Robins
Biggest win: 12-0 v Chippenham Rovers (1935)
Heaviest defeat: 1-10 v Merthyr Tydfil (1952)
Colours: Red-and-white striped shirts, red shorts, red socks

Cheltenham were founded in 1892 but didn't play in the Football League until 1999, the year that the club won the Conference under manager Steve Cotterill. The star of the Robins' promotion-winning side was 41-year-old winger Clive Walker, a former favourite at Chelsea, Sunderland and Fulham.

• The Robins have since twice gained promotion to the third tier via the play-offs, defeating Rushden 3-1 in the final at the Millennium Stadium in 2002 and Grimsby 1-0 four years later at the same venue. The club also

won the FA Trophy in 1998, beating Southport 1-0 at Wembley Stadium.
• Cheltenham splashed out a club record £50,000 in 2003 when they signed Grant McCann from West Ham. The most expensive player to leave Whaddon Road is Steven Gillespie, who signed for Colchester United for a cool £400,000 in June 2008.
• **During the 2008/09 season Cheltenham fielded no fewer than 51 different players, many of them loan signings, over the course of a campaign which ended in relegation to League Two.**
• The Robins staged one of the most remarkable comebacks ever in March 2010 when they won 6-5 at Burton Albion after trailing 5-3 with just five minutes to play.

> HONOURS
> *Conference champions 1999*

CHESTERFIELD

> **Year founded:** 1866
> **Ground:** B2net Stadium (10,338)
> **Previous name:** Chesterfield Town
> **Nickname:** The Spireites
> **Biggest win:** 10-0 v Glossop North End (1903)
> **Heaviest defeat:** 0-10 v Gillingham (1987)
> **Colours:** Blue shirts, white shorts, blue socks

The fourth oldest club in the UK, Chesterfield were founded in 1866. The club was elected to the Second Division in 1899 as Chesterfield Town but lost its league status a decade later, only to return as plain Chesterfield when Division Three (North) was created in 1921.
• **Chesterfield fans still complain about a refereeing decision in the 1997 FA Cup semi-final against Middlesbrough which they believe denied their team a place in the final at Wembley. TV replays showed that Jonathan Howard's shot had crossed the Boro line but referee David Elleray thought otherwise. The game went to a replay in which the Spireites were eventually beaten.**

• Between Christmas Day 1929 and Boxing Day 1930 Chesterfield scored at least one goal in 48 consecutive league and cup matches – the longest such run by any English club.
• **Until the club moved to the 10,600-capacity B2net Stadium in the summer of 2010, Chesterfield's former Saltergate ground was the oldest Football League ground still in use.**

> HONOURS
> *Division 3 (N) champions 1931, 1936*
> *Division 4 champions 1970, 1985*

CLEAN SHEETS

Manchester United goalkeeper Edwin van der Sar holds the British record for league clean sheets, keeping the ball out of his net for 14 Premiership games and a total of 1,311 consecutive minutes in the 2008/09 season. He was finally beaten on 4th March 2009 by Newcastle's Peter Lovenkrands in United's 2-1 victory at St James' Park.
• **The world record for clean sheets is held by Brazilian goalkeeper Mazaropi of Vasco de Gama who went**

Brian Clough led Nottingham Forest to two European Cup triumphs

1,816 minutes without conceding in 1977/78.
• Italy's longserving goalkeeper Dino Zoff holds the international record, going 1,143 minutes without having to pick the ball out of his net between September 1972 and June 1974. Another Italian goalkeeper, Walter Zenga, holds the record for clean sheets at the World Cup, with a run of 517 minutes at the 1990 tournament.
• **England's overall clean sheet record is held by Peter Shilton who shut out the opposition in 66 of his 125 international appearances between 1970-1990.**

BRIAN CLOUGH

> **Born:** Middlesbrough, 21st March 1935
> **Died:** 20th September 2004
> **Managerial career:**
> 1965-67 Hartlepool United
> 1967-73 Derby County
> 1973-74 Brighton
> 1974 Leeds United
> 1975-93 Nottingham Forest

The first post-war manager to win the League championship with two different clubs, Brian Clough is a legendary figure at both Derby County and Nottingham Forest. He transformed the fortunes of both clubs, leading Derby from the old Second Division to the title in 1972 before repeating the trick with Forest in 1978.

• The following year Clough guided Forest to success in the European Cup, new £1 million signing Trevor Francis grabbing the winner against Malmo in the final. The Midlanders retained the trophy in 1980 too, beating Hamburg 1-0 in the final in Madrid. During his 18 years with Forest, Clough also won the League Cup four times, but his final season with the club ended in anguish when Forest were relegated from the Premiership in 1993.

• Brash, opinionated and outspoken, Clough was a prolific striker with Middlesbrough and Sunderland before a knee injury forced his retirement from the game aged 29. He also won two caps for England in 1959.

• Since his death from stomach cancer in 2004 the stretch of the A52 linking Nottingham and Derby has been renamed Brian Clough Way and a statue of one of English football's greatest managers and biggest characters has been unveiled in his home town of Middlesbrough.

COLCHESTER UNITED

Year founded: 1937
Ground: The Colchester Community Stadium (10,000)
Nickname: The U's
Biggest win: 9-1 v Bradford City (1961)
Heaviest defeat: 0-8 v Leyton Orient (1989)
Colours: Blue-and-white striped shirts, blue shorts, white socks

Founded as the successors to amateur club Colchester Town in 1937, Colchester United joined the Football League in 1950. The club lost its league status in 1990, but regained it just two years later after topping the Conference.

• The greatest day in the club's history, though, was in 1971 when the U's sensationally beat Leeds United, then the most powerful side in the country,

TOP 10

FATHERS AND SONS
1. Cesare and Paolo Maldini
2. Johan and Jordi Cruyff
3. Juan Ramon and Juan Sebastian Veron
4. Brian and Nigel Clough
5. Frank snr and Frank Lampard
6. Finn and Michael & Brian Laudrup
7. Miguel and Pepe Reina
8. Arnor and Eidur Gudjohnsen
9. Harry and Jamie Redknapp
10. Terry and Michael Owen

3-2 in an epic fifth round FA Cup tie at their old Layer Road ground. Even a 5-0 defeat at Everton in the next round failed to wipe the smiles off the faces of the Colchester fans.

• Playing away to Hereford in October 1993, Colchester United became the first Football League club to have both their keeper (John Keeley) and sub keeper (Nathan Munson) sent off in the same match – unsurprisingly, the nine men went down to a 5-0 defeat.

• In 1971, the U's became the first English club to win a tournament in a penalty shoot-out after defeating West Brom 4-3 on penalties in the final of the Watney Cup at the Hawthorns.

HONOURS
Conference champions 1992

ASHLEY COLE

Born: Stepney, 20th December 1980
Position: Defender
Club career:
2000-06 Arsenal 156 (8)
2000 Crystal Palace (loan) 14 (1)
2006- Chelsea 111 (6)
International record:
2001- England 82 (0)

Speedy left-back Ashley Cole is the most successful player ever in the history of the FA Cup, having won the competition three times each with Arsenal and his current club Chelsea.

• When Cole helped Chelsea triumph in the FA Cup a week after the Blues' 2009/10 Premier League title success he became the first English player ever to win the Double with two different clubs, having previously achieved the same feat with Arsenal in 2002.

Ashley Cole has won the FA Cup more times than any other player on the planet

• England's first-choice left back for nearly a decade, Cole made his international debut against Albania in 2001. He has since represented his country at the 2002, 2006 and 2010 World Cups and at Euro 2004, where his impressive performances earned him a place in the tournament's all-star squad.

• In 2006 Cole married Girls Aloud singer Cheryl Tweedy, but the couple separated four years later after tabloid reports that he had cheated on his wife with a string of other women.

JOE COLE

Born: 8th November 1981, Islington
Position: Midfielder/winger
Club career:
1998-2003 West Ham 126 (10)
2003- 2010 Chelsea 183 (28)
2010 - Liverpool
International record:
2001- England 56 (10)

One of English football's most creative players, tricky winger Joe Cole attracted much media interest even before he first broke into the West Ham first team as a 17-year-old in 1998. He starred for the Hammers over the next five years, taking over the captaincy in 2003, but left the club for Chelsea that summer in a £6.6 million deal following the Eastenders' relegation from the Premiership.

• Cole picked up seven winners' medals at Stamford Bridge and his dribbling skills and inventive play made him a huge favourite with Blues fans, who voted him their Player of the Year in 2008.

• Despite his undoubted talents, Cole has not always been quite so appreciated by his various managers. Chelsea bosses Jose Mourinho, Guus Hiddink and Carlo Ancelotti all regularly dropped him to the bench and at the end of the 2009/10 season his contract was not renewed by the club. After weeks of intense speculation about his next destination, he joined Liverpool on a four-year deal in July 2010.

• Cole made his international debut against Mexico in 2001 and has gone on to win more than 50 caps for England. He performed well at the 2006 World Cup, scoring a stunning volley against Sweden in the group stage, but only made two brief appearances at the 2010 tournament.

Joe Cole - Liverpool's crafty cockney

COLOURS

In the 19th century, players originally wore different coloured caps, socks and armbands – but not shirts – to distinguish between the two sides. The first standardised kits were introduced in the 1870s with many clubs opting for the colours of the schools or other sporting organisations from which they had emerged.

• In the period after World War II, clothing restrictions forced many teams in Britain to wear unusual kits. For instance, Oldham Athletic, who traditionally wore blue and white, spent two seasons in red and white shirts borrowed from a local rugby league club while Scottish club Clyde turned out in khaki.

• Thanks largely to the longstanding success of Arsenal, Liverpool and Manchester United, teams wearing red have won more trophies in England than those sporting any other colour.

• In April 1996 Manchester United became the first English team to completely change their kit at half-time during a Premiership match at Southampton. Trailing 3-0 at the break, the United players complained that they found it hard to spot each other in the club's grey away shirts and came out for the second half (which they 'won' 1-0) in blue and white stripes. Sir Alex Ferguson ensured that the dreaded grey shirts were never seen again.

COMMUNITY SHIELD

The Community Shield was originally known as the Charity Shield and since 1928 has been an annual fixture usually

TOP 10

COMMUNITY SHIELD WINNERS
1. Manchester United 18 wins
2. Liverpool 15 wins
3. Arsenal 12 wins
4. Everton 9 wins
5. Tottenham Hotspur 7 wins
6. Chelsea 4 wins
   Wolverhampton Wanderers 4 wins
8. Manchester City 3 wins
9. Leeds United 2 wins
   Burnley 2 wins
   West Bromwich Albion 2 wins

Conference side AFC Wimbledon get a big thumbs up

• During the redevelopment of Wembley, the Shield was played at the Millennium Stadium, Cardiff between 2001 and 2006. The first winners of the Community Shield at the new Wembley were Manchester United, who beat Chelsea on penalties in 2007. The following two Shields were also won on spot-kicks, by United in 2008 and Chelsea in 2009.

CONFERENCE

Formed in 1979 as the Alliance Premier League, the Football Conference is the pinnacle of the non-league National League System which feeds into the Football League. The Conference itself has been divided into three sections – National, North and South – since 2004.

• **Promotion and relegation between the Football League and the Conference became automatic in 1987, when Scarborough United replaced Lincoln City.**

• However, clubs have to satisfy the Football League's minimal ground requirements before their promotion can be confirmed and Kidderminster Harriers, Macclesfield Town and Stevenage Borough all failed on this count in the mid-1990s after topping the Conference table.

• **The Conference is currently known as the Blue Square Premier after its sponsors. Previously, the league was sponsored by Gola (1984-86), Vauxhall (1986-98) and the Nationwide Building Society (1998-2007).**

• Aldershot Town won the Conference with a record total of 101 points in 2008, while the biggest win in the league is 9-0, a record jointly held by Sutton United (1990), Hereford United (2004) and Rushden & Diamonds (2009).

played at the start of the season between the reigning League champions and the FA Cup winners. Founded in 1908 to provide funds for various charities, the Charity Shield was initially played between the League champions and the Southern League champions, developing into a game between select teams of amateurs and professionals in the early 1920s.

• **Manchester United were the first club to win the Charity Shield, defeating QPR 4-0 in a replay at Stamford Bridge. With 14 outright wins and four shared, United are also the most successful side in the history**

of the competition.

• In the 1967 Charity Shield Tottenham goalkeeper Pat Jennings scored with a kick from his own penalty area, the ball bouncing over the head of his Manchester United counterpart Alex Stepney and into the net.

• **In the first Charity Shield played at Wembley in 1974, Liverpool's Kevin Keegan and Leeds' Billy Bremner were sent off for fighting, becoming the first British players to be dismissed at the national stadium. To make matters worse, they tore their shirts off as they left the pitch and both were subsequently banned for five weeks.**

IS THAT A FACT?
The last team wearing stripes to win the FA Cup were Coventry City, who beat Tottenham 3-2 in the final in 1987. Meanwhile, no team with a striped kit has won the league since Sunderland in 1936.

Fans of Chile's Colo Colo get in the mood for a Copa Libertadores match

COPA AMERICA

The oldest surviving international football tournament in the world, the Copa America was founded in 1916. The first championships were held in Argentina as part of the country's independence centenary commemorations, with Uruguay emerging as the winners from a four-team field. Originally known as the South American Championship, the tournament was renamed in 1975. Previously, the Copa America was held every two years but in 2007 it was decided to stage future tournaments at four-year intervals.

• **Argentina and Uruguay have both won the tournament a record 14 times, six victories more than current holders Brazil.**

• Norberto Mendez of Argentina and Zizinho of Brazil share the tournament record of 17 goals. Three players have scored a record nine goals in a single tournament: Jair Pinto (Brazil, 1949), Humberto Maschio (Argentina, 1957) and Javier Ambrois (Uruguay, 1957).

COPA LIBERTADORES

The Copa Libertadores is the South American equivalent of the Champions League, played annually between top clubs from all the countries in the continent (in recent years, leading clubs from Mexico have also participated). Argentine club Independiente have the best record in the competition, winning the trophy seven times including four in a row between 1972-75.

• **Ecuadorian striker Albert Spencer is the leading scorer in the history of the competition with 54 goals (48 for Uruguayan club Penarol, helping them to win the first two tournaments in 1960 and 1961, and six for Ecuadorian outfit Barcelona de Guayaquil).**

• In a first round match in 1970, Penarol thrashed Venezuelan club Valencia 11-2 to record the biggest ever win in the competition.

• **Argentinian clubs have won the trophy a record 22 times, nine more than those from Brazil. The most successful player in the**

Copa Libertadores is Argentinian defender Francisco Sa, who won the **tournament six times in the 1970s with Independiente and Boca Juniors.**

CORNERS

Corner kicks were first introduced in 1872, but goals direct from a corner were not allowed until 1924. The first player to score from a corner in League football was

IS THAT A FACT?
Former Yugoslavia international Dejan Petkovic holds the world record for the most goals scored direct from a corner with eight, his most recent effort coming for Brazilian side Flamengo in 2009.

Billy Smith of Huddersfield in the 1924/25 season. On 2nd October 1924 Argentina's Cesareo Onzari scored direct from a corner against reigning Olympic champions Uruguay in Buenos Aires, the first goal of this sort in an international fixture.

• **The first Football League match to feature no corners was the Division One game between Newcastle and Portsmouth at St James' Park on 5th December 1931. Unsurprisingly, the match finished 0-0.**

• A corner count has been proposed as an alternative to penalty shoot-outs as a way of deciding drawn cup ties. This method was used to determine the result of the 1965 All-African Games football tournament, with Congo beating Mali 7-2 on corners after a 0-0 draw.

COVENTRY CITY

Year founded: 1883
Ground: Ricoh Arena (32,609)
Previous name: Singers FC
Nickname: The Sky Blues
Biggest win: 9-0 v Bristol City (1934)
Heaviest defeat: 2-11 v Berwick Rangers (1901)
Colours: Sky blue shirts, white shorts and sky blue socks

Coventry were founded in 1883 by workers from the local Singer's bicycle factory and were named after the company until 1898. The club was elected to the Second Division in 1919 but their league career started unpromisingly with a 5-0 home defeat to Tottenham Hotspur.

• **In 1899 Coventry settled at Highfield Road, their ground for the next 106 years before they moved to the Ricoh Arena in 2005. In November 1940 Highfield Road was bombed by the German Luftwaffe, but fortunately the bombs landed on the pitch rather than in the stands. In 1968, though, the main stand had to be rebuilt after being destroyed in a fire. In 1981 Highfield Road became the first all-seater**

Coventry won the FA Cup in 1987

stadium in England.

• Coventry's greatest moment came in 1987 when the club won the FA Cup for the only time, beating Tottenham 3-2 in an exciting Wembley final. Two years later, though, the Sky Blues were dumped out of the cup by non-league Sutton United in one of the competition's biggest ever upsets.

• **Under innovative manager Jimmy Hill Coventry rose from the Third to the First Division in the mid-1960s and remained there for 34 years until dropping out of the Premiership at the end of the 2000/01 season. At the time, only Everton, Arsenal and Liverpool had stayed in the top flight for a longer period.**

• During the 1919/20 season Coventry went a Football League record 11 games in the old Second Division without scoring a single goal. Happily for their fans, the dismal run came to an end in

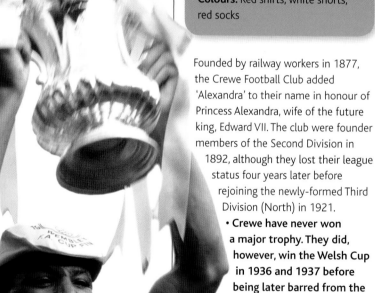

style, with a 3-2 home win over Stoke City on Christmas Day.

• **Stalwart goalkeeper Steve Ogrizovic played in a record 601 games for the club in all competitions between 1984-2000.**

HONOURS
FA Cup 1987
Division 2 champions 1967
Division 3 champions 1964
Division 3 (S) champions 1936

CREWE ALEXANDRA

Year founded: 1877
Ground: Alexandra Stadium (10,118)
Nickname: The Railwaymen
Biggest win: 8-0 v Rotherham (1932)
Heaviest defeat: 2-13 v Tottenham Hotspur (1960)
Colours: Red shirts, white shorts, red socks

Founded by railway workers in 1877, the Crewe Football Club added 'Alexandra' to their name in honour of Princess Alexandra, wife of the future king, Edward VII. The club were founder members of the Second Division in 1892, although they lost their league status four years later before rejoining the newly-formed Third Division (North) in 1921.

• **Crewe have never won a major trophy. They did, however, win the Welsh Cup in 1936 and 1937 before being later barred from the competition for not being a Welsh club.**

• Alex fans endured a miserable spell in the mid 1950s when their club failed to win away from home for a record 56 consecutive matches. The depressing run finally ended with a 1-0 win at Southport in April 1957.

• **Club legend Herbert Swindells scored a record 126 goals for Crewe between 1927-37. Crewe's appearance record is held by Tommy Lowry who turned out in 475 games between 1966-77.**

HONOURS
Welsh Cup 1936, 1937

Peter Crouch is England's tallest player ever

PETER CROUCH

Born: Macclesfield, 30th January 1981
Position: Striker
Club career:
2000-01 QPR 42 (10)
2001-02 Portsmouth 37 (18)
2002-04 Aston Villa 37 (6)
2003 Norwich City (loan) 15 (4)
2004-05 Southampton 27 (12)
2005-08 Liverpool 85 (22)
2008-09 Portsmouth 35 (11)
2009- Tottenham Hotspur 38 (8)
International record:
2005- England 40 (21)

With his gangly physique and stick-thin legs, Peter Crouch may look more like a basketball player than a top-class footballer, but he has proved himself to be an extremely effective striker at both club and international level. Nor is he simply a towering targetman: although an obvious threat in the air, Crouch has a surprisingly deft touch on the ground and can find the net with both feet.
• After initially failing to make the grade at Tottenham, Crouch moved to QPR in 2000 and subsequently played for Portsmouth, Aston Villa, Norwich (on loan) and Southampton, before joining Liverpool in 2005. The following year he won the FA Cup with the Merseysiders and in 2007 played as a sub in the Champions League final defeat to AC Milan. However, following the arrival of Spanish hotshot Fernando Torres at Anfield in the summer of 2008, Crouch returned to Portsmouth in an estimated £11 million deal. A year later he was on the move again, his career coming full circle when he rejoined his first club, Tottenham, for a fee of £10 million.
• Crouch made his England debut against Colombia in 2005 and, despite being in and out of the starting eleven, has enjoyed a prolific scoring record at international level. In fact, his overall strike rate for the Three Lions averages out at a goal every 106 minutes – a figure unmatched by any England player of recent vintage.
• At 6ft 7in, Peter Crouch is the tallest player to appear for England. When he first played for Liverpool his extraordinary height prompted Reds fans to chant, "He's big, he's red, his feet stick out the bed!"

JOHAN CRUYFF

Born: Amsterdam, Holland, 25th April 1947
Position: Midfielder/Striker
Club career:
1964-73 Ajax 240 (190)
1973-78 Barcelona 142 (48)
1979-80 Los Angeles Aztecs 27 (16)
1980-81 Washington Diplomats 32 (12)
1981 Levante 10 (2)
1981-83 Ajax 36 (14)
1983-84 Feyenoord 33 (11)
International record:
1966-78 Holland 48 (33)

Arguably the greatest European player ever, Johan Cruyff was captain of the brilliant Holland side which reached the final of the 1974 World Cup and of the outstanding Ajax team which won the European Cup three times on the trot in the early 1970s.
• Unquestionably the best player in the world at the time, Cruyff became the first man to win the European Player of the Year award three times, topping the poll in 1971, 1973 and 1974.

• Fast, skilful, creative and a prolific scorer, Cruyff was also a superb organiser on the pitch. His talents prompted Barcelona to shell out a world record £922,000 fee to bring him to the Nou Camp in 1973 and the following year Cruyff helped the Catalans win their first title for 14 years.

• After his retirement, Cruyff coached both Ajax and Barcelona. He led the Spanish giants to four consecutive league titles between 1991-94 and, in 1992, guided them to their first ever European Cup success, with a 1-0 victory over Sampdoria at Wembley.

• Cruyff's magnificent contribution to football in Holland was recognised in a 2004 poll when he was voted the sixth greatest Dutch person ever, ahead of two of the world's finest painters, Rembrandt and Vincent Van Gogh.

CRYSTAL PALACE

Year founded: 1905
Ground: Selhurst Park (26,309)
Nickname: The Eagles
Biggest win: 9-0 v Barrow (1959)
Heaviest defeat: 0-9 v Burnley (1909) and v Liverpool (1989)
Colours: Red-and-blue striped shirts, red shorts, red socks

The club was founded in 1905 by workers at the then cup final venue at Crystal Palace, and was an entirely separate entity to the amateur club of the same name which was made up of groundkeepers at the Great Exhibition and reached the first ever semi-finals of the FA Cup in 1871.

• After spending their early years in the Southern League, Palace were founder members of the Third Division (South) in 1920. The club had a great start to their league career, going up to the Second Division as champions in their first season.

• Two Crystal Palace players, striker Johnny 'Budgie' Byrne in 1962 and Peter Taylor in 1977, won England caps while playing in the Third Division. Byrne later

When he played for Holland, Johan Cruyff insisted on having two stripes on his arm instead of three as he was sponsored by Puma not Adidas

Crystal Palace's Gerry Francis and Mike Flanagan scared the life out of opposition defences and little old ladies in the late 1970s!

joined West Ham for a then British record fee of £65,000.

• Palace's greatest moment came in 1990 when they reached the FA Cup final. In the final at Wembley against Manchester United, Ian Wright came off the bench to score twice in a thrilling 3-3 draw before the Eagles went down 1-0 in the replay.

• Pre-war striker Peter Simpson is the club's all-time leading scorer with 153 league goals between 1930-36. Rugged defender Jim Cannon holds the club appearance record, making 660 appearances between 1973-88.

• Defender Aki Riihilahti won a club record 35 international caps for Finland during a five-year stay at Selhurst Park between 2001-06.

• Palace scooped a club record £8.6 million when they sold star striker Andy Johnson to Everton in 2006. The club's record purchase came back in 1998 when they splashed out £2.75 million on Strasbourg defender Valerien Ismael – a bit of a waste of money, as it turned out, since he only played 13 games for the Eagles before joining Lens for a cut-price £1.3 million.

• The Dave Clark Five hit Glad All Over has been the club's anthem since the 1963/64 season and is played with the volume turned up to maximum before every home game at Selhurst Park.

CUP-WINNERS' CUP

A competition for the domestic cup winners of all European countries, the European Cup-Winners' Cup ran for 39 seasons between 1960/61 until 1998/99. The first winners were Italian club Fiorentina, who beat Rangers 4-1 on aggregate in a two-legged final.

• In 1963 Tottenham Hotspur became the first British side to win the competition and the first to triumph in a major European tournament, when they beat Atletico Madrid 5-1 in Rotterdam – a record score for a European final.

• English clubs won the cup eight times, a figure unmatched by any other country. England's successful teams were Tottenham (1963), West Ham (1965), Manchester City (1970), Chelsea (1971 and 1998), Everton (1985), Manchester United (1991) and Arsenal (1994).

• The only club to win the cup three times were Barcelona, who lifted the trophy in 1979, 1982 and 1989.

• In 1963 Sporting Lisbon thrashed APOEL Nicosia 16-1 in a second round first leg tie to record the biggest ever win in any European fixture.

TOP 10

CLUB ANTHEMS

1. *You'll Never Walk Alone*, Liverpool
2. *I'm Forever Blowing Bubbles*, West Ham
3. *Blue Is The Colour*, Chelsea
4. *Glad All Over*, Crystal Palace
5. *On the Ball, City*, Norwich City
6. *Delilah*, Stoke City
7. *Blue Moon*, Manchester City
8. *Keep Right On*, Birmingham City
9. *Marching On Together*, Leeds United
10. *When The Saints Go Marching In*, Southampton

KENNY DALGLISH

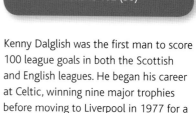

Born: Glasgow, 4th March 1951
Position: Striker
Club career:
1968-77 Celtic 204 (112)
1977-90 Liverpool 354 (118)
International record:
1971-87 Scotland 102 (30)

Kenny Dalglish was the first man to score 100 league goals in both the Scottish and English leagues. He began his career at Celtic, winning nine major trophies before moving to Liverpool in 1977 for a then British record fee of £440,000.

• **A true Liverpool legend, Dalglish won nine championships, two FA Cups and four League Cups with the Reds, plus the European Cup in 1978, 1981 and 1984. He was voted Footballer of the Year in 1979 and 1983.**

• Dalglish won a record 102 caps for Scotland and scored 30 goals. He represented his country at three World Cups in 1974, 1978 and 1982.

• **In 1985 Dalglish became player-manager of Liverpool, winning the Double in his first season and securing three titles before suddenly resigning in 1991. Eight months later he took over at Blackburn and in 1995 steered Rovers to the Premiership title, becoming only the third manager to win the title with two different clubs.**

• In 1997 Dalglish became Newcastle manager, but was sacked after a poor start to the 1998/99 season. He returned to Celtic for a brief spell but was out of the game for nine years before returning to Liverpool as a youth academy coach and club ambassador in 2009.

DIXIE DEAN

Born: Birkenhead, 22nd January 1907
Died: 1st March 1980
Position: Striker
Club career:
1923-25 Tranmere Rovers 30 (27)
1925-37 Everton 399 (349)
1938-39 Notts County 9 (3)
1939 Sligo Rovers 7 (10)
International record:
1927-32 England 16 (18)

Everton legend Dixie Dean scored an all-time record 60 league goals for the Toffees when they won the

Kenny Dalglish: The first man to score 100 goals in both the Scottish and English leagues

DAGENHAM & REDBRIDGE

Year founded: 1992
Ground: Victoria Road (6,000)
Previous name: Dagenham
Nickname: The Daggers
Biggest win: 8-1 v Woking (1994)
Heaviest defeat: 0-9 v Hereford United (2004)
Colours: Red-and blue shirts, blue shorts, blue socks

The self-styled 'pub team from Essex' were formed in 1992 following the merger of local rivals Dagenham and Redbridge Forest, the latter having previously incorporated the once famous amateur clubs Ilford, Leytonstone and Walthamstow Avenue.

• **In 2007 Dagenham & Redbridge were promoted to the Football League for** the first time in their history after winning the Conference. Just three years later the Daggers went up to League One after beating Rotherham 3-2 in a thrilling play-off final.

• Dagenham's Tony Roberts is the only goalkeeper to have scored in the FA Cup, netting in a fourth qualifying round tie against Basingstoke in 2001. Less impressively, the Welsh international is the only keeper to have been sent off in the competition while in the opposition penalty area. The bizarre incident happened late on in the Daggers' 5-2 defeat against Southend in 2008 when Roberts went up for a corner and was red carded for headbutting a Shrimpers' defender.

• **The Daggers' coffers received a welcome boost in August 2009 when they sold midfielder Solomon Taiwo to Cardiff City for a club record £200,000.**

HONOURS
Conference champions 2007

championship in 1927/28. His tally included a hat-trick in the final match of the campaign against Arsenal, enabling Dean to pass the then record of 59 goals, established the previous season by Middlesbrough's George Camsell.

• **Easily Everton's all-time leading scorer, Dean scored a total of 379 league goals with the Toffees, Tranmere and Notts County. In the history of English league football only Arthur Rowley has scored more (434 with West Brom, Fulham, Leicester and Shrewsbury between 1946-65).**

• Famed for his heading ability, Dean hit an impressive 18 goals in 16 appearances for England, including hat-tricks in consecutive games against Belgium and Luxembourg in 1927.

• **His nickname 'Dixie' was given to him by fans in reference to his dark complexion and curly hair which, they believed, were similar to African Americans in the southern United States. However, Dean disliked the moniker and preferred to be called by his real name, Bill.**

• Dean, who won two league titles and one FA Cup with Everton, died in 1980 after suffering a heart attack while watching a Merseyside derby. In 2001 a sculpture of the club's greatest striker was erected outside Goodison Park carrying the inscription 'Footballer, Gentleman, Evertonian'.

DEATHS

The first recorded death as a direct result of a football match came in 1892 when St Mirren's James Delap died of tetanus after cutting his knee during a game against Aberdeen.

• **In 1931 Celtic's brilliant young international goalkeeper John Thompson died in hospital after fracturing his skull in a collision with Rangers forward Sam English. Some 40,000 fans attended his funeral, many of them walking the 55 miles from Glasgow to Thompson's home village in Fife. In the same decade two other goalkeepers, Jimmy Utterson of Wolves and Sunderland's Jimmy Thorpe, also died from injuries sustained on** the pitch. **Their deaths led the Football Association to change the rules so that goalkeepers could not be tackled while they had the ball in their hands.**

• Two players were killed by lightning in the 1948 Army Cup final at Aldershot Military Stadium. Six other players, two spectators and the referee were also struck by the bolt but survived after receiving treatment in hospital.

• **In 1998 11 players were killed by a bolt of lightning which struck the pitch during a game in the Kasai Province of the Democratic Republic of Congo. Remarkably, all those who died were members of the visiting team while the players from the home side, Busanga, were left unscathed.**

• More recently, Cameron international Marc-Vivien Foe collapsed during a match against Colombia in 2003 and

Dixie Dean in the world's biggest shorts

died later the same day. His death was attributed to a previously undiagnosed heart problem.

DEBUTS

The best debut by an England player was probably that of Blackpool striker Stan Mortensen who scored four times in a 10-0 rout of Portugal in Lisbon in 1947. The 'Blackpool Bombshell' went on to notch an impressive 24 goals for his country in just 25 appearances.

• **Conrad Warner, on the other hand, will have had few fond memories of his England debut against Scotland at Hampden Park in 1878. The Upton Park FC goalkeeper conceded seven goals in a 7-2 thrashing and, unsurprisingly, never played international football again.**

• At league level, one of the best starts to a debut came in 1954 when Wrexham's Bernard Evans scored after just 25 seconds against Bradford City. Similarly, goalkeeper Tony Coton was just 83 seconds into his debut with Birmingham City in 1980 when he saved a penalty with his first touch in top-flight football.

• **The worst debut ever has to be that of hapless Halifax Town goalkeeper Stanley Milton, who let in 13 goals against Stockport in 1934.**

• Goal poaching sensation Jimmy Greaves scored on his debuts for all four of his clubs – Chelsea, AC Milan, Tottenham and West Ham – and also found the net on his first appearance for England against Peru in 1959.

> **IS THAT A FACT?**
> In May 2010 Goran Tunjic collapsed and died while playing for Croatian county level side Mladost FC. Unfortunately, the referee completely failed to comprehend the unfolding tragedy... and gave Tunjic a yellow card for diving!

JERMAIN DEFOE

Born: Beckton, London,
7th October 1982
Position: Striker
Club career:
1999-2004 West Ham
United 93 (29)
2000-01 Bournemouth
(loan) 29 (18)
2004-08 Tottenham 139 (43)
2008-2009 Portsmouth 30 (14)
2009- Tottenham 42 (21)
International record:
2004- England 43 (12)

Quicksilver striker Jermain Defoe is one of only three players to have scored five goals in a Premier League game, grabbing his record-equalling haul in Tottenham's 9-1 demolition of Wigan at White Hart Lane in November 2009. In the same match he notched a hat-trick in just seven minutes – the second fastest treble in Premier League history.

• **Defoe started out with Charlton before signing professional forms with West Ham in 1999. During the 2000/01 season he went on loan to Bournemouth and gained national attention when he hit the target in ten consecutive matches, equalling the post-war record set by Liverpool's John Aldridge in 1988.**

• Defoe soon became a regular for the Hammers but angered the club's supporters when he put in a transfer request less than 24 hours after the club were relegated from the Premiership in 2003. He eventually moved on to Tottenham for £6 million in January 2004.

• **He enjoyed a good start for the north Londoners, scoring in a 4-3 win against Portsmouth on his debut, and became a popular figure with the Spurs fans. However, he gradually slipped down the pecking order at White Hart Lane and in January 2008 joined Portsmouth for £9 million.**

• He returned to Tottenham in 2009 in a deal worth £6m more than the club had sold him for less than a year earlier. It was the third time Defoe had been signed by manager Harry Redknapp.

• **Defoe made his England debut as a sub in a friendly against Sweden in March 2004. Six months later he scored in his first start for his country in a World Cup qualifier against Poland, but was a surprise omission** from Sven Goran Eriksson's squad for the finals in Germany in 2006. However, he made the cut for the 2010 tournament in South Africa where he was one of England's few successes, scoring a vital winner against Slovenia in the group stage.

DERBIES

So called because they matched the popularity of the Epsom Derby horserace, 'derby' matches between local sides provoke intense passions among fans and players alike.

• **Probably the most intense derby match in Britain, and possibly the whole world, is between bitter Glasgow rivals Rangers and Celtic.** The Old Firm duo have clashed on a record 388 occasions, Rangers having the edge with 155 wins to Celtic's 139. Sadly, meetings between the two sides have all too often provoked violent scenes either on or off the field. In 1980, for instance, around 9,000 fans fought on on-pitch battle in the aftermath of Celtic's Scottish Cup final victory at Hampden Park – the worst pitch invasion ever reported.

• Other famous derbies include Liverpool v Everton, Arsenal v Tottenham, Manchester City v Manchester United, Newcastle v Sunderland and, on mainland Europe, Inter v AC Milan, Atletico v Real Madrid and Lazio v Roma. To their fans, these matches are as important as any cup final.

The teams line up for the Milan derby at the San Siro

A MILANO, IN EUROPA, OVU

• The most dramatic moment in a Manchester derby was probably in 1974 when former United legend Denis Law scored with a cheeky backheel in the closing stages at Old Trafford. The goal doomed United to relegation from the First Division and prompted thousands of their fans to invade the pitch in an attempt to get the match abandoned. They succeeded in their aim, but the result (a 1-0 win for City) stood.

• Possibly the most important goal in an English derby game, though, came at Tottenham's White Hart Lane in 1971 when Arsenal's Ray Kennedy scored with a last-minute header to win his side the league championship and the first leg of a famous Double.

• In 1986 and 1989 the Merseyside derby came to Wembley as Liverpool and Everton contested the FA Cup final. Liverpool won on both occasions, with Welsh international striker Ian Rush scoring twice in each game. The sides also met in the 1984 League Cup final, the Reds again winning after a replay.

DERBY COUNTY

Year founded: 1884
Ground: Pride Park (33,597)
Nickname: The Rams
Biggest win: 12-0 v Finn Harps (1976)
Heaviest defeat: 2-11 v Everton (1890)
Colours: White shirts, black shorts, white socks

Derby were formed in 1884 as an offshoot of Derbyshire Cricket Club and originally wore an amber, chocolate and blue strip based on the cricket club's colours. Perhaps wisely, they changed to their traditional black and white colours in the 1890s.

• The club were founder members of the Football League in 1888 and seven years later moved from the ground they shared with the cricketers to the Baseball Ground (so named because baseball was regularly played there in the 1890s). Derby had to oust a band

of gypsies before they could move in, one of whom is said to have laid a curse on the place as he left. No doubt, then, the club was pleased to leave the Baseball Ground for Pride Park in 1997... although when Derby's first game at the new stadium had to be abandoned due to floodlight failure there were fears that the curse had followed them!

• Runners-up in the FA Cup final in 1898, 1899 and 1903, Derby reached their last final in 1946. Before the match the club's captain, Jack Nicholas, visited a gypsy encampment and paid for the old curse to be lifted. It worked, as Derby beat Charlton 4-1 after extra-time.

• Under charismatic manager Brian Clough, Derby took the top flight by storm after winning promotion to the First Division in 1969. Three years later they won the league in one of the closest title races ever. Having played all their fixtures ahead of their title contenders, Derby's players were actually sitting on a beach in Majorca when they heard news of their victory. The following season

Derby reached the semi-finals of the European Cup and, in 1975 under the management of former skipper Dave Mackay, they won the championship again.

• Sadly, the club have failed to live up to those glory days in the decades since. By the early 1980s the Rams had sunk as low as the Third Division and were only saved from extinction when publisher Robert Maxwell bailed them out. The club enjoyed a reasonable spell in the Premiership in the late 1990s, but their last season in the top flight in 2007/08 was one to forget. To the dismay of their loyal fans, the Rams only managed to win one game all season (equalling Loughborough's 108-year-old Football League record) and were relegated having accumulated just 11 points, the worst tally since three points for a win were introduced in 1981/82.

• In January 2009, Brian Clough's son Nigel was appointed manager in a move greeted with delight by fans who hope he can re-kindle the glory days. However, a 14th place finish in the Championship in his first full season in charge was something of an anti-climax.

• Derby's best ever goalscorer was one of the true greats of the game in the late 19th and early 20th centuries, Steve Bloomer. He netted an incredible 332 goals in two spells at the club between 1892-1914. Striker Kevin Hector, a two-time title winner with the club in the 1970s, played in a record 485 league games for the Rams during two spells at the Baseball Ground.

HONOURS
Division 1 champions 1972, 1975
Division 2 champions 1912, 1915, 1969, 1987
FA Cup 1946

DISASTERS

The worst disaster at a British football

stadium occurred on 15th April 1989 at Hillsborough when 96 Liverpool fans were killed and a further 170 injured during their team's FA Cup semi-final with Nottingham Forest. The tragedy, which occurred when police opened the gates to the stadium as the game kicked off and fans poured into an already overcrowded section of the Leppings Lane end of the ground, led to the introduction of all-seater stadiums and the abolition of perimeter fencing.

• Four years earlier fighting between Liverpool and Juventus fans before the 1985 European Cup final at the Heysel Stadium in Brussels resulted in 39 (mostly Italian) supporters being crushed to death when a wall collapsed in a corner of the ground. Liverpool fans were largely blamed for the disaster, which led to English clubs being banned from European competition for the next five years.

• Rangers' Ibrox Stadium has been the scene of two major disasters, the first in 1902 when 26 people died after a stand collapsed during a Home International between Scotland and England. Then, in 1971, 66 fans were killed in a crush on a steep stairway after an Old Firm fixture.

• In 1982 at least 66 people were killed just before the end of a match between Spartak Moscow and Haarlem at the Lenin Stadium in Moscow. According to some reports, as many as 340 fans died in the tragedy, which was caused when supporters leaving early attempted to get back into the stadium via an icy ramp when Spartak scored a late goal.

• The worst disaster in African football took place at the Accra Sports Stadium in Ghana near the end of a match in

Derby spared no expense to show off the FA Cup when they won it in 1946

F.A. CUP
DERBY COUNTY 45-46

2001 between two top clubs, Hearts of Oak and Asante Kotoko. After seeing their team concede two late goals to go down to a 2-1 defeat, the Asante fans began tearing up their seats and throwing them on the pitch. The police responded by firing tear gas, leading the Asante supporters to rush to the exits. However, these turned out to be locked and 126 people were killed in the ensuing crush.

DISCIPLINE

Yellow and red cards were introduced into English league football on 2nd October 1976, and on the same day Blackburn's David Wagstaffe received the first red card during his side's match with Leyton Orient. Five years later cards were withdrawn by the Football Association as referees were getting 'too flashy', but the system was re-introduced in 1987.

• **A stormy last 16 match between Holland and Portugal in 2006 was the most ill-disciplined in the history of the World Cup. Russian referee Valentin Ivanov was the busiest man on the pitch as he pulled out his yellow card 16 times and his red one four times, with the match ending as a nine-a-side affair.**

• Incredibly, in December 2006 Dundee striker Andy McLaren was shown the red card three times in the same match against Clyde. Originally dismissed for hitting out at an opponent, McLaren picked up his second red card for throwing a punch at another Clyde player as he trudged off. Called into the referee's room for a post-match ticking off, he kicked a hole in the door on his way out...and was promptly 'sent off' for the third time!

• **Roy McDonough (Walsall, Colchester, Exeter and Southend) and Steve Walsh (Wigan and Leicester) were both sent off a record 13 times during their playing careers.**

• In a Paraguayan league match between Sportivo Ameliano and General Caballero in June 1993 a world record 20 players were sent off following a 10-minute brawl.

DONCASTER ROVERS

Year founded: 1879
Ground: Keepmoat Stadium (15,231)
Nickname: The Rovers
Biggest win: 10-0 v Darlington (1964)
Heaviest defeat: 0-12 v Small Heath (1903)
Colours: Red-and-white hooped shirts, black shorts, black socks

Founded in 1879 by Albert Jenkins, a fitter at Doncaster's Great Northern Railway works, Doncaster turned professional in 1885 and joined the Second Division of the Football League in 1901.

• **Remarkably, Doncaster hold the record for the most wins in a league season (33 in 1946/47) and for the most defeats (34 in 1997/98). At the end of the latter campaign Rovers were relegated to the Football Conference, but they have since bounced back in fine style. In 2003 the Yorkshire club returned to the Football League via the play-offs, and the following season they won the Division Three championship. Then, in 2008, they beat Leeds at Wembley in the League One play-off final to reach the second tier of English football for the first time in 50 years.**

• Doncaster are the only club to have been champions of the fourth tier of League football on more than two occasions – winning the title three times, in 1966, 1969 and 2004.

• **In 1946 Doncaster were involved in the longest ever football match, a Third Division (North) cup tie against**

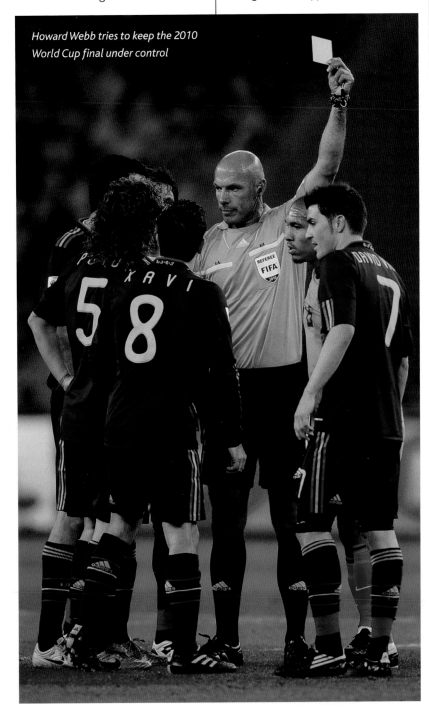

Howard Webb tries to keep the 2010 World Cup final under control

The Spurs team of 1960/61, the first side to win the Double in the modern era

Stockport County at Edgeley Park which the referee ruled could extend beyond extra-time in an attempt to decide a winner. Eventually, the game was abandoned after 203 minutes due to poor light.

• Charlie Williams, who later found fame as Britain's first black stand-up comedian, played over 150 games for Doncaster in the 1950s. A tough-tackling defender, he summed up his playing career by joking "I was never a fancy player, but I could stop them buggers that were!"

> **HONOURS**
> *Division 3 (North) champions 1935, 1947, 1950*
> *Division 4 champions 1966, 1969*
> *Third Division champions 2004*
> *Football League Trophy 2007*

DOUBLES

The first club to win the Double of League Championship and FA Cup were Preston North End, in the very first season of the Football League in 1888/89. The Lancashire side achieved this feat in fine style, remaining undefeated in the league and keeping a clean sheet in all their matches in the FA Cup.

• **Arsenal and Manchester United have both won the Double a record three** times. The Reds' trio of successes all came within a five-year period in the 1990s (1994, 1996 and 1999), with the last of their Doubles comprising two-thirds of a legendary Treble which also included the Champions League. Arsenal first won the Double in 1971, since when the Gunners have twice repeated the feat under manager Arsene Wenger in 1998 and 2002.

• Perhaps, though, the most famous Double of all was achieved by Tottenham Hotspur in 1961 as it was the first such success in the 20th century. The Lillywhites clinched the most-prized honour in the domestic game with a 2-0 victory over Leicester City in the FA Cup final.

• **Northern Ireland side Linfield have won a world record 20 doubles. Rangers with 18 doubles lie in second place, while Greek outfit Olympiacos (14 doubles) are in third place.**

DRAWS

Everton have drawn more matches in the top flight than any other club, having finished on level terms in 1,031 out of 4,176 matches. Even the Toffees, though, can't match Norwich City's record of 23 draws in a single season, set in the First Division in 1978/79.

• **The highest-scoring draw in the top division of English football was 6-6, in a match between Leicester City and Arsenal in 1930. That bizarre scoreline was matched in a Second Division encounter between Charlton and Middlesbrough at The Valley in 1960, with a certain Brian Clough grabbing a hat-trick for the visitors.**

• During the 2009/10 campaign Manchester City drew seven consecutive matches to equal a Premier League record jointly held by Norwich (in 1993/94) and Southampton (in 1994/95).

• **The fourth qualifying round of the FA Cup between Alvechurch and Oxford United in 1971 went to five replays before Alvechurch finally won 1-0 in the sixth game between the clubs. The total playing time of 11 hours is a record for an FA Cup tie.**

• Before penalty shoot-outs were invented in 1970, drawn matches in cup competitions were generally settled by the drawing of lots or the tossing of a coin if a replay was not possible. Possibly the biggest game to hang on the result of a coin toss was the 1968 European Championship semi-final between hosts Italy and the Soviet Union. The Italians' luck was in and they took full advantage, beating Yugoslavia in the final.

DIDIER DROGBA

Born: Abidjan, Ivory Coast,
11th March 1978
Position: Striker
Club career:
1998-2002 Le Mans 63 (12)
2002-03 En Avant Guingamp 45 (20)
2003-04 Marseille 35 (18)
2004- Chelsea 166 (84)
International record:
2002- Ivory Coast 71 (45)

Powerful striker Didier Drogba began his career in France, having moved to the country from his native Ivory Coast as a young child. After starting out with lower division sides Le Mans and Guingamp, Drogba rose to

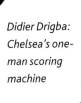

Didier Drigba: Chelsea's one-man scoring machine

prominence with Marseille in the 2003/04 season.

• **In the summer of 2004 Drogba moved to Chelsea for a then club record fee of £24 million. In his first season at the Bridge he helped the Londoners win their first ever Premier League title and also scored in the Blues' Carling Cup final victory over Liverpool.**

• The following year Drogba won a second league title, but was widely criticised by opposition fans and the media for falling over too easily around the penalty box. He responded to the critics in fine style, topping the Premiership scoring charts in 2006/07 and scoring Chelsea's winning goals in both the Carling Cup final victory over Arsenal and the Blues' FA Cup final defeat of Manchester United in the first final played at the new Wembley.

• **Drogba enjoyed his best season with the Blues in 2009/10, scoring the winner in the FA Cup final against Portsmouth. The African also fired in a career-best 29 league goals to win the Golden Boot for a second time.**

• The all-time leading goalscorer for the Ivory Coast, Drogba was voted African Footballer of the Year in 2006.

DRUGS

The use of banned substances to improve performance has been an issue in football since the 1970s, although the problem is not as great as in other sports such as athletics and cycling. Nonetheless, a number of high profile players have been banned from playing after failing drugs tests.

• **Possibly the most famous such case involved the legendary Diego Maradona, who was thrown out of the 1994 World Cup and given a 15-month ban after testing positive for a cocktail of ephedrine substances following Argentina's victory over Greece. The midfielder had previously been hit with a similar ban in 1991 while playing for Napoli when traces of cocaine were found in his test samples.**

• The first player to fail a drugs test at the World Cup was Haiti's Ernest Jean-Joseph at the 1974 tournament in West Germany. Four years later Scotland winger Willie Johnston was sent home in disgrace from Argentina after traces of a banned stimulant were found in his urine sample.

• **Premiership players to have been banned for taking recreational drugs include Lee Bowyer (cannabis), Mark Bosnich (cocaine) and Adrian Mutu (cocaine). Middlesbrough's Abel Xavier, who tested positive for anabolic steroids in 2005, is the only Premiership player to have been banned for taking a performance-enhancing drug.**

• In 2003 Manchester United's Rio Ferdinand missed a drugs test and went shopping instead. The defender's claim that he was distracted by an imminent house move cut no ice with the Football Association, who fined him £50,000 and banned him from playing for eight months.

DUNDEE UNITED

Year founded: 1909
Ground: Tannadice Park (14,209)
Previous name: Dundee Hibernian
Nickname: The Terrors
Biggest win: 14-0 v Nithsdale Wanderers (1931)
Heaviest defeat: 1-12 v Motherwell (1954)
Colours: Tangerine shirts, black shorts, tangerine socks

Originally founded as Dundee Hibernian by members of the city's Irish community in 1909, the club changed to its present name in 1923 to attract support from a wider population.

· **The club emerged from relative obscurity to become one of the leading clubs in Scotland under long-serving manager Jim McLean in the 1970s and 1980s, winning the Scottish Premier Division in 1983. The club's success, allied to that of Aberdeen, led to talk of a 'New Firm' capable of challenging the 'Old Firm' of Rangers and Celtic for major honours.**

· United reached the semi-finals of the European Cup in 1984 and the final of the UEFA Cup in 1987, where they lost to Gothenburg. The club's European exploits also include two home and away victories over Barcelona – a 100 per cent record against the Catalans which no other British team can match. United have played 104 games in Europe, a figure only surpassed by Celtic, Rangers and Aberdeen among Scottish clubs.

· **After being losing finalists on six previous occasions, Dundee United finally won the Scottish Cup in 1994 when they beat Rangers 1-0 in the final. They won the trophy for a second time in 2010, following a comfortable 3-0 win against shock finalists Ross County.**

· Dundee United are known as the Terrors because of the lion in the club's badge. Their supporters, though, are called 'The Arabs', the name possibly stemming from a game the club won on a heavily sanded pitch in the early 1960s.

· **Defender David Narey made an astonishing 612 league appearances for the club between 1973-94. Full back Maurice Malpas is United's most-capped player, winning 55 caps for**

Dundee United celebrate only their second ever Scottish Cup win in 2010

Scotland between 1984-92.

· United's coffers were boosted by a record £4 million when they sold big centre forward Duncan Ferguson to Rangers in 1993, two years before he moved 'down south' to Everton.

· **Tannadice Park, Dundee United's home since their foundation, is situated just a few hundred yards from Dundee's Dens Park, making the two clubs the closest neighbours in British football.**

HONOURS

Premier League champions 1983
Division 2 champions 1925, 1929
Scottish Cup 1994, 2010
Scottish League Cup 1980, 1981

IS THAT A FACT?

In a BBC poll in 2006 Dundee United fan Zippy from Rainbow was named as Britain's favourite celebrity football fan, with nearly 50% of the vote. Rainbow presenter Geoffrey Hayes, a longstanding Terrors' fan himself, had previously insisted on the puppet's bright orange colour to reflect United's famous tangerine shirts.

England at Wembley in 1966 after their one and only World Cup triumph

DUNCAN EDWARDS

Born: Dudley, 1st October 1936
Died: 21st February 1958
Position: Midfielder
Club career:
1953-58 Manchester United 175 (21)
International record:
1955-58 England 18 (5)

The youngest player ever to appear for Manchester United, Duncan Edwards made his debut on Easter Monday 1953 aged just 16 years and 185 days.
• Two years later he became the youngest player since the war to win an England cap, making an impressive debut in a 7-2 thrashing of Scotland at Wembley aged 18 years 183 days. This record stood until beaten by Michael Owen in 1998.
• In 1956 Edwards was the youngest member of the legendary 'Busby Babes' team which won two successive league championships. The following year he also played in the FA Cup final, but finished on the losing side to Aston Villa.
• Edwards was the most complete footballer of his generation. Dominant in the air, strong in the tackle and able to pass and shoot equally well with both feet, he was hailed as a future England captain. His team-mate Bobby Charlton once said of him: "I totally believe he was the best player I

ever saw or am likely to see."
• Two weeks after the Munich air crash on 6th February 1958, Edwards died of his injuries in hospital. On the day of his funeral more than 5,000 people lined the streets of his home town, Dudley, to pay their respects to one of England's greatest players.

ENGLAND

First international: Scotland 0 England 0, 1872
Most capped player: Peter Shilton, 125 caps 1971-90
Leading goalscorer: Bobby Charlton, 49 goals (1958-70)
First World Cup appearance: England 2 Chile 0, 1950
Biggest win: England 13 Ireland 0, 1882
Heaviest defeat: Hungary 7 England 1, 1954
Colours: White shirts, white shorts, white socks

England, along with their first opponents Scotland, are the oldest international team in world football. The two countries met in the first official international in Glasgow in 1872, with

honours being shared after a 0-0 draw. The following year William Kenyon-Slaney of Wanderers FC scored England's first ever goal in a 4-2 victory over Scotland at the Kennington Oval.
• **With a team entirely composed of players from England, Great Britain won the first Olympic Games football tournament in 1908 and repeated the feat in 1912.**
• England did not lose a match on home soil against a team from outside the British Isles until 1953 when they were thrashed 6-3 by Hungary at Wembley. The following year England went down to their worst ever defeat to the same opposition, crashing 7-1 in Budapest.
• **Although Walter Winterbottom was appointed as England's first full-time manager in 1946 the squad was picked by a committee until Alf Ramsey took over in 1963. Three years later England hosted and won the World Cup – the greatest moment in the country's football history by some considerable margin.**
• There were many heroes in that 1966 team, including goalkeeper Gordon Banks, skipper Bobby Moore and striker Geoff Hurst, who scored a hat-trick in the 4-2 victory over West Germany in the final at Wembley. Ramsey, too, was hailed for his part in the success and was knighted soon afterwards.
• **Since then, however, England fans have experienced more than their fair**

TOP 10

MOST CAPPED ENGLAND PLAYERS

1. Peter Shilton (1970–90)
   125 caps
2. David Beckham (1996–)
   115 caps
3. Bobby Moore (1962–73)
   108 caps
4. Bobby Charlton (1958–70)
   106 caps
5. Billy Wright (1946–59)
   105 caps
6. Bryan Robson (1980–91)
   90 caps
7. Michael Owen (1998–)
   89 caps
8. Kenny Sansom (1979–88)
   86 caps
9. Gary Neville (1995–)
   85 caps
10. Ray Wilkins (1976–86)
    84 caps

share of disappointment. A second appearance in the World Cup final was within the grasp of Bobby Robson's team in 1990 but, agonisingly, they lost on penalties in the semi-final to the eventual winners, Germany.

• In 1996 England hosted the European Championships and were again knocked out on penalties by Germany at the semi-final stage. England have since lost four more times on penalties at major tournaments, to leave them with the worst shoot-out record (one win in six) of any country in the world.

• With 49 goals for England, Bobby Charlton is England's leading scorer. His 1960s team-mate Jimmy Greaves scored a record six hat-tricks for the Three Lions.

• The only England player to have appeared in the finals of six major tournaments is Sol Campbell, who played in three European Championships and three World Cups between 1996-2006.

• Since England first entered the World Cup in 1950 they have only lost two qualifying matches at home – 1-0 defeats by Italy and Germany in 1997 and 2000 respectively.

• In 2001 England appointed their first foreign manager Sven Goran Eriksson, a Swede with an excellent track record in club football. Eriksson, though, could not bring back the glory days. Under his hapless successor Steve McClaren, England failed even to qualify for Euro 2008. Fabio Capello took over the job in 2008 but the Italian's first tournament in charge of the team, the 2010 World Cup in South Africa, proved to be one to forget as England crashed out 4-1 to Germany in the last 16.

HONOURS
World Cup 1966
World Cup record
1930 Did not enter
1934 Did not enter
1938 Did not enter
1950 Round 1
1954 Quarter-finals
1958 Round 1
1962 Quarter-finals
1966 Winners
1970 Quarter-finals
1974 Did not qualify
1978 Did not qualify
1982 Round 1
1986 Quarter-finals
1990 Semi-finals
1994 Did not qualify
1998 Round 2
2002 Quarter-finals
2006 Quarter-finals
2010 Round 2

SVEN GORAN ERIKSSON

Born: Sunne, Sweden,
5th February 1948
Managerial career:
1977-78 Degerfors
1979-82 Gothenburg
1982-84 Benfica
1984-87 Roma
1987-89 Fiorentina
1989-92 Benfica
1992-97 Sampdoria
1997-2001 Lazio
2001-2006 England
2007-08 Manchester City
2008-09 Mexico
2010 Ivory Coast

The first foreigner to manage England, Sven Goran Eriksson guided the Three Lions to the quarter-finals of three major tournaments during his five years in charge of the national team between 2001 and 2006. On each occasion, though, he was defeated by a side managed by his nemesis, Luiz Felipe Scolari (Brazil at the 2002 World Cup, and Portugal at Euro 2004 and the 2006 World Cup).

• After an unremarkable playing career in his native Sweden, Eriksson enjoyed a hugely successful 24-year career in club management before taking the England job. He is the only manager to win the league and cup double in three different countries (with Gothenburg in Sweden, Benfica in Portugal and Lazio in Italy) and he also won two European trophies, the UEFA Cup in 1982 and the European Cup-Winners' Cup in 1999.

• During his time as England boss Eriksson's affairs with TV presenter and fellow Swede Ulrika Jonsson and FA secretary Faria Alam made front page headlines. The FA stuck by him on those occasions but were less impressed when he told an undercover reporter that he would be prepared to quit his job to become Aston Villa manager. Soon after this revelation the FA announced that Eriksson's contract would not be renewed after the 2006 World Cup.

• In 2007 Eriksson became manager of Manchester City. However, he only lasted one season at the City of Manchester stadium before being sacked. The bespectacled Swede was soon appointed manager of Mexico but was again sacked in April 2009 after a poor run of results. In an unlikely turn of events he returned to England in July of that year as Director of Football at then League Two side Notts County, before accepting an offer to coach Ivory Coast at the 2010 World Cup.

MICHAEL ESSIEN

Born: Accra, Ghana,
3rd December 1982
Position: Midfielder
Club career:
2000-03 Bastia 65 (11)
2003-05 Lyon 71 (7)
2005- Chelsea 116 (14))
International record:
2002- Ghana 51 (9)

Nicknamed 'The Bison' for his powerhouse displays in midfield, Michael Essien is the second most expensive African player of all time. Having started out with his local club in Ghana, Liberty Professionals, Essien made his name with French side Bastia before joining reigning

SAMUEL ETO'O

Michael Essien is the second most expensive African player ever

his career with Real Madrid but only rose to prominence once he moved to Real Mallorca in 2000. In 2004 he joined Barcelona for around £18 million and the following year helped the Catalans win their first league title of the new millennium.

• Eto'o was the leading scorer in Spain in 2006 as Barca won the title for a second successive season. In the same year he scored in his club's Champions League final victory over Arsenal in Paris. In 2009 he became only the second player to score in two Champions League finals after netting in Barca's 2-0 defeat of Manchester United. That summer he moved to Inter Milan with whom he won the Champions League yet again and the Serie A title the following year.

• Incredibly, Eto'o was one day short of his 15th birthday when he made his international debut for Cameroon in a friendly against Costa Rica in 1996. He has since gone on to win the African Nations Cup with his country in both 2000 and 2002, and is the all-time top scorer in the competition with 18 goals. In 2003, 2004 and 2005 he was voted African Player of the Year.

• Eto'o threatened to walk off the pitch when he was the victim of racist chants at Zaragoza's stadium in 2006. However, his Barcelona team-mates persuaded him that his best response was to carry on playing.

champions Lyon for around £6 million in 2003.

• Essien won two French league titles with Lyon and was voted French Player of the Year in 2005. That same year he moved to Chelsea for a then club record £24.4 million after a long-running transfer saga and helped the Blues retain the Premiership title in his first season at Stamford Bridge.

• In 2007 he added Carling Cup and FA Cup medals to his collection and was voted Chelsea Player of the Year after impressing in a number of positions, including right back and centre half as well as his usual central midfield berth. In recent seasons, however, Essien has often been sidelined through injury, although he did help the Blues win the FA Cup in 2009.

• Essien made his debut for Ghana in a friendly against Egypt in 2002. At the World Cup in Germany in 2006 he helped the Black Stars get further in the tournament than any other African side but missed his country's second round defeat by Brazil through suspension.

SAMUEL ETO'O

Born: Douala, Cameroon, 10th March 1981
Position: Striker
Club career:
1997-2000 Real Madrid 3 (0)
1997-98 Leganes (loan) 28 (3)
1999 Espanyol (loan) 0 (0)
2000 Real Mallorca (loan) 13 (6)
2000-04 Real Mallorca 120 (48)
2004-09 Barcelona 145 (108)
2009- Inter Milan 32 (12)
International record:
1996- Cameroon 103 (48)

One of the most deadly strikers in the modern game, Samuel Eto'o started

Atletico Madrid pictured celebrating their 2010 Europa League triumph, just before the fire brigade turned up!

14-0 at home. Another Dutch side, Feyenoord, hold the record for the biggest aggregate victory, tonking US Rumelange 21-0 in 1972.

EUROPEAN CHAMPIONSHIPS

Originally called the European Nations Cup, the idea for the European Championships came from Henri Delaunay, the then secretary of the French FA. The first championships in 1960 featured just 17 countries (the four British nations, Italy and West Germany were among those who declined to take part). The first winners of the tournament were the Soviet Union, who beat Yugoslavia 2-1 in the final in Paris.

• **Germany have the best record in the tournament, having won the trophy three times (in 1972, 1980 and 1996) and been runners-up on a further three occasions.**

• The most unlikely winners were Denmark in 1992. The Danes had failed to qualify for the finals in Sweden but were invited to compete at the last minute when Yugoslavia were kicked out for political reasons. To the surprise of just about everyone, Denmark – whose players had to be recalled from their holidays to play – went on to lift the trophy after a 2-0 win over Germany in the final.

• **French legend Michel Platini is the leading scorer in the finals of the European Championships with nine goals. England's Alan Shearer is in second place with a total of seven goals at the 1996 and 2000 tournaments.**

• Platini is also the only player to score two hat-tricks at the finals, notching trebles against both Belgium and Yugoslavia in 1984.

EUROPA LEAGUE

The inaugural Europa League final was played between Atletico Madrid and Fulham in Hamburg in 2010, the Spanish side winning 2-1 thanks to a late winner by Uruguayan striker Diego Forlan.

• **The competition is now in its third incarnation, having previously been known as the Fairs Cup (1955-71) and the UEFA Cup (1971-2009). The tournament was originally established in 1955 as a competition between cities, rather than clubs. The first winners were Barcelona who beat London 8-2 on aggregate in the final, which bizarrely did not take place until 1958!**

• The first team to win the newly-named UEFA Cup were Tottenham Hotspur in 1972, who beat Wolves 3-2 on aggregate in the only all-English final. In all, English clubs have won the competition 10 times... an impressive record, although Spanish teams lead the way with 12 victories.

• **Liverpool are the most successful English club in the tournament with three triumphs in 1973, 1976 and 2001. The only other clubs to win the trophy three times are Barcelona, Inter Milan, Juventus and Valencia.**

• The leading goalscorer in the competition is Swedish marksman Henrik Larsson, who notched 40 goals for Feyenoord, Celtic and Helsingborgs.

• **The biggest single win in the competition came in 1984 when Ajax thrashed FA Red Boys Differdange**

IS THAT A FACT?
Germany have played more games (38) at the European Championships than any other country, winning 19 of them – another record. The Germans' tally of 55 goals at the finals is a yet another record, jointly held with Holland.

Spain with their first ever major trophy after winning the 2008 European Championships

• In the qualifying tournament for the 2008 finals Germany recorded the biggest ever win in the history of the competition, thrashing minnows San Marino 13-0 on their home patch.

• Holland's Edwin van der Sar and France's Lilian Thuram share the appearance record at the finals, having both played in 16 games. The pair are also among the six players to have played in a record four tournaments, both featuring between 1996-2008.

EUROPEAN CHAMPIONSHIP FINALS
1960 USSR 2 Yugoslavia 1 (Paris)
1964 Spain 2 USSR 1 (Madrid)
1968 Italy 2 Yugoslavia 0• (Rome)
1972 West Germany 3 USSR 0 (Brussels)
*1976 Czechoslovakia 2^*
West Germany 2 (Belgrade)
1980 West Germany 2 Belgium 1 (Rome)
1984 France 2 Spain 0 (Paris)
1988 Holland 2 USSR 0 (Munich)
1992 Denmark 2 Germany 0 (Gothenburg)
1996 Germany 2 Czech Republic 1 (London)

2000 France 2 Italy 1 (Rotterdam)
2004 Greece 1 Portugal 0 (Lisbon)
2008 Spain 1 Germany 0 (Vienna)
• After 1-1 draw
^ Won on penalties

EUROPEAN FOOTBALLER OF THE YEAR

The first winner of the European Footballer of the Year award (voted for by journalists all over the continent and co-ordinated by *France Football* magazine) was England and Blackpool winger Sir Stanley Matthews.

• **Three players (Johan Cruyff, Michel Platini and Marco Van Basten) have won the award a record three times, with Platini being the only player to win it three times in a row.**

• Until 1995 a player had to be of European nationality to be nominated. Since then, four Brazilians (Ronaldo, Rivaldo, Ronaldinho and Kaka) have won the award, while the reigning European Footballer of the Year is another South American, Argentinian genius Lionel Messi.

• **German and Dutch players have both won the award a record eight times.**

However, players representing Italian clubs have been the most successful with 18 wins in total.

• Six British players have won the award, the most recent being Liverpool's Michael Owen in 2001. The other winners from these shores are: Stanley Matthews (Blackpool, 1956), Denis Law (Manchester United, 1964), Bobby Charlton (Manchester United, 1966), George Best (Manchester United, 1968) and Kevin Keegan, who won the award with Hamburg in both 1978 and 1979.

EUROPEAN FOOTBALLER OF THE YEAR WINNERS
1956 Stanley Matthews
1957 Alfredo di Stefano
1958 Raymond Kopa
1959 Alfredo di Stefano
1960 Luis Suarez
1961 Omar Sivori
1962 Josef Masopust
1963 Lev Yashin
1964 Denis Law
1965 Eusebio
1966 Bobby Charlton
1967 Florian Albert
1968 George Best

1969 Gianni Rivera
1970 Gerd Muller
1971 Johan Cruyff
1972 Franz Beckenbauer
1973 Johan Cruyff
1974 Johan Cruyff
1975 Oleg Blokhin
1976 Franz Beckenbauer
1977 Allan Simonsen
1978 Kevin Keegan
1979 Kevin Keegan
1980 Karl Heinz Rummenigge
1981 Karl Heinz Rummenigge
1982 Paolo Rossi
1983 Michel Platini
1984 Michel Platini
1985 Michel Platini
1986 Igor Belanov
1987 Ruud Gullit
1988 Marco Van Basten
1989 Marco Van Basten
1990 Lothar Matthaus
1991 Jean-Pierre Papin
1992 Marco Van Basten
1993 Roberto Baggio
1994 Hristo Stoichkov
1995 George Weah

1996 Matthias Sammer
1997 Ronaldo
1998 Zinedine Zidane
1999 Rivaldo
2000 Luis Figo
2001 Michael Owen
2002 Ronaldo
2003 Pavel Nedved
2004 Andrei Shevchenko
2005 Ronaldinho
2006 Fabio Cannavaro
2007 Kaka
2008 Cristiano Ronaldo
2009 Lionel Messi

EUROPEAN GOLDEN BOOT

Now officially known as the European Golden Shoe and currently held by Lionel Messi, the European Golden Boot has been awarded since 1968 to the leading scorer in league matches in the top division of every European league. Since 1997 the award has been based on a points system which gives greater weight to goals scored in the leading European leagues.

• The first winner of the award was the legendary Portuguese international Eusebio who picked up the trophy after knocking in an incredible 43 goals for Benfica. He topped the poll again in 1973, aged 30, with a total of 40 goals.
• The first British winner of the award was Liverpool's Ian Rush in 1984, and the most recent was Sunderland's Kevin Phillips in 2000. Since then, Thierry Henry (in 2004 and 2005) and Cristiano Ronaldo (in 2008) have won the Golden Shoe after topping both the Premiership and European goalscoring charts.
• The most controversial winner of the award was Rumania's Rodion Camataru, who scored 20 of his 44 goals for Dynamo Bucharest in the last six games of the 1986/87 season. Suspicions that some of these matches had not been played in a wholly competitive spirit were confirmed by evidence that emerged in the post-Communist era and in 2007 the runner-up in the 1987 list, Austria Vienna striker Toni Polster, was also granted a Golden Boot.

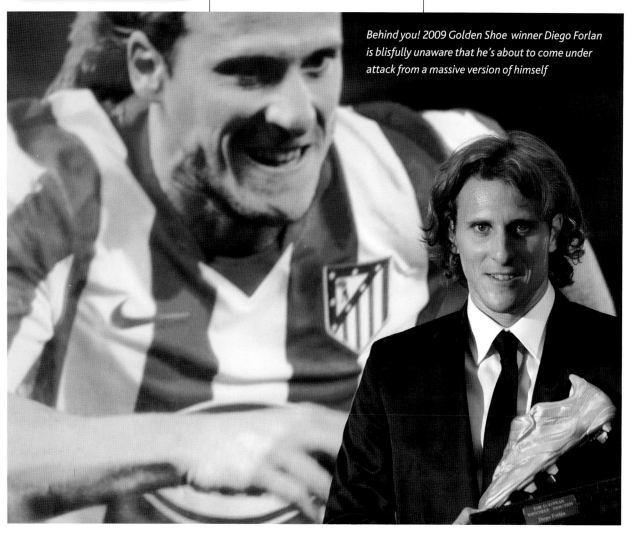

Behind you! 2009 Golden Shoe winner Diego Forlan is blisfully unaware that he's about to come under attack from a massive version of himself

EUSEBIO

Born: Lourenco Marques, Mozambique, 25th January 1942
Position: Striker
Club career:
1957-61 Sporting Lourenco Marques
1961-75 Benfica 301 (317)
1975 Boston Minutemen 7 (2)
1975-76 Monterrey 10 (1)
1976 Toronto Metros-Croatia 25 (18)
1976-77 Beira Mar 12 (3)
1977 Las Vegas Quicksilver 17 (2)
International record:
1961-73 Portugal 64 (41)

A legendary figure for both Benfica and Portugal, Eusebio is the most famous player to appear for his country.

• Known as the 'Black Panther' or the 'Black Pearl', Eusebio was top scorer at the 1966 World Cup with nine goals, including four in one match against North Korea. His performances at the tournament were so impressive that Madame Tussauds added a waxwork of the Portuguese star to their collection. Eusebio's total of 41 goals for his country was a record until 2005, when Pauleta pushed him into second place.

• Born in Mozambique, Eusebio started out with local side Sporting Lourenco Marques, a feeder club for Sporting Lisbon. His decision to sign for Sporting's rivals Benfica led to a huge row between the clubs, which Eusebio escaped by hiding away in a fishing village on the Algarve for several months.

• With an incredible 317 goals in 301 league games, Eusebio is Benfica's all-time leading scorer. He won the Portuguese title 11 times in his 14 years at the club and also picked up five Portuguese cup winners' medals. His greatest triumph, though, came in the 1962 European Cup final when he scored twice in Benfica's 5-3 victory over five-time winners Real Madrid.

• A fast, dynamic striker with an explosive shot, Eusebio was voted European Footballer of the Year in 1965. Three years later he was the first winner of the European Golden Boot, and in 1973 he collected the award for a second time. He ended his career in America, where he won the NASL title with Toronto Metros-Croatia in 1976. In 2003 he was named as the most outstanding Portuguese player of the last 50 years by his country's Football Federation.

The great Eusebio: 317 goals in 301 league games for Benfica

EVERTON

Year founded: 1878
Ground: Goodison Park (40,158)
Previous name: St Domingo
Nickname: The Toffees
Biggest win: 11-2 v Derby County (1890)
Heaviest defeat: 4-10 v Tottenham (1958)
Colours: Blue shirts, white shorts, white socks

The club was formed as the church team St Domingo in 1878, adopting the name Everton (after the surrounding area) the following year. In 1888 Everton joined the Football League as founder members, winning the first of nine league titles three years later.

• One of the most famous names in English football, Everton hold the proud record of spending more seasons in the top flight than any other club. Relegated only twice, in 1930 and 1951, they have spent just four seasons in total outside the top tier.

• The club's unusual nickname, the Toffees, stems from a local business called Ye Ancient Everton Toffee House which was situated near Goodison Park. In the early 1930s Everton's precise style of play earned the club the tag 'The School of Science', a nickname which lingers to this day.

• The club's record goalscorer is the legendary Dixie Dean, who notched an incredible total of 383 goals in all competitions between 1925-37. Dean's best season for the club was in the Toffees' title-winning campaign in 1927/28 when his 60 league goals set a Football League record that is unlikely ever to be beaten.

• Everton's most capped player is long-serving goalkeeper Neville Southall, who made 93 appearances for Wales in the 1980s and 1990s. He is also the club's record appearance maker, turning out in 578 league games.

• In 1931 Everton won the Second Division title, scoring 121 goals in the process. The following season the Toffees banged in 116 goals on their way to lifting the First Division title, becoming the first (and so far only) club to find the net 100 times in consecutive seasons.

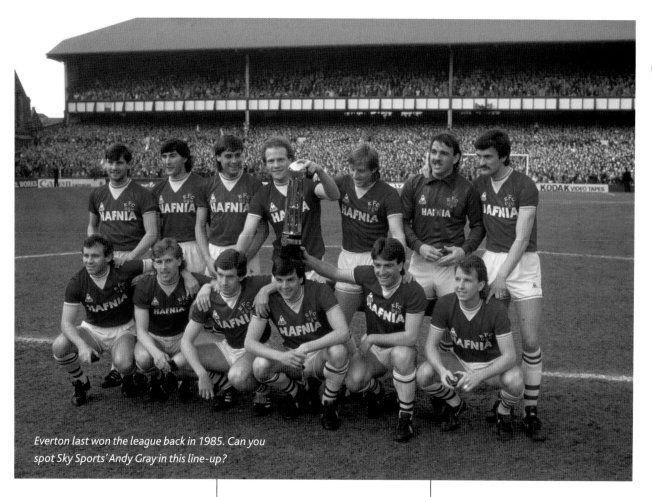

Everton last won the league back in 1985. Can you spot Sky Sports' Andy Gray in this line-up?

• The club's most successful decade, though, was in the 1980s when, under manager Howard Kendall, they won the league championship (1985 and 1987), FA Cup (1984) and the European Cup Winners' Cup (in 1985, following a 3-1 win over Austria Vienna in the final). Since those glory days Everton have had to play second fiddle to city rivals Liverpool, although the Toffees did manage to win the FA Cup for a fifth time in 1995, beating Manchester United in the final thanks to a single goal by striker Paul Rideout.

• **The club's record signing is afro-haired midfielder Morouane Fellaini, who cost £15 million when he signed from Standard Liege in 2008. Local boy Wayne Rooney fetched a record £23 million when he left Everton for Manchester United after starring for England at the Euro 2004 championships.**

• In 1893 Everton's Jack Southworth became the first player in Football League history to score six goals in a match when he fired a double hat-trick in a 7-1 victory against West Bromwich Albion.

• Everton's Louis Saha scored the fastest ever goal in the FA Cup final, when he netted after just 25 seconds against Chelsea at Wembley in 2009. **Sadly for David Moyes' men, the Toffees were unable to hold onto their lead and were eventually beaten 2-1.**

• The oldest ground in the Premiership, Goodison Park is the only stadium in the world to have a church, St Luke the Evangelist, inside its grounds. The stadium was the first in England to feature dug-outs (in the 1930s), undersoil heating (in the 1958/59 season) and a three-tiered stand (in 1971). Goodison Park is also the only ground in the UK to have hosted a World Cup semi-final, staging the West Germany v Russia encounter in 1966.

• **Famous fans of the club include snooker player John Parrott, madcap comedian Freddie Starr and 'Rocky' star Sylvester Stallone.**

HONOURS
Division 1 champions 1891, 1915, 1928, 1932, 1939, 1963, 1970, 1985, 1987
Division 2 champions 1931
FA Cup 1906, 1933, 1966, 1984, 1995
European Cup Winners' Cup 1985

EXETER CITY

Year founded: 1904
Ground: St James' Park (8,830)
Nickname: The Grecians
Biggest win: 9-1 v Aberdare Athletic (1927)
Heaviest defeat: 0-9 v Notts County (1948) and v Northampton Town (1958)
Colours: Red-and-white striped shirts, black shorts, black socks

Exeter City were founded in 1904 following the amalgamation of two local sides, Exeter United and St Sidwell's United. The club were founder members of the Third Division (South) in 1920 and remained in the two lower divisions until they were relegated to the Conference in 2003. Now owned by the Exeter City Supporters Trust, the club rejoined the Football League in 2008 and the following season went up to League One.

• **After a poor start to the 1910/11 season Exeter decided to scrap their 'unlucky' green and white kit. They changed to their current colours of red**

and white stripes and their fortunes took an instant turn for the better, the club winning five of their next six games.

• In 1914 Exeter made an historic tour of South America, playing eight matches against teams in Argentina and Brazil. One of the games was against the newly-formed Brazilian national team in Rio de Janeiro. City lost 2-0.

• **The greatest day in the club's history, though, was in 2005 when they drew 0-0 with Manchester United at Old Trafford in the third round of the FA Cup. Exeter fans packed out their tiny St James' Park ground for the replay but their team failed to rise to the occasion, losing 3-0.**

HONOURS
Division 4 champions 1990

EXTRA TIME

Normally consisting of two halves of 15 minutes each, extra time has been played to produce a winner in knockout tournaments since the earliest days of football. Extra time was first played in an FA Cup final in 1875, Royal Engineers and the Old Etonians drawing 1-1 (Royal Engineers won the replay 2-0). In all, extra time has been played in 18 finals, the most recent in 2007 when Chelsea eventually beat Manchester United 1-0.

• **The first World Cup final to go to extra time was in 1934, when hosts Italy and Czechoslovakia were tied 1-1 at the end of 90 minutes. Seven minutes in to the additional period, Angelo Schiavio scored the winner for Italy. Since then, five other finals have gone to extra time, most recently in 2010 when Spain's Andres Iniesta scored the winner against Holland with just a few minutes to play.**

• In an attempt to encourage attacking football and reduce the number of matches settled by penalty shoot-outs, FIFA ruled in 1993 that the first goal scored in extra time would win the match. The first major tournament to be decided by the so-called 'golden goal' rule was the 1996 European Championships, Germany defeating the Czech Republic in the final thanks to a 94th minute strike by Oliver Bierhoff. The 2000 final of the same competition was also decided in the same manner, David Trezeguet scoring the winner for France against Italy in the 117th minute.

• **Concerns that the 'golden goal' put too much pressure on referees led UEFA to replace it with the 'silver goal' in 2002. Under this rule, which was used at Euro 2004 but scrapped afterwards, only the first half of extra time was played if either team led at the interval.**

"Ok. If you win I'll take you all out for a curry!"

FA CUP

The oldest knockout competition in the world, the FA Cup dates back to 1871 when it was established under the control of the Football Association. The first round of the first FA Cup was played on 11th November 1871, Clapham Rovers' Jarvis Kenrick scoring the very first goal in the competition in a 3-0 win over Upton Park.

• **The following year Wanderers beat Royal Engineers at Kennington Oval in the first ever FA Cup final. The only goal of the game was scored by Morton Peto Betts, who played under the pseudonym A.H. Chequer.**

• Unlike the League Cup, the FA Challenge Cup – the competition's full title – has always retained the same name despite being sponsored since 1994. In 2009 the FA began to search for a new partner after E.ON declined to extend their sponsorship beyond 2010.

• **There have, however, been four different trophies. The first trophy – known as the 'little tin idol' – was stolen from a Birmingham shop window in September 1895 where it was on display, having been won by Aston Villa a few months earlier. Sixty years later the** thief revealed that the trophy was melted down and turned into counterfeit coins. A second trophy was used until 1910 when it was presented to the FA's long-serving President and former five-time cup winner, Lord Kinnaird. A new, larger trophy was commissioned by the FA from Fattorini and Sons Silversmiths in Bradford – and, by a remarkable coincidence, was won in its first year by Bradford City in 1911. This trophy was used until 1992, when it was replaced with an exact replica.

• The only current league team to have won the FA Cup in three consecutive years are Blackburn Rovers, who lifted the trophy in 1884, 1885 and 1886. The most successful club in the competition are Manchester United, who have won the FA Cup a record 11 times.

• **In 2000 Manchester United became the first holders not to defend their title when they failed to enter the FA Cup, opting instead to take part in the inaugural FIFA Club World Championship in Brazil.**

• Five years later United were involved in the first FA Cup final to be decided by penalties, losing 5-4 to Arsenal after a 0-0 draw at the Millennium Stadium, Cardiff. In 2007 the final returned to Wembley, Chelsea becoming the first club to lift the trophy at the new national stadium after a 1-0 victory over Manchester United.

An Everton fan and fashion guru celebrates his team's 1933 FA Cup triumph at Trafalgar Square

• Tottenham Hotspur are the only non-league side to win the competition, lifting the trophy for the first time in 1901 while members of the Southern League. West Ham were the last team from outside the top flight to win the cup, beating Arsenal 1-0 in the 1980 final.

• The first player to be sent off in the FA Cup final was Manchester United's Kevin Moran in 1985, who was dismissed for a foul on Everton's Peter Reid. Nonetheless, United went on to win the match 1-0 after extra time.

• In 1887 Preston North End recorded the biggest win in the history of the competition when they thrashed Hyde 26-0 in a first round tie.

• Ashley Cole has won the FA Cup a record six times. Three of the England full back's triumphs came with his first club, Arsenal (in 2002, 2003 and 2005) and he has also enjoyed three successes with Chelsea (in 2007, 2009 and 2010).

• A record 762 clubs entered the FA Cup in 2009/10, narrowly beating the previous high of 761 set a year earlier.

TOP 10

FA CUP WINNERS
1. Manchester United 11 wins
2. Arsenal 10 wins
3. Tottenham Hotspur 8 wins
4. Liverpool 7 wins
   Aston Villa 7 wins
6. Newcastle United 6 wins
   Blackburn Rovers 6 wins
   Chelsea 6 wins
9. Everton 5 wins
   West Bromwich Albion 5 wins
   Wanderers 5 wins

CESC FABREGAS

Born: Barcelona, 4th May 1987
Position: Midfielder
Club career:
2003-Arsenal 187 (32)
International record:
2006- Spain 54 (6)

One of the most talented midfielders in Europe, Cesc Fabregas is the youngest player ever to appear for Arsenal. He made his debut for the Gunners in a League Cup tie against Rotherham in October 2003, aged just 16 years and 177 days. When he scored against

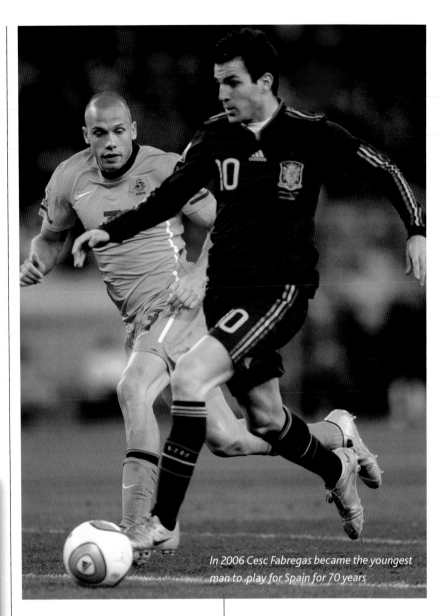

In 2006 Cesc Fabregas became the youngest man to play for Spain for 70 years

Wolves in a later round of the same competition he also became the club's youngest ever goalscorer.

• Fabregas started out as a trainee with Barcelona before signing for Arsenal in September 2003. A superb passer of the ball who can unpick the tightest of defences, he has been compared by Gunners boss Arsene Wenger to French legend Michel Platini. In 2008 Wenger appointed Fabregas as his new skipper after team-mate William Gallas was stripped of the captaincy.

• In his five years at Arsenal Fabregas has won just a single trophy, the FA Cup in 2005. His brilliant performances in the 2007/08 season, though, saw him named PFA Young Player of the Year.

• When Fabregas made his debut for Spain in a friendly against Ivory Coast in 2006 he was the youngest player to represent his country for 70 years. Two years later he helped Spain win Euro 2008 in Austria and Switzerland, his country's first trophy for 44 years.

• At the 2010 World Cup in South Africa he failed to start a single game, but he came off the bench in the final against Holland to set up the winning goal for team-mate Andres Iniesta with a typically clever pass.

FANS

Real Madrid have more fans than any other club in the world. A study at Harvard University in 2006 discovered that the Spanish giants have around 228 million fans worldwide, although presumably most of them have never stepped inside the club's famous Bernabeu Stadium. With 168 million supporters dotted around the globe, Manchester United are the second-best supported club.

• A number of fan groups have realised a common supporters' dream by becoming the owners of their clubs. Two Football League clubs (Brentford and Exeter City) are currently owned by Supporters' Trusts, while non-league clubs AFC Wimbledon, AFC Liverpool and FC United of Manchester were set up by disillusioned supporters of Wimbledon, Liverpool and Manchester United respectively. Fan-owned clubs, meanwhile, are the norm in Germany, while Spanish titans Athletic Bilbao, Barcelona and Real Madrid are also supporter-owned.

• Formed in 1978, the 92 Club is open to all fans who have attended a competitive first-team fixture at the stadium of every Premiership and Football League club in England and Wales. The club's initial membership of 39 had grown to 1,100 by the start of the 2010/11 season.

• **With 142,000 members in England and Wales the Football Supporters'** Federation is the largest fans' organisation in Britain. The FSF campaigns on a variety of issues affecting fans, including ticket pricing, policing and supporter representation on club boards, as well as organising an annual Fans' Parliament at Wembley stadium. The current chairman of the FSF is Malcolm Clarke, a Stoke City fan.

• The must-have accessory for fans at the 2010 World Cup in the South Africa was the vuvuzela, a horn-like instrument that emits a loud, distinctive monotone note when blown. Opinion was divided over whether the noise produced by thousands of vuvuzelas enhanced or spoiled the atmosphere at matches at the tournament, but most European managers and players who expressed a view were in the 'anti' camp. The backlash against the vuvuzela continued as the summer progressed, with the Wimbledon tennis championships placing a blanket ban on the instrument. Tottenham were the first Premier League outfit to follow suit and by the start of the 2010/11 season most top-flight clubs had also decided to ban it.

RIO FERDINAND

Born: Peckham, 7th November 1978
Position: Defender
Club career:
1996-2000 West Ham United 127 (2)
1996 Bournemouth (loan) 10 (0)
2000-02 Leeds United 54 (2)
2002- Manchester United 221 (6)
International record:
1997- England 78 (3)

England captain Rio Ferdinand is the world's most expensive defender, having moved from Leeds United to Manchester United for around £30 million in 2002. Nor was that the first time Ferdinand had been transferred for an eye-watering fee. In 2000 he joined Leeds from West Ham, his first club, for £18 million – also a world record at the time for a defender.

• **A composed and commanding centre-half who likes to bring the ball out from the back to launch attacking moves, Ferdinand won the Premiership title in his first season at Old Trafford. He has since won the title on three further occasions (in 2007, 2008 and 2009) and in 2008 he skippered United when the Reds won the Champions League after beating Premiership rivals Chelsea on penalties in the final in Moscow.**

• A mainstay of the England defence for many years, Ferdinand was first capped against Cameroon in 1997, just one week after his 19th birthday. At the time he was the youngest ever defender to play for England – although this record has since been beaten by Micah Richards. In 2008 Ferdinand captained his country for the first time as England manager Fabio Capello tried out a number of players in the role before finally handing the armband to the United star's defensive partner, John Terry. When Terry was stripped of the captaincy in 2010 after allegations about his private life, Capello handed Ferdinand the armband on a permanent basis. Sadly, injury deprived him of the chance of leading the Three Lions at the 2010 World Cup.

• **Another low point in Ferdinand's**

Rio Ferdinband, the world's most expensive defender

career came in 2003 when he failed to turn up for a drugs test and was subsequently banned from playing for eight months. The ban meant he missed most of the 2003/04 domestic season and the whole of Euro 2004 in Portugal.

• Peckham-born Ferdinand hails from a football family. His younger brother Anton plays for Sunderland while older cousin Les was a prolific striker with QPR, Newcastle, Tottenham and England.

SIR ALEX FERGUSON

Born: Govan, 31st December 1942
Managerial career:
1974 East Stirling
1974-78 St Mirren
1978-86 Aberdeen
1985-86 Scotland (caretaker)
1986- Manchester United

Manchester United boss Sir Alex Ferguson is the most successful British manager in the history of the game. Over his long career he has won more than 30 major trophies and is the only manager from these shores to win the Champions League on two occasions.

• **Ferguson's reputation was forged at Aberdeen between 1978-86**

where he transformed the Dons into Scotland's leading club, breaking the domination of the Glasgow Old Firm in the process. Under Fergie, Aberdeen won three Premier Division titles, four Scottish Cups, one League Cup and the European Cup-Winners' Cup in 1983, making him easily the most successful boss in the club's history.

• He moved to Manchester United in 1986 and, after some difficult early years, established

TOP 10

ALL-TIME MANAGERS*

1. Rinus Michels (Ajax, Barcelona & Holland)
2. Sir Matt Busby (Manchester United)
3. Ernst Happel (Feyenoord, Holland & Hamburg)
4. Sir Alex Ferguson (Aberdeen & Manchester United)
5. Bill Shankly (Liverpool)
6. Bob Paisley (Liverpool)
7. Brian Clough (Derby County & Nottingham Forest)
8. Bela Guttmann (Porto & Benfica)
9. Miguel Munoz (Real Madrid & Spain)
10. Arsene Wenger (Monaco & Arsenal)

* As selected by www.timesonline.co.uk

the Reds as the dominant force of the 1990s and the new millennium. With United Ferguson has won a record 11 Premiership titles, five FA Cups (another record), three League Cups, the European Cup-Winners' Cup and the Champions League in both 1999 and 2008.

• **Fergie's 24-year tenure at Old Trafford means he is currently the longest-serving manager in English football.** Among other United managers, only Sir Matt Busby can match his longevity, with another 24-year stint in the Old Trafford hotseat between 1945-69.

• Ferguson is the only man to guide both Scottish and English clubs to success in all three domestic competitions and in Europe. He is also the only manager to win the English championship in three consecutive seasons with the same club, achieving this feat with United between 1999-2001 and 2007-09. In the first of those years Fergie also won the FA Cup and Champions League to pull off an unprecedented Treble.

• **A committed but not especially skilful striker in his playing days in the 1960s and early 1970s, Ferguson scored over 150 goals for a number of Scottish clubs including Dunfermline, Rangers and Falkirk.**

• Knighted for services to football in 1999, Ferguson has been named Premier League Manager of the Year on a record nine occasions. Still enthusiastic and motivated after all these years he will, no doubt, be looking to add to his staggering roll of honour in seasons to come.

Alex Ferguson: Quite simply the most successful British manager of all time

FIFA

FIFA, the Federation Internationale de Football Association, is the most important administrative body in world football. It is responsible for the organization of major international tournaments, notably the World Cup, and enacts law changes in the game.

• Founded in Paris in 1904, FIFA is now based in Zurich and has 208 members, 16 more than the United Nations. The current President is Sepp Blatter (appointed in 1998), the latest in a distinguished line that includes Jules Rimet (1921-54), Sir Stanley Rous (1961-74) and Joao Havelange (1974-98).

Old skool! Brazil and France wore retro kits for the first half of their friendly match in 2004, played to mark FIFA's centenary

• Law changes FIFA have introduced into the World Cup include the use of substitutes (1970), penalty shoot-outs to settle drawn games (1982) and the banning of the professional foul (1990).
• **The British football associations have twice pulled out of FIFA. First, in 1918 when they were opposed to playing matches against Germany after the end of the First World War, and again in 1928 over the issue of payments to amateurs. This second dispute meant that none of the British teams were represented at the first World Cup in 1930.**
• In 1992 FIFA decided to introduce a ranking index for all its member countries. As of August 2010 the three leading nations were Spain (1,833 points), Holland (1,659 points) and Brazil (1,524 points).

SIR TOM FINNEY

Born: Preston, 5th April 1922
Position: Winger
Club career:
1946-60 Preston North End
433 (187)
International record:
1947-59 England 76 (30)

One of England's greatest ever players, flying winger Sir Tom Finney was the first player to be made Footballer of the Year twice. He won the award in 1954, after starring in Preston's run to the FA Cup final, and was honoured for a second time in 1957.
• **Equally adept on either right or left wing, Finney scored a record 187 league goals for Preston but never won a major club trophy. The closest he got was in 1953 when Preston missed out on the league title on goal average. The following year they lost to West Brom in the FA Cup final, and in 1958 they were again runners-up in the league.**
• In his 76 appearances for England, Finney scored an impressive 30 goals – a record at the time shared with Bolton's Nat Lofthouse. Only four players since have scored more goals for England. His Preston team-mate Bill Shankly once said of him: "Tom Finney would have been great in any team, in any match and in any age – even if he had been wearing an overcoat."
• **Before signing as a pro, Finney served his apprenticeship in the family plumbing business – hence his nickname, the 'Preston Plumber'. Unarguably Preston's best ever player, he was knighted in 1998 and has a stand named after him at the club's Deepdale ground.**

DARREN FLETCHER

Born: Dalkeith, 1st February 1984
Position: Midfielder
Club career:
2001- Manchester United 163 (14)
International record:
2003- Scotland 48 (4)

Darren Fletcher became Scotland's youngest captain for over a century when, at the age of 22, he first wore his country's armband in a 2004 friendly against Estonia in Tallinn. Five years later he was appointed Scotland's captain on a permanent basis by then manager Craig Burley.
• **An industrious midfielder who rarely has a bad game, Fletcher has spent all of his career with Manchester United. He won his first honour with the club, the FA Cup, in 2004 and was a key member of the United squad which won a hat-trick of Premier League titles between 2007-09.**
• Fletcher was an unused substitute when the Red Devils won the Champions League in 2008, and the following year was banned from playing in the final against Barcelona after receiving a harshly awarded red card in his side's semi-final victory over Arsenal.

• Fletcher scored his first goal for Scotland in only his second appearance for his country, a 1-0 win against Lithuania in a Euro 2004 qualifier. Rated by many as the best Scottish player of his generation, he is now approaching a half century of caps.

FLOODLIGHTS

The first ever floodlit match was played at Bramall Lane between two representative Sheffield sides on 14th October 1876 in front of a crowd of 10,000 people (around 8,000 of whom used the cover of darkness to get in without paying). The pitch was illuminated by four lamps, powered by dynamos driven by engines located behind the goals.

• For many years the Football Association banned floodlight football, so the first league match played under lights did not take place until 1956, when Newcastle beat Portsmouth 2-0 at Fratton Park. It was hardly the most auspicious of occasions, though, as floodlight failure meant the kick-off was delayed for 30 minutes.

• Arsenal became the first top flight club in England to install floodlights in 1951 – some 20 years after legendary Gunners manager Herbert Chapman had advocated their use.

Chesterfield were the last Football League club to install floodlights, finally putting up a set in 1967.

• Floodlights were installed at Wembley Stadium in 1955, the first match under lights being the Inter-Cities Fairs Cup encounter between London and Frankfurt on 26th October. Among the scorers

for London in their 3-2 victory was Fulham's Bobby Robson, later the manager of England.

FOOTBALL ASSOCIATION

Founded in 1863 at a meeting at the Freemasons' Tavern in central London, the Football Association is the oldest football organisation in the world and the only national association with no mention of the country in its name.

• The first secretary of the FA was Ebenezer Cobb Morley of Barnes FC, nicknamed 'The Father of Football', who went on to draft the first set of laws of the game. The most controversial of the 14 laws he suggested outlawed kicking an opponent, known as 'hacking'. The first match to be played under the new laws was between Barnes and Richmond in 1863.

• In 1871 the then secretary of the FA, Charles Alcock, suggested playing a national knock-out tournament similar to the competition he had enjoyed as a schoolboy at Harrow School. The idea was accepted by the FA and the competition, named the FA Challenge Cup, has been running ever since. The FA Cup, as it usually called, has long been the most famous national club competition in world football.

• Since 1992, the FA has run the English game's top division, the Premier League, which was formed when the old First Division broke away from the then four division Football League.

• The FA is also responsible for the appointment of the management of the England men's and women's football teams. The FA's main asset is the new Wembley Stadium, which it owns via its subsidiary, Wembley National Stadium Limited.

• Among the innovations the FA has fought against before finally accepting are the formation of an international tournament, the use of substitutes and the use of floodlights.

FOOTBALL LEAGUE

The Football League was founded at a meeting at the Royal Hotel, Piccadilly, Manchester in April 1888. The prime mover behind the new body was Aston Villa director William McGregor, who became the league's first President.

• The 12 founder members were **Accrington, Aston Villa, Blackburn Rovers, Bolton Wanderers, Burnley, Derby County, Everton, Notts County, Preston North End, Stoke City, West Bromwich Albion and Wolverhampton Wanderers. At the end of the inaugural 1888/89 season, Preston were crowned champions.**

• In 1892 a new Second Division, absorbing clubs from the rival Football Alliance, was added to the League and by 1905 the two divisions were made up of a total of 40 clubs. After the First World War the League was expanded again to include a Third Division (later split between North and South sections).

• **A further expansion after 1945 took the number of clubs playing in the league to its long-time total of 92. The formation of the Premier League in 1992 reduced the Football League to three divisions – now known as the Championship, League One and League Two.**

• As well as being the governing body for the three divisions, the Football League also organises two knockout competitions: the League Cup (currently known as the Carling Cup for sponsorship reasons) and the Football League Trophy (aka the Johnstone's Paint Trophy).

• **Liverpool are the most successful club in the history of the Football League, with 18 First Division titles to their name.**

FOOTBALLER OF THE YEAR

Confusingly, there are two Footballer of the Year awards in England and Scotland. The Football Writers' award was inaugurated in 1948 and the first winner was England winger Stanley Matthews. In 1974 the PFA (Professional Footballers' Association) set up their own award, Leeds hard man Norman 'Bites Yer Legs' Hunter being the first to be honoured by his peers.

• **Liverpool midfielder Terry McDermott was the first player to win both awards in the same season after helping Liverpool retain the title in 1980. A total of 13 different**

players have won both Footballer of the Year awards in the same season, most recently Manchester United ace Wayne Rooney in 2010. Arsenal striker Thierry Henry has won a record five awards, landing the 'double' in both 2003 and 2004 and also carrying off the Football Writers' award in 2006.

• In 1977 Aston Villa striker Andy Gray became the first player to win both the main PFA award and the Young Player of the Year trophy. Only Cristiano Ronaldo in 2007 has since matched this achievement.

FOOTBALL WRITERS' PLAYER OF THE YEAR (SINCE 1990)
1990 John Barnes (Liverpool)
1991 Gordon Strachan (Leeds United)
1992 Gary Lineker (Tottenham)
1993 Chris Waddle (Sheffield Wednesday)
1994 Alan Shearer (Blackburn Rovers)
1995 Jurgen Klinsmann (Tottenham)
1996 Eric Cantona (Manchester United)
1997 Gianfranco Zola (Chelsea)
1998 Dennis Bergkamp (Arsenal)
1999 David Ginola (Tottenham)
2000 Roy Keane (Manchester United)
2001 Teddy Sheringham (Manchester United)
2002 Robert Pires (Arsenal)
2003 Thierry Henry (Arsenal)
2004 Thierry Henry (Arsenal)
2005 Frank Lampard (Chelsea)
2006 Thierry Henry (Arsenal)
2007 Cristiano Ronaldo (Manchester United)
2008 Cristiano Ronaldo (Manchester United)
2009 Steven Gerrard (Liverpool)
2010 Wayne Rooney (Manchester United)

PFA FOOTBALLER OF THE YEAR (SINCE 1990)
1990 David Platt (Aston Villa)
1991 Mark Hughes (Manchester United)
1992 Gary Pallister (Manchester United)
1993 Paul McGrath (Aston Villa)
1994 Eric Cantona (Manchester United)
1995 Alan Shearer (Blackburn Rovers)
1996 Les Ferdinand (Newcastle United)
1997 Alan Shearer (Newcastle United)
1998 Dennis Bergkamp (Arsenal)
1999 David Ginola (Tottenham)
2000 Roy Keane (Manchester United)
2001 Teddy Sheringham (Manchester United)
2002 Ruud van Nistelrooy (Manchester United)
2003 Thierry Henry (Arsenal)
2004 Thierry Henry (Arsenal)
2005 John Terry (Chelsea)
2006 Steven Gerrard (Liverpool)
2007 Cristiano Ronaldo (Manchester United)
2008 Cristiano Ronaldo (Manchester United)
2009 Ryan Giggs (Manchester United)
2010 Wayne Rooney (Manchester United)

A rare picture of Roy Keane smiling!

ROBBIE FOWLER

Born: Liverpool, 9th April 1975
Position: Striker
Club career:
1993-2001 Liverpool 236 (120)
2001-03 Leeds United 30 (14)
2003-06 Manchester City 80 (20)
2006-07 Liverpool 30 (8)
2007-08 Cardiff City 13 (4)
2008   Blackburn Rovers 3 (0)
International record:
1996-2002 England 26 (7)

Liverpool legend Robbie Fowler is the fourth highest scorer in the history of the Premiership.

• Fowler's goalscoring feats in his first spell at Anfield earned him the nickname 'God'. In only his fourth senior game he scored five goals in a League Cup match against Fulham in 1993, equalling a Liverpool record held by just three other players.

• The following year Fowler hit the fastest hat-trick in Premiership history, grabbing three goals in under five minutes against Arsenal at Anfield.

• In 1996 Fowler was named Young Player of the Year for the second consecutive season, a feat only matched previously by Ryan Giggs and since by Wayne Rooney.

• Fowler won the League Cup with Liverpool in 1995 and a unique cup treble (League Cup, FA Cup and UEFA Cup) in 2001 before moving on to Leeds. After spending three years with Manchester City, he returned to Liverpool in 2006 but was unable to reproduce his prolific form of the previous decade.

• With a property portfolio estimated at around £137 million, Fowler has had little difficulty paying the fines that have occasionally come his way. In 1999 he was fined £32,000 by the FA after baring his backside to Chelsea's Graeme Le Saux in a game at Stamford Bridge, and later that year he was hit with a £60,000 penalty by his club after celebrating a goal against city rivals Everton by 'sniffing' the six-yard line (a jokey reference to malicious rumours that he was a cocaine user).

TOP 10

PREMIERSHIP SCORERS

1. Alan Shearer (1992-2006)   260
2. Andy Cole (1993-2008)   187
3. Thierry Henry (1999-2007) 174
4. Robbie Fowler (1993-2008) 163
6. Les Ferdinand (1992-2005) 149
7. Teddy Sheringham (1992-2007)   147
   Michael Owen (1996-)   147
8. Frank Lampard (1995-)   129
9. Jimmy Floyd Hasselbaink (1997-2007)   127
10. Dwight Yorke (1992-2009)   123

FRANCE

First international: Belgium 3 France 3, 1904
Most capped player: Lilian Thuram, 142 caps (1994-2008)
Leading goalscorer: Thierry Henry, 51 goals (1997-2010)
First World Cup appearance: France 4 Mexico 1, 1930
Biggest win: France 10 Azerbaijan 0, 1995
Heaviest defeat: France 1 Denmark 17, 1908
Colours: Blue shirts, white shorts, red socks

France have an illustrious World Cup history but their 2010 tournamnt was a nightmate

One of the most successful football nations of recent years, France won the World Cup for the first and only time on home soil in 1998 with a stunning 3-0 victory over Brazil in the final in Paris. Midfield genius Zinedine Zidane was the star of the show, scoring two of his side's goals.

• Two years later France became the first World Cup holders to go on to win the European Championships when they overcame Italy in the final in Rotterdam. This, though, was a much closer affair with the French requiring a 'golden goal' by striker David Trezeguet in extra time to claim the trophy.

• France had won the European Championships once before, in 1984. Inspired by the legendary Michel Platini, who scored a record nine goals in the tournament, les Bleus beat Spain 2-0 in the final in Paris.

• French striker Just Fontaine scored an all-time record 13 goals at the 1958 World Cup finals in Sweden. His remarkable strike rate helped his country finish third in the tournament.

• When World Cup holders France were beaten 1-0 by Senegal in the 2002 World Cup it was one of the biggest shocks in the history of the tournament. Les Bleus slumped out of the competition in the first round on that occasion, but bounced back to reach the final again in 2006... only to suffer the agony of a penalty shoot-out defeat at the hands of Italy. In 2010, though, the French endured another nightmare campaign, internal disputes between leading players and coach Raymond Domenech contributing to a humiliating first-round exit in South Africa.

• In 1908 France suffered one of the biggest ever defeats in international football when they were hammered 17-1 by Denmark in the semi-finals of the Olympic Games tournament in London. The French team were so depressed afterwards that they declined to play for the bronze medal against fellow beaten semi-finalists Holland.

• Defender Lilian Thuram has appeared in more games for France than any other player, donning the famous blue jersey on no fewer than 142 occasions between 1994-2008. Former Arsenal striker Thierry Henry is France's record scorer, with 51 goals.

HONOURS		
World Cup 1998		
European Championship 1984, 2000		
Confederations Cup 2001, 2003		
World Cup Record		
1930	Round 1	
1934	Round 1	
1938	Round 2	
1950	Did not qualify	
1954	Round 1	
1958	Third place	
1962	Did not qualify	
1966	Round 1	
1970	Did not qualify	
1974	Did not qualify	
1978	Round 1	
1982	Fourth place	
1986	Third place	
1990	Did not qualify	
1994	Did not qualify	
1998	Winners	
2002	Round 1	
2006	Runners-up	
2010	Round 1	

FREE KICKS

A method for restarting the game after an infringement, free kicks may either be direct (meaning a goal may be scored directly) or indirect (in which case a second player must touch the ball before a goal may be scored).

• In 2000 a new rule was introduced which allowed the referee to punish dissent by moving a free kick ten yards nearer the defenders' goal. The rule change, though, was deemed not to be a success and was unceremoniously scrapped five years later.

• One of the most memorable free kicks ever was taken by England captain David Beckham in a vital World Cup qualifier against Greece at Old Trafford in 2001. With the last kick of the match Beckham curled a superb free kick over the Greek wall and into the corner of the net to earn England a draw which booked the team's passage to the finals of the tournament in Japan and Korea.

• Managers and coaches are forever dreaming up free kick routines which might confuse the opposition and lead to a goal. Serie A side Catania tried a truly bizarre ploy in 2008 when three of their players stood in front of the Torino goalkeeper and dropped their shorts while team-mate Giuseppe Mascara scored with a well-struck free kick.

• Noted free kick takers today include Real Madrid's Cristiano Ronaldo, Everton's Mikel Arteta and Arsenal's Robin van Persie. Arguably the greatest free kick practitioner of them all, though, was Brazil's Rivelino, whose swerving 'banana' dead ball kicks helped his country win the 1970 World Cup in Mexico..

FRIENDLIES

The first official international friendly took place on 30th November 1872 between Scotland and England at the West of Scotland Cricket Ground, Partick, Glasgow. The Scottish side for the match, which ended in a 0-0 draw, was made up entirely of players from the country's leading club, Queen's Park.

• Not all non-competitive matches live up to their 'friendly' billing. The 1934 encounter at Highbury between England and Italy, for instance, was a famously violent affair. Italian captain Luisito Monti suffered a broken toe and his English counterpart Eddie Hapgood a broken nose as the match threatened to disintegrate into a brawl, before some sort of order was eventually restored. England won the match, which became known as 'The Battle of Highbury', 3-2.

• On 6th February 2007 London played host to a record four international friendlies on the same night – and England weren't even one of the eight teams in action! At the Emirates Stadium Portugal beat Brazil 2-0, Ghana thrashed Nigeria 4-1 at Brentford's Griffin Park, South Korea beat European champions Greece 1-0 at Craven Cottage, while at Loftus Road Denmark were 3-1 winners over Australia.

• Although not as important as competitive matches, high-profile friendlies can still attract big crowds.

IS THAT A FACT?
France's Lucien Laurent scored the first ever goal at the World Cup finals, netting with a 19th-minute volley in his side's 4-1 defeat of Mexico in Uruguay on 13th July 1930.

The record attendance for a club friendly is 104,679 for a Rangers v Eintracht Frankfurt match at Hampden Park in 1961.

• Possibly the most bizarre friendly ever took place between Atletic Bilbao and a 200-strong 'team' of local schoolchildren in May 2010. The youngsters' side consisted of 197 outfield players and three goalkeepers, but despite their huge numerical advantage they were defeated 5-3 by their heroes.

FULHAM

Year founded: 1879
Ground: Craven Cottage (25,700)
Previous name: Fulham St. Andrew's
Nickname: The Cottagers
Biggest win: 10-1 v Ipswich Town (1963)
Heaviest defeat: 0-10 v Liverpool (1986)
Colours: White shirts, black shorts, white socks

London's oldest club, Fulham were founded in 1879 by two clergymen. Originally known as Fulham St Andrew's, the club adopted its present name nine years later. After winning the Southern League in two consecutive seasons Fulham were elected to the Football League in 1907.

• **Before moving to Craven Cottage in 1896, Fulham had played at no fewer than 11 different grounds. Including a stay at Loftus Road in 2002-04 while the Cottage was being redeveloped, Fulham have played at 13 venues, a total only exceeded by QPR.**

• The proudest moment in the club's history came as recently as May 2010 when Fulham met Atletico Madrid in Hamburg in the first Europa League final. Sadly for their fans and their inspirational manager Roy Hodgson, the Cottagers lost 2-1 in extra time despite putting up a spirited fight.

• **In 1975 Fulham reached the FA Cup final for the first (and so far only) time, losing 2-0 to West Ham. The Cottagers have appeared in the semi-final six times, including a forgettable occasion in 1908 when they were hammered 6-0 by Newcastle, to this day the biggest ever winning margin at that stage of the competition.**

• Midfield legend Johnny Haynes holds the club's appearance record, turning out in 594 league games between 1952-70. 'The Maestro', as he was known to Fulham fans, is also the club's most honoured player at international level, with 56 England caps.

• **Haynes starred for the Cottagers during a golden period in the 1960s when they stayed in the top flight for a club record nine consecutive seasons. They had a few narrow escapes, though, notably in the 1965/66 season when they won nine of their last 13 matches to pull clear of the trapdoor by two points.**

• More recently, Fulham pulled off another miraculous escape in 2007/08 when they won their last three Premiership matches of the season, against Manchester City, Birmingham City and Portsmouth, to sensationally avoid the drop on goal difference.

• **Welsh international striker Gordon Davies is Fulham's top scorer with 159 league goals in two spells at the club between 1978-91.**

• Along with opponents Millwall, Fulham were the first British team ever to play a league game on a Sunday. The match at the Den on 20th January 1974 finished 1-0 to Millwall.

• **In 1997 Fulham missed out on the Third Division title on 'goals scored' after finishing level on points with Wigan Athletic, despite having a** superior goal difference. Ironically, then Fulham chairman Jimmy Hill had advocated the change to using goals scored, rather than goal difference, to separate teams who were equal on points.

• Bankrolled by millionaire owner Mohamed Al-Fayed, Fulham climbed from the basement division to the Premiership in just four years between 1997-2001 – a year less than the then Harrods boss had predicted. Only Swansea City have made a quicker rise through the divisions, taking just three years between 1978-81.

• **Livewire striker Andrew Johnson is Fulham's record signing, joining the club from Everton for a cool £13 million in 2008. The club's coffers were boosted by a record £12.8 million four years earlier, when Louis Saha left for Manchester United.**

• In 1987 Fulham took part in the longest ever penalty shoot-out in British football, losing 11-10 to Aldershot in the Freight Rover Trophy quarter-final after the teams had taken 14 spot-kicks each.

• **Famous fans of the club include actor Hugh Grant, singer Lily Allen and veteran DJ David 'Diddy' Hamilton.**

HONOURS
Division 2 champions 1949
First Division champions 2001
Division 3 (S) champions 1932
Second Division champions 1999

Fulham line up for their first ever European final in Hamburg in 2010

GALATASARAY

Year founded: 1905
Ground: Ali Sami Yen (24,990)
Nickname: Cim Bom
Colours: Red-and-yellow halved shirts, white shorts, white socks

Founded in 1905 by members of an elite Istanbul school, Galatasaray are the most successful team in Turkey with 17 league titles and 14 Turkish Cups to their name.

• Galatasaray are the only Turkish club to have won a European trophy, beating Arsenal on penalties in the UEFA Cup final in 2000. Ironically, the winning kick was slotted home by a former Tottenham player, Romanian international Gheorghe Popescu.

• When visiting teams turn up at Galatasaray's Ali Sami Yen stadium they are often greeted with huge 'Welcome to Hell!' banners and the home fans certainly create an intimidating atmosphere with their drums, flags and flares. Time will tell whether the club's new 52,000-capacity Turk Telecom Arena, which Gala plan to move to during the 2010/11 season, will be quite as hostile.

• Galatasaray won a record four consecutive league titles between 1997-2000, a period when they were managed by former Turkey boss Fatih Terim.

TOP 10

SCOTLAND GOALSCORERS

1.	Denis Law (1958-74)	30
	Kenny Dalglish (1971-86)	30
3.	Hughie Gallacher (1924-35)	23
4.	Lawrie Reilly (1948-57)	22
5.	Ally McCoist (1986-98)	19
6.	Robert Hamilton (1899-1911)	15
	James McFadden (2002-)	15
8.	Mo Johnston (1984-91)	14
9.	Robert Smith McColl (1896-1908)	13
10.	Andy Wilson (1920-23)	12
	Billy Steel (1947-53)	12
	Alan Gilzean (1963-71)	12
	John Collins (1988-99)	12

• Galatasaray's top goalscorer is former Turkish international Hakan Suker, who banged in 228 league goals in three spells with the club before retiring in 2008..

HONOURS
Turkish champions 1962, 1963, 1969, 1971, 1972, 1973, 1987, 1988, 1993, 1994, 1997, 1998, 1999, 2000, 2002, 2006, 2008
Turkish Cup 1963, 1964, 1965, 1966, 1973, 1976, 1982, 1985, 1991, 1993, 1996, 1999, 2000, 2005
UEFA Cup 2000
Super Cup 2000

HUGHIE GALLACHER

Born: Bellshill, 2nd February 1903
Died: 11th June 1957
Position: Striker
Club career:
1921 Queen of the South 9 (19)
1921-25 Airdrieonians 111 (90)
1925-30 Newcastle United 160 (133)
1930-34 Chelsea 132 (72)
1934-36 Derby County 51 (38)
1936-37 Notts County 45 (32)
1937-38 Grimsby Town 12 (3)
1938-39 Gateshead 31 (18)
International record:
1924-35 Scotland 20 (23)

With 23 goals for Scotland, Hughie Gallacher is his country's third highest goalscorer of all time. Only Denis Law and Kenny Dalglish managed to find the net more often, but neither of them could match Gallacher's incredible strike rate of more than a goal per game.

• Gallacher's finest hour was as a member of the Scottish side – dubbed the 'Wembley Wizards' – which trounced England 5-1 in 1928. The following year he hit four goals in a 7-3 rout of Northern Ireland, equalling the best return by any Scottish player in an international.

• A prolific goalscorer with all of his clubs, Gallacher joined Newcastle from Airdrieonians in 1925. Two years later he captained the last Magpies team to win the league championship. In 1930 he moved to Chelsea for the then enormous sum of £10,000 but his time in London was marred by disciplinary problems.

• In 1957 Gallacher committed suicide by throwing himself in front of a train, having become depressed by sensational newspaper reports about an incident when he was alleged to have hit his 14-year-old son.

PAUL GASCOIGNE

Born: Gateshead, 25th May 1967
Position: Midfielder
Club career:
1985-88 Newcastle United 92 (21)
1988-92 Tottenham Hotspur 92 (19)
1992-95 Lazio 43 (6)
1995-98 Rangers 74 (30)
1998-2000 Middlesbrough 41 (4)
2000-02 Everton 32 (1)
2002 Burnley 6 (0)
2003 Gansu Tianma 4 (2)
2004 Boston United 5 (0)
International record:
1988-98 England 57 (10)

The most talented English midfielder of his generation, Paul Gascoigne could unlock the tightest of defences with a clever pass or a trademark dribble past a couple of opponents.

• Troubled by injuries throughout his career, he was at his peak at the 1990 World Cup in Italy when his brilliant performances powered England to the last four. 'Gazzamania' completely

Gazza is unleashed on the world, playing for Newcastle in 1985

swept the country after his tears during the England-Germany semi-final (after he picked up a yellow card which meant he would miss the final) perfectly summed up the mood of disappointment that swept the nation as England went on to lose a penalty shoot-out. A few months later he was voted BBC Sports Personality of the Year – only the second footballer, after Bobby Moore in 1966, to receive the award.

• Gazza also starred at Euro 96, scoring a superb solo goal in the local derby with Scotland at Wembley that many rate as the best England goal ever. However, he was controversially left out of England's 1998 World Cup squad after a series of drunken incidents and never added to his 57 caps.

Germany: seven time World Cup finalists

• At club level, Gascoigne is one of a select band of players to have won both the FA Cup (with Spurs in 1991) and the Scottish Cup (with Rangers in 1996). While at Ibrox he also won two league titles and the League Cup.

• A fun-loving character who was once described as being 'as daft as a brush' by then England manager Bobby Robson, Gazza has sadly struggled with alcohol addiction and mental health problems since quitting the game in 2004.

GERMANY

First international: Switzerland 5 Germany 3, 1908
Most capped player: Lothar Matthaus, 150 caps (1980-2000)
Leading goalscorer: Gerd Muller, 68 goals (1966-74)
First World Cup appearance: Germany 5 Belgium 2, 1934
Biggest win: Germany 16 Russia 0, 1912
Heaviest defeat: Austria 6 Germany 0, 1931
Colours: White shirts, black shorts, white socks

Germany (formerly West Germany) have the third-best record in the World Cup behind Brazil and Italy, having won the tournament three times and reached the final on seven occasions (a record shared with Brazil). They have also won the European Championships a record three times and been losing finalists on another three occasions, most recently in 2008.

• Germany are the only country to have won the World Cup after falling two goals behind in the final, fighting back to beat Hungary 3-2 in Bern in 1954 – a match which became known in Germany as 'The Miracle of Bern'. Their other triumphs in the competition came on home soil against Holland in 1974 and at Italia 90 against Argentina.

• Lothar Matthaus, a powerhouse in the German midfield for two decades, played in a record 25 matches at the World Cup in five tournaments between 1982-98. His total of 150 caps for Germany is also a national record.

• With a total of 14 goals at the 1970 and 1974 World Cups German striker Gerd 'der Bomber' Muller set a record for the tournament which stood for 32 years until it was topped by Brazil's Ronaldo in 2006.

• Germany's Oliver Kahn is the only goalkeeper to win the Player of the Tournament award at a World Cup, topping the poll for his performances in 2002 in Japan and Korea.

• Germany have played a record 99 games at the World Cup finals. Along with Brazil, Germany are the only country to have appeared in three consecutive World Cup finals (1982, 1986 and 1990).

HONOURS
World Cup 1954, 1974, 1990
European Championship 1972, 1980, 1996
World Cup record
1930 Did not enter
1934 Third place
1938 Round 1
1950 Did not enter
1954 Winners
1958 Fourth place
1962 Quarter-finals
1966 Runners-up
1970 Third place
1974 Winners
1978 Round 1
1982 Runners-up
1986 Runners-up
1990 Winners
1994 Quarter-finals
1998 Quarter-finals
2002 Runners-up
2006 Third place
2010 Third place

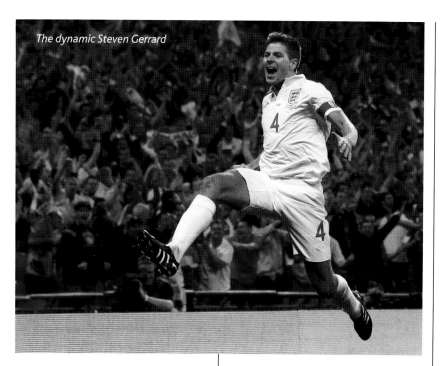

The dynamic Steven Gerrard

STEVEN GERRARD

Born: Whiston, 30th May 1980
Position: Midfielder
Club career:
1998- Liverpool 366 (80)
International record:
2000- England 85 (19)

Liverpool captain Steven Gerrard is the only player to have scored in the FA Cup final, the League Cup final, the UEFA Cup final and the Champions League final. He achieved this feat between 2001-06 while winning all four competitions with the Reds (and, indeed, earning winners' medals in the FA Cup and League Cup on two occasions).

• **A dynamic midfielder who is famed for his surging runs and thunderous shooting, Gerrard made his Liverpool debut in 1998. Five years later, then Anfield boss Gerard Houllier made the Kop idol his skipper and he has retained the armband ever since. A Red to his very core, Gerrard has twice turned down lucrative moves to Chelsea.**

• In the 2006 FA Cup final Gerrard scored two stunning goals against West Ham, including a last-minute equaliser which many rate as the best ever goal in the final. Liverpool went on to win the match on penalties and Gerrard's heroics were rewarded with the 2006 PFA Player of the Year award – the first Liverpool player to top the poll since John Barnes in 1988.

• **Gerrard made his international debut for England against Ukraine in** 2000 and scored his first goal for his country with a superb 20-yarder in the famous 5-1 thrashing of Germany in Berlin in 2001. **In the absence of regular skipper Rio Ferdinand, he captained England at the 2010 World Cup but, despite scoring in a 1-1 draw with the USA, failed to show anything like his best form during the tournament.**

• Gerrard just missed out on leading Liverpool to the Premiership title in 2009, but was rewarded with the Footballer of the Year award at the season's end.

RYAN GIGGS

Born: Cardiff, 29th November 1973
Position: Winger/midfielder
Club career:
1991- Manchester United 588 (108)
International record:
1991-2007 Wales 64 (12)

In a glorious career with Manchester United, Ryan Giggs has become the most decorated player in English football history. At the last count he had won 20 major honours: 11 Premier League titles, four FA Cups, three League Cups and two Champions League trophies. In 2009 he was voted Players' Player of the Year by his fellow professionals.

• **Formerly a flying winger but now more likely to be seen in a deep-lying midfield role, Giggs is the only player to have played and scored in every season since the Premiership** was formed in 1992, having made his debut for United the previous year against Everton.

• When Giggs played for United in their 2008 Champions League final victory over Chelsea in Moscow it was his 759th appearance for the Reds, one more than the club record previously set by Bobby Charlton.

• **Giggs enjoyed his best ever year in 1999 when he won the Premiership, FA Cup and Champions League with United. His goal against Arsenal in that season's FA Cup semi-final, when he dribbled past four defenders before smashing the ball into the roof of the net from a tight angle, is often recalled as one of the greatest ever.**

• Once Wales' youngest ever player, Giggs previously played for England Schoolboys under the name Ryan Wilson (the surname being that of his father, a former Welsh rugby league player). However, having no English grandparents, Giggs was ineligible to play for the England national team and was proud to represent Wales on 64 occasions before retiring from international football in 2007.

Ryan Giggs: superhuman

GIANT-KILLING

Many of the most remarkable instances of giant-killing have occurred in the FA Cup, with a number of non-league clubs claiming the scalps of top flight opposition. One of the biggest such shocks came in 1989 when Coventry City, who had won the FA Cup just two years earlier, were knocked out of the competition by non-league Sutton United in the third round.

• **Hereford United's 2-1 defeat of Newcastle in the third round in 1972 is often remembered as one of the biggest giant-killing acts ever, being particularly memorable for Ronnie Radford's long range equaliser which preceded Ricky George's winner. "The action is constantly replayed on the TV every year and that shows what a big shock it was," said George recently.**

• In their non-league days Yeovil Town beat a record 20 league teams in the FA Cup. The Glovers' most famous win came in the fourth round in 1949 against First Division Sunderland, who they defeated 2-1 on their notorious sloping pitch at Huish Park.

• **Giant-killings also happen occasionally at international level. At the 1950 World Cup in Brazil, for instance, England sensationally lost 1-0 to an unheralded United States team. The result was so unexpected that many people assumed it was a misprint when they saw it in the newspapers. Other major World Cup shocks include North Korea's 1-0 victory over Italy in 1966, Northern Ireland's 1-0 win against Spain in 1982 and Cameroon's 1-0 defeat of holders Argentina in 1990.**

GILLINGHAM

Year founded: 1893
Ground: Priestfield Stadium (11,582)
Previous name: New Brompton
Nickname: The Gills
Biggest win: 12-1 v Gloucester City (1946)
Heaviest defeat: 2-9 v Nottingham Forest (1950)
Colours: Black and blue striped shirts, black shorts, black socks

Founded by a group of local businessmen as New Brompton in 1893, the club changed to its present name in 1913.

Seven years later Gillingham joined the new Third Division but in 1938 were voted out of the league in favour of Ipswich Town. They eventually returned in 1950.

• **The only Kent-based team in the Football League, Gillingham recovered from a financial crisis in the mid-90s to enjoy a first spell in the second tier between 2000-05. They have since plummeted back to the basement tier, after one season in League One in 2009/10.**

• In 1952 the Gills' Jimmy Scarth notched three goals in just two minutes and 30 seconds against Leyton Orient to set a record for the fastest Football League hat-trick which stood until 2004.

• **In 1981 Gillingham were involved in one of the strangest transfers ever when they signed future Republic of Ireland international striker Tony Cascarino from non-league Crockenhill in exchange for a set of tracksuits!**

• Gillingham kept an incredible 29 clean sheets during the 1995/96 season, falling just one short of Port Vale's all-time Football League record.

HONOURS
Division 4 champions 1964

SHAY GIVEN

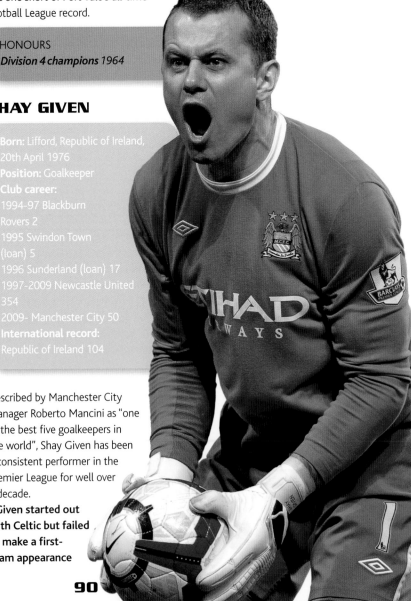

Born: Lifford, Republic of Ireland, 20th April 1976
Position: Goalkeeper
Club career:
1994-97 Blackburn Rovers 2
1995 Swindon Town (loan) 5
1996 Sunderland (loan) 17
1997-2009 Newcastle United 354
2009- Manchester City 50
International record:
Republic of Ireland 104

Described by Manchester City manager Roberto Mancini as "one of the best five goalkeepers in the world", Shay Given has been a consistent performer in the Premier League for well over a decade.

• **Given started out with Celtic but failed to make a first-team appearance** before moving to Blackburn. Again, he failed to establish himself at Ewood Park and his career only really got going after he joined Newcastle for £1.5 million in 1997. During a 12-year stay at St James's Park Given was twice voted into the PFA Team of the Season and played in a total of 462 games for the Magpies – just 34 short of the club's appearance record.

• Frustrated by Newcastle's failure to win major honours, Given put in a transfer request in January 2009 and the following month joined Manchester City for around £6 million. His steadying influence helped City finish fifth in the Premier League in his first full season at Eastlands, the club's highest position since 1992.

• **Given made his international debut for the Republic of Ireland against Russia in 1996 and at the last count won 104 caps – a record for his country held jointly with Hull City winger Kevin Kilbane.**

South African players celebrate the first goal of the 2010 World Cup

GOALS

GOAL CELEBRATIONS

The days when players celebrated a goal by exchanging a simple hand-shake among team-mates before jogging back to the halfway line are long gone. In today's game the celebrations can be even more spectacular than the goals themselves – think, for instance, of the impressive gymnastic routines performed by Manchester United's Nani.

• In the 1990s Middlesbrough striker **Fabrizio Ravanelli would regularly celebrate by pulling his shirt over his head after scoring. Soon players were removing their shirts altogether, sometimes to reveal personal, political or religious messages written on a T-shirt. In 2003 FIFA decided that the craze had got out of hand and ruled that any player removing his shirt would be booked. The first player to be sent off after falling foul of this new law was Everton's Tim Cahill, who was shown a second yellow against Manchester City in 2004.**

• In 1999 Liverpool's Robbie Fowler celebrated a goal against city rivals Everton by 'sniffing' the touchline, apparently in response to rumours that he was a cocaine user. It turned out to be the most expensive goal celebration ever, as Fowler was subsequently fined £60,000 by his club.

• **Ipswich's David Norris was also fined in 2008 after celebrating a goal against Blackpool by making a 'handcuff' gesture in support of his former team-mate Luke McCormick, who had recently been jailed for causing the death of two young boys in a drink-driving incident.**

• In one of the most bizarre goal celebrations ever Manchester United star Carlos Tevez produced a baby's dummy from his shorts and sucked on it after scoring against Birmingham at Old Trafford in 2008. He later explained that the routine was a tribute to his young daughter, Florencia. Earlier in his career, Tevez was sent off while playing for Boca Juniors against arch rivals River Plate when he celebrated a goal in front of the opposition fans by imitating a chicken.

GOAL OF THE SEASON

The Goal of the Season award has been awarded by BBC TV's flagship football programme *Match of the Day* since 1971 (apart from the years 2001-04 when, for broadcasting rights reasons, the award was given by ITV). The first winner was Coventry City's Ernie Hunt, whose spectacular volley against Everton at Highfield Road topped the poll.

• **Liverpool's John Aldridge is the only player to win Goal of the Season in consecutive seasons, taking the award in 1988 and 1989 for his FA Cup strikes against Nottingham Forest and Everton respectively, the second of these goals coming in the final itself. The only other players to win twice are Dennis Bergkamp (in 1998 and 2002) and Wayne Rooney (in 2005 and 2007).**

• Only two players have won the award for goals scored for their countries rather than their clubs: Scotland's Kenny Dalglish in 1983 and England's Bryan Robson in 1986.

• **If John Motson is commentating on a match it's more likely to feature a Goal of the Season winner than if any of his fellow commentators are sat behind the microphone. To date, 'Motty' has provided the commentary for no fewer than 15 of the award-winning goals.**

GOALS

Manchester United have scored more league goals than any other English club. Up to the start of the 2010/11 season, the Red Devils had managed 7,330 goals, 85 more than second-placed Wolves. At the other end of the scale,

IS THAT A FACT?

In 2004 Servette midfielder celebrated a goal he had set up against FC Schaffhausen by jumping on a metal perimeter fence. Unfortunately, his wedding ring caught in the fence and when he jumped down he left much of his finger behind. To add insult to injury, he was then shown the yellow card by the referee for leaving the pitch without permission.

ANDY GRAY

Middlesbrough Ironopolis scored just 37 goals in their one season in the Second Division in 1893/94. No other club has scored so few league goals in total.

• **Peterborough United hold the record for the most league goals in a season, banging in 134 in 1960/61 on their way to claiming the Fourth Division title.**

• Aston Villa hold the top flight record, with 128 goals in 1930/31. Despite their prolific attack, the Villans were pipped to the First Division title by Arsenal (amazingly, the Gunners managed 127 goals themselves). Title-winners Chelsea became the first team to score a century of goals in the Premier League era in 2009/10, the Blues taking their tally to 103 with an 8-0 thrashing of Wigan on the final day of the season.

• **Arthur Rowley scored a record 434 Football League goals between 1946-65, notching four for West Brom, 27 for Fulham, 251 for Leicester City and 152 for Shrewsbury.**

• Joe Payne set an English Football League record for goals in a game by scoring ten times for Luton against Bristol Rovers on 13th April 1936.

Even Aston Villa's unusual home strip couldn't prevent Andy Gray from scoring more than 50 goals for the midlanders!

ANDY GRAY

> **Born:** Glasgow, 30th November 1955
> **Club career:**
> 1973-75 Dundee United 62 (36)
> 1975-79 Aston Villa 113 (54)
> 1979-83 Wolverhampton Wanderers 133 (38)
> 1983-85 Everton 49 (14)
> 1985-87 Aston Villa 54 (5)
> 1987 Notts County (loan) 4 (0)
> 1987-88 West Bromwich Albion 35 (10)
> 1988-89 Rangers 14 (5)

Now synonymous with Sky Sports' coverage of the Premiership, Andy Gray netted an impressive 224 goals for seven English and Scottish clubs in the 1970s and 1980s. In 1979 he became Britain's most expensive player when he left Aston Villa for Wolves in a £1,469,000 deal.

• **The following year Gray scored Wolves' winner in the League Cup final at Wembley and he went on to enjoy more success with his next club Everton, helping the Toffees win the FA Cup in 1984 and the league title and European Cup-Winners' Cup in 1985.**

• While at Aston Villa Gray became the first player to win both the PFA Player of the Year and Young Player of the Year awards in the same season (1977) – only Cristiano Ronaldo in 2007 has since landed the same double.

• **In 1991 Gray gave up his job as Ron Atkinson's assistant at Aston Villa to work full-time for Sky Sports, where his enthusiastic gravel-voiced punditry has made him a favourite with viewers. Gray reportedly earns £20,000 a week with Sky, making him the highest paid football analyst on TV.**

JIMMY GREAVES

> **Born:** London, 20th February 1940
> **Position:** Striker
> **Club career:**
> 1957-61 Chelsea 157 (124)
> 1961-62 AC Milan 14 (9)
> 1962-70 Tottenham 321 (220)
> 1970-71 West Ham United 38 (13)
> **International record:**
> 1959-67 England 57 (44)

With 44 goals for England, Jimmy Greaves is his country's third highest ever goalscorer behind Bobby Charlton and Gary Lineker. He scored on his international debut in 1959 in a 4-1 defeat by Peru, and went on to bag a record six hat-tricks for his country. Famously, Greaves also scored on his debut for all the clubs he played for.

• **A quicksilver striker who always carefully picked his spot when shooting, Greaves began his career at Chelsea. In the 1960/61 season he hit an incredible 41 league goals for the Blues – a post-war record for the top flight.**

• After a brief spell with AC Milan, Greaves moved to Tottenham where he helped the club claim two major trophies, the European Cup-Winners' Cup in 1963 and the FA Cup in 1967. His haul of 220 league goals for Spurs remains a club record.

• **At 21, Greaves was the youngest player to score 100 league goals. He netted his 200th aged 23 years and 290 days, coincidentally exactly the same age at which Dixie Dean reached the**

Barcelona's players give manager Pep Guardiola the bumps on his birthday every year!

same landmark with Everton.

• Arguably English football's most consistent ever striker, Greaves was top scorer in the First Division six times and notched a total of 357 league goals – both top flight records that are unlikely to be broken.

• **He experienced the lowest point of his career in 1966 when, after starting in England's opening matches at the World Cup, he was left out of the team for the triumphant final against West Germany. Bitterly disappointed, he was the only member of the squad not to attend the victory bash in a London hotel.**

• After hanging up his boots Greaves overcame alcoholism to launch a new career as a TV personality, his double act with former Liverpool star Ian St John being especially popular with viewers.

PEP GUARDIOLA

Born: Born: Barcelona, 18th January 1971
Managerial career:
2007-08 Barcelona B
2008- Barcelona

Barcelona coach Pep Guardiola is the only man to lead his side to six trophies in a calendar year, claiming an incredible sextuple in 2009 when Barca won the Spanish league title, the Copa del Rey, the Champions League, the Spanish Super Cup, the UEFA Super Cup and, finally, the FIFA Club World Cup.

• **More silverware followed for Guardiola in 2010 when Barcelona retained their La Liga title with a** record 99 points. Along the way Barcelona did the double over Real Madrid for the second consecutive season, making Guardiola the first coach of the Catalans to record four straight victories over their arch rivals.

• As a defensive midfielder with Barcelona, Guardiola was a key member of Johan Cruyff's 'Dream Team' which won the club's first European Cup and four straight league titles in the early 1990s. Like Cruyff, Guardiola is an advocate of attacking football and, making the best use of the talents of players like Lionel Messi, Andres Iniesta and Xavi in an attractive 4-3-3 formation, has consolidated Barca's reputation as one of the most entertaining club teams in the world.

• **Although he was only appointed Barcelona boss in 2008, having previously impressed with the Catalans' B squad, Guardiola is already the club's longest-serving Spanish manager.**

RUUD GULLIT

Born: Amsterdam, 1st September 1962
Position: Sweeper/midfielder/striker
Club career:
1979-82 Haarlem 91 (32)
1982-85 Feyenoord 85 (31)
1985-87 PSV Eindhoven 68 (46)
1987-93 AC Milan 117 (35)
1993-94 Sampdoria 31 (16)
1994 AC Milan 8 (3)
1994-95 Sampdoria 22 (9)
1995-98 Chelsea 32 (4)
International record:
1981-94 Holland 66 (17)

Once described as 'the Dutch Duncan Edwards', Ruud Gullit was a brilliant performer in a variety of positions, including sweeper, attacking midfielder and striker. In 1987 he became the world's most expensive player when he moved from PSV to AC Milan for a cool £6.5 million.

• **In the same year Gullit became only the third player – after Paolo Rossi and Michel Platini – to be voted both World and European Footballer of the Year in the same season. He dedicated his awards to Nelson Mandela, then still in prison in South Africa.**

• After helping Milan win the Serie A title in 1988 Gullit played a huge part in the club's European Cup success the following year, scoring twice in the Italian club's 4-0 demolition of Steaua Bucharest in the final. In all he won three league titles and two European Cups with Milan.

• **In 1988 he became the first Dutch captain to lift major international silverware when his side beat the Soviet Union 2-0 in the final of the European Championships, Gullit netting the first goal with a trademark power header.**

• In 1997, as player-manager of Chelsea, Gullit became the first foreign boss to win a major domestic competition when the Blues beat Middlesbrough in the FA Cup final at Wembley.

The following year, though, he was sacked and replaced by Gianluca Vialli, one of a number of big-name players he had brought to Stamford Bridge. He later managed Newcastle, taking the Geordies to the FA Cup final in 1999, Feyenoord and LA Galaxy.

• **Gullit is married to Estelle Cruyff, daughter of fellow Dutch legend Johan Cruyff.**

HAMILTON ACADEMICAL

Year founded: 1874
Ground: New Douglas Park (6,096)
Nickname: The Accies
Biggest win: 11-1 v Chryston, 1885
Heaviest defeat: 1-11 v Hibernian, 1965
Colours: Red-and-white hooped shirts, white shorts, white socks

Founded in 1874 by the Rector and pupils of Hamilton Academy, the club is the only one in Britain to be named after a school. Shortly after the start of the 1897/98 season the club joined the Scottish league in place of Renton, who were forced to resign due to financial reasons.

• Hamilton have enjoyed little success over the years, but they did manage to reach the Scottish Cup final in 1911 (losing to Celtic after a replay) and again in 1935 (losing to Rangers).

• In 1971 the club became the first in Britain to recruit players from behind the Iron Curtain, signing three players from Poland. One of the trio, midfielder Roman Strazalkowski, had previously captained his country against Brazil.

• At the end of the 1999/2000 season Hamilton were relegated to the third tier of Scottish football for only the second time in their history. It was a fate they would have avoided if they had not been hit with a 15-point penalty by the Scottish Football League for failing to fulfill a fixture against Stenhousemuir while their players were on strike during a pay dispute.

• The club smashed both its transfer records in July 2009, buying goalkeeper Tomas Cerny from Czech side Sigma Olomouc for £180,000 and selling midfielder James McCarthy to Wigan for £1.2 million.

HONOURS

Division 1 champions 1986, 1988, 2008
Division 2 champions 1904
Division 3 champions 2001

Joe Hart: England's, er, number 29...

JOE HART

Born: Shrewsbury, 19th April 1987
Position: Goalkeeper
Club career:
2003-06 Shrewsbury Town 54
2006- Manchester City 50
2007 Tranmere Rovers (loan) 6
2007 Blackpool (loan) 5
2009-10 Birmingham City (loan) 36
International record:
2008- England 4

Rated by many as the best English goalkeeper in the Premier League, Joe Hart began his career with his hometown club, Shrewsbury Town. His assured performances with the Shrews soon attracted the attention of bigger clubs and in 2006 he moved to Manchester City for an initial £600,000 fee.

• Hart was on his way to establishing himself as City's number one when Republic of Ireland international Shay Given arrived at Eastlands in January 2009. Keen to play first-team football, Hart spent the 2009/10 season on loan at Birmingham where a string of superb displays saw him voted into the PFA Team of the Year.

• While a regular between the sticks for the England Under-21 side, Hart moved up to the senior squad and in June 2008 made his senior debut as a sub in a 3-0 win over Trinidad and Tobago.

• Hart was one of three goalkeepers selected by England coach Fabio Capello for the World Cup in South Africa, but he failed to get off the bench. However, an impressive showing against Hungary at Wembley in August 2010 suggested he could become the first-choice keeper.

HARTLEPOOL UNITED

Year founded: 1908
Ground: Victoria Ground (8,240)
Previous name: Hartlepools United, Hartlepool
Nickname: The Pool
Biggest win: 10-1 v Barrow (1959)
Heaviest defeat: 1-10 v Wrexham (1962)
Colours: Blue and white shirts, blue shorts, white socks

Was it over the line? The Russian linesman says yes and Geoff Hurst has the second of his three goals in the 1966 World Cup final

The club were founded as Hartlepools United in 1908 as a professional team to emulate the success of West Hartlepools, winners of the FA Amateur Cup three years earlier. In 1968 they became 'Hartlepool', adding the word 'United' in 1977.

• The Pool, as they are nicknamed, had to apply for re-election to the Football League a record 11 times, including five times between 1960-64 when they finished bottom or second bottom of the old Fourth Division in five consecutive seasons. On each occasion, though, they earned a reprieve and in recent years they have twice climbed out of the bottom tier into League One.

• Hartlepool's Victoria Ground was the first ever football stadium to be bombed, its wooden stand being destroyed by a bomb dropped from a German Zeppelin in 1917 during the First World War. The ground is also notable for being one of just two (along with Old Trafford) which has staged two matches on the same day, hosting both Hartlepool v Cardiff and Middlesbrough v Port Vale on 23rd August 1983 (Boro's Ayresome Park ground having been shut after the club went into liquidation).

• The legendary Brian Clough started his managerial career at Hartlepool in 1965 at the age of 30, making him the youngest manager in the league at the time.

HAT-TRICKS

Geoff Hurst is the only player to have scored a hat-trick in a World Cup final, hitting three goals in England's 4-2 defeat of West Germany at Wembley in 1966.

• Jimmy O'Connor of Irish club Shelbourne scored the fastest hat-trick in football history, taking just two minutes and 13 seconds to complete a treble against Bohemians in 1967.

• In 2004 Bournemouth's James Hayter struck the fastest hat-trick in English football league history, finding the net three times in just two minutes and 20 seconds against Wrexham. Incredibly, he was only on the pitch for six minutes after coming on as a late substitute!

• The fastest international hat-trick was scored by Willie Hall for England against Ireland in 1938. Hall scored five goals in the game, with the first three of them coming in under four minutes.

• Paraguayan international Jose Luis Chilavert is the only goalkeeper to have notched a hat-trick, scoring three penalties for Argentinean side Velez Sarsfield in their 6-1 win over Ferro Carril Oeste in 1999.

• The last player to score a hat-trick in an FA Cup final was Blackpool's Stan Mortensen in his side's 4-3 victory over Bolton in 1953. Despite Mortensen's feat the match is

remembered as 'the Matthews final', after his veteran team-mate Stanley Matthews.

JOHNNY HAYNES

Born: London, 17th October 1934
Died: 18th October 2005
Position: Midfielder
Club career:
1952-70 Fulham 594 (148)
1970-71 Durban City
International record:
1954-62 England 56 (18)

Fulham and England legend Johnny Haynes became the first £100-a-week player when the maximum wage (then set at £20) was abolished in 1961.

IS THAT A FACT?

In 2002 the Hartlepool mascot H'Angus the Monkey was elected as the town's mayor after campaigning for 'free bananas for schoolchildren'. Somewhat disappointingly, the man inside the monkey outfit, Stuart Drummond, soon binned the costume to become a serious politician.

A loyal one-club man, Haynes spent his entire League career with the Cottagers, with whom he failed to win a single major honour.

• Once described by Pele as "the best passer of the ball I've ever seen", Haynes captained England on 22 occasions before his international career was prematurely ended when he suffered a serious knee injury in a car crash in 1962.

• He played a club record 658 games for Fulham in all competitions and scored 158 goals – another club record until Gordon Davies passed it in 1989. Haynes ended his career in South Africa, winning a championship medal with Durban City in 1971.

• Following his death in 2005 a stand at Craven Cottage was renamed after Haynes and, in 2008, a statue of the man Fulham fans called 'The Maestro' was unveiled outside the ground.

HEADERS

In 2007 Graham Capstick, a 19-year-old defender with Barrow Sunday League side Holker Old Boys, scored with a header against Chadderton from 57 yards out – believed to be the longest range headed goal ever. "I was shocked," Capstick later admitted. "I certainly wasn't aiming for goal – I hadn't scored all season!"

• Huddersfield striker Jordan Rhodes scored the fastest headed hat-trick in Football League history in 2009, nodding in three goals against Exeter City in eight minutes and 23 seconds to smash a record previously held by Everton legend Dixie Dean.

• In 1935 Arsenal's Eddie Hapgood was reported as having scored a penalty against Liverpool with a header. In fact, his shot was saved by the goalkeeper before Hapgood headed in the rebound.

• The world record for non-stop heading of the ball is held by Tomas Lundman from Sweden, who kept it bouncing off his bonce for eight hours, 32 minutes and three seconds on 27th February 2004.

HEART OF MIDLOTHIAN

Year founded: 1874
Ground: Tynecastle (18,000)
Nickname: Hearts
Biggest win: 21-0 v Anchor (1880)
Heaviest defeat: 1-8 v Vale of Leven (1883)
Colours: Maroon and white shirts, white shorts, maroon socks

Hearts were founded in 1874, taking their unusual and romantic-sounding name from a popular local dance hall which, in turn, was named after the famous novel *The Heart of the Midlothian* by Sir Walter Scott. The club were founder members of the Scottish league in 1890, winning their first title just five years later.

• The club enjoyed a golden era in the late 1950s and early 1960s, when they won two league championships and five cups. In the first of those title triumphs in 1958 Hearts scored 132 goals, many of them coming from the so-called 'Terrible Trio' of Alfie Conn, Willie Bauld and Jimmy Wardhaugh. The total is still a record for the top flight in Scotland. In the same year Hearts conceded just 29 goals, giving them the best ever goal difference in the Scottish league, an incredible 103.

• In 1965 Hearts came agonisingly close to winning the championship again when they were pipped by Kilmarnock on goal average after losing 2-0 at home to their title rivals on the last day of the season. Twenty-one years later they suffered a similar fate, losing the title on goal difference to Celtic after a surprise last day defeat against Dundee. Annoyingly for their fans, on both occasions Hearts would have won the title if the alternative method for separating teams level on points had been in use.

• In 1990 Hearts chairman Wallace Mercer proposed that Hearts should merge with their Edinburgh rivals Hibs to form a single club with better prospects of successfully

"On me 'ead son!"

competing with Celtic and Rangers. Understandably, fans of both Hearts and Hibs were appalled at the idea and their noisy protests helped ensure that the scheme was thwarted.

• In recent years Hearts' controversial owner, Lithuanian businessman Vladimir Romanov, has ensured that the club is rarely out of the news. Since taking control of the club in 2005 he has been through a long list of managers and coaches, some of whom have later admitted that Romanov often picks the team himself.

• When Craig Gordon joined Sunderland from Hearts in 2007 for £9 million he became the most expensive goalkeeper in British football history and the most expensive Scottish player ever.

• The club's record goalscorer is John Robertson with 214 goals between 1983-98, and the record appearance holder is Gary Mackay, who played in 640 games between 1980-97. Hearts' highest capped international is Steven Pressley, who won 32 caps for Scotland between 2000-06.

• Famous fans of Hearts include pint-sized comedian Ronnie Corbett, snooker star Steven Hendry and Alex Salmond, Scotland's First Minister.

HONOURS
Division 1 champions 1895, 1897, 1958, 1960
First Division champions 1980
Scottish Cup 1891, 1896, 1901, 1906, 1956, 1998, 2006
League Cup 1955, 1959, 1960, 1963

THIERRY HENRY

Born: Paris, 17th August 1977
Position: Striker
Club career:
1994-98 Monaco 105 (20)
1999 Juventus 16 (3)
1999-2007 Arsenal 254 (174)
10 Barcelona 80 (35)
2010- New York Red Bulls
International record:
1997-2010 France 121 (51)

Arguably Arsenal's greatest ever player, Thierry Henry is the Gunners' all-time top goalscorer. During an eight-year stay in North London after signing from Juventus for a bargain £10.5 million in 1999 he scored 224 goals, many of them memorable ones.

• **Frighteningly quick and a reliably**

Thierry Henry: A Frenchman in New York

clinical finisher, Henry started out with Monaco who he helped win the French title in 1997. He was even more successful at Arsenal, winning two league titles and three FA Cups, and in 2006 become the first ever player to win the Footballer of the Year award three times. The following year he joined Barcelona, with whom he won the Spanish league title and the Champions League in 2009.

• Henry's total of 174 league goals for Arsenal puts him third in the list of all-time Premiership scorers behind Alan Shearer and Andy Cole. In both 2004 and 2005 he won the European Golden Boot, sharing the award with Villarreal's Diego Forlan in 2005.

• **A member of the French squad that won the World Cup in 1998, Henry collected a European Championship winners' medal two years later. In 2006 he had to settle for a runners-up medal in the World Cup final.**

• In October 2007 Henry scored twice against Lithuania to become

TOP 10

MOST CAPPED FRANCE PLAYERS
1. Lilian Thuram (1994-2008) 142 caps
2. Thierry Henry (1997-) 123 caps
3. Marcel Desailly (1993-2004) 116 caps
4. Zinedine Zidane (1994-2006) 108 caps
5. Patrick Vieira (1997-2009) 107 caps
6. Didier Deschamps (1989-2000) 103 caps
7. Laurent Blanc (1989-2000) 97 caps
   Bixente Lizarazu (1989-2000) 97 caps
9. Sylvain Wiltord (1999-2006) 92 caps
10. Fabien Barthez (1994-2006) 87 caps

France's all-time leading goalscorer, passing Michel Platini's previous record of 41 goals. Capped 121 times, he stands second behind Lilian Thuram in France's all-time top appearance makers.

HEREFORD UNITED

Year founded: 1924
Ground: Edgar Street (7,100)
Nickname: The Bulls
Biggest win: 11-0 v Thynnes Athletic (1947)
Heaviest defeat: 0-7 v Middlesbrough (1996)
Colours: White shirts, black shorts, white socks

Founded in 1924 following the merger of a number of local clubs, Hereford United were finally elected to the Football League in 1972. Within four years they had risen to the second tier of English football, but by 1997 they had slid all the way back down to the Conference. They regained league status in 2006 and two years later were promoted to League One, only to suffer relegation in 2009 after finishing bottom of that league.

• In 1972 Hereford gained national attention when, as a Southern League side, they knocked First Division Newcastle out of the FA Cup in one of the competition's biggest ever upsets. It was the first time for 23 years that a non-league side had beaten a top-flight club in the cup.

• 1980s striker Stewart Phillips is the club's leading scorer in league football with 95 goals to his name.

• In 1990 Hereford United became the last English club to win the Welsh Cup,

IS THAT A FACT?
Hibs hold the British record for the biggest away win, thrashing Airdrie 11-1 on their own patch on 24th October 1959. As if to prove that eye-catching result was no fluke they also hit double figures at Partick later that season, winning 10-2.

Hereford's cup exploits of the 1970s were breathtaking... and very muddy!

beating Wrexham 2-1 in the final. Five years later the rules were changed so that only teams playing in the Welsh football league system could enter the competition.

HONOURS
Division 3 champions 1976
Welsh Cup 1990

HIBERNIAN

Year founded: 1875
Ground: Easter Road (20,050)
Previous name: Hibernians
Nickname: Hibs
Biggest win: 22-1 v 42nd Highlanders (1881)
Heaviest defeat: 0-10 v Rangers (1898)
Colours: Green shirts with white sleeves, white shorts, green socks

Founded in 1875 by Irish immigrants, the club took its name from the Roman word for Ireland, Hibernia. After losing many players to Celtic the club disbanded in 1891, but reformed and joined the Scottish League two years later.

• Hibs won the Scottish Cup for the first time in 1887 and lifted the same trophy again in 1902. Since then, however, the club have reached the final on a further eight occasions, but

failed to win once.

• The club enjoyed a golden era after the Second World War, winning the league championship in three out of five seasons between 1948-52 with a side managed by Hugh Shaw that included the 'Famous Five' forward line of Bobby Johnstone, Willie Ormond, Lawrie Reilly, Gordon Smith and Willie Turnbull. All of the Famous Five went on to score 100 league goals for Hibs, a feat only achieved for the club since by Joe Baker.

• When Baker made his international debut against Northern Ireland in 1959 he became the first man to represent England while playing for a Scottish club. In the same season Baker scored an incredible 42 goals in just 33 league games to set a club record.

• Hibs originally wore green-and-white hooped shirts but switched to their famous green shirts with white sleeves in 1938, imitating the kit style of the great Arsenal side of that era.

• In 1955 Hibs became the first British side to enter the European Cup, having been invited to participate in the new competition partly because their Easter Road ground had floodlights. They did Scotland proud, reaching the semi-finals of the competition before falling 3-0 on aggregate to French side Rheims.

• In 1972 Hibs suffered the biggest ever thrashing in a Scottish Cup final when they were hammered 6-1 by Celtic at Hampden Park. Later that year, though, the Edinburgh side got their revenge when they beat The Bhoys 2-1 in the League Cup final, the first of three triumphs in the competition.

• **No player has turned out more often for Hibs than popular left winger Arthur Duncan, who made 446 league appearances between 1969-84.** Lawrie Reilly is the club's record scorer, notching 234 league goals in the 1940s and 1950s, and is also Hibs' highest capped player having played 38 times for Scotland.

• Campaigning under the slogan 'Hands Off Hibs', fans fought off a proposed merger with bitter rivals Hearts in 1990. In the same year Hibs' future was assured when Kwik-Fit owner Sir Tom Farmer took over the club.

> **HONOURS**
> *Division 1 champions 1903, 1948, 1951, 1952*
> *Division 2 champions 1894, 1895, 1933*
> *First Division champions 1981, 1999*
> *Scottish Cup 1887, 1902*
> *League Cup 1972, 1991, 2007*

GLENN HODDLE

> **Born:** Hayes, 27th October 1957
> **Position:** Midfielder
> **Club career:**
> 1975-87 Tottenham Hotspur 377 (88)
> 1987-90 Monaco 69 (27)
> 1991-93 Swindon Town 64 (1)
> 1993-95 Chelsea 31 (1)
> **International record:**
> 1979-88 England 53 (8)

An extravagantly gifted midfielder, Glenn Hoddle gained 53 caps for England and might have won many more but for doubts about his work-rate and tackling ability.

• **During a 12-year playing career with Tottenham Hotspur, Hoddle won the FA Cup twice (in 1981 and 1982) and the UEFA Cup (in 1984). He joined Monaco in 1987, where he played under Arsene Wenger, and the following year became the first Englishman to be part of a championship-winning side in France.** "I couldn't understand why he hadn't been appreciated in England," Wenger said of him. "Perhaps he was a star in the wrong period, years ahead of his time."

• As player-manager of Swindon, Hoddle led the Wiltshire club into the top flight for the first time in their history in 1993. In the same role at Chelsea the following year he guided the Blues to their first FA Cup final for nearly a quarter of a century.

• **In May 1996 Hoddle was appointed England manager, succeeding Terry Venables after Euro 96. Aged 38, he was the youngest man to fill the position since Walter Winterbottom.**

• Hoddle led England to the 1998 World Cup in France, where they were unlucky to lose to Argentina in a penalty shoot-out. The following year, though, he was dismissed from the job after suggesting in a newspaper interview that disabled people were somehow paying for sins committed in a previous life. He has subsequently managed Southampton, Tottenham and Wolves and now runs a football academy in southern Spain.

ROY HODGSON

> **Born:** Croydon, 9th August 1947
> **Managerial career:**
> 1976-80 Halmstads
> 1982 Bristol City
> 1983-85 Orebro
> 1985-90 Malmo
> 1990-92 Neuchatel Xamax
> 1992-95 Switzerland
> 1995-97 Inter Milan
> 1997-98 Blackburn Rovers
> 1999 Inter Milan
> 1999-2000 Grasshoppers
> 2000-01 Copenhagen
> 2001 Udinese
> 2002-04 United Arab Emirates
> 2004-05 Viking
> 2006-07 Finland
> 2007-2010 Fulham
> 2010- Liverpool

Liverpool boss Roy Hodgson is one of the most experienced managers in the game, most recently having turned around the fortunes of Fulham in a three-year stint at Craven Cottage. In his first season at the club Hodgson led his team to an unlikely escape from relegation, when the west Londoners won their final three Premier League fixtures. Two years later he easily topped that achievement, by taking Fulham to the final of the Europa League.

• **After failing to make the grade as a player at Crystal Palace, Hodgson**

Roy of the Reds!

spent much of his early managerial career in Sweden. He won the title with Halmstads in 1979 before leading Malmo to a Swedish record five consecutive championships between 1985-89.

• His next great success came with Switzerland, who he guided to the last 16 of the World Cup in 1994 – the country's best performance for 40 years. A much-travelled manager, Hodgson has also coached both the United Arab Emirates and Finland as well as enjoying two spells with Italian giants Inter Milan.

• **Hodgson's outstanding campaign with Fulham in 2009/10 earned him the League Managers Association Manager of the Year award and saw him touted as a future England manager. In the event, he opted to move to Liverpool, signing a three-year contract with the club in July 2010.**

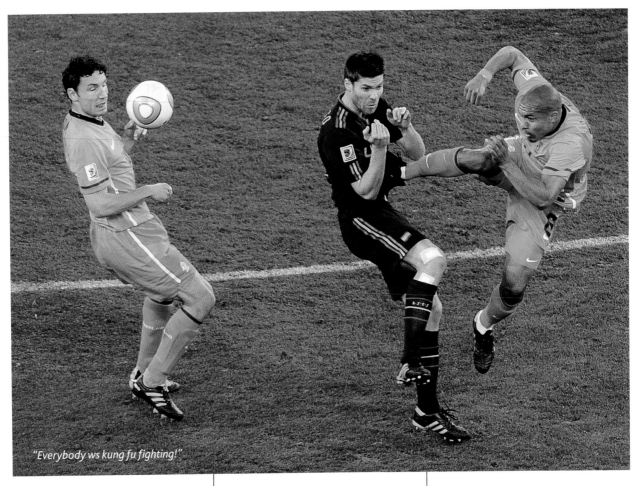

"Everybody ws kung fu fighting!"

HOLLAND

First international:
Belgium 1
Holland 4, 1905
Most capped player:
Edwin van der Sar,
130 caps (1995-2008)
Leading goalscorer:
Patrick Kluivert,
40 goals (1994-2004)
**First World Cup
appearance:** Holland 2 Switzerland 1,
1934
Biggest win: Holland 9 Finland 0,
1912
Heaviest defeat: England
amateurs 9 Holland 1, 1909
Colours: Orange shirts, white
shorts, blue socks

Long associated with an entertaining style of attacking football, Holland have only won one major tournament, the European Championship in 1988. In the final that year the Dutch beat Russia with goals from their two biggest stars of the time, Ruud Gullit and Marco van Basten.

• **Holland have never won the World Cup, although they have been runners-** up three times. On the first two occasions they had the misfortune to meet the hosts in the final, losing to West Germany in 1974 and Argentina in 1978. Then, in the 2010 final, they went down 1-0 in extra-time to Spain in Johannesburg following a negative, at times brutal, Dutch performance which was totally at odds with the country's best footballing traditions.

• A professional league wasn't formed in Holland until 1956 and it took some years after that before the country was taken seriously as a football power. Their lowest ebb was reached in 1963 when they were humiliatingly eliminated from the European Championships by minnows Luxembourg.

• **The following decade, though, saw a renaissance in Dutch football. With exciting players like Johan Cruyff, Johan Neeskens and Ruud Krol in their side, the Dutch were considered the best team in Europe. Pivotal to their success was the revolutionary 'Total Football' system devised by manager Rinus Michels which allowed the outfield players to constantly switch positions during the game.**

• Holland have lost four of the five penalty shoot-outs they have been involved in at major tournaments. Only England have a worse record from the spot, with just one win in six shoot-outs.

HONOURS
European Championship 1988
World Cup record
1930 Did not enter
1934 Round 1
1938 Round 1
1950 Did not enter
1954 Did not enter
1958 Did not qualify
1962 Did not qualify
1966 Did not qualify
1970 Did not qualify
1974 Runners-up
1978 Runners-up
1982 Did not qualify
1986 Did not qualify
1990 Round 2
1994 Quarter-finals
1998 Fourth place
2002 Did not qualify
2006 Round 2
2010 Runners-up

HOME AND AWAY

Brentford hold the all-time record for home wins in a season. In 1929/30 the Bees won all 21 of their home games at Griffin Park in Division Three (South). However, their away form was so poor they missed out on promotion to champions Plymouth.

- **Chelsea hold the record for the longest unbeaten home run in the league, remaining undefeated at Stamford Bridge between February 2004 and October 2008. Ironically, the Blues' 86-game run was eventually broken by Liverpool, the previous holders of the same record.**

- The Blues also hold the record for the most consecutive away wins, with 11 in the Premiership in 2008. The highest number of straight home wins is 25, a record set by Bradford Park Avenue in the Third Division (North) in 1926/27.

- **Doncaster Rovers won a record 18 out of 21 away games while topping the Third Division (North) table in 1946/47.**

- Millwall scored a record 87 goals at home in 1927/28, a total which helped the London club top the Third Division (South) table that season. The away record is held by Arsenal, who scored 60 goals on their travels in their 1930/31 championship-winning campaign.

HUDDERSFIELD TOWN

Year founded: 1908
Ground: Galpharm Stadium (24,500)
Nickname: The Terriers
Biggest win: 11-0 v Heckmondwike (1909)
Heaviest defeat: 1-10 v Manchester City (1987)
Colours: Blue and white shirts, blue shorts, white socks

Huddersfield Town were founded in 1908 following a meeting held at the local Imperial Hotel some two years earlier... it took the club that long to find a ground to play at! The club were elected to the Second Division of the Football League two years later.

- **The Terriers enjoyed a golden era in the 1920s when, under the shrewd management of the legendary Herbert Chapman, they won three consecutive league titles between 1924-26 – no other club had matched this feat at the time and only three have done so since. The Terriers also won the FA Cup in 1922.**

- Huddersfield won the first of their league titles in 1924 by pipping Cardiff

BIGGEST PREMIER LEAGUE HOME WINS

1. Manchester United 9 Ipswich Town 0, 1995
2. Tottenham Hotspur 9 Wigan Athletic 1, 2009
3. Newcastle United 8 Sheffield Wednesday 0, 1999
   Chelsea 8 Wigan Athletic 0, 2010
5. Middlesbrough 8 Manchester City 1, 2008
6. Blackburn Rovers 7 Nottingham Forest 0, 1995
   Manchester United 7 Barnsley 0, 1997
   Arsenal 7 Everton 0, 2005
   Arsenal 7 Middlesbrough 0, 2006
   Chelsea 7 Stoke City 0, 2010

City on goal average, the first time the champions had been decided by this method.

- **The early 1970s were a desperate time for Huddersfield, who slumped from the First to the Fourth Division in just four seasons, becoming the first league champions to be relegated to the bottom tier.**

- In 1996 the Terriers splashed out a club record £1.2 million on Bristol Rovers striker Marcus Stewart. Four years later

Stewart joined Ipswich for £2.75 million, to become the club's most expensive sale.

HONOURS
Division 1 champions 1924, 1925, 1926
Division 2 champions 1970
Division 4 champions 1980
FA Cup 1922

HULL CITY

Year founded: 1904
Ground: KC Stadium (25,404)
Nickname: The Tigers
Biggest win: 11-1 v Carlisle United (1939)
Heaviest defeat: 0-8 v Wolves (1911)
Colours: Amber and black shirts, black shorts, black socks

Hull City were formed in 1904, originally sharing a ground with the local rugby league club. The club joined the Football League in 1905 but failed to achieve promotion to the top flight until 2008.

- **Wracked by financial woes, Hull only narrowly avoided relegation to the Conference in 1998 and 1999,**

Grrrr! Tigers roamed the Premier League between 2008-10

Hungary's famous 6-3 win at Wembley in 1953 shocked the nation that invented football

finishing a worst-ever third bottom in the lowest tier in the first of these years.

• However, their fortunes turned around and in 2008 Hull made it into the Premiership thanks to a play-off final victory over Bristol City, local boy Dean Windass scoring the vital goal. That triumph meant that Hull had climbed from the bottom tier to the top in just five seasons – a meteoric rise only bettered in the past by Swansea City and Wimbledon.

• **After a glorious start to their first ever top-flight campaign, Hull reached the heady heights of third in the Premier League after nine matches – their highest ever position. It couldn't last, though, and after narrowly escaping relegation in 2009 the Tigers dropped back into the second tier the following year.**

• The club's record goalscorer is Chris Chilton, who banged in 193 league goals in the 1960s and 1970s. His sometime team-mate Andy Davidson has pulled on a Hull shirt more than any other player, making 520 league appearances between 1952-68.

• **Hull's first success came in 1933 when they won the Third Division (North) title. Prolific striker Bill McNaughton was a key player in the Tigers' team, scoring a club best 33 goals during the season.**

• The club's record attendance is 55,019 for the visit of Manchester United to Boothferry Park in the sixth round of the FA Cup in 1949. In 2002 Hull moved to the much more compact KC Stadium (which they share with rugby league side Hull FC), so it's a record that is unlikely ever to be beaten.

• **In 2009 Hull splashed out a club record £5 million to bring shaggy-haired midfielder Jimmy Bullard to Humberside from Fulham. In the same year the Tigers received a record £4 million when they sold defender Michael Turner to Sunderland.**

> HONOURS
> ***Division 3 (North) champions*** *1933, 1949*
> ***Division 3 champions*** *1966*

HUNGARY

First international: Austria 5 Hungary 0, 1902

Most capped player: Jozsef Bozsik, 101 caps (1947-62)

Leading goalscorer: Ferenc Puskas, 84 goals (1945-56)

First World Cup appearance: Hungary 4 Egypt 2, 1934

Biggest win: Hungary 13 France 1, 1926

Heaviest defeat: Germany 7 Hungary 0, 1941

Colours: Red shirts, white shorts, green socks

Hungary took part in the first ever international between two non-British European countries, losing 5-0 to Austria in Vienna on 12th October 1902.

• **In the mid-1950s Hungary, inspired by the brilliant Ferenc Puskas, were** indisputably the best football team in the world. They became the first country from outside the British Isles to beat England on home soil in 1953, winning 6-3 at Wembley, before thrashing the same opposition 7-1 in Budapest a year later. This remains England's heaviest ever defeat.

• 'The Magical Magyars', as that great Hungarian side was called, reached the World Cup final in 1954 but lost 3-2 to West Germany in Bern. Hungary had beaten the Germans 8-3 in an earlier round of the competition, but with Puskas hampered by an ankle injury, were unable to hold onto a 2-0 lead in the second match. Hungary were also beaten 4-2 in the 1938 final by Italy.

• **Between 14th May 1950 and 4th July 1954 Hungary were unbeaten in 33 international matches, a record that stood for almost 40 years.**

• At the 1982 World Cup in Spain Laszlo Kiss scored three goals in seven second-half minutes for Hungary in their record 10-1 mauling of El Salvador – the fastest ever hat-trick in the finals of the competition. Kiss had earlier come off the bench and remains the only substitute to score a hat-trick at the World Cup.

WORLD CUP.
World Cup record
1930 Did not enter
1934 Quarter-finals
1938 Runners-up
1950 Did not enter
1954 Runners-up
1958 Round 1
1962 Quarter-finals
1966 Quarter-finals
1970 Did not qualify
1974 Did not qualify
1978 Round 1
1982 Round 1
1986 Round 1
1990 Did not qualify
1994 Did not qualify
1998 Did not qualify
2002 Did not qualify
2006 Did not qualify
2010 Did not qualify

SIR GEOFF HURST

Born: Ashton-under-Lyme, 8th December 1941
Position: Striker
Club career:
1959-72 West Ham United 410 (180)
1972-75 Stoke City 108 (30)
1975-76 West Bromwich Albion 10 (2)
1976 Seattle Sounders 24 (9)
International record:
1966-72 England 49 (24)

Geoff Hurst is the only player to have scored a hat-trick in the World Cup final. His famous treble against West Germany at Wembley helped England to a legendary 4-2 triumph in 1966.

• **Along with Ian Rush, Hurst is the leading scorer in the history of the League Cup with an impressive total of 49 goals. He is also the last player to hit six goals in a top-flight league match, netting a double hat-trick in West Ham's 8-0 thrashing of Sunderland at Upton Park in 1968.**

• A well-built centre forward who was strong in the air and possessed a powerful shot, Hurst won an FA Cup winners' medal with West Ham in 1964 and, the following year, helped the Hammers win the European Cup Winners' Cup.

• **In 1979 he was appointed manager of Chelsea but was sacked two years later after a dismal run of results culminating in a club record sequence of nine matches in which the Blues failed to score a single goal. However, Hurst's great achievements on the pitch remain part of English folklore and earned him a knighthood in 1998.**

Sir Geoff Hurst, Hammers and England legend

IS THAT A FACT?
A study conducted by the Engineering Department at Oxford University in 1996 concluded that Geoff Hurst's controversial second goal against West Germany in the 1966 World Cup final did not actually cross the line and was, in fact, a full 6cm away from being a legitimate goal.

ANDRES INIESTA

Born: Albacete, Spain, 11th May 1984
Position: Midfielder
Club career:
2001-03 Barcelona B 54 (5)
2002- Barcelona 210 (17)
International record:
2006- Spain 49 (8)

Attacking midfielder Andres Iniesta became a hero for the whole Spanish nation when he scored the winning goal in the 2010 World Cup final against Holland at the Soccer City stadium in Johannesburg. To cap a great day for the Barcelona star he also picked up the Man of the Match award and was shortlisted for the Golden Ball.
• Nicknamed 'El Cerebro' ('The Brain') for his brilliant reading of the game, Iniesta made his debut for Spain in 2006 and scored his first goal for his country the following year in a 1-0 friendly win against England at Old Trafford. In 2008 he helped Spain win their first major honour for 44 years, the European Championships in Austria and Switzerland.
• A product of the Barcelona youth system, Iniesta has formed a tremendous midfield partnership with Xavi, his team-mate at both club and international level. Although neither is especially prolific in front of goal, the pair have created numerous opportunities for the likes of Lionel Messi, David Villa and Fernando Torres with their sublime passing skills.
• As well as his international honours, Iniesta has won four league titles with Barcelona plus the Champions League in both 2006 and 2009.

INTER MILAN

Year founded: 1908
Ground: San Siro (82,955)
Nickname: Nerazzurri (The black and blues)
Colours: Black-and-blue-striped shirts, black shorts, blue socks

Founded in 1908 as a breakaway club from AC Milan, Internazionale (as they are known locally) are the only Italian team never to have been relegated from Serie A. Italian champions in the last five seasons, Inter have 18 title wins to their name – a total only bettered by Juventus.
• Inter were the first Italian club to win the European Cup twice, beating the mighty Real Madrid 3-1 in the 1964 final before recording a 1-0 defeat of Benfica the following year. They had to wait 45 years, though, before making it a hat-trick with a 2-0 defeat of Bayern Munich in Madrid in 2010 – a victory that, with the domestic league and cup already in the bag, secured Inter their first ever treble.
• Under legendary manager Helenio Herrera, Inter introduced the 'catenaccio' defensive system to world football in the 1960s. Playing with a sweeper behind two man-markers, Inter conceded very few goals as they powered to three league titles between 1963-66.
• The club endured a barren period domestically until they were awarded their first Serie A title for 17 years in 2006 after Juventus and AC Milan, who had both finished above them in the league table, had points deducted for their roles in a match-fixing scandal. Inter went on to win the championship in more conventional style in the following four years, the last two of these triumphs coming under former Chelsea boss Jose Mourinho.
• Current Fulham boss Roy Hodgson was twice manager of Inter in the 1990s. Only two English players, meanwhile, have played for the club: striker Gerry Hitchens, who joined from Aston Villa in 1961, and Paul Ince, who made a £7 million move from Manchester United in 1995.

HONOURS
Italian champions 1910, 1920, 1930, 1938, 1940, 1953, 1954, 1963, 1965, 1966, 1971, 1980, 1989, 2006, 2007, 2008, 2009, 2010
Italian Cup 1939, 1978, 1982, 2005, 2006, 2010
European Cup /Champions League 1964, 1965, 2010
UEFA Cup 1991, 1994, 1998
World Club Cup 1964, 1965

Diego Milito fired Inter Milan to Champions League glory in 2010

TOP 10

ITALIAN CUP WINNERS

1. Juventus, 9 wins
   Roma, 9 wins
3. Fiorentina, 6 wins
   Inter Milan, 6 wins
5. Torino, 5 wins
   AC Milan, 5 wins
   Lazio, 5 wins
8. Sampdoria, 4 wins
9. Napoli, 3 wins
   Parma, 3 wins

INVERNESS CALEDONIAN THISTLE

Year founded: 1994
Ground: Caledonian Stadium (7,711)
Previous name: Caledonian Thistle
Nickname: Caley Thistle
Biggest win: 8-1 v Annan Athletic (1998)
Heaviest defeat: 0-6 v Airdrie (2001)
Colours: Blue-and-red- striped shirts, blue shorts, blue socks

Founded as Caledonian Thistle in 1994 following the amalgamation of Highland league sides Caledonian and Inverness Thistle, the club was elected to the Scottish Third Division in the same year. In 1996, at the request of Inverness District Council, the club added 'Inverness' to its name.

• The club has steadily climbed up the league ladder in the years since, eventually gaining promotion to the SPL in 2004 after winning the First Division title. The club was relegated from the SPL in 2009 but bounced back the following season under manager Terry Butcher, a former England international defender.

• In February 2000 Thistle pulled off one of the biggest ever shocks in the Scottish Cup when they beat Celtic 3-1 at Parkhead. The Sun newspaper reported this famous giant-killing under the witty headline "Super Caley go ballistic, Celtic are atrocious".

• Incredibly, Caley went 'ballistic' again in 2003 when they knocked Celtic out of the cup for a second time, winning 1-0 at their tiny Caledonian Stadium.

Ipswich parade the FA Cup after beatiing Arsenal 1-0 in 1978

• In 2007 Thistle fielded the first ever Romanian to appear in the Scottish league system, midfielder Marius Nicalae.

> HONOURS
> **First Division champions** 2004
> **Third Division champions** 1997

IPSWICH TOWN

Year founded: 1878
Ground: Portman Road (30, 311)
Nickname: The Blues
Biggest win: 10-0 v Floriana (1962)
Heaviest defeat: 1-10 v Fulham (1963)
Colours: Blue shirts, white shorts, blue socks

The club was founded at a meeting at the town hall in 1878 but did not join the Football League until 1938, two years after turning professional.

• **Ipswich were the last of just four clubs to win the old Second and First Division titles in consecutive seasons, pulling off this remarkable feat in 1962 under future England manager Alf Ramsey. The team's success owed much to the strike partnership of Ray Crawford and Ted Phillips, who together scored 61 of the club's 93 goals during the title-winning campaign.**

• Two years after that title win, though,

Ipswich were relegated after conceding 121 goals. Only Blackpool in 1930/31 (125 goals against) have had a worse defensive record in the top flight.

• **However, the club enjoyed more success under Bobby Robson, another man who went on to manage England, in the following two decades. In 1978 Ipswich won the FA Cup, beating favourites Arsenal 1-0 in the final at Wembley, and three years later they won the UEFA Cup with attacking midfielder John Wark contributing a record 14 goals during the club's continental campaign.**

• Ipswich were founder members of the Premier League in 1992 but were relegated in 1995 after a dismal season which included a 9-0 thrashing against Manchester United at Old Trafford – the biggest defeat in Premiership history.

• With 203 goals for the Tractor Boys between 1958-69, Ray Crawford is the club's record goalscorer. Mick Mills is the club's record appearance maker, turning out 591 times between 1966-82. Another defender from that era, Allan Hunter, is Ipswich's most capped international, winning 47 of his 53 caps for Northern Ireland while at Portman Road.

> HONOURS
> **Division 1 champions** 1962
> **Division 2 champions** 1961
> **Division 3 (S) champions** 1954, 1957
> **FA Cup** 1978
> **UEFA Cup** 1981

Italy: worse than New Zealand!!!!

ITALY

First international:
Italy 6 France 2, 1910
Most capped player:
Fabio Cannavaro, 136
caps (1997-2010)
Leading goalscorer:
Luigi Riva, 35 goals
(1965-74)
**First World Cup
appearance:** Italy 7
USA 1, 1934
Biggest win: Italy 11 Egypt 3,1928
Heaviest defeat: Hungary 7
Italy 1, 1924
Colours: Blue shirts, blue shorts,
blue socks

Italy have the best record of any
European nation at the World Cup,
having won the tournament four times
(in 1934, 1938, 1982 and 2006). Only
Brazil with five wins have done better in
the competition.
• **The Azzurri, as they are known to
their passionate fans, are the only
country to have been involved in**
two World Cup final penalty shoot-
outs. In 1994 they lost out to Brazil,
but in 2006 they beat France on
penalties after a 1-1 draw in the
final in Berlin.
• When Italy won 1-0 at Wembley in
1997 in a World Cup qualifier they
became the first country to beat England
on home soil in a World Cup match.
• **The most humiliating moment in
Italy's sporting history came in 1966
when they lost 1-0 to minnows North
Korea at the World Cup in England.
The Italians had a remarkably similar
embarrassment at the 2002
tournament when they were knocked
out by hosts South Korea after a 2-1
defeat. Fortunately for the Azzurri,
neither 'East Korea' or 'West Korea'
exist as independent countries!**
• To the dismay of their fans, Italy had
another World Cup to forget in 2010
when they defended their trophy in
lamentable style, finishing bottom
of their group behind Paraguay,
Slovakia and, most embarrassingly,
New Zealand.
• **Italy have won the European
Championship just once, beating**
Yugoslavia 2-0 in the final in Rome in
1968. They reached the final again in
2000, but lost to France.

HONOURS
World Cup 1934, 1938, 1982, 2006
European Championship 1968
World Cup record
1930 Did not enter
1934 Winners
1938 Winners
1950 Round 1
1954 Round 1
1958 Did not qualify
1962 Round 1
1966 Round 1
1970 Runners-up
1974 Round 1
1978 Fourth place
1982 Winners
1986 Round 2
1990 Third place
1994 Runners-up
1998 Quarter-finals
2002 Round 2
2006 Winners
2010 Round 1

JAIRZINHO

Born: Caxias, Brazil, 25th December 1944
Position: Striker
Club career:
1959-74 Botofago 413 (186)
1974-75 Marseille 18 (9)
1976 Cruzeiro
1977 Portuguesa
1978-79 Noroeste 10 (2)
1979 Fast Club 2 (0)
International record:
1963-82 Brazil 87 (38)

Jairzinho is the last player to have scored in every game at the World Cup finals. He achieved this feat at the 1970 tournament, scoring a total of seven goals as Brazil won the Jules Rimet trophy for a record third time, but was beaten to the Golden Boot by West Germany's Gerd Muller (who scored 10 goals).

• Jairzinho spent most of his club career with Brazilian side Botofago. After a brief spell in France with Marseille he returned home to play for Cruzeiro, with whom he won the Copa Libertadores in 1976.

• He later became the coach of local Rio de Janeiro side Sao Cristovao, where one of the promising young players he brought through the youth system was future world superstar Ronaldo.

DAVID JAMES

Born: Welwyn Garden City, 1st August 1970
Position: Goalkeeper
Club career:
1989-92 Watford 89
1992-99 Liverpool 214
1999-2001 Aston Villa 67
2001-04 West Ham United 90
2004-06 Manchester City 93
2006-10 Portsmouth 134
2010 Bristol City
International record:
1997- England 53

David James has played more Premiership matches than any other player since the league was founded in 1992, his total at the end of the 2009/10 season standing at 573 games.

• James started out at Watford before moving to Liverpool in 1992 for £1

David James became the World Cup's oldest debutant in 2010

million. He won the League Cup with the Reds in 1995 but his occasional blunders also earned him the nickname 'Calamity James'.

• He left Anfield for Aston Villa and later played for West Ham and Manchester City. While at Eastlands he played the last five minutes of the club's final home game of the 2004/05 season against Middlesbrough as a striker (substitute keeper Nicky Weaver taking his place in goal) as City vainly sought the winning goal that would see them qualify for the UEFA Cup.

• In 2006 James joined Portsmouth and two years later he helped the south coast side win the FA Cup. It was his first success in the competition, although he had previously been a runner-up with Liverpool (in 1996) and Villa (in 2000). In 2010 he became the oldest player ever to captain a team in the FA Cup final, when he skippered Pompey against eventual winners Chelsea aged 39 and 287 days.

• James made his England debut against Mexico back in 1997 and has been in and out of the side ever since. He was dropped by Sven Goran Eriksson before the 2006 World Cup and was largely ignored by Steve McClaren, but he came back into favour as England's number one when Fabio Capello took charge in 2008. Two years later James made his first appearance in the World Cup finals against Algeria, in the process becoming the tournament's oldest ever debutant aged 39 years and 321 days.

PAT JENNINGS

Born: Newry, 12th June 1945
Position: Goalkeeper
Club career:
1961-63 Newry
1963-64 Watford 48
1964-77 Tottenham Hotspur 472
1977-85 Arsenal 237
International record:
1964-86 Northern Ireland 119

In an international career spanning 22 years, Pat Jennings made a record 119 appearances for Northern Ireland. He won his first cap in 1964 against Wales and his last against Brazil, on his 41st birthday, during the 1986 World Cup. At the time he was the oldest ever player to appear in the finals.

• For four years Jennings held the world record for the most international caps, until his total was surpassed by

IS THAT A FACT?
David James holds the record for the most clean sheets in Premier League history, with 173.

England keeper Peter Shilton at the 1990 World Cup finals.
• Jennings is the only goalkeeper in the modern era to have played for both Arsenal and Tottenham. He won the FA Cup with Spurs in 1967, before repeating the feat with the Gunners 12 years later.
• Voted Footballer of the Year in 1973, Jennings is one of a handful of goalkeepers to have scored with a kick from his hands, his huge punt downfield bouncing over Manchester United 'keeper Alex Stepney and into the net during the 1967 Charity Shield.

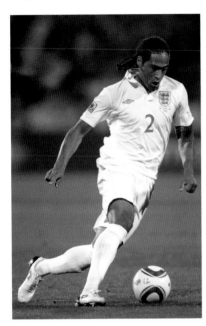

GLEN JOHNSON

Born: Dartford, 23rd August 1984
Position: Defender
Club career:
2001-03 West Ham United 15 (0)
2002 Millwall (loan) 8 (0)
2003-07 Chelsea 42 (3)
2006-07 Portsmouth (loan) 26 (0)
2007-09 Portsmouth 68 (5)
2009- Liverpool 25 (3)
International record:
2003- England 26 (1)

Glen Johnson started his career at West Ham United and later played for Chelsea and Portsmouth before signing for Liverpool for a cool £17 million in the summer of 2009.
• He won the League Cup with Chelsea in 2005 but increasingly became a squad player at Stamford Bridge and in 2006 he was allowed to join Portsmouth on loan. The move became permanent the following year and at the end of the season Johnson

collected an FA Cup winners' medal with Pompey.
• Before leaving Fratton Park Johnson won the 2009 Goal of the Season award for a brilliant 35-yard strike against Hull.
• An attacking right back, Johnson made his England debut as a substitute in a friendly against Denmark in November 2003. He took some time to establish himself in the team, but was Fabio Capello's preferred choice in his position at the 2010 World Cup.

JUVENTUS

Year founded: 1897
Ground: Stadio Olimpico (28,000)
Nickname: The Zebras
Colours: Black-and-white-striped shirts, black shorts, black socks

The most famous and the most successful club in Italy, Juventus were founded in 1897 by pupils at a school in Turin – hence the team's name, which means 'youth' in Latin. Six years later the club binned their original pink shirts and adopted their distinctive black-and-white-striped kit after an English member of the team had a set of Notts County shirts shipped out to Italy.

• Juventus emerged as the dominant force in Italian football in the 1930s when they won five titles in a row. They currently have a record 27 titles to their name and are the only team in Italy allowed to wear two gold stars on their shirts, signifying 20 Serie A victories.
• When, thanks to a single goal by their star player Michel Platini, Juventus beat Liverpool in the European Cup final in 1985 they became the first ever club to win all three European trophies. However, their triumph at the Heysel Stadium in Brussels was overshadowed by the death of 39 of their fans, who were crushed to death as they tried to flee from crowd trouble before the kick-off.
• Juventus have won the Italian Cup nine times, a record matched only by Roma, although they haven't raised the trophy since 1995.

HONOURS
Italian champions 1905, 1926, 1931, 1932, 1933, 1934, 1935, 1950, 1952, 1958, 1960, 1961, 1967, 1972, 1973, 1975, 1977, 1978, 1981, 1982, 1984, 1986, 1995, 1997, 1998, 2002, 2003
Italian Cup 1938, 1942, 1959, 1960, 1965, 1979, 1983, 1990, 1995
European Cup/Champions League 1985, 1996
European Cup Winners' Cup 1984
UEFA Cup 1977, 1990, 1993
European Super Cup 1984, 1996
World Club Cup 1985, 1996

"Are you Notts County in disguise?"

The 2010 World Cup is all a bit of a blur to Brazil star Kaka

KAKA

Born: Brasilia, 22nd April 1982
Position: Midfielder
Club career:
2001-03 Sao Paulo 59 (23)
2003-09 AC Milan 193 (70)
2009- Real Madrid 22 (8)
International record:
2002- Brazil 82 (27)

Ricardo Izecson dos Santos Leite, better known as 'Kaka', is widely considered the best midfielder playing in the world today. After impressing with Brazilian club Sao Paulo, he moved to AC Milan in 2003 for £5 million – a fee later described by Milan owner Silvio Berlusconi as "peanuts".

• Kaka helped Milan win the Serie A title in 2004, and the following year he finished as a runner-up in the Champions League after the Italians lost to Liverpool in the final. Two years later, though, Kaka got his revenge against the same opponents in Athens, having scored 10 goals en route to the final. In the same year, 2007, he was named World Footballer of the Year.

• Kaka first played for Brazil in 2002 and was a member of his country's squad which won the World Cup in the same year – although he only actually appeared on the pitch for 25 minutes of the tournament. Since then he has become a regular in the side.

• **In 2009 Kaka signed for Real Madrid for a then world record £56 million. His first season at the Bernabeu, though, was something of a disappointment as Real were pipped to the Spanish title by arch rivals Barcelona.**

• When he was 18 Kaka suffered a spinal fracture in a swimming pool accident that could easily have left him in a wheelchair for the rest of his life. A committed Christian who wears a T-shirt bearing the legend "I Belong to Jesus" under his football jersey, he attributed his remarkable recovery to the power of God.

ROBBIE KEANE

Born: Dublin, 8th July 1980
Position: Striker
Club career:
1997-99 Wolves 74 (24)
1999-2000 Coventry City 31 (12)
2000-01 Inter Milan 6 (0)
2001 Leeds United (loan) 18 (9)
2001-02 Leeds United 28 (4)
2002-08 Tottenham Hotspur 197 (80)
2008-09 Liverpool 19 (5)
2009- Tottenham Hotspur 34 (11)
2010 Celtic (loan) 16 (14)
International record:
1998- Republic of Ireland 100 (43)

Livewire striker Robbie Keane began his club career with Wolves, for whom he scored twice on his debut against Norwich in 1997. Two years later, aged 19, he joined Coventry City for £6 million – then a record fee for a teenager.

• **After brief spells with Inter Milan and Leeds, Keane moved to Tottenham in 2002. While at White Hart Lane he finally won the first trophy of his career, the Carling Cup in 2007/08 – a**

TOP 10

MOST CAPPED REPUBLIC OF IRELAND INTERNATIONALS

1. Shay Given (1996-) 104 caps
   Kevin Kilbane (1997-) 104 caps
3. Steve Staunton (1988-2002) 102 caps
4. Robbie Keane (1998-) 100 caps
5. Niall Quinn (1986-2002) 91 caps
6. Tony Cascarino (1986-2000) 88 caps
7. Paul McGrath (1985-97) 83 caps
8. Damien Duff (1998-) 82 caps
9. Packie Bonner (1981-96) 80 caps
10. Ray Houghton (1986-98) 73 caps

season in which he hit a personal best-ever 23 goals in all competitions.

• His goals record prompted Liverpool to pay £20 million for him in the summer of 2008. It was a dream move for Keane, a childhood fan of the Reds, but he was used irregularly by then Liverpool boss Rafa Benitez and, in the January 2009 transfer window, he returned to Tottenham for £15 million. The following year he spent the second half of the season on loan at Celtic.

• Keane made his debut for the Republic of Ireland in 1998 against the Czech Republic. In 2006 he was appointed captain and he is now his country's all-time leading goalscorer with an impressive 43 goals in 100 appearances.

ROY KEANE

Born: Cork, 10th August 1971
Position: Midfielder
Club career:
1989/90 Cobh Ramblers 12 (1)
1990-93 Nottingham Forest 114 (22)
1993-2005 Manchester United 323 (33)
2005-06 Celtic 10 (1)
International record:
1991-2005 Republic of Ireland 66 (9)

Manchester United legend Roy Keane is the club's most successful captain ever, leading the Reds to nine major trophies while wearing the armband between 1997-2005.

• The driving force in United's midfield for over a decade after arriving from Nottingham Forest for a then British record fee of £3.75 million in 1993, Keane won seven league titles and four FA Cups while at Old Trafford but he missed out on the Reds' 1999 Champions League triumph through suspension.

• A fiery, volatile character, Keane was sent off 13 times during his career – a record for English football. He set another unwanted record in 2002 when he was fined £150,000 by the FA for bringing the game into disrepute when he admitted in his autobiography that he had intended to hurt an opponent, Manchester City's Alf-Inge Haaland.

Roy Keane does not appear to be best pleased!

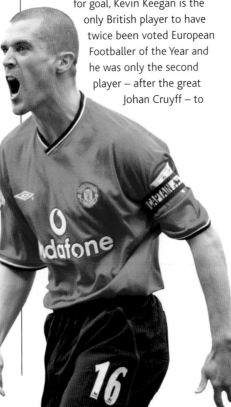

• Keane starred for the Republic of Ireland at the 1994 World Cup, being named his country's best player. However, before the 2002 tournament in Japan and Korea he stormed out of Ireland's training camp on the Pacific island of Saipan after a furious row with manager Mick McCarthy. Despite the intervention of Irish Prime Minister Bertie Ahern, Keane refused to return, although he later played for his country again under new boss Brian Kerr.

• Once tipped by Sir Alex Ferguson to succeed him at Old Trafford, Keane became manager of Sunderland in 2006 but walked out in November 2008. Five months later he was unveiled as the new manager of Ipswich Town, but he has so far failed to bring back the glory days to the Suffolk club.

KEVIN KEEGAN

Born: Doncaster, 14th February 1951
Position: Striker
Club career:
1968-71 Scunthorpe United 124 (18)
1971-77 Liverpool 230 (68)
1977-80 Hamburg 90 (32)
1980-82 Southampton 68 (37)
1982-84 Newcastle United 78 (48)
International record:
1972-82 England 63 (21)

A busy, all-action striker with a sharp eye for goal, Kevin Keegan is the only British player to have twice been voted European Footballer of the Year and he was only the second player – after the great Johan Cruyff – to win the award in consecutive seasons (1978 and 1979).

• Keegan was also the first English player to appear in the European Cup final with two different clubs. In 1977 he was a winner with Liverpool against Borussia Monchengladbach, but three years later he had to settle for a runners-up medal after Hamburg were beaten by Nottingham Forest.

• After making his England debut against Wales in 1972 Keegan went on to win 63 caps for his country, 31 of them as captain. His last match for England was as a substitute against Spain at the 1982 World Cup.

• Nicknamed 'Mighty Mouse' during his spell with Hamburg, Keegan had a top 10 hit in Germany with Head Over Heels in 1979. The single fared less well in the UK, stalling at number 31.

• Keegan finished his playing days at Newcastle in the early 1980s, returning to St James' Park a decade later as manager. But, after five years in charge, he dramatically quit the club a few months after his entertaining Toon team had narrowly missed out on the Premiership title. A brief second spell in charge of the Geordies ended in similar fashion in 2008 following a long-running disagreement with owner Mike Ashley about the club's management structure.

• Keegan also walked out on the England job in October 2000 just a few minutes after his team had lost a vital World Cup qualifier to Germany in the last ever match played at the old Wembley. He had only been in charge for 18 months, but had increasingly come under fire after a poor England showing at Euro 2000.

KICK-OFF

Scottish club Queens Park claim to have been the first to adopt the traditional kick-off time of 3pm on a Saturday, which allowed those people who worked in the morning time to get to the match.

• The fastest ever goal from a kick-off was scored in just 2.5 seconds by Marc Burrows for Cowes Sports reserves against Eastleigh reserves on the Isle of Wight in 2004. "The wind was so strong I thought it was worth a go," he said of his shot from the halfway line. "The ball just sailed over their poor keeper. I was so stunned I didn't even celebrate. I just put my hands in the air and burst out laughing."

• Until the start of the 20th century teams used to change ends before kicking off after every goal.
• **Celebrities used to take a ceremonial kick-off at important matches, including members of the Royal Family at cup finals.**
• Singer Diana Ross was supposed to kick off the 1994 World Cup in the USA by kicking a ball into an enormous inflatable goal, but she missed!

KILMARNOCK

Year founded: 1869
Ground: Rugby Park (18,128)
Nickname: Killie
Biggest win: 13-2 v Saltcoats Victoria (1896)
Heaviest defeat: 1-9 v Celtic (1938)
Colours: Blue-and-white-striped shirts, blue shorts, blue socks

The oldest professional club in Scotland, Kilmarnock were founded in 1869 by a group of local cricketers who were keen to play another sport during the winter months. Originally, the club played rugby (hence the name of Kilmarnock's stadium, Rugby Park) before switching to football in 1873.
• **That same year Kilmarnock entered the inaugural Scottish Cup and on 18th October 1873 the club took part in the first ever match in the competition, losing 2-0 in the first round to Renton.**
• Kilmarnock's greatest moment was back in 1965 when they travelled to championship rivals Hearts on the last day of the season requiring a two-goal win to pip the Edinburgh side to the title on goal average. To the joy of their travelling fans, Killie won 2-0 to claim the title by 0.04 of a goal.
• **Kilmarnock have won the Scottish Cup three times, most recently in 1997 when they beat Falkirk 1-0 at Ibrox.**
• Killie's match-winner on that occasion was striker Paul Wright, who remains the club's most expensive signing after moving from St Johnstone for £300,000 in 1995. The club's record sale is Steven Naismith, who left Rugby Park for Rangers for £2 million in 2007.

Jurgen Klinsmann seems pretty chuffed to have won the 1990 World Cup

HONOURS
Division 1 champions 1965
Division 2 champions 1898, 1899
Scottish Cup 1920, 1929, 1997

JURGEN KLINSMANN

Born: Goppingen, Germany, 30th July 1964
Position: Striker
Club career:
1981-84 Stuttgart Kickers 61 (22)
1984-89 VfB Stuttgart 156 (79)
1989-92 Inter Milan 123 (40)
1992-94 Monaco 65 (29)
1994-95 Tottenham Hotspur 41 (21)
1995-97 Bayern Munich 65 (31)
1997-98 Sampdoria 8 (2)
1997-98 Tottenham Hotspur (loan) 15 (9)
International record:
1987-98 Germany 108 (47)

Jurgen Klinsmann is the third-highest scorer for Germany. His total of 47 goals for his country is only bettered by Gerd Muller and Miroslav Klose. Klinsmann also lies second in the list of appearance makers for Germany, his 108 caps only being surpassed by former team-mate Lothar Matthaus.
• **In 1990 Klinsmann won a World Cup winners' medal after Germany defeated holders Argentina 1-0 in a bad-tempered final. He also captained Germany to success at Euro 96 in England.**
• In a varied club career, Klinsmann played in four different countries with seven clubs, including two spells with Tottenham in the 1990s. He won the UEFA Cup with both Inter Milan and Bayern Munich but only once played in a title-winning side, with Bayern in 1997.
• **In 2004 Klinsmann was appointed manager of Germany and two years later led his country to a creditable third place at the World Cup. He quit the job after the tournament but returned to management with Bayern Munich in 2008, having previously been strongly linked with both Chelsea and Liverpool. He was sacked by Bayern in April 2009 after a string of poor results.**

FRANK LAMPARD

Born: Romford, 20th June 1978
Position: Midfielder
Club career:
1995-2001 West Ham United
148 (24)
1995-96 Swansea City 9 (1)
2001- Chelsea 320 (105)
International record:
1999- England 83 (20)

With 129 goals to his name, Frank Lampard is the highest scoring midfielder in Premier League history. The vast majority of those strikes have come for Chelsea, who Lampard joined from West Ham in an £11 million deal back in 2001.
• **A key figure in Chelsea's success in recent years, Lampard has won both the league and the FA Cup three times during his nine years with the Blues, including the Double in 2010. Despite scoring in the 2008 Champions League final he had to settle for a runners' up medal after the Londoners lost to Manchester United on penalties.**
• A model of consistency, Lampard played in a then record 164 consecutive Premiership games until illness forced him out of Chelsea's visit to Manchester City in December 2005. Goalkeepers David James and Brad Friedel have since passed his total, but Lampard still holds the Premiership record for an outfield player.
• **Along with Southampton's Matt Le Tissier and the Manchester United pair of Ryan Giggs and Paul Scholes, Lampard is one of just four midfielders to have scored more than 100 goals in the Premier League.**

• The son of former England and West Ham defender Frank senior, Lampard made his international debut in 1999 against Belgium, but took a while to establish himself in the England team. He starred at the European championships in 2004, scoring in three of his country's four games, but fared less well at the 2006 World Cup where he was one of three England players to miss a penalty in the quarter-final shoot-out defeat at the hands of Portugal. His luck was also out at the 2010 tournament in South Africa, when the officials failed to spot that his shot against Germany in England's second-round defeat had clearly crossed the line.

TOP 10

SPL GOALSCORERS

1.	Kris Boyd (1999-2010)	164
2.	Henrik Larsson (1998-2004)	158
3.	Scott McDonald (2004-10)	93
4.	John Hartson (2001-06)	88
5.	Derek Riordan (2001-)	84
6.	Nacho Novo (2002-10)	73
7.	Stevie Crawford (1998-2008)	65
	Billy Dodds (1994-2006)	65
	Chris Sutton (2000-06)	65
10.	Colin Nish (2003-)	59

Frank Lampard: The highest scoring midfielder in Premier League history

HENRIK LARSSON

Born: Helsingborg, Sweden, 20th September 1971
Position: Striker
Club career:
1988-92 Hogaborg 74 (23)
1992-93 Helsingborg 56 (50)
1993-97 Feyenoord 101 (26)
1997-2004 Celtic 221 (174)
2004-06 Barcelona 40 (13)
2006-09 Helsingborg 77 (34)
2007 Man United (loan) 7 (1)
International record:
1993-2009 Sweden 106 (37)

Celtic legend Henrik Larsson is the club's leading scorer in the Scottish Premier League era, 158 of his 174 league goals for the Glasgow giants coming after the formation of the SPL in 1998. For many years he was the top scorer in SPL history, but in December 2009 Kris Boyd set a new record and the ex-Rangers striker went on to a total 164 goals.
• **In a hugely successful seven-year stay at Celtic Park, Larsson won four league titles and was top scorer in the SPL on five occasions. His greatest season was in 2000/01 when he notched 53 goals in all competitions as the Celts won the domestic treble. In the same year Larsson was voted Scottish Player of the Year (an award he had previously won in 1999) and picked up the European Golden Boot. It was a remarkable comeback for a player who, just two years earlier, had suffered a career-threatening double fracture of the leg in a UEFA Cup tie against Lyon.**
• In 2004 Larsson moved to Barcelona, where he won two more league title medals and, in 2006, the Champions

League after his side's 2-1 victory over Arsenal in the final in Paris.
• With 37 goals for Sweden, Larsson is his country's third highest scorer ever and one of just seven Swedish players to have won over 100 caps. After hanging up his boots in 2009 he became the manager of Swedish second division side Landskrona.

DENIS LAW

> **Born:** Aberdeen, 24th February 1940
> **Position:** Striker
> **Club career:**
> 1956-60 Huddersfield Town 81 (16)
> 1960-61 Manchester City 44 (21)
> 1961-62 Torino 27 (10)
> 1962-73 Manchester United 309 (171)
> 1973-74 Manchester City 24 (9)
> **International record:**
> 1958-74 55 (30)

Along with Kenny Dalglish, Denis Law is Scotland's leading scorer with 30 international goals. Law, though, scored his goals in roughly half the number of games as 'King Kenny'.
• Law made his international debut in 1958, scoring in a 3-0 win against Wales. Aged 18, he was the youngest player to appear for Scotland since before the war. He went on to represent Scotland for 16 years, taking his bow at the 1974 World Cup in Germany.
• On two occasions Law was sold for fees that broke the existing British transfer record. In 1960 he moved from Huddersfield to Manchester City for a record £55,000 and two years later his £115,000 transfer from Torino to Manchester United set a new benchmark figure.
• With United, Law won two league titles and the FA Cup in 1963, but he missed out on the club's European Cup triumph in 1968 through a knee injury. He remains the only Scottish player to have been voted European Footballer of the Year, an award he won in 1964.
• The last goal Law scored, a clever backheel for Manchester City against United at Old Trafford in 1974, gave him no pleasure at all as it condemned his old club to relegation to the Second Division. "I have seldom felt so depressed as I did that weekend," he remarked later.

• In 2002 a statue of Law was unveiled at Old Trafford, scene of many of his greatest triumphs. The following year the Scottish Football Association marked UEFA's Jubilee by naming him as Scotland's 'Golden Player' of the previous 50 years.

LAWS

Thirteen original laws of association football were adopted at a meeting of the Football Association in 1863, although these had their roots in the 'Cambridge Rules' established at Cambridge University as far back as 1848.
• No copy of those 1848 rules now exists, but they are thought to have included laws relating to throw-ins, goal-kicks, fouls and offside. They even allowed for a length of string to be used as a cross bar.
• Perhaps the most significant rule change occurred in 1925 when the offside law was altered so that an attacking player receiving the ball would need to be behind two opponents, rather than three. The effect of this rule change was dramatic, with the average number of goals per game in the Football League rising from 2.55 in 1924/25 to 3.44 in 1925/26.
• The laws of the game are governed by the International Football Association Board, which was founded in 1886 by the four football associations of the United Kingdom. Each of these associations still has one vote on the IFAB, with FIFA having four votes. Any changes to the laws of the game require a minimum of six votes.
• In recent years the most important change to the laws of the game was

the introduction of the 'back pass' rule in 1992, which prevented goalkeepers from handling passes from their own team-mates. The rule was introduced to discourage time-wasting and overly defensive play, following criticisms of widespread negative tactics at the 1990 World Cup.

LEAGUE CUP

With seven wins to their name, Liverpool have won the League Cup more often than any other club. The Reds have also appeared in the most finals, ten.
• The competition has been known by more names than any other in British football. Originally called the Football League Cup (1960-81), it has subsequently been rebranded through sponsorship deals as the Milk Cup (1981-86), Littlewoods Cup (1986-90), Rumbelows Cup (1990-92), Coca-Cola Cup (1992-98), Worthington Cup (1998-2003) and, since 2003, the Carling Cup.
• Ian Rush won a record five winners' medals in the competition with Liverpool (1981-84 and 1995) and, along with Geoff Hurst, is also the leading scorer in the history of the League Cup with 49 goals. In the 1986/87 season Tottenham's Clive Allen scored a record 12 goals in the competition.
• Oldham's Frankie Bunn scored a record six goals in a League Cup match when Oldham thrashed Scarborough 7-0 on 25th October 1989.
• Liverpool won the competition a record four times in a row between 1981-84, going undefeated for an unprecedented 25 League Cup matches.

LEEDS UNITED

• Liverpool were also the first club to win the trophy on penalties, beating Birmingham City 5-4 in the shoot-out in 2001 in the first final to be played at the Millennium Stadium, Cardiff.

• Norman Whiteside, the youngest player ever to score in an FA Cup final (for Manchester United v Brighton in 1983), is also the youngest man ever to score in the League Cup final (for Manchester United v Liverpool, also in 1983), aged 17 years and 324 days.

• **The youngest player to captain a side in the League Cup final was Sunderland's Barry Venison, who was aged just 20 years, seven months and eight days when he led out his team to play Norwich at Wembley in 1985. Unfortunately for Bazza, the Wearsiders lost 1-0.**

• The first League Cup final to be played at Wembley was between West Brom and QPR in 1967. QPR were then a Third Division side and pulled off a major shock by winning 3-2. Prior to 1967, the final was played on a home and away basis over two legs.

• **The first player to score in every round of the League Cup was West Brom's Tony Brown in 1965/66.**

• Chelsea striker Didier Drogba has scored a record four goals in League Cup finals, finding the target against Liverpool in 2005, Arsenal in 2007 (two goals) and Tottenham in 2008.

• **In 1983 West Ham walloped Bury 10-0 to record the biggest ever victory** in the League Cup. Three years later Liverpool equalled the Hammers' tally with an identical thrashing of Fulham.

LEEDS UNITED

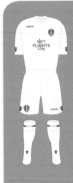

Year founded: 1919
Ground: Elland Road (40,242)
Nickname: United
Biggest win: 10-0 v Lyn Oslo (1969)
Heaviest defeat: 1-8 v Stoke City (1934)
Colours: White shirts, white shorts, white socks

Leeds United were formed in 1919 as successors to Leeds City, who had been expelled from the Football League after making illegal payments to their players. United initially joined the Midland League before being elected to the Second Division in 1920.

• **Leeds' greatest years were in the 1960s and early 1970s under legendary manager Don Revie. The club were struggling in the Second Division when he arrived at Elland Road in 1961 but, building his side around the likes of Jack Charlton, Billy Bremner and Johnny Giles, Revie soon turned Leeds into a powerful force.**

• During the Revie years Leeds won two league titles in 1969 and 1974, the FA Cup in 1972, the League Cup in 1968, and two Fairs Cup in 1968 and 1971. There were any number of near misses, too, as the Yorkshiremen's unique blend of skill and steel saw them challenge for just about every trophy going.

• **Leeds also reached the final of the European Cup in 1975, losing 2-0 to Bayern Munich. Sadly, rioting by the club's fans resulted in Leeds becoming the first English club to be suspended from European competition. The ban lasted three years.**

• Peter Lorimer, another Revie-era stalwart, is the club's leading scorer, hitting 168 league goals in two spells at Elland Road: 1962-79 and 1983-86. Jack Charlton holds the club appearance record, turning out in 773 games in total between 1952-73.

• **On 15th April 1970 Leeds appeared in front of the biggest crowd ever to watch a European Cup tie when 135,826 fans crammed into Hampden Park in Glasgow to see Celtic beat them 2-1 in the semi-final second leg.**

• In 1992 Leeds pipped Manchester United to the title to become the last club to win the old First Division before it became the Premiership. Ironically, Leeds's star player at the time, Eric Cantona, joined the Reds the following season. The club remained a force over the next decade, even reaching the Champions League semi-final in 2001, but financial mismanagement

Darren Beckford fires Leeds back into the Championship

saw them plummet to League One in 2007 before they climbed back into the Championship three years later.

• **Longserving defender Lucas Radebe is Leeds's most capped player, winning 61 caps for South Africa in the 1990s.**

• In 1982 Elland Road was the venue for the replay of the rugby league Challenge Cup final between Hull and Widnes – the first football stadium to host the event. The ground was also used by rugby league side Hunslet between 1982-94.

> **HONOURS**
> *Division 1 champions* 1969, 1974, 1992
> *Division 2 champions* 1924, 1964, 1990
> *FA Cup* 1972
> *League Cup* 1968
> *Fairs Cup* 1968, 1971

LEICESTER CITY

Year founded: 1884
Ground: Walkers Stadium (32,500)
Previous name: Leicester Fosse
Nickname: The Foxes
Biggest win: 13-0 v Notts Olympic (1894)
Heaviest defeat: 0-12 v Nottingham Forest (1909)
Colours: Blue shirts, white shorts, blue socks

Founded in 1884 as Leicester Fosse by old boys from Wyggeston School, the club were elected to the Second Division a decade later. In 1919 they changed their name to Leicester City, shortly after Leicester was given city status.

• **Leicester have been promoted a joint record 11 times to the top flight (six times as champions, a figure only bettered by Manchester City). But they've also been relegated 11 times from the top division, which is also a record.**

• The Foxes have enjoyed great success in the League Cup, winning the trophy three times. Their first victory came against Stoke in 1964 and more recently they won the trophy twice under then manager Martin O'Neill, against Middlesbrough in 1997 and Tranmere Rovers in 2000.

• **Only Crystal Palace can match**

Leicester's Portuguese midfielder Moreno has one of the finest haircuts in the Championship

Leicester's record of playing in four Championship play-off finals since the system was introduced in 1987. The club's record in these games is mixed with two wins and two defeats.

• In 1909, while still known as Leicester Fosse, the club suffered their worst ever defeat, losing 12-0 to East Midland neighbours Nottingham Forest. The score is still a record for a top flight match.

• **Leicester City are the only club to have played in four FA Cup finals and lost them all. Beaten in 1949, 1961 and 1963 they were defeated again by Manchester City in 1969 – the same season that they were relegated from the First Division. Only four other teams, most recently Portsmouth in 2010, have suffered a similar double blow.**

• Arthur Chandler holds the club goalscoring record, netting 259 times between 1923-35. Remarkably, he scored in a record 16 consecutive matches during the 1924/25 season. The club's

appearance record is held by defender and ex-Leicestershire county cricketer Graham Cross, who turned out 599 times in all competitions for the Foxes between 1960-76.

> **HONOURS**
> *Division 2 champions* 1925, 1937, 1954, 1957, 1971, 1980
> *League One champions* 2009
> *League Cup* 1964, 1997, 2000

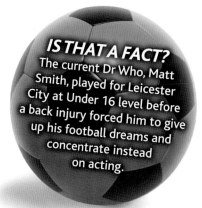

IS THAT A FACT?
The current Dr Who, Matt Smith, played for Leicester City at Under 16 level before a back injury forced him to give up his football dreams and concentrate instead on acting.

*Spurs' super-quick winger
Aaron Lennon*

AARON LENNON

Born: Leeds, 16th April 1987
Position: Winger
Club career:
2003-05 Leeds United 38 (1)
2005- Tottenham Hotspur 139 (15)
International record:
2006- England 19 (0)

A livewire winger whose pace and dribbling skills make him a threat to any defence, Aaron Lennon has represented England in two World Cups despite still being only 23 years old.

• Lennon was selected by then England manager Sven Goran Eriksson for the 2006 tournament in Germany despite not being capped at senior level, and he also featured in Fabio Capello's squad for the 2010 finals in South Africa.

• A teenage prodigy with his hometown club Leeds, Lennon became the youngest player ever to wear sponsored boots when he signed a deal with Adidas when he was just 14. Two years later he made his first-debut as a sub against

Tottenham when aged just 16 and 129 days – at the time the youngest ever player to appear in the Premier League.

• In 2005 Lennon moved to Spurs for £1 million and has since become a favourite with the White Hart Lane fans. At the end of the 2008/09 campaign his blistering displays down the right wing earned him the supporters' Player of the Season award, while his last-gasp equaliser in a dramatic 4-4 draw at arch rivals Arsenal was voted the club's best moment of the season.

CRAIG LEVEIN

Born: Dunfermline, 22nd October 1964
Managerial career:
1997-2000 Cowdenbeath
2000-04 Hearts
2004-06 Leicester City
2006 Raith Rovers
2006-09 Dundee United
2009-Scotland

Appointed as Scotland manager in December 2009 as the successor to George Burley, Craig Levein got off to a great start when his team beat the Czech Republic 1-0 at Hampden Park in his first match in charge of the national team. Incredibly, the victory was Scotland's first in a home friendly for 14 years.

• Levein began his managerial career at Cowdenbeath, before moving to Hearts in 2000. In four years with the Edinburgh club he guided them to consecutive third-place finishes in the SPL, but was unable to break the Old Firm's monopoly of the top two positions.

• In his next job, at Championship side Leicester City, he was less successful but he did oversee a famous victory in the FA Cup third round in January 2006, when the Foxes came from two goals down to beat Tottenham 3-2.

• Later that month, though, he was sacked but Levein was soon back in management at Dundee United, via a short spell at Raith Rovers. He spent three years at Tannadice before taking the Scotland job, the highlight coming in 2008 when he led the Terrors to the League Cup final, which United eventually lost to Rangers on penalties.

• A tough-tackling defender in his playing days, Levein started out at Cowdenbeath before spending many years at Hearts. He also won 16 caps for Scotland, representing his country at the 1990 World Cup in Italy.

LEYTON ORIENT

Year founded: 1881
Ground: Brisbane Road (9,271)
Previous name: Eagle FC, Clapton Road, Orient
Nickname: The O's
Biggest win: 9-2 v Aldershot (1934) and v Chester (1962)
Heaviest defeat: 0-8 v Aston Villa (1929)
Colours: Red shirts, red shorts, red socks

Originally founded by members of a local cricket team, the club chose the name 'Orient' in 1888 following a suggestion by one of the players

Not again! Lincoln suffer play-off heartache yet again, this time against Southend in 2005

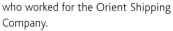

who worked for the Orient Shipping Company.

• **Over 40 Orient players and staff fought in the First World War, three of them dying in the conflict. In recognition of this sacrifice, The Prince of Wales (later King Edward VIII) watched an Orient match in 1921 – the first time a member of the Royal Family had attended a Football League fixture.**

• Orient are the only club to have played league matches at the old Wembley stadium. During the 1931/32 season, while still named Clapton Orient, the club played matches against Brentford and Southend at 'the home of football' after their own Lea Bridge ground was temporarily closed for failing to meet official standards. More recently, along with West Ham, the club has expressed an interest in moving into the Olympic Stadium at Stratford after the London Games in 2012.

• **Success has generally proved elusive for the east enders but the club did enjoy a single season in the top flight in 1962/63 and in 1978 the O's reached the semi-finals of the FA Cup before losing 3-0 to Arsenal.**

• Orient's record scorer is Tommy Johnston, who banged in 121 goals in two spells at the club between 1956-61. In 2009 the South Stand at Brisbane Road was named after the prolific striker.

• **In the Third Division play-off final in 2001, Orient's Chris Tate scored against Blackpool after just 27**

seconds – the fastest ever goal at the Millennium Stadium. Sadly for the O's, they lost the game 4-2.

HONOURS
***Division 3 (S) champions** 1956*
***Division 3 champions** 1970*

LINCOLN CITY

Year founded: 1884
Ground: Sincil Bank (10,120)
Nickname: The Imps
Biggest win: 11-1 v Crewe Alexandra (1951)
Heaviest defeat: 3-11 v Manchester City (1895)
Colours: Red-and-white striped shirts, black shorts, black socks

The oldest club never to have played in the top flight, Lincoln City were founded as successors to Lincoln Rovers in 1884. The club were founder members of Division Two in 1892 but have spent most of their history in the lower reaches of the League.

• **Former England manager Graham Taylor started his managerial career at Lincoln in 1972 and four years later led the Imps to the Fourth Division title with a record haul of 74 points (the highest ever total until 1981/82**

when wins earned an extra point).

• During the 1901/02 season Lincoln conceded just four goals at home in 17 Second Division fixtures to set a record for defensive meanness that has only since been matched by two clubs, Plymouth and Liverpool.

• **In January 1932 Lincoln scored an amazing seven goals in just 21 second-half minutes against Halifax Town, with striker Frank Keetley grabbing six of them. The Imps won the match 9-1 and, at the end of the season, won the Division Three (North) title on goal average.**

• In 1987 Lincoln became the first club to be relegated automatically from the Football League but they bounced back the following year as Conference champions.

• **More recently, Lincoln reached the League Two play-offs for a record five years in succession but failed to win promotion every time, losing three semi-finals and two finals.**

• The theme from *The Dambusters* film is played at Sincil Bank whenever Lincoln score – a tradition which stems from the fact that the Dambusters squadron was based at RAF Scampton, just outside the city, during World War II.

HONOURS
***Division 3 (N) champions** 1932, 1948, 1952*
***Division 4 champions** 1976*
***Conference champions** 1988*

GARY LINEKER

Born: Leicester,
30th November 1960
Position: Striker
Club career:
1978-85 Leicester City 194 (95)
1985-86 Everton 41 (30)
1986-89 Barcelona 103 (43)
1989-92 Tottenham Hotspur
105 (67)
1992-94 Nagoya Grampus 8 23 (9)
International record:
1984-92 England 80 (48)

Now a popular BBC sports presenter known for his excruciating puns, Gary Lineker is England's second highest scorer, with 48 goals, just one behind the legendary Bobby Charlton. He had a great chance to beat the record, but failed to score in any of his final six matches and even missed a penalty to equal Charlton's tally against Brazil.

• He is, though, England's leading scorer at the finals of the World Cup with ten goals. At the 1986 tournament in Mexico Lineker scored six goals to win the Golden Boot and he added another four at Italia 90.

• Lineker is the only player to have twice scored all four England goals in a match, grabbing all his side's goals in 4-2 away wins over Spain in 1987 and Malaysia in 1991. In all, he hit five hat-tricks in his 80 international appearances.

• At club level Lineker won the European Cup-Winners' Cup with Barcelona in 1989 and the FA Cup with Spurs two years later. He was also voted PFA Player of the Year in 1986 after a single goal-filled season with Everton.

• In his last international, against Sweden at the 1992 European championships, Lineker was controversially substituted by England boss Graham Taylor. The

TOP 10

FOOTBALLERS IN TV ADS

1. Gary Lineker, Walkers crisps (1994-)
2. David Beckham, Pepsi (2000-08)
3. Thierry Henry, Renault Clio (2001-05)
4. Kevin Keegan, Brut (1976)
5. Wayne Rooney, Powerade (2010)
6. Alan Shearer, McDonald's (1999)
7. Gareth Southgate, Chris Waddle & Stuart Pearce, Pizza Hut (1996)
8. Ruud Gullit, M & Ms (1996)
9. John Terry, King of Shaves (2007-08)
10. Ian Wright, Chicken Tonight (1999-2001)

move backfired as England lost the match and were eliminated.

• A revered figure in his hometown, Lineker has a stand named after him at Leicester City's Walkers Stadium.

LIVERPOOL

Year founded: 1892
Ground: Anfield
(45,362)
Nickname: The Reds
Biggest win: 11-0 v
Stromsgodset (1974)
Heaviest defeat:
1-9 v Birmingham
City (1954)
Colours: Red shirts,
red shorts, red socks

Liverpool were founded as a splinter club from local rivals Everton following a dispute between the Toffees and the landlord of their original ground at Anfield, John Houlding. When the majority of Evertonians decided to decamp to Goodison Park in 1892, Houlding set up Liverpool FC after his attempts to retain the name 'Everton' had failed.

• With 18 league titles to their name, Liverpool are (with Manchester United) the most successful club in the history of English football. For

In 1992 Gary Lineker missed a penalty that would have seen him equal Bobby Charlton's England goalscoring record

Liverpool have won the European Cup five times, more that any other English club

two years later. In the same season the Reds' mean defence conceded just 16 goals, a record for a 42-game top-flight campaign, and kept a record 28 clean sheets.

• In 1986 Liverpool became only the third English side in the twentieth century to win the Double, pipping rivals Everton to the league title and then beating the Toffees 3-1 in the FA Cup final at Wembley.

• **England international striker Roger Hunt is the club's leading scorer in league games, with 245 goals between 1958-69. His team-mate Ian Callaghan holds the Liverpool appearance record, turning out in 640 league games between 1960-78.**

• Spanish hitman Fernando Torres is the club's record signing, joining the Reds' from Atletico Madrid for £20 million in 2007. The most expensive player to leave Anfield is Robbie Keane, who cost Tottenham £15 million when he returned to White Hart Lane in 2009.

• **In 2001 Liverpool became only the second English club to win the League Cup and FA Cup in the same season. For good measure, the Reds made it a 'Treble' by lifting the UEFA Cup as well after a thrilling 5-4 victory over Spanish club Alaves in the final.**

• Kop hero Steven Gerrard is the club's most capped international, having played 85 games for England since making his debut in 2000.

• **In 1944 Liverpool made one of the most unlikely signings ever when they recruited world heavyweight boxing champion Joe Louis on an amateur contract. Despite hopes that he might play for the Reds, he never did, although he did train a couple of times with the squad at Anfield.**

many years the Reds held top spot on their own, but their failure to win a single championship since 1990 has seen their deadly rivals from Old Trafford draw level with them.

• Liverpool dominated English football in the 1970s and 1980s after the foundations of the club's success were laid by legendary manager Bill Shankly in the previous decade. Under Shankly's successor, Bob Paisley, the Reds won 13 major trophies – a haul only surpassed by Sir Alex Ferguson.

• **While Liverpool have been unable to match Manchester United's achievements in domestic football in recent years, they remain the most successful English side in Europe having won the European Cup/ Champions League on five occasions. The Reds first won the trophy in 1977, beating Borussia Monchengladbach 3-1 in Rome, and the following year became the first British team to retain the cup (after a 1-0 win in the final against Bruges at Wembley).**

• In 1984 Liverpool became the first club to win the European Cup on penalties

when they beat Roma by this method after a 1-1 draw. In 2005 the Reds won the trophy on spot-kicks again, this time against AC Milan, and remain the only club to have twice triumphed in the competition after a penalty shoot-out.

• **Liverpool have won the League Cup a record seven times, including four times in a row between 1981-84. Reds striker Ian Rush is the joint leading scorer in the history of the competition with 49 goals, hitting all but one of these for Liverpool in two spells at the club in the 1980s and 1990s.**

• Rush also scored a record five goals in three FA Cup finals for Liverpool in 1986, 1989 and 1992 – all of which were won by the Reds. In all, the Merseysiders have won the trophy seven times, most recently in 2006 when they became only the second team (after Arsenal the previous year) to claim the cup on penalties.

• **In 1979 Liverpool won the league title with 68 points, a record for the old First Division before the introduction of three points for a win**

HONOURS

Division 1 champions *1901, 1906, 1922, 1923, 1947, 1964, 1966, 1973, 1976, 1977, 1979, 1980, 1982, 1983, 1984, 1986, 1988, 1990*
Division 2 champions *1894, 1896, 1905, 1962*
FA Cup *1965, 1974, 1986, 1989, 1992, 2001, 2006*
League Cup *1981, 1982, 1983, 1984, 1995, 2001, 2003*
European Cup/Champions League *1977, 1978, 1981, 1984, 2005*
UEFA Cup *1973, 1976, 2001*
European Super Cup *1977, 2001, 2005*

NAT LOFTHOUSE

Born: Bolton, 27th August 1925
Position: Striker
Club career:
1946-60 Bolton Wanderers
452 (255)
International record:
1950-58 England 33 (30)

The top scorer in the history of Bolton Wanderers, Nat Lofthouse banged in a phenomenal 285 goals for the Trotters in 505 matches in all competitions.

• Of all those goals the most important two came in the 1958 FA Cup final, when Bolton defeated Manchester United 2-0 at Wembley to claim their last major trophy.

• Lofthouse is one of four players to score in every round of the cup, including the final, but finish on the losing side at Wembley. His goals helped the Trotters reach the 1953 final but, in an epic match, they went down 4-3 to Blackpool.

• A superb header of the ball, Lofthouse scored twice on his debut for England in a 2-2 draw with Yugoslavia at Highbury in 1950. He went on to score 30 goals for his country and for a while was England's leading scorer – he has since dropped down the rankings to joint fifth position with Tom Finney and Alan Shearer.

• After scoring two goals in a 3-2 victory over Austria in 1952, Lofthouse was dubbed 'the Lion of Vienna' by the press. The nickname stayed with him for the rest of his career and even became the name of a popular pub in Bolton.

• A genuine one-club man who was voted Footballer of the Year in 1953, Lofthouse went on to manage Bolton from 1968-71 and was appointed the Trotters' president in 1986.

LYON

Year founded: 1950
Ground: Stade Gerland (41,494)
Nickname: Les Gones ('The Boys')
Colours: White shirts with red and blue trim, white shorts, white socks

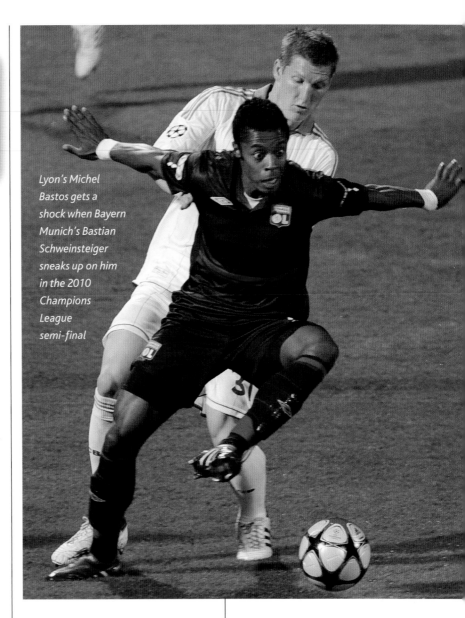

Lyon's Michel Bastos gets a shock when Bayern Munich's Bastian Schweinsteiger sneaks up on him in the 2010 Champions League semi-final

Lyon only came into existence in 1950 when the football section of the multisports club Lyon Olympique fell out with the rugby section and decided to form its own club.

• After winning the French title for the first time in 2002, Lyon went on to top the table in each of the subsequent six seasons before losing out to Bordeaux in 2009. All the same, the club's total of seven successive championship victories is an all-time record for the French league.

• Lyon's recent success stems from the arrival of businessman Jean-Michel Aulas, who took control of the club in 1987. Since then he has invested heavily in the club, signing top French players and recruiting leading managers such as Paul Le Guen and Gerard Houllier.

• Lyon's 7-2 thrashing of Werder Bremen in the Champions League in 2005 was a record for the knock-out phase until Manchester United annihilated Roma 7-1 two years later.

HONOURS
French championship 2002, 2003, 2004, 2005, 2006, 2007, 2008
French Cup 1964, 1967, 1973, 2008

TOP 10

FRENCH LEAGUE WINNERS

1. Saint Etienne, 10 titles
   Marseille, 10 titles
3. Nantes, 8 titles
4. Monaco, 7 titles
   Lyon, 7 titles
6. Reims, 6 titles
   Bordeaux, 6 titles
8. Standard Athletic Club, 5 titles
   Roubaix, 5 titles
10. Lille, 4 titles
    Nice, 4 titles

ALLY McCOIST

Born: Bellshill, 24th September 1962
Position: Striker
Club career:
1979-81 St Johnstone 57 (22)
1981-83 Sunderland 56 (8)
1983-98 Rangers 418 (251)
1998-2001 Kilmarnock 59 (12)
International record:
1986-98 Scotland 61 (19)

With an incredible 355 goals for Rangers in all competitions, Ally McCoist is the highest scorer in the Glasgow club's history. His tally of 251 league goals is also a club record.

• During a 15-year career with Rangers, McCoist won no fewer than ten league titles (including nine in a row between 1989-97), nine Scottish League Cups and one Scottish Cup. His haul of medals is unmatched by any other Scottish player in the last quarter of a century.

• In 1992 McCoist hit a personal best

"You're fired!" Alex McLeish does his famous Sir Alan impression

34 goals and won the European Golden Boot. In the same year he was voted Scottish Player of the Year. A Scotland international for over a decade, his total of 19 goals for his country is only bettered by four players.

• In 2007 McCoist became assistant manager of Rangers. Previously he was part of the Question of Sport team for over a decade, his cheeky quips gaining him a huge following of fans. On his final appearance in 2007 he failed to spot that the 'Mystery Guest' was none other than Rangers boss Walter Smith!

ALEX McLEISH

Born: Barrhead, 21st January 1959
Position: Defender
Club career:
1978-94 Aberdeen 493 (25)
1994-95 Motherwell 3 (0)
International record:
1980-93 Scotland 77 (0)

A year after leading Birmingham back into the Premier League in 2009, Alex McLeish guided the Blues to a highly creditable ninth position in the table – their best showing for over half a century.

• He began his managerial career with spells at Motherwell and Hibs before landing the Rangers job in 2001. In five years at Ibrox, McLeish won two SPL titles and five cups, his best season coming in 2002/03 when he led the 'Gers to the domestic treble. In 2007 he became Scotland manager but only stayed in the role for ten months before moving to St Andrews.

• As a tough central defender with Aberdeen, McLeish enjoyed huge success in the early 1980s while Alex Ferguson was in charge at Pittodrie. His impressive medal haul included three

Scottish league titles, five Scottish Cups and the European Cup-Winners' Cup in 1983.

• In an international career spanning 13 years, McLeish won 77 caps for Scotland – a total only surpassed by the legendary Kenny Dalglish and goalkeeper Jim Leighton.

MACCLESFIELD TOWN

Year founded: 1874
Ground: Moss Rose (6,335)
Nickname: The Silkmen
Biggest win: 6-0 v Stockport County (2005)
Heaviest defeat: 0-7 v Walsall (1997) and v Coventry City (1998)
Colours: Blue shirts, white shorts, blue socks

Previously a rugby union club, Macclesfield switched to football in 1874 but had to wait until 1997 before finally achieving league status.

• Under former Manchester United and Northern Ireland midfielder Sammy McIlroy the club were Conference champions in 1995 but were denied promotion as their Moss Rose ground failed to meet league requirements. Two years later, though, the Silkmen were admitted to the Football League in place of Hereford United after topping the Conference once again.

• Remarkably, the club were promoted to the third tier in their first season as a league club but dropped straight back down again the following year.

• During Euro 1996 eventual champions Germany used Moss Rose as a training base. One of the stars of that tournament for England, Paul Ince, later had two spells in charge of Macclesfield.

• In the 1933/34 season, when Macclesfield were playing in the Cheshire County League, striker Albert Valentine scored an incredible 83 goals for the Silkmen to set a club record that will surely never be beaten.

HONOURS
Conference champions 1995, 1997

PAOLO MALDINI

Born: Milan, 26th June 1968
Position: Defender
Club career:
1985-2009 AC Milan 647 (29)
International record:
1988-2002 Italy 126 (7)

Former AC Milan full back Paolo Maldini is Italy's second most capped player ever. A regular for the azzurri until his retirement from international football in 2002, he played for his country 126 times, captaining Italy a record 74 times.

• In 1994 Maldini was the first defender to be voted World Player of the Year, an honour he described as "a particular matter of pride because defenders generally receive so much less attention from fans and the media than goalscorers."

• Maldini played in eight Champions League finals (winning five of them) with Milan, equalling the record set by Real Madrid winger Francisco Gento in the 1960s. In the 2005 final against Liverpool he scored after just 51 seconds, to become both the fastest and oldest scorer in the history of Champions League finals.

• A loyal one-club man, Maldini also won seven league titles and one Coppa Italia with Milan. In 2005 he passed Dino Zoff's Serie A appearance record and, three years later, played his 1,000th senior game for club and country.

MANAGER OF THE YEAR

Manchester United boss Sir Alex Ferguson has won the FA Premier League Manager of the Year award a record nine times, once more than all the other winning managers put together. He also won the old Manager of the Year award in 1993, a total of ten triumphs.

• Arsene Wenger (in 1998, 2002 and 2004) and Jose Mourinho (2005 and 2006) are the only other managers to win the current award on more than one occasion since it was introduced in the 1993/94 season.

• Only two managers have won the award while in charge of a club which did not win the title that season: George Burley, who was honoured in 2001 after leading Ipswich to fifth place in the Premiership a year after winning promotion; and Harry Redknapp, who claimed top spot in 2010 after guiding Tottenham to fourth place.

• The most successful manager in the pre-Premiership era was Liverpool's Bob Paisley, who won six Manager of the Year awards between 1976-83.

MANCHESTER CITY

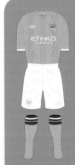

Year founded: 1887
Ground: City of Manchester Stadium (47,726)
Previous name: Ardwick
Nickname: The Citizens
Biggest win: 12-0 v Liverpool Stanley (1890)
Heaviest defeat: 1-9 v Everton (1906)
Colours: Sky blue shirts, white shorts, sky blue socks

City have their roots in a church team which was renamed Ardwick in 1887 and became founder members of the Second Division five years later. In 1894, after suffering financial difficulties, the club was reformed under its present name.

• Now owned by a company belonging to a member of the Abu Dhabi Royal Family, City are the richest club in the world. Their newfound spending power was underlined in September 2008 when they outbid Chelsea to buy Brazilian striker Robinho from Real Madrid for a British record fee of £32.5 million.

• Time will tell whether the club can buy success, but there's no doubt that a trophy can't come soon enough for City's long suffering fans who have watched their bitter rivals Manchester United gorge on silverware in the past two decades. City, meanwhile, have to go back to a 1976 victory in the League Cup for their last major triumph.

• The club, though, did enjoy a hugely successful era just a few years before that when a City team featuring the likes of Colin Bell, Francis Lee and Mike Summerbee won the league title (1968), the FA Cup (1969), the League Cup (1970) and the European Cup-Winners' Cup (also in 1970).

• City also won the league title in 1937. Incredibly, the following season they were relegated to the Second Division despite scoring more goals than any other side in the division. To this day they remain the only league champions to suffer the drop in the following campaign.

• Eric Brook, an ever-present in that initial title-winning season, is City's joint leading scorer (along with 1920s marksman Tommy Johnson) with 158 league goals between 1928-40. The club's record appearance maker is Alan Oakes, who turned out 564 times in the sky blue shirt between 1958-76.

• City have won the FA Cup four times and, in 1926, were the first club to reach the final and be relegated in the same season. A 1-0 defeat by Bolton at Wembley ensured a grim season ended on a depressing note.

• The 1957/58 season was more enjoyable, especially for fans who like goals, as City scored 104 times while conceding 100 – the first and only time this 'double century' has been achieved. At the other end of the scale, City managed to score just ten goals at home in the 2006/07 season, the lowest ever total by an English club.

• City have won the title for the second tier of English football a record seven times, most recently in 2002 when they returned to the Premiership under then manager Kevin Keegan. Four years earlier the club experienced their lowest ever moment when they dropped into the third tier for the first and only time in their history – the first European trophy winners to sink this low.

• The highest attendance ever at an English club ground, 84,569, saw City beat Stoke 1-0 at their old Maine Road stadium in the sixth round of the FA Cup in 1934.

• City's most famous supporters are Liam and Noel Gallagher of rock band Oasis, while boxer Ricky Hatton is also a devoted fan of the club.

IS THAT A FACT?
The only player to pull on the famous blue shirt of Italy more often than Paolo Maldini is Fabio Cannavaro, the azzurri's captain when they won the World Cup in 2006. After making his international debut in 1997 the Juventus defender went on to play 136 times for his country.

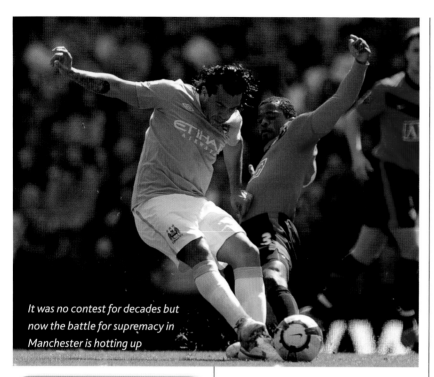

It was no contest for decades but now the battle for supremacy in Manchester is hotting up

HONOURS

Division 1 champions 1937, 1968
Division 2 champions 1899, 1903, 1910, 1928, 1947, 1966
First Division champions 2002
FA Cup 1904, 1934, 1956, 1969
League Cup 1970, 1976
European Cup Winners' Cup 1970

MANCHESTER UNITED

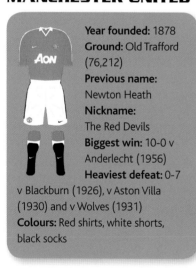

Year founded: 1878
Ground: Old Trafford (76,212)
Previous name: Newton Heath
Nickname: The Red Devils
Biggest win: 10-0 v Anderlecht (1956)
Heaviest defeat: 0-7 v Blackburn (1926), v Aston Villa (1930) and v Wolves (1931)
Colours: Red shirts, white shorts, black socks

The club was founded in 1878 as Newton Heath, a works team for employees of the Lancashire and Yorkshire Railway. In 1892 Newton Heath (who played in yellow-and-green-halved shirts) were elected to the Football League but a decade later went bankrupt, only to be immediately reformed as Manchester United with the help of a local brewer, John Davies.

• United are the most successful club in the history of English football, having won the league title 18 times (a record jointly held with Liverpool) and the FA Cup a record 11 times. The Red Devils have been the dominant force of the Premiership era, winning the title a record 11 times under long-serving manager Sir Alex Ferguson and never finishing outside the top three since the league was formed in 1992.

• United were the first English club to win the Double on three separate occasions, in 1994, 1996 and 1999. The last of these triumphs was particularly memorable as the club also went on to win the Champions League, beating Bayern Munich 2-1 in the final in Barcelona thanks to two late goals by Teddy Sheringham and Ole Gunner Solskjaer, to record English football's first ever Treble.

• **Under legendary manager Sir Matt Busby, who was in charge of the Red Devils for a record 24 years between 1945-69, United became the first ever English club to win the European Cup in 1968, when they beat Benfica 4-1 in the final at Wembley. Victory was especially sweet for Sir Matt who, a decade earlier, had narrowly survived the Munich air crash which claimed the lives of eight of his players as the team returned from a European Cup fixture in Belgrade. United also won European football's top club prize in 2008, beating Chelsea in the Champions League final on penalties in Moscow.**

• United won the FA Cup for the first time in 1909, beating Bristol City 1-0 in the final. The club's total of 18 appearances in the final (11 wins, seven defeats) is a record for the competition.

• **The club's history, though, has not always been glorious. The 1930s were a particularly grim decade for United, who were threatened with relegation to the old Third Division on the final day of the 1933/34 season. In a bid to change their luck United swapped their red shirts for cherry and white hoops for the first and only time, and beat Millwall 2-0 away to stay in the Second Division.**

• Old Trafford currently has the highest capacity of any club ground in Britain but, strangely, when United set an all-time Football League attendance record of 83,260 for their home game against Arsenal on 17th January 1948 they were playing at Maine Road, home of local rivals Manchester City. This was because Old Trafford was badly damaged by German bombs during the Second World War, forcing United to use their neighbours' ground in the immediate post-war period.

• **United's leading appearance maker is the evergreen Ryan Giggs, who has played in 838 games in all competitions for the club since making his debut in 1991. He is also the only player to have scored at least one goal in every Premier League season.**

• The club's highest goalscorer is Sir Bobby Charlton, who banged in 199 league goals for the club between 1956-73. Charlton is also United's most capped international, playing 106 times for England in an illustrious career.

• **United recorded the biggest ever victory in Premier League history on 4th March 1995 when they thrashed Ipswich 9-0 at Old Trafford, with striker Andy Cole scoring five of the goals to set another Premiership record.**

• In the last of a record-equalling three consecutive title-winning campaigns, in 2008/09, United went a record 14 league games (a total of 1,334 minutes) without conceding a single goal.

• **Known for many years as a big-spending club, United's record signing is Bulgarian international striker Dimitar Berbatov, who cost £30.75 million when he moved from Tottenham in 2008. The club's most expensive sale is former Old Trafford**

hero Cristiano Ronaldo, who joined Real Madrid for a world record £80 million in 2009.

• One of the most widely supported clubs around the world, United are followed by a host of celebrity fans including actor Steve Coogan (aka Alan Partridge), Simply Red singer Mick Hucknall and broadcaster Eamonn Holmes.

HONOURS

Division 1 champions 1908, 1911, 1952, 1956, 1957, 1965, 1967
Premier League champions 1993, 1994, 1996, 1997, 1999, 2000, 2001, 2003, 2007, 2008, 2009
Division 2 champions 1936, 1975
FA Cup 1909, 1948, 1963, 1977, 1983, 1985, 1990, 1994, 1996, 1999, 2004
League Cup 1992, 2006, 2009, 2010
European Cup/Champions League 1968, 1999, 2008
European Cup Winners' Cup 1991
European Super Cup 1991
World Club Cup 1999, 2008

ROBERTO MANCINI

Born: Jesi, Italy, 27th November 1964
Managerial career:
2001-02 Fiorentina
2002-04 Lazio
2004-08 Inter Milan
2009- Manchester City

Only the second foreigner to manage Manchester City, Roberto Mancini replaced Mark Hughes in the Eastlands hotseat in December 2009. The Italian's main priority was to help his new club qualify for the Champions League, but he failed to achieve his goal after City were narrowly pipped for fourth place in the Premier League by Tottenham.

• Mancini began his managerial career at cash-strapped Fiorentina, who he led to the Coppa Italia before moving to Lazio in 2002. He won another Coppa Italia with the Rome club, but after two years moved on to Inter Milan.

• During a four-year stint at the San Siro, Mancini turned Inter into the dominant force in Italian football. His team were awarded the 2006 Serie A title after Juventus were stripped of the honour, but the following season Inter won the championship in some style, winning an Italian record 17 consecutive league games at one stage and ending the campaign with a record 97 points – an amazing 22 points ahead of runners-up Roma. A third title followed in 2008 but Mancini's incredible domestic success was counterbalanced by repeated failures in the Champions League and he was sacked at the end of the season.

• An intelligent striker in his playing days, Mancini won the Scudetto and the Cup-Winners' Cup with both Sampdoria and Lazio and played 36 times for Italy. He also enjoyed a brief spell in the Premier League with Leicester City in 2001 before moving into management.

"Look, if you don't do well I'll just go and buy a completely new team."

DIEGO MARADONA

Born: Buenos Aires, 30th October 1960
Position: Striker/midfielder
Club career:
1976-80 Argentinos Juniors 167 (115)
1980-82 Boca Juniors 40 (28)
1982-84 Barcelona 36 (22)
1984-91 Napoli 186 (83)
1992-93 Sevilla 25 (4)
1995-97 Boca Juniors 29 (7)
International record:
1977-94 Argentina 91 (34)

The best player in the world in the 1980s, Diego Maradona is considered by many to be the greatest footballer ever.

• During his career in his native Argentina, then in Spain and Italy, he smashed three transfer records. First, his £1 million move from Argentinos Juniors to Boca Juniors in 1980 was a world record for a teenager. Then he broke the world transfer record when he joined Barcelona from Boca for £4.2 million in 1982, and again when he signed for Napoli for £6.9 million in 1984.

• A superb dribbler who used his low centre of gravity to great effect, Maradona was almost impossible to mark. He was idolised at Napoli, who he led to a first ever Italian title in 1987 and a first European trophy two years later, when they won the UEFA Cup.

• He made his international debut aged 16 in 1977 and went on to play at four World Cups, captaining his country in a record 16 games at the finals. His greatest triumph came in 1986 when, after scoring the goals that beat England (including the infamous 'Hand of God' goal which he punched into the net) and Belgium in the quarter and semi-finals, he skippered Argentina to victory in the final against West Germany.

Diego Maradona runs rings round the England defence in 1986, this time without using his hand

He also led his side to the 1990 final against the same opponents.

• However, Maradona's international career ended in disgrace when he was thrown out of the 1994 World Cup in the USA after failing a drugs test. He had previously been hit with a worldwide 15-month ban from football in 1991 after testing positive for cocaine.

• Despite these blots on his reputation, Maradona was voted 'The Player of the Century' by more than half of those who took part in a worldwide FIFA internet poll in 2000. In 2008 he became head coach of Argentina, but resigned two years later after his side were thrashed 4-0 by Germany in the World Cup quarter-finals.

TOP 10

WORLD PLAYERS OF THE CENTURY*

1. Diego Maradona (Argentina, 1977-94) 53.60%
2. Pele (Brazil, 1957-71) 18.53%
3. Eusebio (Portugal, 1961-73) 6.21%
4. Roberto Baggio (Italy, 1988-2004) 5.42%
5. Romario (Brazil, 1987-2005) 1.69%
6. Marco van Basten (Holland, 1983-92) 1.57%
7. Ronaldo (Brazil, 1994-2006) 1.55%
8. Franz Beckenbauer (West Germany, 1965-77) 1.50%
9. Zinedine Zidane (France, 1994-2006) 1.34%
10. Rivaldo (Brazil, 1993-2003) 1.19%

* As selected in a 2000 poll on www.fifa.com

MARSEILLE

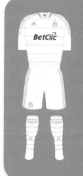

Year founded: 1899
Ground: Stade Velodrome (60,031)
Nickname: l'OM
Colours: White shirts with light blue trim, white shorts, white socks

Olympique de Marseille were formed as a multisports club in 1899 but only began playing football three years later thanks to the influence of expats from Germany and England.

• Marseille's greatest moment came in 1993 when they beat favourites AC Milan in the European Cup final to become the first ever French club to win a European trophy. However, the celebrations turned sour when it later emerged that Marseille had fixed a vital league match against Valenciennes to ensure their players were fresh for the final a few days later. As a result of the scandal Marseille were expelled from the European Cup the following season – the first time the holders had not defended their trophy.

• The club were also stripped of their 1993 French title and relegated to the Second Division as an additional punishment. After winning five French titles on the trot between 1989-93, Marseille's glory days had ended in ignominy. The club soon returned to the top flight, but had to wait until 2010 before winning the French title for a record-equalling tenth time.

• In 1988 Marseille splashed out £4.5 million for Tottenham winger Chris Waddle, then a record British fee. Two years later they smashed the Scottish transfer record, signing midfielder Trevor Steven from Rangers for £5 million.

HONOURS
French title 1937, 1948, 1971, 1972, 1989, 1990, 1991, 1992, 1993 (withdrawn), 2010
French Cup 1924, 1926, 1927, 1935, 1938, 1943, 1969, 1972, 1976, 1989
European Cup 1993

"If that Goldilocks has eaten my porridge again I'll be furious," says Bayern Munich mascot Bertil

MASCOTS

In one of the most bizarre football sights ever, Wolves mascot Wolfie traded punches with his Bristol City counterpart City Cat during a half-time penalty shoot-out competition at Ashton Gate in 2002. City Cat, who was backed up by three little piggies representing a local company, got the better of the fracas which had to be broken up by stewards.

• **Bury mascot Robbie the Bobby – who, ironically, has the appearance of a policeman – was sent off from the touchline three times in as many months in 2001. Two of his dismissals were for over-exuberant goal celebrations, while the third was for fighting with Cardiff City mascot, Barclay the Bluebird.**

• In 2008 Fulham's Billy the Badger mascot was sent off by referee Chris Foy during the Cottagers' 2-1 home defeat of Aston Villa after his dancing antics delayed the start of the second half.

• **The first World Cup mascot, a Union Jack-draped lion called World**

Cup Willie, was designed for the 1966 tournament in England. The most recent mascot, for the 2010 tournament in South Africa, was Zakumi, a green-haired lion.

MATCH-FIXING

The first recorded incidence of match-fixing occurred in 1900 when Jack Hillman, goalkeeper with relegation-threatened Burnley, was alleged to have offered a bribe to the Nottingham Forest captain. Hillman was found guilty of the charges by a joint Football Association and Football League commission and banned for one year.

• **Nine players received bans after Manchester United beat Liverpool at Old Trafford in April 1915. A Liverpool player later admitted the result had been fixed in a Manchester pub before the match. For his part in the scandal, United's Enoch West was banned for life – although the punishment was later waived... when West was 62!**

• In the mid-1960s English football was rocked by a match-fixing scandal when former Everton player Jimmy Gauld revealed in a newspaper interview that a number of games had been rigged as part of a betting coup. Gauld implicated three Sheffield Wednesday players in the scam, including England internationals Tony Kay and Peter Swan. The trio were later sentenced to four months in prison and banned for life from football. Ringleader Gauld fared even worse, receiving a four-year prison term.

• **In 1978 World Cup hosts Argentina needed to beat Peru by four clear**

goals to reach the final of the competition. It has been alleged (though never proved) that the Argentinian military junta offered the Peruvian government 35,000 tonnes of free grain and the unfreezing of $50 million in credits for their team to play below par. Argentina cruised to a 6-0 victory and went on to win the tournament.

• In 2005 German referee Robert Hoyzer was jailed for more than two years after admitting fixing, or trying to fix, nine matches. He told the court that after fixing a German Cup game by awarding two dubious penalties, a Croatian organised crime syndicate gave him more than £46,000 and a flat-screen television

SIR STANLEY MATTHEWS

Born: Stoke, 1st February 1915
Died: 23rd February 2000
Position: Winger
Club career:
1932-47 Stoke City 259 (51)
1947-61 Blackpool 379 (17)
1961-65 Stoke City 59 (3)
International record:
1934-57 England 54 (11)

Nicknamed 'the Wizard of the Dribble' for his magnificent skills on the ball, Stanley Matthews was one of the greatest footballers of all time. His club career spanned a record 33 years and, incredibly, he played his last game in the First Division for Stoke City five days after his 50th birthday. He remains the oldest player to appear in the top flight.

• **Matthews' England career was almost as lengthy, his 54 appearances for his country spanning 23 years between 1934-57. He made his last appearance for the Three Lions at the age of 42, setting another record.**

• A brilliant winger who possessed superb close control, Matthews inspired Blackpool to victory in the 1953 FA Cup final after the Seasiders came back from 3-1 down to beat Bolton 4-3. Despite a hat-trick by his team-mate Stan Mortensen, the match is remembered as 'the Matthews final'. He had never won an FA Cup winners' medal before and the whole country (outside of Bolton) was willing Matthews to succeed.

• **The first player to be voted Footballer of the Year (in 1948) and European Footballer of the Year**

IS THAT A FACT?
The Mascot Grand National, an annual race over hurdles between football and other sporting mascots, has been held at Huntingdon Racecourse since 1999. The first winner was Birmingham's Beau Brummie Bulldog, while Oldham's Chaddy the Owl was the first mascot to retain the title.

As the name suggests, the 1953 'Matthews final' was all about one man...and it wasn't Bolton's number five!

(another first in 1956), Matthews was knighted in 1965 – the only footballer to be so honoured while still playing. When he died in 2000 more than 100,000 people lined the streets of Stoke to pay tribute to one of the true legends of world football.

LIONEL MESSI

Born: Rosario, Argentina, 24th June 1987
Position: Winger
Club career:
2004- Barcelona 144 (88)
International record:
2005- Argentina 49 (13)

Rated by many as the best player in the world, Lionel Messi has attracted headlines around the globe since making his debut for Barcelona as a 17-year-old in 2004.

• Life, though, could have been very different for Messi, who suffered from a growth hormone deficiency as a child in Argentina. However, his outrageous talent was such that Barcelona were prepared to move him and his family to Europe when he was aged just 13 and pay for his medical treatment.

• Putting these problems behind him, he has flourished to the extent that in 2009 he was named both World Player of the Year and European Player of the Year, a year after being runner-up in both polls. A brilliant dribbler who can bamboozle the most experienced of defenders with his ball skills, Messi helped Barcelona win the domestic double and the Champions League in 2008/09. The following year was his most prolific in front of goal yet, his 34 league strikes winning him the European Golden Boot.

• Messi made his international debut in 2005 but it was a forgettable occasion – he was sent off after just 40 seconds for elbowing a Hungarian defender who was pulling his shirt. Happier times followed in 2007 when he was voted Player of the Tournament at the Copa America and in 2008 when he won a gold medal with the Argentine football team at the Beijing Olympics. At the 2010 World Cup in South Africa Messi produced some thrilling displays, but he failed to score a single goal and was left in tears after Argentina's 4-0 thrashing by Germany at the quarter-final stage.

• The legendary Diego Maradona has hailed Messi as his true successor, saying, "He has something different to any other player in the world."

MIDDLESBROUGH

Year founded: 1876
Ground: Riverside Stadium (35,100)
Nickname: Boro
Biggest win: 11-0 v Scarborough (1890)
Heaviest defeat: 0-9 v Blackburn Rovers (1954)
Colours: Red shirts with white trim, white shorts, red socks

Founded by members of the Middlesbrough Cricket Club at the Albert Park Hotel in 1876, the club turned professional in 1889 before reverting to amateur status three years later. Winners of the FA Amateur Cup in both 1895 and 1898, the club turned pro for a second time in 1899 and was elected to the Football League in the same year.

• **In 1905 Middlesbrough became the first club to sign a player for a four-figure transfer fee when they forked out £1,000 for Sunderland and England striker Alf Common. On his Boro debut Common paid back some of the fee by scoring the winner at Sheffield United… the Teesiders' first away win for two years!**

• The club had to wait over a century before winning a major trophy but finally broke their duck in 2004 with a 2-1 victory over Bolton in the League Cup final at the Millennium Stadium, Cardiff.

• **Two years later Middlesbrough reached the UEFA Cup final, after twice overturning three goal deficits earlier in the competition. There was no happy ending, though, as Boro' were thrashed 4-0 by Sevilla in the final in Eindhoven.**

• In 1997 the club were deducted three points by the FA for calling off a Premier League fixture at Blackburn at short notice after illness and injury ravaged their squad. The penalty resulted in Boro being relegated from the Premier League at the end of the season. To add to their supporters' disappointment the club was also beaten in the finals of the League Cup and FA Cup in the same campaign.

• **The lowest moment in Middlesbrough's history, though, came in the summer of 1986 when a financial crisis led to the club almost being wound up. At the last minute a consortium led by current chairman Steve Gibson stepped in to save the club from bankruptcy.**

• In 1926/27 striker George Camsell hit an astonishing 59 league goals, including a record nine hat-tricks, for Boro as the club won the Second Division championship. His tally set a new Football League record and, although it was beaten by Everton's Dixie Dean the following season, Camsell still holds the divisional record. An ex-miner, Camsell went on to score a club record 325 league goals for Boro and also notched an impressive 18 goals in just nine appearances for England.

• **Tim Williamson is the club's longest-serving player, appearing in 563 league games between 1902-23. A goalkeeper, Williamson also scored two goals for Boro, both strikes coming from the penalty spot.**

HONOURS
Division 2 champions 1927, 1929, 1974
First Division champions 1995
League Cup 2006

JACKIE MILBURN

Born: Ashington, 11th May 1924
Died: 9th October 1988
Position: Striker
Club career:
1946-57 Newcastle United 353 (177)
1957-60 Linfield 54 (68)
International record:
1948-55 England 13 (10)

One of the greatest players in Newcastle's history, 'Wor' Jackie Milburn was the star of the Magpies team which enjoyed a trio of FA Cup triumphs in the 1950s.

• **In 1951 Milburn scored in every round of the cup, including two goals in the final against Blackpool, and in 1955 he scored the then fastest goal in a Cup Final, after just 45 seconds, to help Newcastle record a 3-1 win over Manchester City.**

• In all, he scored 200 goals for the Toon, a club record until another Gallowgate hero, Alan Shearer, set a new benchmark of 206 goals in 2006.

• **An uncle of Bobby and Jack Charlton, Milburn left Newcastle to become player/coach of Linfield in 1957. He later had a brief spell in charge of Ipswich before becoming a sports journalist.**

• When Milburn died from lung cancer in 1988, 30,000 people attended his funeral. A genuine Geordie legend, he is commemorated by a bronze statue in the centre of Newcastle and has a stand named after him at St James' Park.

Toon legend Jackie Milburn scored 200 goals for the Magpies

ROGER MILLA

Born: Yaounde, Cameroon,
20th May 1952
Position: Striker
Club career:
1965-70 Éclair de Douala 61 (6)
1971-74 Leopard de Douala 117 (89)
1974-77 Tonerre Yaounde 87 (69)
1977-79 Valenciennes 28 (6)
1979-80 Monaco 17 (2)
1980-84 Bastia 113 (35)
1984-86 St Etienne 59 (31)
1986-89 Montpellier 95 (37)
1989-90 JS Saint-Pierroise
1990-94 Tonerre Yaounde 117 (89)
1994-96 Pelita Jaya 23 (23)
International record:
1978-94 Cameroon 102 (28)

The oldest player ever to appear at the World Cup finals, Roger Milla was 42 when he appeared for Cameroon at the 1994 tournament in the USA. In his side's final match he scored a consolation goal in a 6-1 defeat by Russia to become the oldest player ever to score at the World Cup.

• Remarkably, the record Milla broke was his own, as he had previously scored no fewer than four goals at the 1990 tournament in Italy. Celebrating his goals with a dance around the corner flag, Milla started a craze that was copied all over the world.

• In the same year Milla was named African Footballer of the Year, becoming the first player to win the award twice – his previous honour had come way back in 1976.

• Milla played much of his club football in France, winning the French Cup with Monaco in 1980 and again with Bastia the following year.

MILLWALL

Year founded: 1885
Ground: The New Den (20,146)
Previous name:
Millwall Rovers
Nickname: The Lions
Biggest win: 9-1 v Torquay (1927) and v Coventry (1927)
Heaviest defeat: 1-9 v Aston Villa (1946)
Colours: Blue shirts, blue shorts, white socks

The Millwall Lions are roaring again!

The club was founded as Millwall Rovers in 1885 by workers at local jam and marmalade factory, Morton and Co. In 1920 they joined the Third Division, gaining a reputation as a club with some of the most fiercely partisan fans in the country.

• In 1988 Millwall won the Second Division title to gain promotion to the top flight for the first time in their history. The Lions enjoyed a few brief weeks at the top of the league pyramid in the autumn of 1988 but were brought back to earth with a bump when they were relegated two years later.

• The club's greatest moment, though, came in 2004 when they reached their first FA Cup final. Despite losing 3-0 to Manchester United, the Lions made history by becoming the first club from outside the top flight to contest the final in the Premiership era. The following season Millwall made a first foray into Europe, but were beaten by Hungarian champions Ferencvaros in the first round of the UEFA Cup.

• In 2006, however, Millwall suffered a major blow when they were relegated from the Championship. The club had to wait until 2010 before returning to the second tier, courtesy of a goal by defender Paul Robinson in the League One play-off final against Swindon Town.

• Neil Harris is the club's all-time leading scorer after passing Teddy Sheringham's record of 111 goals for the Lions in a 3-2 win at Crewe in January 2009. Harris has since taken his goals tally to 135.

• Hardman defender Barry Kitchener has made more appearances for Millwall than any other player, turning out in 602 games in all competitions between 1967-82.

• On their way to winning the Division Three (South) championship in 1928 Millwall scored 87 goals at home, an all-time Football League record.

• In 1974 Millwall hosted the first league match to be played on a Sunday. To get around the law at the time, admission for the Lions' game with Fulham was by 'programme only' – the cost of the programme being the same as a match ticket.

HONOURS
Division 2 champions 1988
Division 3 (S) champions 1928, 1938
Second Division champions 2001
Division 4 champions 1962

TOP 10

LEAGUE GOALS IN A SEASON

1. Peterborough United, 134 goals (Division 4, 1960/61)
2. Bradford City, 128 goals (Division 3 North, 1928/29)
   Aston Villa, 128 goals (Division 1, 1930/31)
4. Millwall, 127 goals (Division 3 South, 1927/28)
   Arsenal, 127 goals (Division 1, 1930/31)
6. Doncaster Rovers, 123 goals (Division 3 North, 1946/47)
7. Middlesbrough, 122 goals (Division 2, 1926/27)
8. Everton, 121 goals (Division 2, 1930/31)
   Lincoln City, 121 goals (Division 3 North, 1951/52)
10. Chester, 119 goals (Division 4, 1964/65)

JAMES MILNER

Born: Leeds, 4th January 1986
Position: Midfield
Club career:
2002-04 Leeds United 48 (5)
2003 Swindon Town (loan) 6 (2)
2004-08 Newcastle United 94 (6)
2005-06 Aston Villa (loan) 27 (1)
2008- Aston Villa 72 (10)
2010- Manchester City
International record:
2009- England 11 (0))

A versatile player who can play on the wing, in midfield or at full back, James Milner came through the ranks at Leeds to make his debut as a 16-year-old in 2002. When he scored his first goal for the club, in a 2-1 victory over Sunderland on Boxing Day that year, he became the youngest ever scorer in the Premier League, although his record was beaten by Everton's James Vaughan three years later.

• In 2004 Milner moved from cash-strapped Leeds to Newcastle for £3.6 million. The following year he teamed up again with his old Leeds manager David O'Leary when he went on loan to Aston Villa. He returned to St James's Park in 2006 before making a permanent move to Villa Park two years later. In August 2010 he moved to Manchester City.

• Between 2004-09 Milner made a record 46 appearances for the England Under-21 team and was a member of the team which reached the 2009 Under-21 European Championship final, only to be thrashed 4-0 by Germany.

• PFA Young Player of the Year in 2010, Milner made his full England debut as a sub in a friendly against Holland in 2009. He made an excellent start to his international career, too, setting up Jermain Defoe's equaliser in a 2-2 draw with a trademark low cross from the wing. At the 2010 World Cup finals in South Africa Milner played a key role in the one major highlight of England's dismal campaign, drilling over the cross from which Jermain Defoe scored the winner against Slovenia.

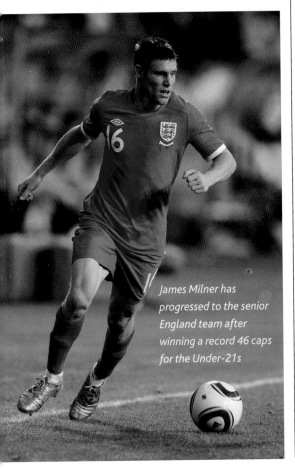

James Milner has progressed to the senior England team after winning a record 46 caps for the Under-21s

MILTON KEYNES DONS

Year founded: 2004
Ground: stadium:mk (22,000)
Nickname: The Dons
Biggest win: 5-0 v Accrington (2007)
Heaviest defeat: 0-5 v Hartlepool (2005), v Huddersfield (2006), v Tottenham (2006) and v Rochdale (2007)
Colours: White shirts, white shorts, white socks with black trim

The club was effectively formed in 2004 when Wimbledon FC were controversially allowed to re-locate to Milton Keynes on the ruling of a three-man FA commission despite the opposition of the club's supporters, the Football League and the FA.

• Despite pledging to Wimbledon fans that they would not change their name, badge or colours, within a few seasons all three of these things had happened, reinforcing the impression amongst many in the game that the MK Dons are English football's first 'franchise'.

• The MK Dons have since handed back to Merton Council all the honours and trophies won by Wimbledon FC and claimed by AFC Wimbledon, the club started up by angry Wimbledon supporters which was promoted to the Conference Premier in 2009 despite the claim by the FA Commission that the creation of such a team would "not be in the wider interests of football".

• The MK Dons won their first trophy in 2008 when, under then manager Paul Ince, they beat Grimsby Town 2-0 in the Football League Trophy final at Wembley. Later that season they lifted the League Two title to earn their first promotion.

• In 2009, to the surprise of many, stadium:mk was named as a venue for the 2018 World Cup in the event of England's bid to host the finals proving successful.

BOBBY MOORE

Born: Barking, 12th April 1941
Died: 24th February 1993
Position: Defender
Club career:
1958-74 West Ham United 544 (22)
1974-77 Fulham 124 (1)
1976 San Antonio Thunder 24 (1)
1978 Seattle Sounders 7 (0)
International record:
1962-73 England 108 (2)

The first and only Englishman to lift the World Cup, Bobby Moore captained England on 90 occasions – a record shared with Billy Wright.

• Moore's total of 108 caps was a record until it was surpassed by Peter Shilton in 1989, but he was England's most capped outfield player until David Beckham passed him in 2009.

• At club level, Moore won the FA Cup with West Ham in 1964 and the European Cup-Winners' Cup the following year. Then, in 1966, he made it a Wembley treble when England beat West Germany in the World Cup final. England boss Sir Alf Ramsey later paid tribute to his skipper and most reliable defender, saying, "He was the supreme professional. Without him England would never have won the World Cup."

• In the same year Moore was voted the BBC Sports Personality of the Year – the first footballer to win the honour.

• The world of football mourned Moore's death when he died of cancer in 1993, but he has not been forgotten. A decade later he was selected by the FA as England's 'Golden Player' of the previous 50 years and, in 2007, a huge bronze statue of England's greatest captain was unveiled outside the new Wembley.

Bobby Moore, West Ham's (and England's) greatest ever captain

MORECAMBE

Year founded: 1920
Ground: Globe Arena (6,476)
Nickname: The Shrimps
Biggest win: 8-0 v Fleetwood Town (1993)
Heaviest defeat: 0-7 v Leek Town (1998)
Colours: Red shirts, white shorts, red socks

Founded in 1920 after a meeting at the local West View Hotel, Morecambe joined the Lancashire Combination League that same year and subsequently spent the next 87 years in non-league football.

• **The greatest moment in the club's history came in 2007 when The Shrimps beat Exeter 2-1 in the Conference play-off final at Wembley to win promotion to the Football League.**

• Morecambe's first outing in the League Cup in 2007 saw them pull off a major shock when they beat Championship outfit Preston 2-1 at Deepdale. The Shrimps then knocked out Wolves before

crashing out to Sheffield United, who beat them 5-0 in the third round.

• **In 2010 Morecambe reached the League Two play-offs, but a 6-0 hammering by Dagenham and Redbridge – the biggest ever play-off defeat – in the first leg of the semi-final ended their promotion hopes.**

MOTHERWELL

Year founded: 1886
Ground: Fir Park (13,742)
Nickname: The Well
Biggest win: 12-1 v Dundee United (1954)
Heaviest defeat: 0-8 v Aberdeen (1979)
Colours: Amber shirts with claret hoop, claret shorts, claret socks

Motherwell were founded in 1886 following the merger of two local factory-based sides, Alpha and Glencairn. The club turned pro in 1893 and, in the same year, joined the newly-formed Scottish Second Division.

• **The club enjoyed its heyday in the 1930s, winning the league title for the first and only time in 1932 and finishing as runners-up in the Scottish Cup three times in the same decade.**

• Striker Willie McFadyen scored a remarkable 52 league goals for The Well when they won the title in 1931/32, a Scottish top flight record that still stands today. The club's all-time leading scorer, though, is Hugh Ferguson, who notched 284 goals between 1916-25.

• **Motherwell had to wait until 1952 before they won the Scottish Cup for the first time, and they did it in some style thrashing Dundee 4-0 in the final. Another success followed in 1991, The Well beating Dundee United 4-3 in an exciting final.**

• Scottish international striker John Spencer is the most expensive player to arrive at Fir Park, costing £500,000 when he joined the club from Everton in 1999. Five years earlier Motherwell received a club record £1.75 million when they sold Phil O'Donnell to Celtic. O'Donnell later returned to Fir Park but, tragically, died after collapsing on the pitch during a match against Dundee United in January 2007.

HONOURS
Division 1 champions 1932
First Division champions 1982, 1985
Division 2 champions 1954, 1969
Scottish Cup 1952, 1991
League Cup 1951

JOHN MOTSON

Born: Salford, 7th October 1945

John Motson has commentated on a record 29 FA Cup finals for the BBC, a figure that rises to 34 when replays are included.

• **His first final was the 1977 clash between Manchester United and Liverpool. Aged 31 at the time, Motson was the youngest man ever to commentate on an FA Cup final.**

• Five years earlier his commentary career had been launched by non-league Hereford's dramatic 2-1 victory over Newcastle in an FA Cup third round replay. "I was very lucky indeed to tumble on to such a phenomenal and famous match in my first season as a commentator on *Match of the Day*", Motson later admitted.

• **Famed for his sheepskin coats and well-stocked store of football facts, 'Motty' also covered 18 World Cups and European Championships before retiring from international football commentary in 2008.**

• Classic Motson quotes include "For those of you watching in black and white, Spurs are playing in yellow", "Steve Bruce has got the taste for Wembley in his nostrils" and, after Greece's surprise triumph at Euro 2004, "This is the biggest thing that's happened in Athens since Homer put down his pen!"

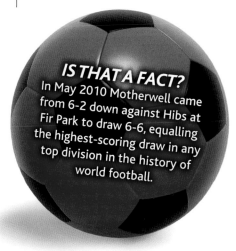

IS THAT A FACT?
In May 2010 Motherwell came from 6-2 down against Hibs at Fir Park to draw 6-6, equalling the highest-scoring draw in any top division in the history of world football.

JOSE MOURINHO

Born: Setubal, Portugal,
26th January 1963
Managerial career:
2000 Benfica
2001-02 Uniao Leiria
2002-04 Porto
2004-07 Chelsea
2008-10 Inter Milan
2010- Real Madrid

Outspoken manager Jose Mourinho is Chelsea's most successful boss ever, leading the Blues to five major trophies in a three-year spell at Stamford Bridge before sensationally leaving the club in 2007 after falling out with owner Roman Abramovich.

• Mourinho started out as Bobby Robson's assistant at Sporting Lisbon, Porto and Barcelona before briefly managing Benfica in 2000. Two years later he returned to Porto, where he won two Portuguese league titles and the UEFA Cup before becoming Europe's most sought after young manager when his well-drilled side claimed the Champions League trophy in 2004.

• Shortly after this triumph, Mourinho

Jose Mourinho: He may be 'The Special One' but some of his dance moves are a bit dodgy!

replaced Claudio Ranieri as Chelsea manager, styling himself as a "Special One" in his first press conference. He certainly lived up to his billing, as his expensively-assembled Blues team won back-to-back Premiership titles in 2005 and 2006, the FA Cup in 2007 and the League Cup in both 2005 and 2007.

• Often embroiled in controversy, Mourinho was fined a record £200,000 (later reduced to £75,000 on appeal) in 2005 for breaking Premier League rules by secretly meeting Arsenal defender Ashley Cole to talk about a possible move to Chelsea.

• A year after quitting Chelsea, Mourinho took charge of Italian giants Inter Milan. In his first season at the San Siro he underlined his reputation as one of the world's top coaches by leading Inter to the Serie A title. The following year he did even better, guiding Inter to a treble which included the Champions League, before leaving the San Siro to take over the reins at Real Madrid.

DAVID MOYES

Born: Glasgow, 25th April 1963
Managerial career:
1998-2002 Preston North End
2002- Everton

Having joined Everton in 2002 as successor to fellow Scot Walter Smith, David Moyes is now the third longest-serving Premiership manager behind Arsene Wenger and Sir Alex Ferguson.

• Moyes' first managerial job was at Preston who he led to the Division Two (now League One) title in 2000. The following year North End almost made it into the Premiership, but lost out to Bolton in the play-off final.

• In his first season in charge at Goodison Park in 2002/03, Moyes was voted the League Managers' Association Manager of the Year after guiding the Toffees to a creditable seventh place in the Premiership. Two years later he won the award again after Everton finished fourth, one place ahead of deadly rivals Liverpool, and qualified for the preliminary stage of the Champions League.

• A journeyman centre half in his playing days, Moyes won a championship medal with Celtic in 1982 and later played for a number of clubs, including Bristol City, Dunfermline and Preston.

GERD MULLER

Born: Nordlingen, Germany,
3rd November 1945
Position: Striker
Club career:
1963-64 TVS Nordlingen 32 (51)
1964-79 Bayern Munich 427 (365)
1979-81 Fort Lauderdale Strikers 80 (40)
International record:
1966-74 West Germany 62 (68)

Gerd 'der Bomber' Muller is Germany's most prolific goalscorer with a record of 68 goals in just 62 internationals.

• 14 of those goals came at the World Cup, an all-time record for the tournament until his total was passed by Brazil's Ronaldo in 2006.

• A deadly poacher inside the penalty box, Muller won an impressive haul of medals during his glittering career, including the 1972 European Championships, the World Cup in 1974 and an amazing hat-trick of European Cups with Bayern Munich between 1974-76. He was also voted European Footballer of the Year in 1970.

• Twice winner of the European Golden Boot, Muller scored a record 365 goals in the Bundesliga.

TOP 10

LEADING WORLD CUP GOALSCORERS

1.	Ronaldo (Brazil, 1998-2006)	15
2.	Gerd Muller (West Germany, 1970-74)	14
	Miroslav Klose (Germany, 2002-10)	14
4.	Just Fontaine (France, 1954-58)	13
5.	Pele (Brazil, 1958-70)	12
6.	Sandor Kocsis (Hungary, 1954)	11
	Jurgen Klinsmann (Germany, 1990-98)	11
8.	Helmut Rahn (West Germany, 1954-58)	10
	Teofilio Cubillas (Peru, 1970-82)	10
	Grzegorz Lato (Poland, 1974-82)	10
	Gary Lineker (England, 1986-90)	10
	Gabriel Batistuta (Argentina, 1994-2002)	10

NEWCASTLE UNITED

Year founded: 1892
Ground: St James's Park (52,387)
Nickname: The Magpies
Biggest win: 13-0 v Newport County (1946)
Heaviest defeat: 0-9 v Burton Wanderers (1895)
Colours: Black-and-white-striped shirts, black shorts, black socks

The club was founded in 1892 following the merger of local sides Newcastle East End and Newcastle West End, gaining election to the Football League just a year later.

• In 1895 Newcastle suffered their worst ever defeat, going down 9-0 to Burton Wanderers in a Second Division match. The Magpies recorded their best ever win in 1946, thrashing Newport County 13-0 to equal Stockport County's record for the biggest ever victory in a Football League match. Star of the show at St James' Park was Len Shackleton, who scored six of the goals on his Newcastle debut to set a club record.

• Newcastle have a proud tradition in the FA Cup, having won the competition on six occasions. In 1908 the Magpies reached the final after smashing Fulham 6-0, the biggest ever win in the semi-final. Then, in 1924, 41-year-old defender Billy Hampson became the oldest player ever to appear in the Cup Final, when he turned out for the Toon in their 2-0 defeat of Aston Villa at Wembley.

• The club's best cup era was in the 1950s when they won the trophy three times. Legendary centre forward Jackie Milburn was instrumental to Newcastle's success, scoring in every round in 1951 and then notching after just 45 seconds in the 1955 final against Manchester City... the fastest Wembley cup final goal ever until Roberto di Matteo scored for Chelsea after 43 seconds in 1997.

• Milburn is the club's leading goalscorer in league matches with 178 strikes between 1946-57. However, Alan Shearer holds the overall club goalscoring record, finding the net 206 times in all competitions after his then world record £15 million move from Blackburn Rovers in 1996. Another famous Newcastle centre forward, Hughie Gallagher, scored a record 36 goals in the 1926/27 season to help the Magpies win the last of their four league titles.

• The club's leading appearance maker is goalkeeper Jimmy Lawrence, who featured in 432 league games between 1904-21. Another goalkeeper, Shay Given, is easily Newcastle's most honoured international with 83 caps for the Republic of Ireland between 1997-2009.

• Newcastle supporters have not had much to cheer about in recent years, their team having failed to win a major trophy since 1969. That was the Fairs Cup, the Magpies beating Hungarian side Ujpest Dozsa 6-2 on aggregate in a two-legged final.

• The mid-1990s, though, promised much. A swashbuckling side managed by Toon legend Kevin Keegan swept to the new First Division title in 1993 before emerging as Premiership title contenders in the 1995/96 season. At one stage during that campaign Newcastle held a 12-point lead over eventual winners Manchester United but they were unable to hold their advantage and ultimately finished in second place.

• Michael Owen is Newcastle's most expensive player, joining the club from Real Madrid for £16 million in 2005. A year earlier the Magpies made their record sale to the same club, Jonathan Woodgate moving to Spain for £13.67 million.

• Relegated from the Premier League in 2009, Newcastle bounced back the following season under manager Chris Hughton with a mammoth total of 102 points – only four short of the all-time Football League record set by Reading in 2005/06.

• Newcastle are followed by an army of devoted fans who include TV presenters Ant and Dec, former Prime Minister Tony Blair and eccentric racing pundit John McCririck.

There was no way that anyone was going to pinch the FA Cup trophy from Newcastle captain Frank Hudspeth in 1924

HONOURS
Division 1 champions 1905, 1907, 1909, 1927
Division 2 champions 1965
First Division champions 1993
Championship champions 2010
FA Cup 1910, 1924, 1932, 1951, 1952, 1955
Fairs Cup 1969

BILL NICHOLSON

Born: Scarborough,
26th January 1919
Died: 23rd October 2004
Managerial career:
1958-74 Tottenham Hotspur

Legendary Tottenham boss Bill Nicholson was the first manager to win the Double in the 20th century, steering Spurs to the League Championship and FA Cup in 1961.

• **Two years later he became the first British manager to win a European trophy when his brilliant Spurs side thrashed Atletico Madrid 5-1 in the final of the European Cup-Winners' Cup. During a 16-year stint in the White Hart Lane hot seat he also won two more FA Cups in 1962 and 1967, the League Cup in 1971 and 1973 and the UEFA Cup in 1972.**

• As a player Nicholson won the league title with Spurs in 1951. In the same year he made his one and only appearance for England, scoring with his first touch after just 19 seconds against Portugal at Goodison Park. He remains the fastest-scoring England debutant ever.

• **In later life Nicholson became Tottenham's Club President. His achievements with the club were marked in 1999 when an approach road to White Hart Lane was renamed Bill Nicholson Way.**

NORTHAMPTON TOWN

Year founded: 1897
Ground: Sixfields Stadium (7,653)
Nickname:
The Cobblers
Biggest win: 11-1 v Southend United (1909)
Heaviest defeat:
0-11 v Southampton (1901)
Colours: Maroon shirts with white side panels, white shorts, white socks

The club was founded at a meeting of local schoolteachers at the Princess Royal Inn in Northampton in 1897. After turning professional in 1901 Northampton were founder members of the Third Division in 1920.

David Healy scored a record 13 goals in the Euro 2008 qualifiers, but it wasn't enough to take Northern Ireland to the finals

• No other club can match the extraordinary decade Northampton experienced in the 1960s. After starting the era in the Fourth Division the Cobblers rose to the First Division in 1965 – in the process becoming the first club to reach the top flight via all three lower divisions – before swiftly plummeting back to the basement by 1969.

• Northampton's best run in the FA Cup came in 1970 when they reached the fifth round before going down 8-2 at home to Manchester United, with a certain George Best scoring six of the visitors' goals.

• **The Cobblers' record goalscorer is Jack English, who banged in 135 league goals between 1947-60. His team-mate Tommy Fowler, meanwhile, played in a record 521 matches for the club.**

• Veteran entertainer Des O'Connor was evacuated from London to Northampton in the Second World War and later played for the Cobblers' youth team.

HONOURS
Division 3 champions 1963
Division 4 champions 1987

NORTHERN IRELAND

First international:
Northern Ireland 2 England 1, 1923
Most capped player:
Pat Jennings, 119 caps (1964-86)
Leading goalscorer:
David Healy, 35 goals (2000-)
First World Cup appearance: Northern Ireland 1 Czechoslovakia 0 (1958)
Biggest win: 7-0 v Wales, 1930
Heaviest defeat: 2-9 v England, 1949
Colours: Green shirts, white shorts, green socks

Until Trinidad and Tobago appeared at the 2006 tournament, Northern Ireland were the smallest country to qualify for a World Cup finals tournament. They have made it on three occasions, reaching the quarter-finals in 1958 and memorably beating the hosts Spain in 1982 on their way to the second round.

• **Northern Ireland's Norman Whiteside is the youngest player ever to appear at the World Cup. He was aged just 17**

The Canaries are flying!!!

years and 42 days when he played at the 1982 tournament in Spain, beating the previous record set by Pele in 1958.

• When Northern Ireland thrashed Wales 7-0 on 1st February 1930 to record their biggest ever win striker Joe Bambrick scored six of the goals – a record for a Home International match.

• **After going a record ten matches without a goal Northern Ireland's fortunes picked up when Lawrie Sanchez became manager in 2003. Their revival included a famous 1-0 win over England in the 2006 World Cup qualifying campaign and a 3-2 victory over champions-to-be Spain in the Euro 2008 qualifiers.**

• During that Euro 2008 campaign Northern Ireland's highest ever scorer David Healy scored 13 goals to set a new record for the European Championships.

WORLD CUP RECORD
1930 Did not enter
1934 Did not enter
1938 Did not enter
1950 Did not qualify
1954 Did not qualify
1958 Quarter-finalists
1962 Did not qualify
1966 Did not qualify
1970 Did not qualify
1974 Did not qualify
1978 Did not qualify
1982 Round 2
1986 Round 1
1990 Did not qualify
1994 Did not qualify
1998 Did not qualify
2002 Did not qualify
2006 Did not qualify
2010 Did not qualify

NORWICH CITY

Year founded: 1902
Ground: Carrow Road (27,000)
Nickname: The Canaries
Biggest win: 10-2 v Coventry City (1930)
Heaviest defeat: 2-10 v Swindon Town (1908)
Colours: Yellow shirts, green shorts, yellow socks

Founded in 1902 by two schoolteachers, Norwich City soon found themselves in

hot water with the FA and were expelled from the FA Amateur Cup in 1904 for being 'professional'. The club joined the Football League as founder members of the Third Division in 1920.

• **Norwich fans enjoyed the greatest day in their history when they beat Sunderland 1-0 at Wembley in 1985 to win the League Cup. However, joy soon turned to despair when the Canaries were relegated from the top flight at the end of the season. No other club before or since has experienced this particular mix of sweet and sour.**

• Ron Ashman is the club's leading appearance maker, turning out in 592 league matches between 1947-64. The Canaries' leading scorer is Ashman's team-mate John Gavin, who notched 122 league goals between 1948-58.

• **Norwich's most capped player is Mark Bowen, who played 35 times for Wales during his Carrow Road career.**

• In 2006 the Canaries splashed out a club record £3.5 million to bring striker Robert Earnshaw to Carrow Road from West Brom. In the same year Norwich received a club record £7.25 million when they sold striker Dean Ashton to West Ham United.

• **Under the ownership of cook and recipe book author Delia Smith, Norwich finished a best ever third in the inaugural Premiership season in 1992/93. The club enjoyed a spirited run in the UEFA Cup in the following campaign, defeating Vitesse Arnhem and German giants Bayern Munich before going out to Inter Milan.**

• Norwich City's anthem, On the Ball City, is a music hall song that has been associated with the club throughout their history and is believed to be the

oldest fans' song anywhere in the world that is still regularly heard at matches.

HONOURS
***Division 2 champions** 1972, 1986*
***First Division champions** 2004*
***Division 3 (S) champions** 1934*
League One champions 2010
League Cup 1985

NOTTINGHAM FOREST

Year founded: 1865
Ground: The City Ground (30,062)
Nickname: The Reds
Biggest win: 14-0 v Clapton (1891)
Heaviest defeat: 1-9 v Blackburn Rovers (1937)
Colours: Red shirts, white shorts, red socks

One of the oldest clubs in the world, Nottingham Forest were founded in 1865 at a meeting at the Clinton Arms in Nottingham by a group of former players of 'shinty' (a form of hockey), who decided to switch sports to football.

• **Over the following years the club was at the forefront of important innovations in the game. For instance, shinguards were invented by Forest player Sam Widdowson in 1874, while four years later a referee's whistle was first used in a match between Forest and Sheffield Norfolk. In 1890, a match between Forest and Bolton Wanderers was the first ever to feature goal nets.**

• Forest adopted their famous red tops in tribute to the Italian patriot Giuseppe

Garibaldi, whose followers were known as the 'redshirts'. In 1886 the club donated a spare kit to newly-formed Arsenal and the Londoners have worn red ever since.

• Forest enjoyed a golden era under charismatic manager Brian Clough, who sat in the City Ground hotseat from 1975 until his retirement in 1993. After winning promotion to the top flight in 1977, the club won the league championship the following season – a feat that no promoted team has achieved since. Even more incredibly, the Reds went on to win the European Cup in 1979 with a 1-0 victory over Malmo in the final. The next year Forest retained the trophy, beating Hamburg 1-0 in the final in Madrid.

• Forest also won the League Cup in 1978, and the following year became the first club to retain the trophy. The Reds' record of four wins in the competition is only bettered by Liverpool and Aston Villa.

• In 1959, in the days before subs, Forest won the FA Cup despite being reduced to ten men when Roy Dwight, a cousin of pop star Elton John, was carried off with a broken leg after 33 minutes of the final against Luton Town. It was the first time that a club had won the cup with fewer than 11 players.

• Defender Bobby McKinlay, a member of that 1959 team, is Forest's longest-serving player, turning out in 614 league games in 19 seasons at the club. The Reds' record scorer is Grenville Morris, who fell just one short of a double century of league goals for the club in the years before the First World War.

• Nottingham Forest's City Ground is just 330 yards from Notts County's Meadow Lane, making the two clubs the nearest neighbours in the Football League.

• Forest cashed a club record cheque for £8.5 million when they sold striker Stan Collymore to Liverpool in 1995. Two years later they splashed out a record £4.8 million to bring Dutch striker Pierre van Hooijdonk to the City Ground from Celtic.

HONOURS

Division 1 champions 1978
Division 2 champions 1907, 1922
First Division champions 1998
Division 3 (South) champions 1951
FA Cup 1898, 1959
League Cup 1978, 1979, 1989, 1990
European Cup 1979, 1980
European Super Cup 1979

TOP 10

BRITISH WINS IN EUROPEAN CUP/ CHAMPIONS LEAGUE FINAL

1. Manchester United 4 Benfica 1, 1968
2. Celtic 2 Inter Milan 1, 1967
3. Liverpool 3 Borussia Monchengladbach 1, 1977
4. Aston Villa 1 Bayern Munich 0, 1982
5. Nottingham Forest 1 Hamburg 0, 1980
6. Manchester United 2 Bayern Munich 1, 1999
7. Liverpool 1 Real Madrid 0, 1981
8. Nottingham Forest 1 Malmo 0, 1979
9. Liverpool 3* AC Milan 3, 2005
10. Manchester United 1* Chelsea 1, 2008

* Won on penalties

NOTTS COUNTY

Year founded: 1862
Ground: Meadow Lane (13,725)
Nickname: The Magpies
Biggest win: 15-0 v Rotherham (1885)
Heaviest defeat: 1-9 v Aston Villa (1888), v Blackburn (1889) and v Portsmouth (1927)
Colours: Black-and- white striped shirts, black shorts, black socks

Notts County are the oldest professional football club in the world. Founded in 1862, the club were founder members of the Football League in 1888.

• In their long history County have swapped divisions more often than any other league club, winning 13 promotions – most recently, to League One in 2010 – and suffering the agony of relegation 15 times.

• The club's greatest ever day was way back in 1894 when, as a Second Division outfit, they won the FA Cup – the first time a team from outside the top flight had won the trophy. In the final at Goodison Park County beat Bolton 4-1, with Jimmy Logan scoring the first ever hat-trick in the FA Cup final.

• Striker Henry Cursham scored a record 48 goals for Notts County in the FA Cup between 1880 and 1887, playing alongside his two brothers in the same County team.

• Giant goalkeeper Albert Iremonger played in a club record 564 games for County between 1905-26, the last occasion when he was 42, making him the club's oldest ever player. A temperamental character, Iremonger was known for running out of his goal to argue with the ref.

• Along with Brentford, Notts County are one of just two clubs to have won the fourth tier of English football under its three historical names: Division 4 in 1971, the Third Division in 1998 (by a record margin of 17 points), and League Two in 2010.

HONOURS

Division 2 champions 1897, 1914, 1923
Division 3 (S) champions 1931, 1950
Division 4 champions 1971
League Two champions 2010
Anglo-Italian Cup 1995

NUMBERS

Shirt numbers were first used in a First Division match by Arsenal against Sheffield Wednesday at Hillsborough on 25th August 1928. On the same day Chelsea also wore numbers for their Second Division fixture against Swansea at Stamford Bridge.

• Numbers were first used in an FA Cup final in 1933. Everton's players were numbered 1-11 while Manchester City's wore 12-22. Six years later, in 1939, the Football League made the use of shirt numbers obligatory for all teams.

• England and Scotland first wore numbered shirts on 17th April 1937 for the countries' Home International fixture at Hampden Park. Scotland won 3-1. The following year numbers were introduced for the World Cup tournament in France.

• Squad numbers were adopted by Premiership clubs at the start of the 1993/94 season. The highest number worn to date by a Premiership player is 52 by Arsenal striker Nicklas Bendtner in the 2009/10 season. In the Football League both Ade Akinbiyi and Dominik Werling have worn the number 55 shirt for Crystal Palace and Barnsley, respectively.

• In 2000 Aberdeen's Moroccan striker

Hicham Zerouaki was allowed to wear the number 0 on his back after being nicknamed 'Zero' by Dons fans. The following season, however, the SPL outlawed the number.

• In 2010 Australia's Thomas Oar set a world record for a high shirt number when he turned out in a top with 121 on his back for an Asian Cup qualifier against Indonesia.

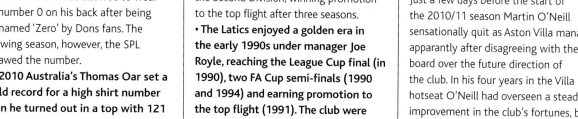

Number 121! Now that's just being silly...

OLDHAM ATHLETIC

Year founded: 1895
Ground: Boundary Park (10,368)
Previous name: Pine Villa
Nickname: The Latics
Biggest win: 11-0 v Southport (1962)
Heaviest defeat: 4-13 v Tranmere Rovers (1935)
Colours: Blue shirts with white trim, white shorts, white socks

Originally known as Pine Villa, the club was founded by the landlord of the Featherstone and Junction Hotel in 1895. Four years later the club changed to its present name and in 1907 Oldham joined the Second Division, winning promotion to the top flight after three seasons.

• **The Latics enjoyed a golden era in the early 1990s under manager Joe Royle, reaching the League Cup final (in 1990), two FA Cup semi-finals (1990 and 1994) and earning promotion to the top flight (1991). The club were founder members of the Premier League in 1992 but were relegated two years later and since 1997 they have been stuck in the third tier.**

• In 1915 Oldham looked almost certain to win the First Division championship but they blew the opportunity by losing their last two games, at home to Burnley and Liverpool. Everton took full advantage of the Latics' loss of nerve, claiming the title by a single point.

• **In 1989 Oldham striker Frankie Bunn scored six of his side's goals in a 7-0 hammering of Scarborough in the third round of the League Cup. He remains the only player to have notched a double hat-trick in the competition.**

• Ian Wood appeared in a record 525 league games for the club between 1966-80, including one four-year spell in the early 1970s when he missed just one match. The Latics' leading scorer is Roger Palmer, who banged in 141 goals between 1980-92.

HONOURS
Division 2 champions 1991
Division 3 (N) champions 1953
Division 3 champions 1974

MARTIN O'NEILL

Born: Kilrea, 1st March 1952
Managerial career:
1990-95 Wycombe Wanderers
1995 Norwich City
1995-2000 Leicester City
2000-05 Celtic
2006-10 Aston Villa

Just a few days before the start of the 2010/11 season Martin O'Neill sensationally quit as Aston Villa manager, apparently after disagreeing with the board over the future direction of the club. In his four years in the Villa hotseat O'Neill had overseen a steady improvement in the club's fortunes, but had failed to land any silverware.

• **One of the brightest, most articulate managers in the game, O'Neill has enjoyed huge success since starting out at Wycombe Wanderers in 1990. He led the Chairboys out of the Conference and into the third tier before briefly managing Norwich. From Carrow Road he went to Leicester, who he guided into the Premiership via the play-offs in 1996. The following year he led the Foxes to triumph in the League Cup, a competition the club won again three years later.**

• In 2000 O'Neill joined Celtic, where he again made an immediate impact, winning the treble in his first season. Dubbed 'Martin the Magnificent' by the fans, O'Neill led the Glasgow giants to two more league titles, four more cups and the final of the UEFA Cup in 2003 before quitting the club in 2005 to care for his sick wife.

Martin O'Neill: A regular contender for the 'Most Excitable Manager' award

• O'Neill's playing career was mostly spent at Nottingham Forest under legendary manager Brian Clough. A hard-working midfielder with no little skill, O'Neill won the league championship and two European Cups with Forest, before later playing for Norwich, Manchester City and Notts County. He also won 64 caps for Northern Ireland, captaining his country at the 1982 World Cup.

• Formerly a law student at Queen's University in Belfast, O'Neill has retained a keen interest in the subject and has attended some of the most notorious trials in British legal history, including those of the Yorkshire Ripper and serial killer Rosemary West.

MICHAEL OWEN

Born: Chester, 14th December 1979
Position: Striker
Club career:
1997-2004 Liverpool 216 (118)
2004-05 Real Madrid 35 (13)
2005-09 Newcastle United 71 (26)
2009- Manchester United 19 (3)
International record:
1998-2008 England 89 (40)

Manchester United striker Michael Owen is England's fourth highest scorer of all time. He once seemed certain to become his country's record scorer but his international career stalled under current England boss Fabio Capello and would now appear to be over.

• Frighteningly quick in his heyday with Liverpool, Owen enjoyed a golden year in 2001 when he won the FA Cup, League Cup and UEFA Cup in the same season with the Merseysiders, scoring both the Reds' goals in their 2-1 FA Cup final defeat of Arsenal at the Millennium Stadium. In

Michael Owen is England's top scorer in competitive matches

the same year he was voted European Footballer of the Year, the last English player to achieve that distinction.

• Owen joined Real Madrid for £8 million in 2004, but the following year moved back to England when he signed for Newcastle for £16 million. His unveiling at St James' Park was attended by 20,000 excited Toon fans, but after failing to set Tyneside alight he made a surprise move to Manchester United in 2009. In his first season at Old Trafford he helped United win the Carling Cup, scoring in the final against Aston Villa before limping off injured.

• Owen is the only England player to have scored at four international tournaments, notching at two World Cups and two European Championships. His strike against Argentina at the 1998 World Cup, when he sped past two defenders before slamming the ball high into the net, is one of the most famous England goals of all time. In the same year he was voted BBC Sports Personality of the Year, becoming only the third footballer to win the award.

• Of Owen's 40 international goals, 26 of them have come in competitive matches – a figure unmatched by any other

OWN GOALS

The first ever own goal in the Football League was scored on the opening day of the inaugural 1888/89 season, the unfortunate George Cox of Aston Villa putting through his own net in his team's 1-1 draw with Wolves.

• The record number of own goals in a single match is, incredibly, 149. In 2002 Madagascan team Stade Olympique l'Emyrne staged a predetermined protest against alleged refereeing bias by constantly whacking the ball into their own net, their match against

TOP 10

INFAMOUS OWN GOALS

1. Andreas Escobar, Colombia v USA, World Cup 1994
2. Gary Mabbutt, Tottenham v Coventry, FA Cup Final, 1987
3. Tommy Boyd, Scotland v Brazil, 1998 World Cup
4. Des Walker, Nottingham Forest v Tottenham, FA Cup Final, 1991
5. Gary Neville, England v Croatia, Euro 2008 qualifier, 2006
6. Steven Gerrard, Liverpool v Chelsea, Carling Cup Final, 2005
7. Jorge Costa, Portugal v USA, World Cup 2002
8. John Arne Riise, Liverpool v Chelsea, Champions League semi-final, 2008
9. Berti Vogts, West Germany v Austria, World Cup 1978
10. Tommy Hutchison, Manchester City v Tottenham, FA Cup Final, 1981

AS Adema finishing in a 149-0 win for their opponents. The Madagascan FA took a dim view of the incident and promptly handed out long suspensions to four SOE players.

• Three players have scored at both ends in the same FA Cup final: Charlton's Bert Turner in his side's 4-1 defeat to Derby in 1949, Manchester City's Tommy Hutchison in a 1-1 draw with Tottenham in 1981, and Spurs' Gary Mabbutt in a surprise 3-2 defeat to Coventry City in 1987.

• The only own goal ever credited to two players was scored in a match between Chelsea and Leicester in 1954. Attempting to clear the ball at the same time, Leicester's Stan Milburn and Jack Froggart only managed to send it flying into the back of their net.

• A record 43 own goals were scored in the 2009/10 Premier League season, with Manchester United being gifted an incredible 12 of them (another record).

• The most notorious own goal ever was scored by Colombia's Andreas Escobar in his country's 2-1 defeat by hosts USA at the 1994 World Cup. Ten days later Escobar was shot dead in his home town Medellin, reportedly as a punishment for the gambling losses the city's drug lords had suffered as a result of his error.

OXFORD UNITED

Year founded: 1893
Ground: Kassam Stadium (12,500)
Previous name: Headington, Headington United
Nickname: The U's
Biggest win: 11-0 9-1 v Dorchester Town, 1995
Heaviest defeat: 0-7 v Sunderland, 1998
Colours: Yellow and blue shirts, navy blue shorts, navy blue socks

The club was founded by a local vicar and doctor in 1893 as Headington, primarily as a way of allowing the cricketers of Headington CC to keep fit during the winter months. The club's current name was adopted in 1956, six years before Oxford were elected to the Football League.

• **In 1964 Oxford became the first Fourth Division side to reach the quarter-finals of the FA Cup. However, despite being backed by a record crowd of 22,750 at their old Manor Ground, the U's went down 2-1 to eventual finalists Preston.**

• The club enjoyed a golden era under controversial owner Robert Maxwell in the 1980s, although the decade began badly when the newspaper proprietor proposed that Oxford and Reading should merge as the 'Thames Valley Royals'. The fans' well-organised campaign against the idea was successful, and their loyalty was rewarded when Oxford gained consecutive promotions to reach the top flight in 1985.

• **The greatest day in the club's history, though, came in 1986 when Oxford defeated QPR 3-0 at Wembley to win the League Cup. The following two decades saw a period of decline, however, and by 2006 Oxford had become the first major trophy winners to sink into the Conference.**

• Fours years later the U's booked their return to the Football League with a 3-1 play-off victory over York City at Wembley.

HONOURS

Division 2 champions 1985
Division 3 champions 1968, 1984
League Cup 1986

Bob Paisley, Liverpool's most successful ever manager, is still revered at Anfield

BOB PAISLEY

Born: Sunderland, 23rd January 1919
Died: 14th February 1996
Managerial career:
1974-83 Liverpool

The most successful manager in Liverpool's history, Bob Paisley won no fewer than 13 major trophies in his nine years in charge of the club between 1974-83: six league titles, three European Cups, three League Cups and one UEFA Cup. Surprisingly, he never managed to win the FA Cup with the Reds.

• **Paisley was the first manager to win the European Cup with the Merseysiders, leading his team to a 3-1 victory over Borussia Monchengladbach in Rome in 1977. On arriving in the** Italian capital, referring to his wartime exploits, Paisley had quipped: "The last time I was here I was in a tank!"

• After taking over from the equally legendary Bill Shankly in 1974, Paisley won at least one trophy every season apart from his first in the Anfield hot seat. His success was rewarded with six Manager of the Year awards – a total only surpassed by Sir Alex Ferguson, with ten.

• **As a player Paisley won the league title with Liverpool in 1947 and later captained the club. He joined the back-room staff as a physiotherapist after retiring in 1954, serving the club in a variety of roles before becoming manager.**

• Paisley died in 1996, aged 77, after a long illness. His memory was subsequently honoured by the club with the opening of the Paisley Gates at one of the entrances to Anfield.

PELE

Born: Tres Coracoes, Brazil,
23rd October 1940
Position: Striker
Club career:
1956-74 Santos 412 (470)
1975-77 New York Cosmos 56 (31)
International record:
1957-71 Brazil 92 (77)

Born Edson Arantes do Nascimento, but known throughout the world by his nickname, Pele is generally recognised as the greatest footballer ever to play the game.

• In 1957, aged just 16 years and nine months, he scored on his debut for Brazil against Argentina to become the youngest international goalscorer ever. The following year he made headlines around the globe when he scored twice in Brazil's 5-2 World Cup final defeat of hosts Sweden, in the process making history as the youngest ever World Cup winner.

• Four years later he missed most of Brazil's successful defence of their trophy through injury but was later awarded a winners' medal by FIFA. After being kicked out of the 1966 World Cup, he was back to his best at the 1970 tournament in Mexico,

opening the scoring in the final against Italy and inspiring a magnificent Brazilian side to a comprehensive 4-1 victory. He remains the only player in the world with three World Cup winners' medals.

• Fast, strong, tremendously skilful and powerful in the air, Pele was the complete footballer. He was also a phenomenal goalscorer who remains Brazil's top scorer of all time with an incredible 77 goals (in just 92 games), a record only surpassed in international football by two players. Twelve of those goals came at the World Cup, making him the fourth highest scorer in the history of the tournament.

• Since his retirement Pele's legend has continued to grow, helped in part by the man himself. "Football is like music, where there is Beethoven and the rest," he once said. "In football, there is Pele and the rest."

PENALTIES

Penalty kicks were first proposed by goalkeeper William McCrum of the Irish FA in 1890 and adopted the following year. Wolves's John Heath was the first player to take and score a penalty in a Football League match, against Accrington at Molineux on 14th September 1891.

• **Francis Lee holds the British record for the most penalties in a league season, scoring 13 for Manchester City in Division One in 1971/72. He earned many of the penalties himself, leading fans to dub him 'Lee Won Pen'.**

• Alan Shearer is the most prolific penalty-taker in the Premier League era, scoring 58 times from the spot.

• **Mexican international Manuel Rosas scored the first penalty in a World Cup match, netting from the spot in his side's 6-3 defeat by Argentina in 1930. In the same match Argentina's Fernando Paternoster became the first player to miss a World Cup penalty.**

The brilliant Pele scored a world record 1,281 goals

• The most penalties ever awarded in a British match is five in the game between Crystal Palace and Brighton at Selhurst Park in 1989. Palace were awarded four penalties (one scored, three missed) while Brighton's consolation goal in a 2-1 defeat also came from the spot.

• **Argentina's Martin Palermo missed a record three penalties in a Copa America match against Colombia in 1999. His first effort struck the crossbar, his second penalty sailed high over the bar, but remarkably Palermo still insisted on taking his side's third spot-kick of the match. Perhaps he shouldn't have bothered, as his shot was palmed away by the goalkeeper.**

• Ipswich goalkeeper Paul Cooper saved a record eight out of the ten penalties he faced during the 1979/80 season. His technique was to leave a slightly bigger gap on one side of the goal, tempting the penalty taker to shoot there.

PENALTY SHOOT-OUTS

Penalty shoot-outs were first used in England as a way to settle drawn matches in the Watney Cup in 1970. In the first ever shoot-out Manchester United beat Hull City in the semi-final of the competition, United legend George Best being the first player to take a penalty while his team-mate Denis Law was the first to miss.

• **On 25th November 1991 Rotherham United**

Van der Sar saves in the 2008 Community Shield shoot-out between United and Chelsea

made FA Cup history by becoming the first club to win an FA Cup tie on penalties, the Yorkshire side beating Scunthorpe United 7-6 in the shoot-out after their first round replay finished 3-3. In 2005 Arsenal became the first team to win the final on penalties, defeating Manchester United 5-4 after a 0-0 draw.

• The first World Cup match to be settled by penalties was the 1982 semi-final between France and West Germany. The Germans won 5-4 in the shoot-out after an exciting 3-3 draw. In 1994 the final was decided by penalties for the first time, Brazil defeating Italy 3-2 on spot-kicks after a dull 0-0 draw. The 2006 final also went to penalties, Italy beating France 5-3. In all, 22 World Cup matches have been settled by penalties.

• **The first country to win a major international tournament on penalties, though, was Czechoslovakia, who beat West Germany 5-3 in the shoot-out of the 1976 European Championship final. The winning penalty was scored by Antonin Panenka with a delicate chip into the middle of the net.**

• Among major nations who have taken part in more than two shoot-outs, Germany have the best record with five wins out of six. England, on the other hand, have the poorest record, with just one win in six attempts.

• The longest ever penalty shoot-out was between KK Palace and Civics in the first round of the 2005 Namibian Cup. After an incredible total of 48 kicks, KK Palace emerged victorious 17-16. At junior level, Under-10 sides Mickleover Lightning Blue Sox and Chellaston required an extraordinary 66 penalties to settle their Derby County Cup match in 1998, before Blue Sox narrowly won 2-1.

PETERBOROUGH UNITED

Year founded: 1934
Ground: London Road (15,460)
Nickname: The Posh
Biggest win: 9-1 v Barnet (1998)
Heaviest defeat: 1-8 v Northampton Town (1946)
Colours: Blue shirts, blue shorts, white socks

Peterborough were founded in 1934 at a meeting at the Angel Hotel to fill the void left by the collapse of local club Peterborough and Fletton United two years earlier.

• The club's unusual nickname, The Posh, stemmed from Peterborough and Fletton manager Pat Tirrel's remark in 1921 that the club wanted "Posh players for a Posh team". When the new club played its first game against Gainsborough Trinity in 1934 there were shouts of "Up the Posh!" and the nickname stuck.

• Peterborough were finally elected to the Football League in 1960... at the 21st attempt. The fans' long wait was rewarded when Peterborough stormed to the Fourth Division title in their first season, scoring a league record 134 goals. Striker Terry Bly notched an amazing 52 of the goals to set a hard-to-beat club record.

• **In 1968 the club became the first since the Second World War to be relegated for non-football reasons, dropping from the Third to the Fourth Division after making illegal payments to players and collecting a 19-point deduction as a punishment.**

• Left winger Terry Robson has made more appearances for The Posh than any other player, turning out 482 times between 1968-81. The club's record scorer is Jim Hall, who banged in 122 goals between 1967-75.

HONOURS
Division 4 champions 1961, 1974

141

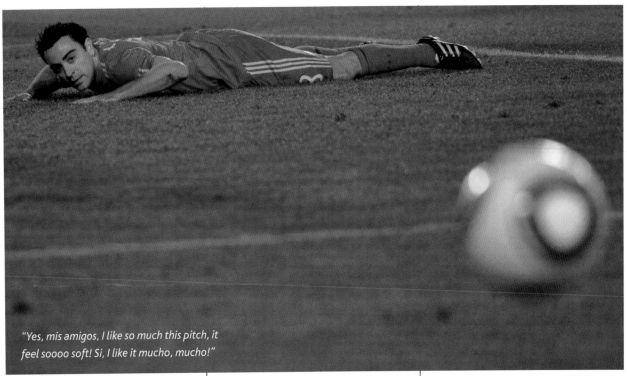

"Yes, mis amigos, I like so much this pitch, it feel soooo soft! Si, I like it mucho, mucho!"

MARTIN PETERS

Born: Plaistow, 8th November 1943
Position: Midfielder
Club career:
1962-70 West Ham United 302 (81)
1970-75 Tottenham Hotspur 189 (46)
1975-80 Norwich City 206 (44)
1980 Sheffield United 24 (3)
International record:
1966-74 England 67 (20)

But for a last-minute West German equaliser which forced the match into extra-time, Martin Peters would be remembered as the man whose goal won England the World Cup in the 1966 final.
• Described by England manager Alf Ramsey as being "ten years ahead of his time", Peters was a key member of the England team for nearly a decade, his well-timed runs from midfield into the opposition penalty area and composure in front of goal marking him out as a top-class player.
• One of a trio of West Ham players in the 1966 side, along with Bobby Moore and Geoff Hurst, Peters won the European Cup-Winners' Cup with the Hammers in 1965. In 1970 he moved to Tottenham for £200,000, a British record fee at the time, where he won the League Cup in 1971 and 1973 and the UEFA Cup in 1972.
• He later spent five more years in the top flight with Norwich City, but after

an unsuccessful spell as Sheffield United manager he left the game to work in the insurance business.

PITCHES

According to FIFA rules, a football pitch must measure between 100-130 yards in length and 50-100 yards in breadth. It's no surprise, then, that different pitches vary hugely in size.
• Of current Premiership clubs, Manchester City have the largest pitch, their surface at the City of Manchester Stadium measuring 116 yards by 77 yards to give a total playing area of 8,932 square yards.
• At the opposite end of the scale, West Ham have the smallest pitch in the top flight. The playing surface at Upton Park is just 7,700 (110 x 70yds) square yards.
• The first portable natural grass pitch was used for the 1993 America Cup clash between America and England at the Detroit Silverdome. The grass was grown in hexagonal segments in the stadium car park and then reassembled in the covered stadium.
• The world's highest pitch was marked out on the summit of Mount Sajama in Bolivia in 2001. Carrying two goalposts and four orange balls, the players climbed 6,542 metres before playing a ten-a-side game (two players having dropped out with altitude sickness) on the snow-capped peak. To prevent other players succumbing to altitude sickness the match lasted just 20 minutes.

MICHEL PLATINI

Born: Joeuf, France, 21st June 1955
Position: Midfielder
Club career:
1972-79 Nancy 181 (98)
1979-82 St Etienne 104 (58)
1982-87 Juventus 147 (68)
International record:
1976-87 France 72 (41)

The only man to be voted European Footballer of the Year in three consecutive years (1983, 1984 and 1985), Michel Platini is a legendary figure in world football.
• An elegant attacking midfielder with a striker's scoring instinct, Platini starred in the French team that reached the World Cup semi-final in 1982 and 1986, only to lose on both occasions to West Germany.
• In between those disappointments, however, Platini captained France to their first ever trophy when, as the host nation, they won the 1984 European Championships. Again, Platini was the main inspiration, scoring a record nine goals in the tournament, including one from a free kick in his side's 2-0 defeat of Spain in the final.
• After playing for Nancy and St Etienne, Platini joined Juventus for £1.2 million in 1982. Three times top scorer in Serie A, he scored the winning goal for the Italian giants in the 1985 European Cup final against

Liverpool, although Juventus' victory was completely overshadowed by the deaths of 39 fans in the Heysel tragedy.

• After managing France for four years between 1988-1992, Platini was elected President of UEFA in 2007. In this role he has become embroiled in a number of controversies, particularly over his backing of the proposed '6 + 5' rule which would have reduced the number of overseas players in team line-ups.

PLAY-OFFS

The play-off system was introduced by the Football League in the 1986/87 season. Initially, one club from the higher division competed with three from the lower division at the semi-final stage but this was changed to four teams from the same division in the 1988/89 season. The following season a one-off final at Wembley replaced the original two-legged final.

• **Ipswich Town have featured in the Championship play-offs a record seven times but have only reached the final once, defeating Barnsley 4-2 in 2000.**

• The highest-scoring play-off final was a thrilling 4-4 draw between Charlton Athletic and Sunderland in 1998. The Londoners won the subsequent penalty shoot-out 7-6 to gain promotion to the Premier League. Dagenham & Redbridge recorded the biggest ever play-off victory

TOP 10

MOST DRAMATIC PLAY-OFF FINALS

1. Charlton* 4 Sunderland 4, First Division, 1998
2. Bolton 4 Reading 3, First Division, 1995
3. Manchester City* 2 Gillingham 2, Second Division, 1999
4. Leicester City 2 Crystal Palace 1, First Division, 1996
5. Scunthorpe 3 Millwall 2, League One, 2009
6. Swindon 4 Leicester City 3, First Division, 1993
7. Blackpool 3 Cardiff City 2, Championship, 2010
8. Ipswich 4 Barnsley 2, First Division, 2000
9. Stockport 3 Rochdale 2, League Two, 2008
10. Sheffield Wednesday 4 Hartlepool 2, League One, 2005

* Won on penalties

when they smashed Morecambe 6-0 in the League Two semi-final first leg in 2010.

• **The Championship play-off final is the most financially rewarding sporting event in the world, its worth to the winners in prize money, TV and advertising revenue and increased gate receipts being estimated at** around £90 million.

• Between 2003 and 2007 Lincoln City reached the League Two play-offs a record five times on the trot, but failed to gain promotion every time.

PLYMOUTH ARGYLE

Year founded: 1886
Ground: Home Park (19,500)
Previous name: Argyle FC
Nickname: The Pilgrims
Biggest win: 8-1 v Millwall (1932) and v Hartlepool (1994)
Heaviest defeat: 0-9 v Stoke City (1960)
Colours: Green shirts, white shorts, white socks

The club was founded as Argyle FC in 1886 in a Plymouth coffee house, the name deriving from the Argyll and Sutherland Highlanders who were stationed in the city at the time. The current name was adopted in 1903, when the club became fully professional and entered the Southern League.

• **After joining the Football League in 1920 Plymouth just missed out on promotion from the Third Division (South) between 1922-27, finishing**

The Championship play-off final: the winners get the glory, a place the Premier League and a big pot of cash. Best not to mention the losers...

in second place in six consecutive seasons... a record of misfortune no other club can match.

• Sammy Black, a prolific marksman during the 1920s and 1930s, is the club's leading goalscorer with 185 league goals. The Pilgrims' longest-serving player is Kevin Hodges, with 530 appearances between 1978-92.

• **In 1984 Plymouth became only the sixth Third Division club to reach the FA Cup semi-finals, but were beaten 1-0 by Watford at Villa Park.**

• In one of the most bizarre incidents ever in the history of football, Plymouth conceded a goal scored by the referee in a Division Three fixture against Barrow in 1968. A shot from a Barrow player was heading wide until it deflected off the boot of referee Ivan Robinson and into the Pilgrims' net for the only goal of the match.

• **The largest city in England never to have hosted top-flight football, Plymouth were crowned Third** Division champions in 2001/02 with an impressive 102 points – a joint-record total for the fourth tier and the third-highest points haul in Football League history.

> HONOURS
> *Division 3 (S) champions 1930, 1952*
> *Division 3 champions 1959*
> *Second Division champions 2004*
> *Third Division champions 2002*

POP SONGS

The most successful football pop song of all time is England's official anthem at Euro 96, Three Lions, by the Lightning Seeds and comedians David Baddiel and Frank Skinner. The song topped the charts in both 1996 and 1998, when it was re-released to coincide with England's participation in the World Cup in France.

• **The England World Cup squad has recorded two number one hit singles, Back Home in 1970 and World In** Motion with the band New Order in 1990. The latter song featured a memorable rap by winger John Barnes, which was parodied by tubby comedian James Corden when he performed a Comic Relief sketch with the England squad in 2009.

• Among the clubs to enjoy chart success are Chelsea with *Blue is the Colour* in 1972, Tottenham (supported by Chas and Dave) with *Ossie's Dream* in 1981, and Liverpool with *The Anfield Rap* in 1988.

• **Of the numerous individual footballers to release singles, Paul Gascoigne enjoyed most success with a version of Lindisfarne's 'Fog on the Tyne', which reached number two in the charts in 1990.**

PORT VALE

Year founded: 1876
Ground: Vale Park (22,356)
Previous name: Burslem Port Vale
Nickname: The Valiants
Biggest win: 9-1 v Chesterfield (1932)
Heaviest defeat: 0-10 v Sheffield United (1892) and v Notts County (1895)
Colours: White shirts, black shorts, white socks

Port Vale's name derives from the house where the club was founded in 1876. Initially, the club was known as Burslem Port Vale – Burslem being the Stoke-on-Trent town where the Valiants are based – but the prefix was dropped in 1911.

• **Loyal defender Roy Sproson is Port Vale's longest-serving player, appearing in a phenomenal 761 league games between 1950-72. Only two other players in the history of league football have made more appearances for the same club. With 154 league goals in two spells at the club between 1923-33 Wilf Kirkham is the Valiants' record goalscorer.**

• Port Vale were the only English team managed by the legendary Sir Stanley Matthews. The 'Wizard of Dribble' took charge at Vale Park in 1967 but left the club the following year after the Valiants were briefly expelled from the Football League for making illegal payments to players.

Kevin Keegan found a good use for his 1979 single Head Over Heels...as a sun visor!

- In their first season as a league club, in 1892/93, Port Vale suffered the worst ever home defeat in Football League history when Sheffield United hammered them 10-0. However, Vale's defence was in much better nick in 1953/54 when they kept a league record 30 clean sheets on their way to the Third Division (North) championship.
- Port Vale's most famous fan is singer Robbie Williams, who in 2006 became the club's majority shareholder. Darts legend Phil 'The Power' Taylor is also a keen supporter of the Valiants.

> HONOURS
> **Division 3 (N) champions** 1930, 1954
> **Division 4 champions** 1959
> **Football League trophy** 1993, 2001

FC PORTO

Year founded: 1893
Ground: Estadio do Dragao (50,399)
Nickname: The Dragons
Colours: Blue-and-white-striped shirts, blue shorts, blue socks

Easily the most successful Portuguese side of recent years, Porto were founded in 1893 by a local wine salesman who had been introduced to football on his regular business trips to England.
- Six league title wins in the last seven seasons have taken Porto's total of domestic championships to 24, seven behind arch rivals Benfica. The club was also the dominant force of the 1990s, winning eight titles during the decade including a record five on the trot between 1995-99.
- Porto have the best record in Europe of any Portuguese side, with two victories in the European Cup/Champions League (in 1987 and 2004) and one in the UEFA Cup (in 2003), the latter two of these triumphs coming while the charismatic Jose Mourinho was in charge at the Estadio do Dragao.
- Porto are the only Portuguese club to have been crowned world champions, claiming the World Club Cup in both 1987 and 2004.

Portsmouth have appeared in two FA Cup finals already this century

> HONOURS
> **Portuguese League champions** 1935, 1939, 1940, 1956, 1959, 1978, 1979, 1985, 1986, 1988, 1990, 1992, 1993, 1995, 1996, 1997, 1998, 1999, 2003, 2004, 2006, 2007, 2008, 2009
> **Portuguese Cup** 1922, 1925, 1932, 1937, 1956, 1958, 1968, 1977, 1984, 1988, 1991, 1994, 1998, 2000, 2001, 2003, 2006, 2009
> **European Cup/Champions League** 1987, 2004
> **UEFA Cup** 2003
> **European Super Cup** 1987
> **World Club Cup** 1987, 2004

PORTSMOUTH

Year founded: 1898
Ground: Fratton Park (20,688)
Nickname: Pompey
Biggest win: 9-1 v Notts County (1927)
Heaviest defeat: 0-10 v Leicester City (1928)
Colours: Blue shirts with white trim, white shorts, red socks

Portsmouth were founded in 1898 by a group of sportsmen and businessmen at a meeting in the city's High Street. After starting out in the Southern League the club joined the Third Division in 1920.
- In 1949 the club became the first team to rise from the third tier to claim the league championship, and the following year became the first of just five clubs to retain the title since the end of the Second World War.
- The most influential player in that team was half-back Jimmy Dickinson, who went on to play a record 764 times for Pompey, the second highest number of Football League appearances with any single club. Dickinson is also Portsmouth's most decorated international, winning 48 caps for England.
- Another legendary figure from that period, right-winger Peter Harris, is the club's leading marksman, with 193 goals between 1946-60.
- The club won the FA Cup for the first time in 1939, when Pompey thrashed favourites Wolves 4-1 in the final at Wembley. The club's success was attributed to the 'lucky' white spats worn by manager Jack Tinn throughout the cup run.
- In 2008 the famous Pompey Chimes ("Play up Pompey, Pompey play up!") were heard at Wembley again as Portsmouth took on Cardiff in only the second FA Cup final to be played at the new national stadium. A single goal by Portsmouth's Nigerian striker Kanu was enough to see off the Welshmen, sparking ecstatic celebrations across the city.
- Already relegated from the Premier League and suffering grave financial difficulties, Pompey made it to the FA Cup final again in 2010 but their

miserable season ended on a low note when they lost 1-0 to champions Chelsea.

• Portsmouth's record signing is gangly striker Peter Crouch, who re-joined the club from Liverpool for £11 million in 2008 having previously signed for Pompey from QPR in 2001 (also for a then club record fee of £1.5 million). Later in 2008, Pompey made their record sale when midfielder Lassana Diarra joined Real Madrid for a cool £20 million.

HONOURS

Division 1 champions 1949, 1950
First Division champions 2003
Division 3 (South) champions 1924
Division 3 champions 1962, 1983
FA Cup 1939, 2008

IS THAT A FACT?

After winning the FA Cup in 1939 Portsmouth remained holders of the trophy for a record seven years as the disruption caused by the Second World War prevented the competition being played until the 1945/46 season.

PORTUGAL

First international: Spain 3 Portugal 1, 1921
Most capped player: Luis Figo, 127 caps (1991-2006)
Leading goalscorer: Pauleta, 47 goals (1997-2006)
First World Cup appearance: Portugal 3 Hungary 1, 1966
Biggest win: Portugal 8 Liechtenstein 0, 1994 and 1999
Heaviest defeat: Portugal 0 England 10, 1947
Colours: Red shirts with a single green hoop, red shorts, red socks

Portugal have never won a major trophy, although led by then manager Luiz Felipe Scolari they did reach the final of the European Championships in 2004. Playing on home soil they were

Despite sporting a very snazzy kit at the 2010 World Cup, Portugal failed once more to get their hands on the trophy

hot favourites to beat Greece, but went down to a surprise 1-0 defeat.

• **Portugal's best showing at the World Cup was in 1966 when they finished third after going out to hosts England in the semi-finals. Much of their success was down to legendary striker Eusebio, who topped the goalscoring charts at the tournament with nine goals.**

• The southern Europeans also reached the semi-finals of the World Cup in 2006, after beating Holland in 'The Battle of Nuremburg' in the last 16 and England on penalties in the quarter-finals. A 1-0 defeat to France, though, ended their hopes of appearing in the final.

• **Portugal were the first country to beat West Germany at home in a competitive match, winning 1-0 in Stuttgart in a World Cup qualifier in 1985. That victory booked Portugal's passage to the 1986 World Cup in Mexico where they went out in the first round despite recording a shock 1-0 victory over England in their first match.**

WORLD CUP RECORD

1930-38 *Did not enter*
1950-62 *Did not qualify*
1966 *Third place*
1970-82 *Did not qualify*
1986 *Round 1*
1990-98 *Did not qualify*
2002 *Round 1*
2006 *Fourth place*
2010 *Round 2*

PREMIER LEAGUE

The Premier League was founded in 1992 and is now the most watched and most lucrative sporting league in the world, with revenues of around £2 billion in the 2009/10 season.

• **Initially composed of 22 clubs, the Premier League was reduced to 20 teams in 1995. A total of 44 clubs have played in the league but just four – Manchester United, Blackburn Rovers, Arsenal and Chelsea – have won the title. Of this quartet, United are easily the most successful, having won the league 11 times.**

• The first ever Premier League goal was scored by Sheffield United striker Brian Deane on 15th August 1992 five minutes into the Blades' 2-1 victory against Manchester United at Bramall Lane.

• **Only seven clubs have appeared in the league in every season since its inception: Arsenal, Aston Villa, Chelsea, Everton, Liverpool, Manchester United and Tottenham Hotspur. United lead the all-time table with 1,494 points (including a record 449 wins in 696 games), followed by Arsenal (1,311 points) and Chelsea (1,267 points).**

• Alan Shearer is the leading scorer in the history of the Premier League with a total of 260 goals for Southampton, Blackburn Rovers and Newcastle between 1992 and 2006.

• **David James is the leading appearance-maker in the history of the Premier League, turning out in a total of 537 games for five clubs between 1992-2010.**

PRESTON NORTH END

Year founded: 1879
Ground: Deepdale (24,525)
Nickname: The Lilywhites
Biggest win: 26-0 v Hyde (1887)
Heaviest defeat: 0-7 v Blackpool (1948)
Colours: White shirts, navy blue shorts, white socks

Preston were founded in 1879 as a branch of the North End Cricket and Rugby Club, playing football exclusively from 1881.

• Founder members of the Football League in 1888, Preston won the inaugural league title the following year, going through the entire 22-game season undefeated and conceding just 15 goals (a league record). For good measure the club also won the FA Cup, beating Wolves 3-0 in the final, to become the first club to win the Double. During their cup run, Preston demolished Hyde 26-0 to record the biggest ever win in any English competition, striker Jimmy Ross scoring seven of the goals to set a club record that has never been matched.

• Of the 12 founder members of the league, Preston are the only club still playing at the same ground, making Deepdale the oldest league football stadium anywhere in the world.

• The legendary Tom Finney is Preston's most capped international, turning out for England in 76 games. The flying winger is also the club's highest scorer, with 187 strikes between 1946-60. North End's leading appearance maker is Alan Kelly, who played in goal for the club in 447 league games between 1958-73.

• Along with Wolves and Burnley, Preston are one of just three clubs to have won all four divisions of English football, achieving this feat in 1996 when they topped the Third Division (now League Two).

• Preston have appeared in the play-offs on a record eight occasions but, strangely, have yet to be promoted via this route.

HONOURS
Division 1 champions 1889, 1890
Division 2 champions 1904, 1913, 1951
Division 3 champions 1971
Second Division champions 2000
Third Division champions 1996
FA Cup 1889, 1938
Double 1889

PROFESSIONAL FOOTBALLERS' ASSOCIATION

Founded in 1907 as the successor to the short-lived Association Footballers' Union, the PFA is the world's oldest professional sportsmen's association and has 4,000 members.

• Former chairmen of the PFA include Garth Crooks, Derek Dougan and, most famously of all, Jimmy Hill (1957-61), who led an ultimately successful campaign to abolish the then maximum wage of £20 per week. The current chairman is ex-Leicester City defender Chris Powell.

• In 1974 the PFA established three major awards: Players' Player of the Year (first won by Leeds United defender Norman Hunter); Young Player of the Year (first won by Ipswich defender Kevin Beattie) and the Merit award for services to football (first won by Bobby Charlton and PFA secretary Cliff Lloyd).

• The PFA chairman heads a ten-strong Management Committee of elected players who currently include Manchester United defender Gary Neville and Wolves goalkeeper Marcus Hahnemann. The chief executive of the body is the long-serving Gordon Taylor, a former winger with Bolton and Birmingham City. He is reputed to be the highest paid union official in the world, receiving an annual salary well in excess of £1 million.

PROFESSIONAL FOOTBALLERS' ASSOCIATION

Preston captain Tom Smith shows off the FA Cup in 1938, the club's last major trophy

PROGRAMMES

PROGRAMMES

Football programmes started out in the 1870s as simple teamsheets and have since evolved to become full-colour magazines of 50 or more pages. The programme for the 2007 FA Cup Final between Chelsea and Manchester United provided the event's biggest ever read, running to 146 pages.

• On 25th December 1948 Chelsea became the first club to issue a 16-page magazine-style programme for their home match against Portsmouth.

• Between 1904-35 Everton and Liverpool issued a shared programme, which covered both the first team game of whichever club happened to be at home that week and the reserve team home game of the other club.

• In 2006 a single sheet programme from the 1889 FA Cup final between Wolves and Preston fetched £21,850 at auction, a world record price for a football programme. Before the auction the document was expected to sell for £7,000-£10,000 but a lively bidding war, which was eventually won by Giles Lyon, a bookseller from Farnham, Surrey, pushed the price up.

PROMOTION

Automatic promotion from the Second to First Division was introduced in the 1898/99 season, replacing the previous 'test match' play-off style system. The first two clubs to go up automatically were Glossop North End and Manchester City.

• Birmingham City and Notts County have gained a record 13 promotions, while the Brummies and Leicester have both gone up to the top flight on a record 11 occasions.

• Not all clubs who have been promoted have done so through playing merit. The most notorious case involved Arsenal in 1919 who were elected to the First Division at the expense of local rivals Tottenham, allegedly thanks to the underhand tactics employed by the Gunners' then chairman, Sir Henry Norris.

• In the Premiership era promoted clubs have often struggled against relegation the following season. The worst season for the new boys was in 1997/98 when all three promoted clubs – Barnsley, Bolton and Crystal Palace – were relegated at the end of the campaign. Four years later, on the other hand, Blackburn, Bolton and Fulham all stayed up – the only season in Premiership history when

Zakaria Labyad scores for Dutch giants PSV

the promoted trio have managed to maintain their new status.

PSV EINDHOVEN

Year founded: 1913
Ground: Philips Stadium (35,119)
Nickname: Boeren ('The Farmers')
Colours: Red-and-white striped shirts, black shorts, red and white socks

As their name indicates PSV, or Philips Sport Vereniging (Union in English), were founded in 1913 as a works team for the giant electronics company Philips.

• PSV have dominated Dutch football in recent times and are now their country's second most successful club ever, after Ajax, with 21 league titles. Their greatest moment, though, came in 1988 when they beat Benfica on penalties to win the European Cup, a feat previously achieved by both their arch rivals in domestic football, Ajax and Feyenoord.

• The club had also won the UEFA Cup a decade earlier, beating French side Bastia 3-0 in a two-legged final in 1978.

• Twice managed by former Chelsea boss Guus Hiddink, PSV appointed Bobby Robson as their new manager shortly before he led England into the 1990 World Cup. In three years Robson won the league twice, but was sacked after a lack of success in Europe.

• Famous players to turn out for PSV

include Ruud Gullit, Ronaldo, Ruud van Nistelrooy and Arjen Robben. Still owned by Philips, PSV have sported the company's names on their shirts since 1982, a record for Dutch football.

HONOURS
Dutch League champions 1929, 1935, 1951, 1963, 1975, 1976, 1978, 1986, 1987, 1988, 1989, 1991, 1992, 1997, 2000, 2001, 2003, 2005, 2006, 2007, 2008
Dutch Cup 1950, 1974, 1976, 1988, 1989, 1990, 1996, 2005
European Cup 1988
UEFA Cup 1978

FERENC PUSKAS

Born: Budapest, 2nd April 1927
Died: 17th November 2006
Position: Striker
Club career:
1943-49 Kispest 177 (187)
1949-56 Honved 164 (165)
1958-66 Real Madrid 182 (157)
International record:
1945-56 Hungary 84 (83)
1962 Spain 4 (0)

The greatest Hungarian player ever and the all-time top scorer for his country with an incredible 83 goals, Ferenc Puskas is one of the legendary names of world football.

• Nicknamed 'the Galloping Major' during his time with the Hungarian army team Honved, the left-footed Puskas captained his country to Olympic victory in 1952 and, two years later, to the World Cup final.

Although not fully fit, he got on the scoresheet in the biggest match of his career, but finished on the losing side as West Germany recovered from 2-0 down to win 3-2.

• Puskas skippered Hungary to their most famous victory in 1953, scoring twice as the central Europeans became the first country from outside the British Isles to beat England on home soil. The 6-3 score that day was remarkable, but the next year England went down to their biggest ever thrashing, losing 7-1 in Budapest with Puskas grabbing another brace.

• After the Hungarian revolution in 1956, Puskas fled his homeland and was banned from playing by UEFA for two years. He took centre stage again with Real Madrid, starring alongside the brilliant Alfredo di Stefano, won five league titles and was top scorer in La Liga on four occasions.

• In 1960 Puskas won the European Cup with Real, notching four goals in the final as the Spanish giants overwhelmed Eintracht Frankfurt 7-3 at Hampden Park in a game considered by many to be the greatest ever played. Two years later he hit another hat-trick in the final, although Real went down 5-3 to Benfica.

• Puskas later managed Greek side Panathinaikos, who he led to the European Cup final in 1971. A revered figure in Hungary, the national stadium in Budapest was renamed in his honour in 2002 and, following his death in 2006 he was given a full state funeral.

QUEENS PARK

Year founded: 1867
Ground: Hampden Park (52,500)
Nickname: The Spiders
Biggest win: 16-0 v St Peters (1885)
Heaviest defeat: 0-9 v Motherwell (1930)
Colours: Black-and-white hooped shirts, white shorts, white socks

Founded in 1867 at a meeting at a house in south Glasgow, Queen's Park are Scotland's oldest club.

• **The dominant force in the game north of the border in the 19th century, Queen's Park won the first ever Scottish Cup in 1874 and held the** trophy for the next two years as well. In all, they have won the competition ten times... a cup record only bettered by Old Firm giants Celtic and Rangers.

• Queen's Park's star player of the Victorian era was Charles Campbell, who won a record eight Scottish Cup winners' medals.

• **Queen's Park are the only Scottish side to have played in the final of the FA Cup, losing to Blackburn Rovers in both 1884 and 1885 before the Scottish FA banned its clubs from entering the competition two years later.**

• Despite being the only amateur club in senior football anywhere in Britain, Queen's Park play their games at the home of Scottish football, Hampden Park, but rarely attract more than a few hundred spectators to the 52,500-capacity stadium.

HONOURS
Division Two champions 1923, 1956
Second Division champions 1981
Third Division champions 2000
Scottish Cup 1874, 1875, 1876, 1880, 1881, 1882, 1884, 1886, 1890, 1893

QUEENS PARK RANGERS

Year founded: 1882
Ground: Loftus Road (19,128)
Nickname: The R's
Biggest win: 9-2 v Tranmere Rovers (1960)
Heaviest defeat: 1-8 v Mansfield Town (1965) and v Manchester United (1969)
Colours: Blue-and-white hooped shirts, white shorts, white socks

Founded in 1882 following the merger of St Jude's and Christchurch Rangers, the club was called Queens Park Rangers because most of the players came from the Queens Park area of north-west London.

• **A nomadic outfit in their early days, QPR have staged home matches at no fewer than 19 different venues, a record for a Football League club.**

• The club enjoyed its finest moment in 1967 when Rangers came from two goals down to defeat West Bromwich Albion 3-2 in the first ever League Cup final to be played at Wembley. In the same season the R's won the Third Division title to pull off a unique double.

• **Loftus Road favourite Rodney Marsh hit a club record 44 goals that season, 11 of them coming in the League Cup.** George Goddard, though, holds the club

Rodney Marsh

record for league goals with 37 in 1929/30. Goddard is also the club's leading scorer, notching 174 league goals between 1926-34.

• In 1976 QPR finished second in the old First Division, being pipped to the league championship by Liverpool in the last game of the season. Six years later Rangers reached the FA Cup final for the only time in their history, but went down 1-0 to London rivals Tottenham in a replay.

• **No other player has pulled on Rangers' famous hoops more often than Tony Ingham, who made 519 league appearances over 13 years after signing from Leeds in 1950.**

• Now partly owned by Formula 1 tycoons Flavio Briatore and Bernie Ecclestone, QPR splashed out a club record £3.5 million in 2009 when they signed midfielder Alejandro Faurlin from Argentinean club Instituto de Cordoba. In 1995 the R's made their record sale when striker Les Ferdinand joined Newcastle for a cool £6 million.

HONOURS
Division Two champions 1983
Division Three (S) champions 1948
Division Three champions 1967
League Cup 1967

'Right, we've beaten them once, now go out there and... er, sorry, lads, I think you've already heard that one!'

SIR ALF RAMSEY

Born: Dagenham,
21st January 1920
Died: 28th April 1999
Managerial career:
1955-63 Ipswich Town
1963-74 England
1977-78 Birmingham City

England manager between 1963 and 1974, Alf Ramsey is the only man to have guided the Three Lions to victory in a World Cup final.

• At the 1966 tournament England were one of the favourites, primarily because they had the advantage of being hosts and playing all their matches at Wembley. Ramsey still had to get the team to perform, though, and he did so brilliantly, devising a 4-4-2 formation without wide men which earned England the nickname of 'the Wingless Wonders'.

• His most important single contribution came just after West Germany scored a last-minute equaliser to take the final into extra-time. "You've beaten them once," he told his disappointed players, "now go out there and bloody beat them again." England did precisely that, scoring two more goals to win 4-2.

• Ramsey was sacked from the England job after failing to lead the team to the 1974 World Cup in West Germany.

Under his management, England won 69 of 113 matches and only lost 17.

• As a club manager, Ramsey took over Third Division Ipswich Town in 1955, taking them into the second tier in 1957. In 1961 they won the Second Division title and the following season Ipswich were crowned league champions for the first and only time in their history. In recognition of these remarkable achievements a statue of Ramsey was erected outside Portman Road a year after his death in 1999.

• A solid right-back for Southampton and Spurs in his playing days, Ramsey won 32 caps for England and scored three goals, including one from the penalty spot in the infamous 6-3 thrashing by Hungary at Wembley in 1953.

RANGERS

Year founded: 1873
Ground: Ibrox Stadium (51,082)
Nickname: The Gers
Biggest win: 14-2 v Blairgowrie (1934)
Heaviest defeat: 2-10 v Airdrieonians (1886)
Colours: Royal blue shirts, white shorts, black socks with red trim

The most decorated club in the history of world football, Rangers were founded by a group of rowing enthusiasts in 1873. The club were founder members of the Scottish League in 1890, sharing the inaugural title with Dumbarton.

• **Rangers have won the league title 52 times, a record of domestic success which is unmatched by any club on the planet. Between 1989-97 the Gers topped the league in nine consecutive seasons, initially under Graeme Souness then under current boss Walter Smith, to equal a record previously set by arch rivals Celtic.**

• In 2000 Rangers became the first club in the world to win 100 major trophies. The Glasgow giants have since extended their tally to 113, most recently adding the League Cup in 2010. The club's tally of seven domestic trebles is also unequalled anywhere in the world.

• **Way back in 1898/99 Rangers enjoyed their best ever league season, winning all 18 of their matches to establish yet another world record.**

• The club's record goalscorer is current assistant manager, and former *Question of Sport* captain, Ally McCoist. In a 15-year Ibrox career between 1983-98 McCoist banged in an incredible 251 goals (355 in all competitions), including a record 28 hat-tricks. McCoist is also the club's most-capped international, winning 59 of his 61 Scotland caps while with the Gers.

• Rangers also hold two important records in the Scottish League Cup, with more wins (26) and more appearances in the final (32) than any other club. The Gers' first win in the competition came in its inaugural year when they thrashed Aberdeen 4-0 in the final in 1947.

• The club's record in the Scottish Cup is not quite as impressive, the Gers' 33 triumphs in the competition being bettered by Celtic's 34. However, it was in the Scottish Cup that Rangers recorded their biggest ever victory, thrashing Blairgowrie 14-2 in 1934. Striker Jimmy Fleming scored nine of the goals on the day to set a club record.

• Despite all their domestic success, Rangers have only won a single European trophy. That was the Cup Winners' Cup, which they claimed in 1972 after beating Dynamo Moscow 3-2 in the final in Barcelona. The club, though, did reach the final of the same competition in both 1961 and 1967 and were also runners-up in the UEFA Cup in 2008, when an estimated 150,000 (mostly ticketless) Rangers fans followed their team to the final in Manchester.

• No player has turned out in the royal blue shirt of Rangers more often than former captain John Greig, who made 755 appearances in all competitions between 1961-78. The league record, though, is held by Sandy Archibald (513 games between 1917-34).

• In two spells with Rangers between 1994-2009 midfielder Barry Ferguson made 82 European appearances, a record for a Scottish player.

• In 2000 Rangers splashed out a club record £12 million when they signed lanky Norwegian striker Tore Andre Flo from Chelsea. Eight years later, in 2008, the Ibrox coffers were boosted by a record £9 million when full back Alan Hutton moved south of the border to join Spurs.

> HONOURS
> **Division 1 champions** *1891 (shared), 1899, 1900, 1901, 1902, 1911, 1912, 1913, 1918, 1920, 1921, 1923, 1924, 1925, 1927, 1928, 1929, 1930, 1931, 1933, 1934, 1935, 1937, 1939, 1947, 1949, 1950, 1953, 1956, 1957, 1959, 1961, 1963, 1964, 1975*
> **Premier League champions** *1976, 1978, 1987, 1989, 1990, 1991, 1992, 1993, 1994, 1995, 1996, 1997, 1999, 2000, 2003, 2005, 2009, 2010*
> **Scottish Cup** *1894, 1897, 1898, 1903, 1928, 1930, 1932, 1934, 1935, 1936, 1948, 1949, 1950, 1953, 1960, 1962, 1963, 1964, 1966, 1973, 1976, 1978, 1979, 1981, 1992, 1993, 1996, 1999, 2000, 2002, 2003, 2008, 2009*
> **Scottish League Cup** *1947, 1949, 1961, 1962, 1964, 1965, 1971, 1976, 1978, 1979, 1982, 1984, 1985, 1987, 1988, 1989, 1991, 1993, 1994, 1997, 1999, 2002, 2003, 2005, 2008, 2010*
> **European Cup Winners' Cup** *1972*

IS THAT A FACT?
On 2nd January 1939 the Old Firm derby between Rangers and Celtic at Ibrox attracted a crowd of 118,567, a record for a British league match.

RAUL

> **Born:** Madrid, 27th June 1977
> **Position:** Striker
> **Club career:**
> 1994-2010 Real Madrid 521 (223)
> 2010- Schalke
> **International record:**
> 1996-2006 Spain 102 (44)

Raul Gonzalez Blanco, usually known simply as Raul, is Spain's record scorer with 44 goals and his country's highest-capped outfield player with 102 international appearances between 1996-2006.

• **A three-time winner of the Champions League with Real Madrid, Raul was the first player to score in two finals of the competition, netting in Real's victories against Valencia in 2000 and Bayer Leverkusen two years later. He is**

Cleverly camouflaged for the conditions, Rangers ran out easy 10-0 winners!!!

also the all-time leading scorer in the Champions League, having scored an incredible 66 goals in 130 appearances (another record).

• Raul was the club's youngest ever player when he made his debut in 1994 aged 17 and four months. He went on to win six La Liga titles with the Spanish giants and in 2009 became Real's all-time leading scorer when he passed Alfredo di Stefano's longstanding club record of 216 goals. By the time he left for German club Schalke in 2010 he was third on the list of all-time scorers in Spain with 228 goals in La Liga, while his total of 550 La Liga appearances is only exceeded by former Barcelona goalkeeper Andoni Zubizarreta.

• **Surprisingly, Raul has never won the Copa del Rey, the Spanish equivalent of the FA Cup. He has also missed out on international honours, failing to be selected for the Spanish squad which won Euro 2008.**

Real Madrid's Carvalho is really not going to let Bayern's Ribery get past is he!

READING

Year founded: 1871
Ground: Madjeski Stadium (24,224)
Nickname: The Royals
Biggest win: 10-2 v Crystal Palace (1946)
Heaviest defeat: 0-18 v Preston (1894)
Colours: Navy-and-white hooped shirts, blue shorts, navy socks

Reading were founded in 1871, making them the oldest Football League club south of Nottingham. After amalgamating with local clubs Reading Hornets (in 1877) and Earley FC (in 1889), the club was eventually elected to the new Third Division in 1920.

• **The oldest club still competing in the FA Cup never to have won the trophy, Reading experienced their worst ever defeat in the competition when they were hammered 18-0 by Preston in 1894.**

• Happier days followed, though, when Reading toured Italy in 1913. After beating AC Milan 5-0 and the Italian national team 2-0, the club were hailed as "the finest foreign team seen in Italy" by the Corriere della Sera newspaper.

• **In the 1985/86 season Reading set a Football League record by winning their opening 13 matches, an outstanding**

start which provided the launchpad for The Royals to go on to top the old Third Division at the end of the campaign.

• Reading's greatest moment, though, came in 2006 when, under manager Steve Coppell, they won promotion to the top flight for the first time in their history. They went up in fine style, too, claiming the Championship title with a Football League record 106 points and going 33 matches unbeaten (a record for the second tier) between 9th August 2005 and 17th February 2006.

• **Prolific marksman Ronnie Blackman holds two scoring records for the club, with a total of 158 goals between 1947-54 and a seasonal best of 39 goals in the 1951/52 campaign.**

• Stalwart defender Martin Hicks is Reading's longest-serving player, making precisely 500 league appearances for the club between 1978-91.

• **In 2001 Reading became the first English club to register their supporters as an official member of the squad when their fans were allotted the vacant number 13 shirt.**

• During their brief Premier League sojourn, Reading were involved in the competition's highest-scoring match,

losing 7-4 to Portsmouth in 2007.

HONOURS
Championship champions 2006
Division 3 (South) champions 1926
Division 3 champions 1986
Second Division champions 1994
Division 4 champions 1979

REAL MADRID

Year founded: 1902
Ground: Estadio Bernabeu (80,354)
Previous name: Madrid FC
Nickname: Los Meringues ('The Merengues')
Colours: White shirts, white shorts, white socks

Founded by students as Madrid FC in 1902, the title 'Real' (meaning 'Royal') was bestowed on the club by King Alfonso XIII in 1920.

• **One of the most famous names**

in world football, Real Madrid won the first ever European Cup in 1956 and went on to a claim a record five consecutive victories in the competition with a side featuring greats such as Alfredo di Stefano, Ferenc Puskas and Francisco Gento. Real's current total of nine victories in the European Cup/Champions League is also a record.

• The club have dominated Spanish football over the years, winning a record 31 league titles (11 more than nearest rivals Barcelona) including a record five on the trot on two occasions (1961-65 and 1986-90).

• As Madrid FC the club won silverware for the first time, the Spanish Cup, in 1905. They went on to win the trophy four times in succession, a record later equalled by their opponents in the final, Athletic Bilbao.

• Between 17th February 1957 and 7th March 1965 Real Madrid were undefeated at home in the league for an incredible 121 consecutive matches, a sequence unmatched by any European team.

HONOURS
Spanish League *1932, 1933, 1954, 1955, 1957, 1958, 1961, 1962, 1963, 1964, 1965, 1967, 1968, 1969, 1972, 1975, 1976, 1978, 1979, 1980, 1986, 1987, 1988, 1989, 1990, 1995, 1997, 2001, 2003, 2007, 2008*
Spanish Cup *1905, 1906, 1907, 1908, 1917, 1934, 1936, 1946, 1947, 1962, 1970, 1974, 1975, 1980, 1982, 1989, 1993*
European Cup/Champions League *1956, 1957, 1958, 1959, 1960, 1966, 1998, 2000, 2002*
UEFA Cup *1985, 1986*
European Super Cup *2002*
Club World Cup *1960, 1998, 2002*

HARRY REDKNAPP

Born: Poplar, 2nd March 1947
Managerial career:
1983-92 Bournemouth
1994-2001 West Ham United
2002-04 Portsmouth
2004-05 Southampton
2005-08 Portsmouth
2008- Tottenham Hotspur

Tottenham boss Harry Redknapp is one of the most experienced managers in the game, having previously been in charge

of Bournemouth, West Ham, Portsmouth (twice) and Southampton.

• Redknapp enjoyed his greatest successes with Pompey, leading the south coast club into the Premiership in 2003 in his first spell at Fratton Park and then guiding Portsmouth to a first triumph in the FA Cup for 69 years in 2008 after returning to the club from local rivals Southampton three years earlier.

• Redknapp then moved on to Tottenham, the London club paying £5 million to Portsmouth in compensation when he succeeded the hapless Juande Ramos at White Hart Lane. Spurs were in the relegation zone when he arrived but, thanks in part to big money signings like Jermain Defoe, Peter Crouch and Wilson Palacios, Redknapp was able to guide his new club to mid-table safety by the end of the 2008/09 season. The following year he led Spurs to fourth place in the Premier League, the club's best finish since they came third in 1990. The achievement helped him to the title of Premiership Manager of the Year.

• One of the most quotable managers in the Premiership, Redknapp has a sharp sense of humour. After Darren Bent missed a sitter for Spurs in a

2009 encounter with Portsmouth he told the press pack, "My missus could have scored that one".

• The father of former Liverpool and England player Jamie and the uncle of Chelsea's Frank Lampard, Redknapp spent most of his playing career with West Ham and Bournemouth.

REFEREES

In the 19th century Colonel Francis Marinden was the referee at a record nine FA Cup finals, including eight on the trot between 1883-90. His record will never be beaten as the FA now appoints a different referee for the FA Cup final every year.

• The first referee to send off a player in the FA Cup final was Peter Willis, who dismissed Manchester United defender Kevin Moran in the 1985 final for a foul on Everton's Peter Reid. Video replays showed that it was a harsh decision.

• Modern-day referees have to put up with plenty of abuse but at least none of them have suffered the unfortunate fate of William Ernest Williams, who was attacked and killed in his dressing room in 1912 after a match between Wattstown and Aberaman Athletic in south Wales. His attacker was later jailed for manslaughter.

• During the 2009/10 season Martin Atkinson was the most officious referee on the Premier League list, showing 119 yellow cards and five reds in 30 games.

Thank goodness Harry Redknapp isn't directing traffic!

PEPE REINA

Born: Madrid, 31st August 1982
Position: Goalkeeper
Club career:
1999-2000 Barcelona B 41
2000-02 Barcelona 30
2002-05 Villarreal 109
2005- Liverpool 182
International record:
2005- Spain 20

A model of consistency since he arrived from Villarreal in 2005, Liverpool goalkeeper Pepe Reina has won the Barclays Golden Glove (awarded to the keeper with the most clean sheets in the Premier League) a record four times, most recently sharing the honour with Chelsea stopper Petr Cech at the end of the 2009/10 season.

• In his five years on Merseyside, Reina has won just one major honour with the Reds, the FA Cup in 2006. Despite having a poor game by his own high standards, the Madrid-born goalkeeper ended the afternoon as the Reds' hero after he sensationally saved three of West Ham's penalties in the shoot-out that followed a gripping 3-3 draw.

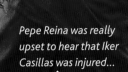

Pepe Reina was really upset to hear that Iker Casillas was injured...

• The following year Reina became only the third player to follow his father by featuring in a European Cup final when he lined up against AC Milan in Athens. Unfortunately, Reina finished on the losing side, just as his father, Miguel, had done in 1974 with Atletico Madrid.

• Reina made his international debut for Spain in 2005 but has had to be content with being his country's number two behind Real Madrid's Iker Casillas. He did, though, make a small contribution to Spain's Euro 2008 triumph, appearing in a group stage win against Greece.

RELEGATION

Birmingham City and Leicester City share the unwanted record of having been relegated from the top flight more often than any other club, both having taken the drop 11 times. Neither club, though, has experienced that sinking feeling as often as Notts County, who have suffered 15 relegations.

• In the Premiership era Crystal Palace have been the most unfortunate club, dropping out of the top flight on no fewer than four occasions.

• Of longstanding members of the Football League or Premiership, Arsenal have the best relegation record having only once been demoted (in 1913) in a proud 123-year history.

• When Derby County went down from the Premiership in 2008 they did so with the lowest points total of any club in the history of the English league football. The Rams accumulated only 11 points in a miserable campaign, during which they managed to win just one match out of 38.

REPLAYS

In the days before penalty shoot-outs, the FA Cup fourth qualifying round tie between Alvechurch and Oxford City went to a

record five replays before Alvechurch reached the first round proper with a 1-0 win in the sixth match between the two clubs.

• The first FA Cup final to go to a replay was the 1875 match between Royal Engineers and Old Etonians, Engineers winning 2-0 in the second match. The last FA Cup final to require a replay was the 1993 match between Arsenal and Sheffield Wednesday, the Gunners eventually triumphing 2-1 in the second game. In 1999 the FA scrapped final replays, ruling that any drawn match would be settled on the day by penalties.

• Five League Cup finals have gone to replays, the first in 1977 between Aston Villa and Everton requiring a third match before Villa eventually won 3-2 at Old Trafford.

• Only one European Cup final went to a replay, Bayern Munich defeating Atletico Madrid 4-0 in 1974 after the original final ended in a 0-0 draw.

• In 1999 the FA ordered a rematch of Arsenal's fifth round FA Cup tie with Sheffield United after Marc Overmars' controversial winning goal for the Gunners was deemed to have breached the spirit of the game, although it was not against the rules. Arsenal won the rematch 2-1, the same score as in the first game between the two clubs.

Robbie Keane celebrates one of his record 43 goals for the Republic of Ireland

REPUBLIC OF IRELAND

First international: Republic of Ireland 1 Bulgaria 0, 1924

Most capped players: Shay Given and Kevin Kilbane, 104 caps (1996/1997-)

Leading goalscorer: Robbie Keane, 43 goals (1998-)

First World Cup appearance: Republic of Ireland 1 England 1, 1990

Biggest win: 8-0 v Malta (1983)

Heaviest defeat: 0-7 v Brazil (1982)

Colours: Green shirts, white shorts, green socks

The Republic of Ireland enjoyed their most successful period under English manager Jack Charlton in the late 1980s and early 1990s. 'Big Jack' became a legend on the Emerald Isle after guiding the Republic to their first ever World Cup in 1990, taking the team to the quarter-finals of the tournament before they were eliminated by hosts Italy.

• Under Charlton, Ireland were undefeated in four matches against arch-rivals England, pulling off a famous 1-0 win in the 1988 European Championships and drawing three other competitive matches 1-1. This record prompted the gleeful chant whenever the teams met of, "You'll never beat the Irish!".

• The Republic were the first country from outside the United Kingdom to beat England on home soil, winning 2-0 at Goodison Park in 1949.

• **In 2009, in a World Cup play-off against France, the Republic were on the wrong end of one of the worst refereeing decisions of all time when Thierry Henry's blatant handball went unpunished before he crossed for William Gallas to score the goal that ended Ireland's hopes of reaching the 2010 finals in South Africa.**

• Tottenham striker Robbie Keane is easily the most prolific scorer in the Republic's history, with a total of 43 goals since making his international debut in 1998.

WORLD CUP RECORD
1930 *Did not enter*
1934 *Did not qualify*
1938 *Did not qualify*
1950 *Did not enter*
1954-86 *Did not qualify*
1990 *Quarter-finals*
1994 *Round 2*
1998 *Did not qualify*
2002 *Round 2*
2006 *Did not qualify*
2010 *Did not qualify*

DON REVIE

Born: Middlesbrough, 10th July 1927
Died: 26th May 1989
Managerial career:
1961-74 Leeds United
1974-77 England
1977-80 United Arab Emirates
1980-84 Al-Nasr
1984-85 Al-Ahly

Legendary Leeds boss Don Revie is the most successful manager in the club's history, guiding the Yorkshiremen to a string of triumphs in the 1960s and early 1970s.

• **Revie took over the club in 1961 when Leeds were threatened by relegation to the Third Division, but he built a combative team featuring the likes of Jack Charlton, Billy Bremner and Norman 'Bites Your Legs' Hunter that soon became the most feared in England. He led Leeds to two league titles, the FA Cup in 1972 (the only time the club have won the trophy), the League Cup in 1968 and the Fairs Cup in 1968 and 1971. In recognition of his achievements the kop at Elland Road was later renamed the Don Revie stand.**

• In 1974 Revie became England manager but he came under pressure after his team failed to qualify for the 1976 European

Championships. With qualification for the 1978 World Cup also looking remote, Revie resigned from the England job to negotiate a secret deal to manage the United Arab Emirates... making him one of the most unpopular men in the country for a while.

• In his playing days Revie was a fine deep-lying centre forward who won six England caps and helped Manchester City win the FA Cup in 1956. The previous year he was voted Footballer of the Year and he also picked up the Manager of the Year award on three separate occasions.

RIVER PLATE

Year founded: 1901
Ground: El Monumental (65,645)
Nickname: Los Millonarios ('The Millionaires')
Colours: White shirts with red diagonal sash, black shorts, white socks

The most successful club in Argentina, River Plate were founded in 1901 by English residents of Buenos Aires, who decided to name the club after the river which the city sits on.

• The best year of the club's long and distinguished history was in 1986, when River Plate won an unprecedented quadruple made up of the World Club Cup, the South American Copa Libertadores, the Inter-American Cup and the Argentinian league championship.

• In Argentina, though, the most respected River Plate side ever was the attack-minded one of the 1940s, whose forward line was nicknamed 'La Maquina' or 'the Machine'.

• Among the many famous names to have played for the club are the legendary Alfredo di Stefano, former Chelsea striker Hernan Crespo and current Liverpool star Javier Mascherano.

• River Plate's derby with local rivals Boca Juniors is the most intense in Argentine football and, arguably, the whole world. The two sides first met in 1913, when River Plate won 2-1 and have been involved in numerous fiercely-fought matches since, including one in 1931 which had to be abandoned after three River players were sent off for complaining about a Boca goal and the rest of their team-mates walked off in protest.

HONOURS
Argentinian league champions 1932, 1936, 1937, 1941, 1942, 1945, 1947, 1952, 1953, 1955, 1956, 1957, 1975, 1979, 1980, 1981, 1986, 1990, 1993, 1996, 1997, 1999, 2000, 2002, 2003, 2004, 2008
Copa Libertadores 1986, 1996
World Club Cup 1986
Inter-American Cup 1986

ARJEN ROBBEN

Born: Holland, 23rd January 1984
Position: Winger
Club career:
2000-02 Groningen 50 (8)
2002-04 PSV 56 (17)
2004-07 Chelsea 67 (15)
2007-09 Real Madrid 50 (11)
2009- Bayern Munich 24 (16)
International record:
2003- Holland 52 (15)

One of the stars of Holland's impressive 2010 World Cup campaign, Arjen Robben might well have won the trophy for the Dutch if his carefully placed shot when clean through in the final had found the net rather than deflecting just wide after hitting the outstretched leg of Spain goalkeeper Iker Casillas.

• As it turned out, the flying Dutch winger had to settle for a runners-up medal in South Africa. That was the second major disappointment of 2010 for Robben, who also finished on the losing side in the Champions League final with his club Bayern Munich. However, he did win the domestic double with Bayern in his first season at the Allianz Arena, and he was also voted Player of the Year in Germany – the first Dutchman to receive this honour.

• After starting out with Groningen, Robben made his name with PSV, with whom he was named Dutch Young Player of the Year in 2003. The following year he

Even River Plate's stadium in far away Argentina was enveloped by the Icelandic volcanic ash cloud

The Bald v Hairy All-in Wrestling Final was briefly interrupted when a spectator threw a football into the ring

SIR BOBBY ROBSON

Born: Sacriston, County Durham, 18th February 1933
Died: 31st July 2009
Managerial career:
1968 Fulham
1969-82 Ipswich Town
1982-90 England
1990-92 PSV Eindhoven
1992-94 Sporting Lisbon
1994-96 Porto
1996-97 Barcelona
1998-99 PSV Eindhoven
1999-2004 Newcastle United

Apart from the legendary Sir Alf Ramsey, who won the trophy in 1966, no other England manager has come closer than Bobby Robson to claiming football's greatest prize. At the 1990 World Cup in Italy Robson's England reached the semi-finals, where they were desperately unlucky to be knocked out by Germany in a nail-biting penalty shoot-out.

• **Robson also guided England to the quarter-finals of the 1986 tournament in Mexico during an eight-year reign as his country's boss. Overall, his record was pretty good but a failure to qualify for the 1984 European championships and a poor showing at the 1988 finals made him a target for the tabloid press.**

• He made his managerial reputation with Ipswich, who he led to triumphs in the FA Cup (in 1978) and the UEFA Cup (in 1981). His achievements with the unfashionable East Anglian outfit prompted the club to erect a statue of Robson outside Portman Road in 2002. In the same year he received a knighthood for services to football.

• After resigning as England manager, Robson worked on the continent for a number of famous clubs. He won two league titles with PSV Eindhoven, another brace with Porto and, in 1997, the European Cup-Winners' Cup with Barcelona. His ended his managerial career with Newcastle, the club he had supported as a boy, twice leading the Geordies to Champions League qualification.

• Robson's playing career was spent with Fulham and West Bromwich Albion. He played 20 times for England, scoring twice on his debut in a 4-0 Wembley win over France in 1957. The following year he played in the World Cup in Sweden.

---

joined Chelsea where, despite suffering a number of injuries and a testicular cancer scare during his three years in London, he enjoyed huge success, helping the Blues win two Premier League titles, two Carling Cups and the FA Cup before departing for Real Madrid in 2007.

• **Robben made his debut for Holland in 2003. The following year he impressed at the Euro 2004 finals in Portugal, scoring the deciding penalty in the quarter-final against Sweden to clinch his country's first ever shoot-out victory. Still only 26, he has already won more than 50 international caps.**

ROBINHO

Born: Sao Vicente, Brazil, 25th January 1984
Position: Winger
Club career:
2002-05 Santos 104 (44)
2005-08 Real Madrid 101 (25)
2008- Manchester City 31 (14)
2010- Santos (loan) 12 (5)
International record:
2003- Brazil 79 (25)

In August 2008 Robinho became the most expensive player in the history of British football when he joined Manchester City from Real Madrid for £32.5 million. Moneybags City immediately made him the highest paid player in the Premiership, reportedly paying the Brazilian winger a cool £160,000 a week.

• **Robinho, real name Robson de Souza, made a great start to his City career, scoring on his debut against Chelsea, ironically the club he had previously been linked with for much of the summer. In his first season Robinho's dazzling close control and clever tricks made him a firm fans' favourite, but after a poor start to the following campaign he fell down the pecking order at City and in January 2010 went on loan to his first club, Santos, with whom he had won the Brazilian league in 2002 and 2004.**

• Robinho joined Real Madrid in 2005 and two years later helped the Spanish giants win La Liga on the last day of the season.

• **He made his international debut in 2003 in a 1-0 defeat against Mexico. Four years later Robinho was a key figure as Brazil won the Copa America, claiming the Golden Boot with a total of six goals in the competition.**

BRYAN ROBSON

Born: Chester-le-Street,
11th January 1957
Position: Midfielder
Club career:
1974-81 West Bromwich
Albion 198 (40)
1981-94 Manchester United 345 (74)
1994-96 Middlesbrough 25 (1)
International record:
1980-91 England 90 (26)

Bryan Robson was the most
expensive player in Britain in
the 1980s

Dubbed 'Captain Marvel' for his inspirational midfield performances for Manchester United and England, Bryan Robson captained his country on 65 occasions – a figure only surpassed by Billy Wright and Bobby Moore.

• Robson's £1.5 million move from West Bromwich Albion to Manchester United in 1981 broke the British transfer record and he remained the UK's most expensive player for the next six years. However, it proved money well spent as 'Robbo' went on to lead United to three FA Cups and the European Cup-Winners' Cup, as well as winning two Premier League titles later in his career.

• Robson won 90 caps for England, and would have gained many more but for a string of serious injuries. He scored 26 goals for his country, including one after just 27 seconds against France in 1982 which at the time was the fastest goal ever scored at the World Cup.

• In 1994 Robson became player-manager of Middlesbrough. In seven years in charge at the Riverside he led the Teesiders to three Wembley finals, all of which they lost. He has since managed West Brom, Bradford City and Sheffield United and is currently the coach of Thailand.

IS THAT A FACT?
Rochdale failed to win a single game in the FA Cup for 18 years from 1927 – the longest period of time any club has gone without tasting victory in the competition. The appalling run finally came to an end in 1945 when The Dale beat Stockport 2-1 in a first round replay.

ROCHDALE

Year founded: 1907
Ground: Spotland stadium (10,249)
Nickname: The Dale
Biggest win: 8-1 v Chesterfield (1926)
Heaviest defeat: 1-9 v Tranmere Rovers (1931)
Colours: Black-and-blue striped shirts, white shorts, blue socks

Founded at a meeting at the town's Central Council Office in 1907, Rochdale were elected to the Third Division (North) as founder members in 1921.

• In their long history, Rochdale have gained promotion just twice, climbing into the third tier for the first time in 1969. They stayed there until a disastrous season in 1973/74 when they finished bottom of the pile after winning just two matches... a Third Division record.

• For years opposition fans had cruelly referred to League Two as 'the Rochdale division', but The Dale had the last laugh when they won a second promotion from the basement division in 2010.

• The proudest day in the club's history, though, came in 1962 when they reached the League Cup final. Rochdale lost 4-0 on aggregate to Norwich City, then in the Second Division, but it remains the only time a club from the bottom division has reached a major cup final.

• Current Rochdale midfielder Gary Jones has made more appearances for the club than any other player, turning out in 370 games in two spells at Spotland.

ROMA

Year founded: 1927
Ground: Stadio Olimpico (72,000)
Nickname: I Lupi ('The Wolves')
Colours: Maroon red shirts with yellow trim, white shorts, black socks

Associazione Sportiva Roma were founded in 1927 following the merger of four clubs from the Italian capital and have since spent all but one season in the top flight of Italian football.

• The club, though, have only occasionally managed to break the domination of their main rivals in northern Italy, winning just three

Italian league titles. The most recent of these triumphs came in 2001 when the Roma side contained the likes of Brazilian defender Cafu, Argentinian striker Gabriel Batistuta and playmaker Francisco Totti, the club's all-time leading scorer with 192 goals in Serie A.

• Roma have just one European title to their name, beating Birmingham City 4-2 on aggregate in the 1961 Fairs Cup final. I Lupi, as they are known by fans, came close to winning the European Cup in 1984 but lost on penalties to Liverpool in a final played on their home ground.

• The Stadio Olimpico, which Roma share with city rivals Lazio, is the second biggest stadium in Italy (behind Milan's San Siro) with a capacity of over 72,000.

> HONOURS
> *Italian championship 1942, 1983, 2001*
> *Italian Cup 1964, 1969, 1980, 1981, 1984, 1986, 1991, 2007, 2008*
> *Fairs Cup 1961*

ROMARIO

> **Born:** Rio de Janeiro, Brazil, 29th January 1966
> **Position:** Striker
> **Club career:**
> 1985-88 Vasco da Gama 47 (17)
> 1988-93 PSV Eindhoven 109 (98)
> 1993-95 Barcelona 46 (34)
> 1995-96 Flamengo 16 (8)
> 1996 Valencia 5 (4)
> 1996-97 Flamengo 7 (3)
> 1997 Valencia 6 (1)
> 1998-99 Flamengo 39 (26)
> 1999-2002 Vasco da Gama 46 (41)
> 2002-03 Fluminense 26 (16)
> 2003 Al-Sadd 3 (0)
> 2003-04 Fluminense 34 (18)
> 2005-06 Vasco da Gama 32 (22)
> 2006 Miami FC 25 (19)
> 2006 Adelaide United 4 (1)
> 2007-08 Vasco da Gama 6 (3)
> **International record:**
> 1987-2005 Brazil 85 (71)

One of the most prolific strikers of all time, Romario was a key member of Brazil's 1994 World Cup-winning team. He scored five goals in the tournament and one in the shoot-out in the final when Brazil beat Italy on penalties to win the competition for a record fourth time. In the same year

he was voted FIFA World Player of the Year, having been runner-up 12 months earlier.

• Romario – real name Romario de Souza Faria – had an itinerant club career, playing for nine teams in four different continents. His best days were with PSV Eindhoven, with whom he won the Dutch league in 1989, 1991 and 1992, and with Barcelona, where he won the Spanish league in 1994 after top-scoring with an impressive 30 goals in just 33 games.

• A pint-sized penalty box predator, Romario claimed to have scored his 1,000th goal in professional football on 20th May 2007 when he netted from the penalty spot for Vasco da Gama in a match against Sport Recife. The game was held up for 20 minutes by celebrating fans, but since Romario's total included goals scored in junior football and friendly matches the validity of his claim is highly dubious.

• In an 18-year international career Romario banged in 71 goals for Brazil, making him his country's second highest scorer of all time behind the legendary Pele, who notched 77.

RONALDINHO

> **Born:** Porto Alegre, Brazil, 21st March 1980
> **Position:** Midfielder
> **Club career:**
> 1998-2001 Gremio 35 (14)
> 2001-03 Paris St Germain 53 (17)
> 2003-08 Barcelona 145 (70)
> 2008- AC Milan 65 (20)
> **International record:**
> 1999-2006 Brazil 97 (62)

A truly original talent who has more tricks than the average conjurer, Ronaldinho is only the second man (after fellow Brazilian Ronaldo) to retain the FIFA World Player of the Year title, topping the poll in both 2004 and 2005.

• Ronaldinho started out with Brazilian club Gremio before moving to Paris St Germain in 2001. Two years later he joined Barcelona, helping the Catalan giants win the Spanish league in 2005 and the Champions League in 2006.

• However, his love of the local nightlife and his frequent absences from training sessions made Ronaldinho a focus of dressing-room discontent, and in 2008 the buck-toothed midfielder signed for AC Milan in a £16.7 million deal after turning down a substantially bigger bid from Manchester City.

• One of a handful of players to represent Brazil from under-17 level upwards, Ronaldinho starred as his country won the World Cup for a record fifth time in 2002. His biggest contribution to the team's cause came in the quarter-final, when he scored the winning goal with a long-range free-kick that sailed over England goalkeeper David Seaman and into the top corner of the net.

RONALDO

> **Born:** Rio de Janeiro, September 22nd 1976
> **Position:** Striker
> **Club career:**
> 1993-94 Cruzeiro 14 (12)
> 1994-96 PSV Eindhoven 45 (42)
> 1996-97 Barcelona 37 (34)
> 1997-2002 Inter Milan 68 (49)
> 2002-07 Real Madrid 127 (83)
> 2007-08 AC Milan 20 (9)
> 2009- Corinthians 21 (13)
> **International record:**
> 1994- Brazil 97 (62)

'I learnt this trick from Sammy the Seal!'

Ronaldo, real name Ronaldo Luis Nazario de Lima, is the leading scorer in the history of the World Cup with 15 goals in the tournament. The toothy Brazilian striker passed Gerd Muller's old record of 14 goals at the 2006 World Cup in Germany.

• Ronaldo was top scorer at the 2002 World Cup with eight goals, two of them coming in the final when Brazil beat Germany 2-0 to win the trophy for

CRISTIANO RONALDO

a record fifth time. This triumph made up for the disappointment Ronaldo experienced four years earlier, when he suffered a convulsive fit 24 hours before the final against France and performed poorly as Brazil went down to a 3-0 defeat.

• Along with French legend Zinedine Zidane, Ronaldo is the only player to have been voted FIFA World Player of the Year on three occasions, in 1996, 1997 and 2002. He has also won the European Footballer of the Year award twice.

• Ronaldo spent most of his club career in Europe with some of the continent's leading names, including Barcelona, Real Madrid and both Inter and AC Milan. Until both Diego Forlan and Samuel Eto'o reached the milestone in 2008/09, he was the last player to score 30 or more goals in a La Liga season, hitting 33 for Barca in 1996/97.

CRISTIANO RONALDO

Born: Madeira, Portugal,
5th February 1985
Position: Winger/Striker
Club career:
2001-03 Sporting Lisbon 25 (3)
2003-09 Manchester United
196 (84)
2009- Real Madrid 29 (26)
International record:
2003- Portugal 76 (23)

In July 2009 Cristiano Ronaldo became the most expensive footballer ever when he joined Real Madrid from Manchester United for £80 million on a six-year contract worth a reported £10 million a year. Despite scoring 26 goals in his first season at the Bernabeu, Ronaldo missed out on silverware as Real endured a rare trophy-less campaign.

• Born on the Portuguese island of Madeira, Ronaldo began his career with Sporting Lisbon before joining Manchester United in a £12.25 million deal in 2003. The following year he won his first trophy with the Red Devils, opening the scoring as United beat Millwall 3-0 in the FA Cup final. He later helped United win a host of major honours, including three Premiership titles and the

The worlds's most expensive footballer

Champions League in 2008.

• In 2007 Ronaldo was voted PFA Player of the Year and Young Player of the Year, the first man to achieve this double since Andy Gray in 1977. The following season he scored a remarkable 42 goals for United in all competitions, just four short of the club record set by Denis Law in 1963/64.

• **Ronaldo made his international debut for Portugal against Kazakhstan in 2003 and the following year played for his country in their surprise Euro 2004 final defeat by Greece. He first captained Portugal in 2007 and now wears the armband on a regular basis.**

• Arguably the most exciting talent in world football today, Cristiano Ronaldo is the only player from the Premiership to have been voted World Footballer of the Year, having collected this most prestigious of awards in 2008. In the same year he was also voted European Footballer of the Year.

WAYNE ROONEY

Born: Liverpool,
24th October 1985
Position: Striker
Club career:
2002-04 Everton 67 (15)
2004- Manchester United 189 (91)
International record:
2003- England 65 (25)

When Wayne Rooney scored his first goal for England, against Macedonia in a Euro 2004 qualifier on 6th September 2003, he was aged just 17 years and 317 days... the youngest player ever to find the net for the Three Lions.

• **Rooney burst onto the scene with Everton in 2002, scoring his first league goal for the Toffees with a magnificent 20-yarder against reigning champions Arsenal at Goodison Park just five days before his 17th birthday. At the time** he was the youngest ever Premiership scorer but his record has since been surpassed by both James Milner and James Vaughan.

• After starring for England at Euro 2004 Rooney signed for Manchester United later that summer for £25.6 million, to become the world's most expensive teenage footballer. He started his Old Trafford career in sensational style with a hat-trick against Fenerbahce and has since played a pivotal part in the Red Devils' recent success, winning three Premier League titles, two League Cups and the Champions League. He enjoyed his most prolific season in 2009/10, hitting 26 Premier League goals as United just missed out on a record fourth consecutive title.

• **When Rooney made his England debut against Australia on 12th February 2003 he was his country's youngest ever player, but he has since lost this particular record to Arsenal's Theo Walcott.**

CRISTIANO RONALDO

The one and only Wayne Rooney

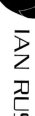
IAN RUSH

Born: St Asaph, 20th October 1961
Position: Striker
Club career:
1979-80 Chester City 34 (18)
1980-87 Liverpool 224 (139)
1987-88 Juventus 29 (8)
1988-96 Liverpool 245 (90)
1996-97 Leeds United 36 (3)
1997-98 Newcastle United 10 (2)
1998 Sheffield Wednesday
(loan) 4 (0)
1998-99 Wrexham 18 (0)
1999 Sydney Olympic 2 (0)
International record:
1980-96 Wales 73 (28)

• Famously hot-tempered, Rooney endured his worst moment in an England shirt at the 2006 World Cup when he was sent off in the quarter-final against Portugal after clashing with Ricardo Carvalho. He fared little better at the 2010 finals in South Africa, where he completely failed to live up to his pre-tournament billing as one of the best players in the world.

ROTHERHAM UNITED

Year founded: 1925
Ground: Don Valley Stadium (25,000)
Nickname: The Millers
Biggest win: 8-0 v Oldham Athletic (1947)
Heaviest defeat: 1-11 v Bradford City (1928)
Colours: Red shirts, white shorts, red socks

The club had its origins in Thornhill FC (founded in 1878, later becoming Rotherham County) and Rotherham Town, who merged with County to form Rotherham United in 1925.

• **The club's greatest moment came in 1961 when they reached the first ever League Cup final, losing 3-2 on aggregate to Aston Villa. Six years earlier Rotherham had missed out on goal average on promotion to the First Division for the first time in the club's history... the closest they've ever been to playing top-flight football.**

• In 1991 Rotherham made history by becoming the first ever side to win a penalty shoot-out in the FA Cup, defeating Scunthorpe United 7-6 on spot-kicks after a first round replay.

• **Less happily, in 1925 Rotherham failed to keep a clean sheet in 45 consecutive league matches. The run was a record at the time, but Bristol City extended it to 49 games seven years later.**

• Stalwart midfielder Danny Williams holds the record for club league appearances with 459 between 1946-62.

HONOURS

Division 3 (North) champions 1951
Division 3 champions 1981
Division 4 champions 1989
Football League Trophy 1996

One of the most prolific strikers ever, Ian Rush is Liverpool's leading scorer of all time with a total of 346 goals for the club in two spells at Anfield in the 1980s and 1990s.

• **Rush has scored more goals in the FA Cup final than any other player, with a total of five for Liverpool in the 1986, 1989 and 1992 finals. His strikes helped the Reds win all three games, two of them against local rivals Everton. With 44 goals in the competition as a whole, Rush is the second highest scorer in the history of the tournament and the leading FA Cup marksman of the 20th century.**

• 'Rushie', as he was known to Liverpool fans, is also the joint leading scorer in the League Cup with Geoff Hurst, the pair both ending their careers on 49 goals. He enjoyed huge success in the tournament, winning the trophy in 1981, 1982, 1983, 1984 and 1995 to become the first player to collect five League Cup winners' medals.

• **Rush tops the scoring charts for his native Wales, with 28 goals in 73 appearances. However, he never played in the finals of either the World Cup or the European Championships.**

• Rush is the all-time leading scorer in the Merseyside derby with 25 goals against Everton, including a post-war record four goals in a 5-0 thrashing of the Toffees at Goodison Park on 6th November 1982.

• **In 1988 Rush returned to Liverpool from Juventus for a then British record £2.7 million. He had only spent a year on the continent and seemed pleased to be back, famously complaining that life in Italy "was like being in a foreign country."**

SACKINGS

In May 2007 Leroy Rosenoir was sacked as manager of Conference side Torquay United after just ten minutes in charge! No sooner had the former West Ham and QPR striker been unveiled as the Gulls' new boss when he was told that the club had been bought by a business consortium and his services were no longer required.

• In 1959 Bill Lambton got the boot from Scunthorpe United after just three days in the managerial hot seat, an English league record. His reign at the Old Showground took in just one match – a 3-0 defeat at Liverpool in a Second Division fixture. The shortest Premier League reign, meanwhile, was Les Reed's seven-game stint at Charlton in 2006.

• Crystal Palace have sacked more managers since the Second World War than any other league club. The Eagles have made 42 different managerial appointments since 1945, although Steve Coppell and Steve Kember have filled the role on four occasions each.

• The safest job in football, on the other hand, is manager of Manchester United. Since the war the Reds have only made eight managerial appointments, helped by the lengthy tenures of Sir Matt Busby (1945-69) and Sir Alex Ferguson, who arrived at Old Trafford way back in 1986.

ST JOHNSTONE

Year founded: 1884
Ground: McDiarmid Park (10,673)
Nickname: The Saints
Biggest win: 13-0 v Tulloch (1887)
Heaviest defeat: 0-12 v Cowdenbeath (1928)
Colours: Blue shirts, blue shorts, blue socks

• St Johnstone were founded in 1884 by a group of local cricketers in Perth who wanted to keep fit in winter.

• The club have experienced little in the way of success over the years, but they did reach the League Cup final in 1969 (losing 1-0 to Celtic) and again in 1998 (losing 2-1 to Rangers).

• The Saints' record scorer is John Brogan, who hit 114 league goals for the club between 1976-84.

• In winning promotion back to the SPL after a seven-year absence in 2009, St Johnstone went a club record 22 league matches without defeat. They then enjoyed a decent season in the top flight, finishing in mid-table and beating Rangers 4-1 to record their biggest ever win against the Old Firm giants.

HONOURS
Division 2 champions 1924, 1960, 1963
First Division champions 1983, 1990, 1997, 2009

ST MIRREN

Year founded: 1877
Ground: St Mirren Park (8,016)
Nickname: The Buddies
Biggest win: 15-0 v Glasgow University (1960)
Heaviest defeat: 0-9 v Rangers (1897)
Colours: Black-and-white-striped shirts, black shorts, white socks

Named after the patron saint of Paisley, St Mirren were founded in 1877 by a group of local cricketers and rugby players. The club were founder members of the Scottish League in 1890, but have never finished higher than third in the top flight.

• The Buddies, though, have won the Scottish Cup on three occasions, most recently in 1987 when they beat Dundee United 1-0 in the final after extra time – the last time that the winners have fielded an all-Scottish line-up.

• St Mirren were the only Scottish club to win the Anglo-Scottish Cup in the six years of its existence, thrashing Bristol City 5-1 on aggregate in 1980. Seven years later they were involved in a short-lived attempt to revive the tournament, but after their match with Coventry City attracted a poor attendance the competition was unceremoniously scrapped.

• Assistant manager Andy Millen is the oldest player ever to appear in the SPL, turning out for St Mirren against Hearts for the final time on 15th March 2008 when he was aged 42 and 279 days.

• St Mirren reached the Scottish League Cup final for only the second time in 2010 but lost 1-0 to Rangers despite playing against nine men for the last 20 minutes.

HONOURS
Division 2 champions 1968
First Division champions 1977, 2000, 2006
Scottish Cup 1926, 1959, 1987

PETER SCHMEICHEL

Born: Gladsaxe, Denmark, 18th November 1963
Position: Goalkeeper
Club career:
1981-84 Gladsaxe-Hero 46 (0)
1984-87 Hvidovre 78 (6)
1987-91 Brondby 119 (2)
1991-99 Manchester United 292 (0)
1999-2001 Sporting Lisbon 50 (0)
2001-02 Aston Villa 29 (1)
2002-03 Manchester City 29 (0)
International record:
1987-2001 Denmark 129 (1)

One of the greatest goalkeepers ever, Peter Schmeichel played a record 129 times for Denmark. The highlight of his international career came in 1992 when the Danes won the European championship, beating hot favorites Germany 2-0 in the final. Incredibly, Denmark had already been eliminated in the qualifying round, but sneaked into the finals through the back door after the withdrawal of Yugoslavia.

• At club level, Schmeichel enjoyed huge success with Manchester United whom he joined from Brondby for £530,000 in 1991 – a deal later described by Sir Alex Ferguson as "the bargain of the century". The Great Dane went on to win five Premiership titles and three FA Cups with the Reds, before skippering his side to victory in the 1999 Champions League final against Bayern Munich.

• After winning the Portuguese title with Sporting Lisbon, Schmeichel returned to England with Aston Villa in 2001. His son, Kaspar, is also a goalkeeper and helped Notts County win the League Two title in 2010 before moving on to Leeds United.

PAUL SCHOLES

Born: Salford,
16th November 1974
Position: Midfielder
Club career:
1994- Manchester United 444 (101)
International record:
1997-2004 England 66 (14)

A busy midfielder who often scores spectacular goals, Paul Scholes is one of just nine players to have made more than 500 competitive appearances for Manchester United.

• **A product of United's youth system, Scholes scored twice against Port Vale on his first-team debut in September 1994 and has since gone on to enjoy a glittering career with the club. Among the many honours he has won at Old Trafford are eight Premiership titles, three FA Cups and two Champions League titles.**

• Scholes made his England debut against South Africa in 1997 and the following year he played for his country at France 98, scoring in the group stage against Tunisia. In 1999 he hit a hat-trick at Wembley in a European championship qualifier against Poland and, later that year, secured England's place at Euro 2000 with two goals against Scotland in a play-off decider.

• **Less happily, Scholes was the first and last England player to be sent off at the old Wembley, receiving his marching orders for a rash tackle in a friendly against Sweden in 2000. Four years later, aged just 29, he announced his retirement from international football.**

The ever brilliant Paul Scholes

If only Scotland's history had included more moments like John Collins' goal against Brazil at the 1998 World Cup...

SCOTLAND

First international:
Scotland 0 England 0, 1872
Most capped player:
Kenny Dalglish, 102 caps (1971-86)
Leading goalscorer:
Denis Law (1958-74) and Kenny Dalglish (1971-86), 30 goals
First World Cup appearance:
Scotland 0 Austria 1, 1954
Biggest win: Scotland 11 Ireland 0, 1901
Heaviest defeat: Scotland 0 Uruguay 7, 1954
Colours: Dark blue shirts, white shorts, red socks

Along with England, Scotland are the oldest international team in the world. The two countries played the first official international way back in 1872, the match at Hamilton Crescent, Partick, finishing 0-0. Since then, honours have been more or less even between the 'Auld Enemies', with England winning 45 matches, Scotland winning 41 and 20 ending in a draw.

• **It took the Scots a while to make an impression on the world scene. After withdrawing from the 1950 World Cup, Scotland competed in the finals** for the first time in 1954 but were eliminated in the first round after suffering their worst ever defeat, 7-0 to reigning champions Uruguay.

• Scotland have taken part in the World Cup finals on eight occasions but have never got beyond the group stage. They have been unlucky, though, going out of the 1974, 1978 and 1982 tournaments only on goal difference.

• **Scotland have a pretty poor record in the European Championships, only qualifying for the finals on two occasions, in 1992 and 1996. Again, they failed to reach the knockout stage both times, although they were unfortunate to lose out on the 'goals scored' rule to Holland at Euro 96. More recently, the Scots made a brave**

IS THAT A FACT?
Scotland's record win was an 11-0 hammering of Ireland in 1901, the Old Firm pair of Sandy 'Duke' McMahon (Celtic) and Bob Hamilton (Rangers) helping themselves to four goals apiece.

attempt to qualify for Euro 2008 but were narrowly pipped by Italy and France despite beating the French home and away.

• Scotland had a good record in the Home Championships until the tournament was scrapped in 1984, winning the competition 24 times and sharing the title another 17 times. Only England (34 outright wins and 20 shared) have a better overall record.

• Two of Scotland's most famous wins, both against England, came in the Home Championships. In 1928 a Scottish team later dubbed 'the Wembley Wizards' won 5-1 at the Twin Towers, England's worst ever home defeat. Then in 1967, a year after England had won the World Cup, Scotland triumphed 3-2 at Wembley, leading the 'Tartan Army' to hail their team as the unofficial world champions.

WORLD CUP RECORD
1930-38 Did not enter
1950 Withdrew
1954 Round 1
1958 Round 1
1962-70 Did not qualify
1974 Round 1
1978 Round 1
1982 Round 1
1986 Round 1
1990 Round 1
1994 Did not qualify
1998 Round 1
2002 Did not qualify
2006 Did not qualify
2010 Did not qualify

SCOTTISH CUP

The Scottish Cup was first played for in 1873/74, shortly after the formation of the Scottish FA. Queen's Park, who the previous year had competed in the English FA Cup, were the first winners, beating Clydesdale 2-0 in the final in front of a crowd of 3,000 at the original Hampden Park.

• Queen's Park were the dominant force in the early years of the competition, winning ten of the first 20 finals, including one in 1884 when their opponents, Vale of Leven, failed to turn up! Since then, Celtic (34 wins) and Rnagers (33 wins) have ruled the roost, although Queen's Park (ten wins) remain third in the list of all-time winners ahead of Aberdeen (7 wins).

• The final has only twice been settled on penalties, the first time in 1990 when Aberdeen beat Celtic 9-8 in the shoot-out after a 0-0 draw.

• Incredibly, the biggest ever victories in the history of British football took place in the Scottish Cup on the same day, 12th September 1885. Dundee Harp beat Aberdeen Rovers 35-0 and were confident that they had set a new record. Yet, no doubt to their utter amazement, they soon discovered that Arbroath had thrashed Bon Accord, a cricket club who had been invited to take part in the competition by mistake, 36-0!

• Minted in 1885, the Scottish Cup trophy is the oldest national trophy in the world.

SCUNTHORPE UNITED

Year founded: 1899
Ground: Glanford Park (9,088)
Previous name: Scunthorpe & Lindsey United
Nickname: The Iron
Biggest win: 9-0 v Boston United (1953)
Heaviest defeat: 0-8 v Carlisle United (1952)
Colours: Claret and blue shirts, claret shorts, claret socks

The club was founded in 1899 when Brumby Hall linked up with some other local teams. Between 1910-58 they were known as Scunthorpe and Lindsey United after amalgamating with the latter team.

• Elected to the Third Division (North) when the league expanded in 1950, Scunthorpe won the division eight years later. Their only other honour came in 2007 when The Iron were crowned League One champions under former physio Nigel Adkins. Scunny fans celebrated that triumph by singing, "Who needs Mourinho, we've got our physio!"

• Among the famous names to play for Scunthorpe are England and Liverpool legends Kevin Keegan and Ray Clemence and, somewhat bizarrely, former England cricket captain Ian Botham, who made 11 appearances as a striker for Scunthorpe in the early 1980s.

• Steve Cammack is the club's leading scorer. In two spells with Scunthorpe between 1979-86 he notched a total of 109 league goals.

• Nobody has worn Scunthorpe's claret shirt more often than loyal defender Jack Brownsword. Between 1950-65 he turned out in 595 league games for The Iron, making his last appearance at the age of 41 to become the club's oldest ever player.

• The club's record signing is defender Rob Jones, who joined Scunthorpe from Hibs for £700,000 in 2009. Two

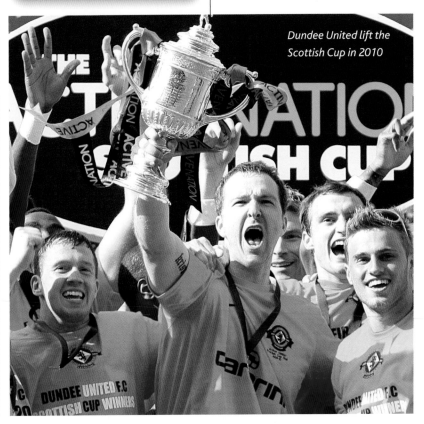

Dundee United lift the Scottish Cup in 2010

years earlier The Iron sold striker Billy Sharp, top scorer in their League One title-winning campaign with 30 goals, to Sheffield United for a club record £2 million.

• In 1988 Scunthorpe became the first club in the modern era to move to a new purpose-built stadium when they left their former ground, the Old Showground, for Glanford Park.

> HONOURS
> *Division 3 (North) champions 1958*
> *League One champions 2007*

BILL SHANKLY

> **Born:** Glenbuck, 2nd September 1913
> **Died:** 29th September 1981
> **Managerial career:**
> 1949-51 Carlisle United
> 1951-54 Grimsby Town
> 1954-55 Workington
> 1956-59 Huddersfield Town
> 1959-74 Liverpool

Liverpool legend Bill Shankly turned the Reds from a mediocre Second Division outfit into the most formidable side in England and laid the foundations for the Merseysiders' domination of Europe under his successor, Bob Paisley.

• **Shankly arrived at Anfield in 1959 and led the Reds to the Second Division title in 1962. His slick-passing, hard-working team won the league title just two years later before winning the FA Cup for the first time in the club's history in 1965. By the time he retired in 1974, the always quotable Scot had added two more League Championships, another FA Cup and Liverpool's first European trophy, the UEFA Cup in 1973.**

• Most of his playing days were spent with Preston, with whom he won the FA Cup in 1938. A tenacious right half, he also won five caps for Scotland before his career was interrupted by the Second World War.

• **Although he died in 1981 Shankly remains a revered**

Legendary Liverpool boss Bill Shankly famously said there were two top teams on Merseyside: Liverpool...and Liverpool reserves!

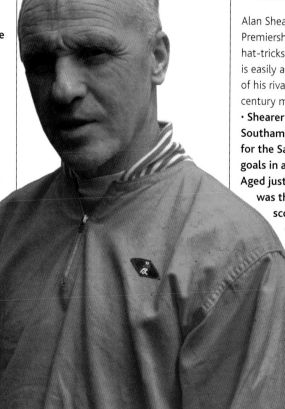

figure at Anfield, where his memory is preserved both by a huge statue and the Shankly Gates entrance.

• Much like ordinary Liverpool fans, Shankly hugely enjoyed winding up the Reds' city rivals and near neighbours. "If Everton were playing at the bottom of the garden, I'd pull the curtains," he once told a reporter.

Alan Shearer: 260 Premier League goals... and his celebration never got any more exciting than this!

ALAN SHEARER

> **Born:** Newcastle, 13th August 1970
> **Position:** Striker
> **Club career:**
> 1988-92 Southampton 118 (23)
> 1992-96 Blackburn Rovers 138 (112)
> 1996-2006 Newcastle United 303 (148)
> **International record:**
> 1992-2000 England 63 (30)

Alan Shearer's incredible total of 260 Premiership goals (including a record 11 hat-tricks) for Blackburn and Newcastle is easily a record for the league, none of his rivals having passed the double century mark.

• **Shearer began his career with Southampton, marking his full debut for the Saints in 1988 by scoring three goals in a 4-2 victory over Arsenal. Aged just 17 years and 240 days, he was the youngest ever player to score a top-flight hat-trick.**

• In 1992 Shearer moved to Blackburn for a then British record £3.3 million. He helped Rovers win the Premiership title in 1994/95, his impressive tally of 34 goals that campaign earning him one of his three Golden Boots.

• **A then world record £15 million move**

to Newcastle followed in 1996, to the delight of the Geordie faithful. Shearer's goalscoring feats made him an icon at St James' Park, and he eventually became the club's all-time record goalscorer, his total of 206 goals in all competitions for the Magpies eclipsing the 49-year-old record of another Toon legend, Jackie Milburn.

• Strong, good in the air and possessing a powerful shot in both feet, Shearer proved a real handful for international defences, too. His five goals at Euro 96 powered England to the semi-finals of the tournament and won him the competition's Golden Boot. By the time he quit international football after Euro 2000 he had scored 30 goals for his country, a figure only surpassed by four other England players.

• Shearer became a pundit for the BBC after hanging up his boots in 2006 but three years later he sensationally returned to his beloved St James' Park as Newcastle caretaker manager. However, in his eight matches in charge he was unable to prevent the Geordies from dropping out of the Premiership for the first time.

SHEFFIELD UNITED

Year founded: 1889
Ground: Bramall Lane (32,702)
Nickname: The Blades
Biggest win: 10-0 v Port Vale (1892) and v Burnley (1929)
Heaviest defeat: 0-13 v Bolton (1890)
Colours: Red-and-white-striped shirts, black shorts, black socks

The club was founded at a meeting at the city's Adelphi Hotel in 1899 by the members of the Sheffield United Cricket Club, partly to make greater use of the facilities at Bramall Lane.

• **The Blades enjoyed their heyday in the late Victorian era, winning the title in 1898, and lifting the FA Cup in both 1899 and 1902. The club won the FA Cup again in 1915, in what was to be the last final to be played before the First World War brought a halt to the sporting calendar. They chalked up another victory in 1925.**

• The club's leading scorer is Harry

United v Wednesday: The biggest derby match in Sheffield by some distance

Johnson, who bagged 201 league goals between 1919-30. His successor at centre forward, Jimmy Dunne, scored a record 41 goals in the 1930/31 season, helped by a purple patch when he found the net in 12 consecutive matches (another club record).

• **The Blades' home, Bramall Lane, is one of the oldest sporting arenas in the world. It first hosted cricket in 1855, before football was introduced to the ground in 1862. Sixteen years later, in 1878, the world's first ever floodlit match was played at the stadium between two sides picked from the Sheffield Football Association, the lights being provided by two generators.**

• During an 18-year career with the club between 1948-66, Joe Shaw made a record 631 appearances for the Blades.

• **In 2006 Sheffield United became the first foreign club to take over a Chinese team when they purchased Chengdu Wuniu (now known as Chengdu Blades).**

• The following year United broke their transfer record when they bought James Beattie from Everton for £4 million. In 2009 the Blades received a club record £6 million when they sold England Under-21 full back Kyle Naughton to Tottenham.

• **The club's most famous fan is the actor Sean Bean. In 1996 he fulfilled** a childhood fantasy by playing at Bramall Lane when he starred as a park footballer who is signed up by Sheffield United in the football film *When Saturday Comes*.

> HONOURS
> *Division 1 champions 1898*
> *Division 2 champions 1953*
> *Division 4 champions 1982*
> *FA Cup 1899, 1902, 1915, 1925*

SHEFFIELD WEDNESDAY

Year founded: 1867
Ground: Hillsborough (39,812)
Previous name: The Wednesday
Nickname: The Owls
Biggest win: 12-0 v Halliwell (1891)
Heaviest defeat: 0-10 v Aston Villa (1912)
Colours: Blue-and-white-striped shirts, black shorts, blue socks

The club was formed as The Wednesday in 1867 at the Adelphi Hotel in Sheffield by members of the Wednesday Cricket Club, who originally met on that particular

day of the week. In 1929 the club added 'Sheffield' to their name, but are still often referred to simply as 'Wednesday'.

• In 1904 the Owls became the first club in the 20th century to win consecutive league championships. They did so again in 1929-1930, but have not won the league since.

• In 1935 Wednesday won the FA Cup for the third and last time, striker Ellis Rimmer scoring in every round of the competition.

• Sheffield Wednesday have won the second tier of English football five times (a total only surpassed by Manchester City and Leicester City). Their last triumph came in 1959 when they banged in a club record 106 goals on their way to the title.

• Andrew Wilson holds two significant records for the club. Between 1900-20 he played in 501 league matches, scoring 199 goals. No Wednesday player, before or since, can match these figures.

• In 1991, while residing in the old Second Division, the Owls won the League Cup for the first and only time in their history, beating Manchester United 1-0 at Wembley. It was the last time that a club from outside the top flight has lifted a major domestic cup.

• On the opening day of the 2000/01 season Wednesday goalkeeper Kevin Pressman was sent off after just 13 seconds at Molineux for handling a Wolves shot outside the penalty area... the fastest dismissal ever in British football.

> HONOURS
> *Division 1 champions* 1903, 1904, 1929, 1930
> *Division 2 champions* 1900, 1926, 1952, 1956, 1959
> *FA Cup* 1896, 1907, 1935
> *League Cup* 1991

PETER SHILTON

> **Born:** Leicester, 18th September 1949
> **Position:** Goalkeeper
> **Club career:**
> 1965-75 Leicester City 286 (1)
> 1975-78 Stoke City 110
> 1978-82 Nottingham Forest 202
> 1982-87 Southampton 188
> 1987-92 Derby County 175
> 1995-96 Bolton Wanderers 1
> 1997 Leyton Orient 9
> **International record:**
> 1970-90 England 125

Peter Shilton is the only player in the history of English football to have played 1,000 league games. He reached the landmark, aged 47, while keeping a clean sheet for Leyton Orient in their 2-0 win over Brighton on 22nd December 1996.

• Shilton is currently England's highest capped player with 125 appearances to his name. In his 20-year international career he played at three World Cups, where he kept ten clean sheets – a goalkeeping record shared with France's Fabien Barthez.

• A losing FA Cup finalist with Leicester City in 1969 at the age of 19, Shilton had to wait almost ten years before he collected his first honour, the League Championship with Nottingham Forest in 1978. He went on to win two European Cups with Forest before moving on to Southampton in 1982.

• Shilton is the last goalkeeper to be voted PFA Player of the Year, collecting the award in 1978. The only other keeper to be so honoured was Tottenham's Pat Jennings, two years earlier.

TOP 10

MOST CAPPED GOALKEEPERS

1. Mohamed Al-Deayea (Saudi Arabia, 1993-2006) 181 caps
2. Thomas Ravelli (Sweden, 1981-97) 143 caps
3. Edwin van der Sar (Holland, 1995-2008) 130 caps
4. Jorge Campos (Mexico, 1991-2004) 129 caps
5. Andoni Zubizarreta (Spain, 1985-98) 126 caps
6. Peter Shilton (England, 1970-90) 125 caps
7. Peter Schmeichel (Denmark, 1988-2001) 121 caps
8. Essam El-Hadary (Egypt, 1996-) 120 caps
   Mart Poom (Estonia, 1992-2009) 120 caps
   Rustu Recber (Turkey, 1994-2009) 120 caps

England's Peter Shilton kept a record ten World Cup clean sheets

SHREWSBURY TOWN

Year founded: 1886
Ground: New Meadow (9,875)
Nickname: The Shrews
Biggest win: 11-2 v Marine (1995)
Heaviest defeat: 1-8 v Norwich City (1952) and v Coventry City (1963)
Colours: Blue shirts, white shorts, blue socks

Founded at the Lion Hotel in Shrewsbury in 1886, the club played in regional football for many years until being elected to the Football League in 1950.

• Prolific striker Arthur Rowley is the club's record scorer, hitting 152 goals between 1958-65 to complete his all-time league record of 434 goals (he also turned out for West Bromwich Albion, Fulham and Leicester City). His best season for the Shrews was in 1958/59 when he banged in a club best 38 goals.

• 'Sir' Mickey Brown is the club's leading appearance maker, playing in 418 league games in three spells at the club between 1986-2001. He was 'knighted' by the fans after scoring the winning goal against Exeter on the last day of the 1999/2000 season, thus preserving the club's league status and sending down local rivals Chester City instead.

• Shewsbury pulled off one of the biggest ever shocks in the FA Cup when they beat Premiership titans Everton 2-1 in 2003. However, at the end of the season they were relegated to the Conference (happily, the Shrews bounced back the next year).

• Shrewsbury have won the Welsh Cup six times – a record for an English club.

HONOURS
Division 3 champions 1979
Third Division champions 1994
Welsh Cup 1891, 1938, 1977, 1979, 1984, 1985

SIZE

The heaviest player in the history of the professional game was Willie 'Fatty' Foulke, who played in goal for Sheffield United, Chelsea and Bradford City. By the end of his career, the tubby custodian weighed in at an incredible 24 stone.

• At just five feet tall, Fred Le May is the shortest player ever to have appeared in the Football League. He played for Thames, Clapton Orient and Watford between 1930-33.

• No prizes for guessing who the tallest ever England international is. It is, of course, giraffe-like striker Peter Crouch, who stands six feet seven inches in his socks. Crouch, though, is half an inch shorter than Wolves' Austrian international striker Stefan Maierhofer and Birmingham's Serbian striker Nikola Zigic, who jointly claim the record as the tallest ever Premier League players.

• The shortest England international ever was Frederick 'Fanny' Walden, a five feet two inch winger with Tottenham who won the first of two caps in 1914.

They didn't call 24-stone William Foulke 'Fatty' for nothing...

WALTER SMITH

Born: Lanark, 24th February 1948
Managerial career:
1991-98 Rangers
1998-2002 Everton
2004-07 Scotland
2007- Rangers

One of the most successful managers ever, Walter Smith was first appointed Rangers manager in 1991 having previously been Graeme Souness's assistant at Ibrox. He led the club to seven successive league titles before joining Everton in 1998.

• Smith's four-year reign at Goodison, though, proved to be deeply disappointing. After the Toffees had finished in the bottom half of the Premiership table in three consecutive seasons he was sacked in March 2002 following a 3-0 defeat at Middlesbrough in the FA Cup sixth round.

Appointed Scotland manager in 2004 in place of Berti Vogts, Smith failed to lead his country to the 2006 World Cup. However, results improved considerably during his tenure, helping Scotland to climb 70 places in the FIFA world rankings.

• In January 2007 Smith returned to Ibrox. In his first full season back Rangers won both the Scottish Cup and League Cup, narrowly missing out on a cup treble when they lost in the final of the UEFA Cup to Zenit St Petersburg. Since then, Smith has claimed two more SPL titles, taking his total to nine.

• A former defender with Dundee United and Dumbarton, Smith has been voted Scottish Manager of the Year on a record seven occasions.

WESLEY SNEIJDER

Born: Utrecht, Holland, 9th June 1984
Position: Midfielder
Club career:
2002-07 Ajax 127 (44)
2007-09 Real Madrid 52 (11)
2009- Inter Milan 26 (14)
International record:
2003- Holland 68 (19)

Dutch midfielder Wesley Sneijder enjoyed the best season of his career in 2009/10, winning the Treble with his club Inter Milan, before starring at the 2010 World Cup in South Africa. Although Sneijder had to settle for a runners-up medal after Holland's defeat by Spain in the final, there was some consolation for him when he was voted the second best player at the tournament behind Uruguay's Diego Forlan.

• A product of the famous Ajax Academy, Sneijder played for the Amsterdam club for five years before

Theo Walcott is Southampton's youngest ever player and record sale at £9.1 million

joining Real Madrid for around £19 million in 2007. The fee made him the second most expensive Dutch player ever after Ruud van Nistelrooy, who moved from PSV to Manchester United for a slightly higher fee in 2001.

• Sneijder won the title with Real in 2008, but dropped out of favour at the Bernabeu and joined Inter Milan the following year. Under then Inter manager Jose Mourinho he became a key player for the Italian giants as they swept all before them, winning the Serie A title, the Coppa Italia and the Champions League, with a 2-0 victory over Bayern Munich in the final.

• A clever player who likes to drop into the spaces between the midfield and the attack, Sneijder made his debut for Holland as an 18-year-old in 2003. He has since developed into a mainstay of the Dutch side, earning rave reviews at Euro 2008 as well as the last World Cup.

• Sneijder is married to Dutch actress and TV presenter Yolanthe Cabau van Kasbergen, a three-time winner of Dutch FHM's 'Sexiest babe of the year' award.

SOUTHAMPTON

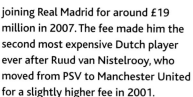

Year founded: 1885
Ground: St Mary's (32, 689)
Previous name: Southampton St Mary's
Nickname: The Saints
Biggest win: 14-0 v Newbury (1894)
Heaviest defeat: 0-8 v Tottenham (1936) and v Everton (1971)
Colours: With shirts with a diagonal red slash, black shorts, red/white socks

Founded as Southampton St Mary's by members of St Mary's Church Young Men's Association in 1885, the club joined the Southern League in 1894 and became simply 'Southampton' the following year.

• **The Saints won the Southern League six times in the decade up to 1904 and also appeared in two FA Cup finals during that period, losing to Bury in 1900 and to Sheffield United two**

years later.

• The club finally won the cup in 1976. Manchester United were hot favourites to beat the Saints, then in the Second Division, but the south coast side claimed the trophy thanks to Bobby Stokes's late strike. As scorer of the first (and only) goal in the final Stokes was rewarded with a free car... unfortunately, he still hadn't passed the driving test!

• **Mick Channon, a member of that cup-winning team and now a successful racehorse trainer, is the**

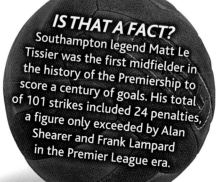

IS THAT A FACT?
Southampton legend Matt Le Tissier was the first midfielder in the history of the Premiership to score a century of goals. His total of 101 strikes included 24 penalties, a figure only exceeded by Alan Shearer and Frank Lampard in the Premier League era.

Viva Espana!: Spain celebrate their 2010 World Cup victory

Saints' leading scorer with a total of 185 goals in two spells at The Dell, the club's old ground. Derek Reeves holds the record for most goals in a season, notching 39 when the Saints won the Division Three title in 1959/60.

• Legendary winger Terry Paine, a member of England's 1966 World Cup-winning squad, is Southampton's longest serving player. Between 1956-74 he wore the club's colours in no fewer than 713 league games before moving to Hereford United. Paine's amazing total of 824 league games puts him third in the all-time list, behind Peter Shilton and Tony Ford.

• **England goalkeeper Shilton is the club's most capped player, winning 49 of his record 125 caps while at The Dell.**

• In 2001 the Saints forked out a record £4 million to buy long-throw expert Rory Delap from Derby. Five years later the club received a record cash injection of £9.1 million when teenage prodigy Theo Walcott, the Saints' youngest ever player, signed for Arsenal.

HONOURS
Division 3 (South) champions 1922
Division 3 champions 1960
FA Cup 1976
Football League Trophy 2010

SOUTHEND UNITED

Year founded: 1906
Ground: Roots Hall (12,306)
Nickname: The Shrimpers
Biggest win: 10-1 v Golders Green (1934), v Brentwood (1968) and v Aldershot (1990)
Heaviest defeat: 1-9 v Brighton and Hove Albion (1965)
Colours: Blue shirts, blue shorts, blue socks

Southend United were founded in 1906 at the Blue Boar pub, just 50 yards away from the club's current home, Roots Hall.

• **After joining the Football League in 1920 the Shrimpers remained in the third tier for a record 46 years, before dropping into the Fourth Division in 1966.**

• The club's top appearance maker is Sandy Anderson, who turned out in 452 league games between 1950-62. His team-mate Roger Hollis is Southend's leading marksman, rifling in 120 league goals in just six years at the club between 1954-60.

• **A number of famous names have managed the club, including England World Cup-winning captain Bobby Moore and fellow England internationals Alvin Martin and Peter Taylor.**

• None of that illustrious trio, however, brought as much success to Roots Hall as former boss Steve Tilson. He guided the Shrimpers to consecutive promotions from the fourth tier to the Championship in 2005-06 and also presided over the club's greatest ever victory, a 1-0 League Cup win against holders Manchester United in 2006.

HONOURS
League One champions 2006
Division 4 champions 1981

SPAIN

First international: Spain 1 Denmark 0, 1920
Most capped player: Andoni Zubizarreta, 126 caps (1985-98)
Leading goalscorer: Raul, 44 goals (1996-present)
First World Cup appearance: Spain 3 Brazil 1, 1934
Biggest win: Spain 13 Bulgaria 0, 1933
Heaviest defeat: Italy 7 Spain 1, 1928 and England 7 Spain 1, 1931
Colours: Red shirts, blue shorts, red socks

Currently considered the best and most attractive international side in the world, Spain are only the third country in football history to hold the World and European championships at the same time following their successes at Euro 2008 and the 2010

World Cup in South Africa.

• Spain secured their first ever World Cup triumph with a 1-0 victory over Holland at the Soccer City stadium in Johannesburg, midfielder Andres Iniesta rifling home the all-important goal four minutes from the end of extra time. Despite their entertaining close passing style of play, Spain only managed to score eight goals in the tournament – the lowest total ever by the winning nation at a World Cup.

• Apart from their victory in 2008, when striker Fernando Torres scored the winning goal in the final against Germany, Spain also won the second edition of the European Championships in 1964 when they had the advantage of playing both the semi-final and the final, against holders the Soviet Union, on home soil at Real Madrid's Bernabeu stadium.

• Between 2007-09 Spain went 35 matches without defeat (winning 32 and drawing just three) to equal the world record set by Brazil in the 1990s. The run came to an end when Spain lost 2-0 to USA at the 2009 Confederations Cup, but the Spanish were soon back on form, going into the 2010 World Cup on the back of 18 consecutive victories before they surprisingly lost their opening match at the finals against Switzerland. That setback, though, was soon forgotten as Vicente del Bosque's men went on to lift the trophy, sparking jubilant scenes across Spain from Santander to Seville.

HONORS

European championship 1964, 2008

World Cup record

1930 Did not enter
1934 Quarter-finals
1938 Did not enter
1950 Fourth place
1954 Did not qualify
1958 Did not qualify
1962 Round 1
1966 Round 1
1970 Did not qualify
1974 Did not qualify
1978 Round 1
1982 Round 2
1986 Quarter-finals
1990 Round 2
1994 Quarter-finals
1998 Round 1
2002 Quarter-finals
2006 Round 2
2010 Winners

SPONSORSHIP

The first competition in England to be sponsored was the Watney Cup in 1971, a pre-season tournament between the highest-scoring teams in the different divisions of the Football League.

• On 24th January 1976 Kettering Town became the first senior football club in the UK to feature a sponsor's logo on their shirts, Kettering Tyres, for their Southern League Premier Division match against Bath City. The Football Association ordered the removal of the logo, but finally accepted shirt sponsorship in June 1977. Two years later Liverpool became the first top-flight club to sport a sponsor's logo after signing a deal with Hitachi.

• The biggest shirt sponsorship deal in English football was agreed between Manchester United and American insurance giants Aon Corp in 2009. The four-year partnership will boost the Old Trafford coffers by a staggering £80 million.

• Barcelona are the only major football club in the world never to have had a commercial shirt sponsor, the Catalan giants believing that a company logo would sully their famous blue and red stripes. Since 2006, however, Barca have proudly sported the logo of the United Nations Children's Fund (UNICEF) on their shirts.

• The League Cup was the first major English competition to be sponsored, being renamed the Milk Cup after receiving backing from the Milk Marketing Board in 1982. It has since been rebranded as the Littlewoods Cup, the Rumbelows Cup, the Littlewoods Cup, the Coca-Cola Cup, the Worthington Cup and the Carling Cup. Since 1994 the FA Cup has been sponsored by Littlewoods, AXA and E.ON, but the competition is still known by its original name.

Man United's sponsorship deal with AON is the biggest in English football history

ALFREDO DI STEFANO

Born: Buenos Aires, 4th July 1926
Position: Striker
Club career:
1943-49 River Plate 65 (49)
1946-47 Huracan (loan) 25 (10)
1949-53 Millionarios 102 (88)
1953-64 Real Madrid 282 (216)
1964-66 Espanyol 47 (11)
International record:
1947-49 Argentina 6 (6)
1949-54 Colombia 4 (0)
1954-61 Spain 31 (23)

The inspiration behind Real Madrid's domination of the European Cup in the late 1950s and early 1960s, Alfredo di Stefano is considered one of the best players of all time.

• Known as 'the White Arrow', Di Stefano scored in all five finals when Real Madrid won the European Cup five times on the trot between

1956-60, including a hat-trick in the Spanish giants' famous 7-3 demolition of Eintracht Frankfurt in 1960.

• Di Stefano's total of 49 goals in the European Cup was a record in the competition until the Champions League era, while only Raul has scored more than his 216 league goals for Real Madrid.

• **Twice winner of the European Footballer of the Year award, Di Stefano is one of a handful of players to have represented three countries: his native Argentina, Colombia and Spain.**

• A successful manager in later life, Di Stefano led Valencia to the league championship in 1971 before twice taking charge of his beloved Real. In 2003 he was officially named as the greatest Spanish player of the previous 50 years.

JOCK STEIN

Born: Burnbank, 5th October 1923
Died: 10th September 1985
Managerial career:
1960-64 Dunfermline Athletic
1964-65 Hibernian
1965/66 Scotland
1965-78 Celtic
1978 Leeds United
1978-85 Scotland

Legendary Celtic boss Jock Stein was the first British manager to win the European Cup, guiding the Glasgow club to victory over Inter Milan in the 1967 final in Lisbon. During that same season, Stein's Celtic won every competition they entered – European Cup, Scottish League, Scottish Cup and Scottish League Cup.

• **Stein turned Celtic into the dominant force in Scottish football, leading his side to an incredible nine consecutive league title triumphs between 1966-74 after arriving from Hibs in 1965. He added a tenth title in 1977 before leaving the club the following year.**

• As a centre half with Celtic, Stein had previously helped The Bhoys win the league and Scottish Cup in 1954... their first Double since 1914.

• **Stein began his managerial career at Dunfermline, with whom he won the Scottish Cup in 1961. After leaving Celtic he managed Leeds for just 45 days before taking over as Scotland manager, a job he had previously held on a part-time basis in the mid-1960s.**

• He led Scotland to the 1982 World Cup finals and had just seen his side qualify for the 1986 tournament when he died from a heart attack after the end of the 1985 qualifier against Wales at Ninian Park. His sudden death was mourned by the whole of Scotland.

• **He is remembered, though, primarily, for his great achievements at Celtic. Summing up what it meant to play for one of Britain's greatest clubs, Stein once said: "Celtic jerseys are not for second best... they don't fit inferior players."**

Jock Stein led Celtic to the European Cup and nine league titles in a row

STEVENAGE

Year founded: 1976
Ground: Broadhall Way (7,100)
Previous name: Stevenage Borough
Nickname: The Boro
Biggest win: 7-0 v Merthyr (2006)
Heaviest defeat: 1-6 v Farnborough (2002)
Colours: White shirts, red shorts, red socks

The club was founded in 1976 as Stevenage Borough, following the bankruptcy of the town's former club, Stevenage Athletic. In 2010 the club decided to become simply 'Stevenage'.

• **Stevenage rose through the football pyramid to gain promotion to the Conference in 1994. Two years later they won the title but were denied**

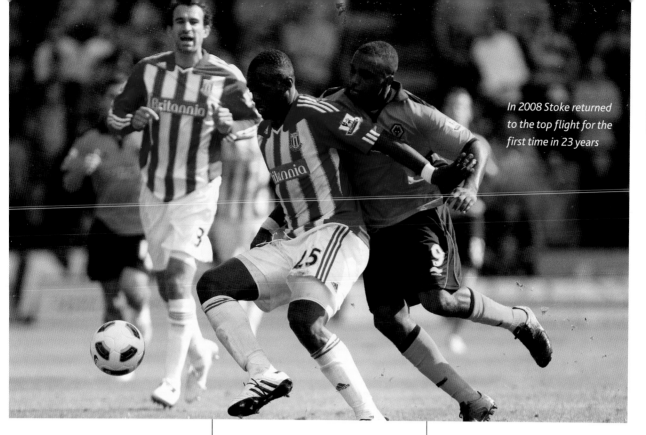

In 2008 Stoke returned to the top flight for the first time in 23 years

promotion to the Football League as their tiny Broadhall Way stadium did not meet the league's standards.

• Stevenage finally made it into the league in 2010 after topping the Conference table with an impressive 99 points. If the club's two victories against Chester City, who were expelled from the league during the season, had not been expunged then Stevenage would have set a new Conference record of 105 points.

• In 1998 the club reached the fourth round of the FA Cup for the first time in their history. Amazingly, they managed to hold mighty Newcastle to a 1-1 draw at Broadhall Way before going down 2-1 in the replay at St James' Park.

Honours
Conference champions 1996, 2010

STOCKPORT COUNTY

Year founded: 1883
Ground: Edgeley Park (10,852)
Previous name: Heaton Norris Rovers
Nickname: The Hatters
Biggest win: 13-0 v Halifax Town (1934)
Heaviest defeat: 1-8 v Chesterfield (1902)
Colours: Blue shirts, white shorts, white socks

Founded as Heaton Norris Rovers in 1883 by members of Wycliffe Congregational Church, the club adopted the name Stockport County in 1890, a year after the town became a county borough.

• **The Hatters enjoyed their best ever win in 1934 when they thrashed Halifax Town 13-0 in a Third Division (North) fixture. The result set a new record for the biggest margin of victory in a Football League fixture which stands to this day, although Newcastle matched it in 1946 when they beat Newport County by the same score.**

• Between January and March 2007 Stockport set a Football League record when they won nine consecutive League Two matches without conceding a goal.

• **The club's leading scorer is Jack Connor who banged in 140 goals, with 17 hat-tricks, between 1951-56.**

• Recently struggling with financial problems, Stockport's best season was in 1996/97 when they won promotion to the second tier and reached the semi-final of the League Cup, beating no fewer than three Premiership clubs en route.

• **The first father and son to play together in an English league game were Alec and David Herd, who appeared for Stockport in a Third Division (North) match against Hartlepools in May 1951.**

HONOURS
Division 3 (North) champions 1922, 1937
Division 4 champions 1967

STOKE CITY

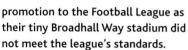

Year founded: 1863
Ground: Britannia Stadium (28,383)
Previous name: Stoke Ramblers, Stoke
Nickname: The Potters
Biggest win: 11-0 v Stourbridge (1914)
Heaviest defeat: 0-10 v Preston (1889)
Colours: Red-and-white-striped shirts, white shorts, white socks

Founded in 1863 by employees of the North Staffordshire Railway Company, Stoke are the second oldest league club in the country. Between 1868-70 the club was known as Stoke Ramblers, before simply becoming Stoke and then adding the suffix 'City' in 1925.

• **Stoke were founder members of the Football League in 1888 but finished bottom of the table at the end of the season. After another wooden spoon in 1890 the club dropped out of the league, but returned to the big time after just one season.**

• The club's greatest moment came in 1972 when they won the League Cup, beating favourites Chelsea 2-1 in the final at Wembley, thanks to a late winner by George Eastham. Aged 35 and 161 days at the time, Eastham is the oldest player ever to win the League Cup.

• **While playing in his second spell at**

Stoke, the great Stanley Matthews became the oldest player ever to appear in the top flight. On 6th February 1965 Matthews played his last game for the club against Fulham just five days after celebrating his 50th birthday.

• The legendary Gordon Banks is Stoke's most capped player. The brilliant goalkeeper, a World Cup winner in 1966, won 37 of his 73 England caps while with the Staffordshire outfit.

• Freddie Steele is Stoke's leading scorer with 140 league goals between 1934-49, including a club record 33 in the 1936/37 season. Stalwart defender Eric Skeels played in a record 507 league games for the Potters between 1960-76.

• On 23rd February 1957 Stoke thrashed Lincoln City 8-0 in a Second Division match. Incredibly, Neville Coleman bagged seven of the goals to set a club record which has never been matched since.

• In the summer of 2008, shortly after returning to the top flight for the first time in 23 years, Stoke splashed out a club record £5.5 million to bring Reading striker Dave Kitson to the Britannia Stadium. The following year the Potters made their record sale when Nigerian midfielder Seyi Olofinjana moved to Hull City in a £3 million deal.

• On 27th January 1974 Stoke became the first top-flight club to host Sunday football when they played Chelsea at their former home, The Victoria Ground. Ignoring the complaints of religious groups, a crowd of nearly 32,000 turned up to see Stoke win 1-0.

• Stoke's most famous fan is former *They Think It's All Over* TV presenter Nick Hancock. In 2001 Hancock forked out £20,000 at an auction to buy Stanley Matthews's 1953 FA Cup winners' medal, even though the wing wizard won the trophy with Blackpool!

IS THAT A FACT?
Wolves striker Jimmy Mullen was the first substitute to play for England, coming off the bench in a friendly against Belgium in Brussels on 18th May 1950. He did well, too, scoring a goal in a 4-1 win.

"Hurry up, Wayne, I've got less than two seconds to score the fastest ever goal by a substitute!"

HONOURS
Division 2 champions 1933, 1963
Division 3 (North) champions 1927
Second Division champions 1993
League Cup 1972
Football League Trophy 1992, 2000

SUBSTITUTES

Substitutes were first allowed in the Football League in the 1965/66 season. The first player to come off the bench was Charlton's Keith Peacock, who replaced injured goalkeeper Mike Rose after 11 minutes of the Addicks' match away to Bolton on 21st August 1965. On the same afternoon Barrow's Bobby Knox became the first substitute to score a goal when he notched against Wrexham.

• The fastest ever goal scored by a substitute was by Arsenal's Nicklas Bendtner, who headed in a corner against Tottenham at the Emirates on 22nd December 2007 just 1.8 seconds after replacing Emmanuel Eboue.

• The most goals ever scored in a game by a substitute is four by Ole Gunnar Solskjaer in Manchester United's 8-1 win at Nottingham Forest in 1999. Incredibly, the Norwegian striker was only on the pitch for 19 minutes. During his United career Solskjaer scored a record 28 goals off the bench.

• Substitutes were first allowed at the World Cup in 1970. The most goals scored by a sub at the tournament is three by Poland's Lazlo Kiss against El Salvador in 1982. At France 98 Denmark's Ebbe Sand scored the fastest goal by a sub, netting against Nigeria just 16 seconds after coming off the bench.

• Newcastle goalkeeper Steve Harper has sat on the bench a record 304 times in Premier League fixtures, while Portsmouth striker Kanu has made a record 118 sub appearances.

TOP 10

PREMIER LEAGUE SUBSTITUTE APPEARANCES

1. Kanu (Arsenal, West Brom, Portsmouth) 118 sub apps
2. Jermain Defoe (West Ham, Tottenham, Portsmouth) 89 sub apps
3. Ole-Gunnar Solskjaer (Manchester United) 84 sub apps
4. Duncan Ferguson (Everton, Newcastle United) 83 sub apps
5. James Beattie (Blackburn Rovers, Southampton, Everton, Stoke City) 81 sub apps
   Shoala Ameobi (Newcastle United) 81 sub apps
7. Danny Murphy (Liverpool, Charlton, Tottenham, Fulham) 79 sub apps
   Joe Cole (West Ham United, Chelsea) 79 sub apps
9. Paul Scholes (Manchester United) 78 sub apps
10. Ryan Giggs (Manchester United) 77 sub apps

SUNDERLAND

Year founded: 1879
Ground: Stadium of Light (49,000)
Previous name: Sunderland and District Teachers' AFC
Nickname: The Black Cats
Biggest win: 11-1 v Fairfield (1895)
Heaviest defeat: 0-8 v Sheffield Wednesday (1911), v West Ham (1968) and v Watford (1982)
Colours: Red-and-white-striped shirts, black shorts, red socks

The club was founded as the Sunderland and District Teachers' AFC in 1879 but soon opened its ranks to other professions and became simply 'Sunderland' the following year.

• Sunderland were the first 'new' club to join the Football League, replacing Stoke in 1890. Just two years later they won their first league championship and they retained the title the following year, in the process becoming the first club to score 100 goals in a league season. In 1895 Sunderland became the first club ever to win three championships and their status was further enhanced when they beat Scottish champions Hearts 5-3 in a one-off 'world championship' match.

• In 1958 Sunderland were relegated after a then record 57 consecutive seasons in the top flight. Arsenal passed this particular landmark in 1983/84 and can now boast an impressive run of 85 successive seasons at the top level.

• Sunderland were the first Second Division team in the post Second World War era to win the FA Cup, beating Leeds 1-0 at Wembley in one of the biggest upsets of all time thanks to a goal by the late Ian Porterfield.

• Goalkeeper Jim Montgomery, a hero of that cup winning side, is the Black Cats' record appearance maker, turning out in 537 league games between 1960-77.

• Sunderland's record victory was an 11-1 thrashing of Fairfield in the FA Cup in 1895. However, the club's best ever league win, a 9-1 demolition of eventual champions and arch rivals Newcastle at St James' Park in 1908, probably gave their fans more pleasure. To this day, it remains the biggest ever victory by an away side in the top flight.

• Sunderland last won the league championship in 1935/36, the last time, incidentally, that a team wearing stripes has topped the pile. The Wearsiders' success, though, certainly wasn't based on a solid defence... the 74 goals they conceded that season is more than any other top-flight champions before or since.

• In 1990 Sunderland became the only team to lose a play-off final yet still gain promotion, the Wearsiders going up to the old First Division in place of Swindon after the Robins were punished for financial irregularities.

• Inside forward Charlie Buchan is Sunderland's record scorer with 209 league goals between 1911-25. Dave Halliday holds the record for a single season, hitting the target 43 times in 1928/29.

• Famed for their spending power in the late 1940s and early 1950s, when they were dubbed 'The Bank of England' club, Sunderland coughed up a record £10 million in August 2009 when they signed Darren Bent from Tottenham. In his first season at The Stadium of Light Bent was the Premier League's third highest scorer with 24 goals, including a bizarre strike against Liverpool that deflected into the net off a stray red beach ball.

• Well-known fans of the club include former middle distance runner Steve Cram, England cricketer Paul Collingwood and Heather Mills, ex-wife of Paul McCartney.

HONOURS
Division 1 champions 1892, 1983, 1895, 1902, 1913, 1936
Division 2 champions 1976
Championship champions 2005, 2007
Division 3 champions 1988
FA Cup 1937, 1973

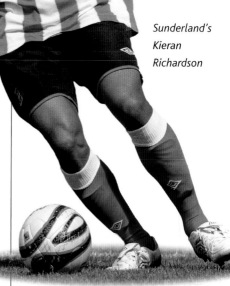

Sunderland's Kieran Richardson

SUNDERLAND

"I kizz le baldie 'ead and, voila!, France win le match...eez tres clever, non?"

Lewis let in a soft goal against Cardiff. He later blamed his mistake on the ball slipping from his grasp and over the line as it brushed against the shiny surface of his new jumper.

SWANSEA CITY

Year founded: 1912
Ground: Liberty Stadium (20,532)
Previous name: Swansea Town
Nickname: The Swans
Biggest win: 12-0 v Sliema Wanderers (1982)
Heaviest defeat: 0-8 v Liverpool (1990) and v Monaco (1991)
Colours: White shirts, white shorts, white socks

The club was founded as Swansea Town in 1912 and entered the Football League eight years later. The present name was adopted in 1970.

• **Under former Liverpool striker John Toshack the Swans climbed from the old Fourth Division to the top flight in just four seasons between 1978-81, the fastest ever ascent through the Football League. The glory days soon faded, though, and by 1986 Swansea were back in the basement division.**

• In 1961 the club became the first from Wales to compete in Europe, but were knocked out of the Cup-Winners' Cup in the first round by East German side

SUPERSTITIONS

Many footballers, including some of the great names of the game, are highly superstitious and believe that performing the same personal routines before every game will bring them good luck. Republic of Ireland goalkeeper Shay Given, for instance, has a 'lucky' vial of Holy Water which he places in the back of his net before kick-off.

• Former England striker Gary Lineker never used to shoot at goal during the warm up, believing that if he hit the back of the net it would be a 'waste' of a goal. Then, if he didn't score in the first half he would always change his shirt at half-time.

• Another England legend, 1966 World Cup-winning captain Bobby Moore, was always the last player in the team to put on his shorts.

• Kolo Toure's superstition almost cost his then club Arsenal dear in their 2009 Champions League clash with Roma. Believing that it would be bad luck to leave the dressing room before team-mate William Gallas, who was receiving treatment, Toure failed to appear for the start of the second half, leaving the Gunners to restart the match with just nine players!

• France developed a number of superstitions around Fabien Barthez at the 1998 World Cup, one of which demanded that skipper Laurent Blanc had to kiss the goalkeeper's bald head just before kick-off. It may all have been mumbo-jumbo, but the routine worked for the French who won the competition for the first time in their history.

• **Some superstitions are not entirely irrational. For example, Arsenal always make sure that a new goalkeeper's jersey is washed before it is used for the first time. The policy stems from the 1927 FA Cup final, which the Gunners lost when goalkeeper Dan**

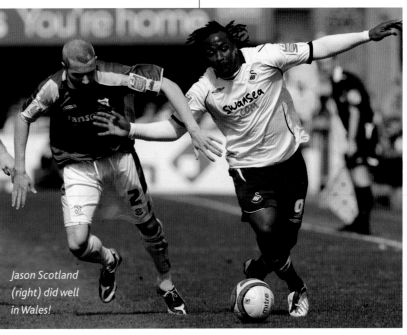

Jason Scotland (right) did well in Wales!

The Robins are bobbin'

Carl Zeiss Jena.

• **Ivor Allchurch is the Swans' leading scorer, banging in 166 goals in two spells at the club between 1949-68. Allchurch is also the club's most decorated international, winning 42 caps for Wales while with Swansea.**

• Some of the club's most famous victories have come in the FA Cup. In 1926 Swansea knocked out Arsenal before losing in the semi-finals to Bolton and in 1964 the Swans again reached the last four after sensationally beating Liverpool at Anfield. Then, in 2009, the Welshmen pulled off another major shock when they beat holders Portsmouth 2-0 at Fratton Park.

• **Unusually, the Swans made their record sale when manager Roberto Martinez moved to Wigan in 2009. The Lancashire club forked out £2 million in total for the Spaniard and Trinidad & Tobago striker Jason Scotland.**

> HONOURS
> *Division 3 (South) champions 1925, 1949*
> *League One champions 2008*
> *Third Division champions 2000*
> *Football League Trophy 1994, 2006*
> *Welsh Cup 1913, 1932, 1950, 1961, 1966, 1981, 1982, 1983, 1989, 1991*

SWINDON TOWN

> **Year founded:** 1879
> **Ground:** The County Ground (14,700)
> **Previous name:** Swindon Spartans
> **Nickname:** The Robins
> **Biggest win:** 10-1 v Farnham United Breweries (1925)
> **Heaviest defeat:** 1-10 v Manchester City (1930)
> **Colours:** Red shirts with white trim, red shorts, red socks

The club was founded by the Reverend William Pitt in 1879, becoming Swindon Spartans two years later before adopting its current name in 1883. In 1920 Swindon were founder members of the Third Division, kicking off their league career with a best ever 9-1 thrashing of Luton in their first match.

• **The Robins' finest moment came in 1969 when, as a Third Division club, they beat mighty Arsenal 3-1 in the League Cup final on a mud-clogged Wembley pitch. Legendary winger Don Rogers was the star of the show, scoring two of Swindon's goals.**

• Rogers' team-mate John Trollope

is Swindon's longest-serving player, appearing in an astounding 770 league games for the club between 1960-80. This is a record for a single club, beating Roy Sproson's 761 for Port Vale between 1950-72.

• **Prolific marksman Harry Morris holds all Swindon's goalscoring records. He is the club's leading scorer with 216 league goals, the highest scorer in a season with 47 in 1926/27 and the only player to have twice scored five in a match for the Robins (against QPR in 1926 and Norwich in 1930).**

• In 1993, three years after being denied promotion to the top flight for the first time because of a financial scandal, Swindon earned promotion to the Premiership via the play-offs. The following campaign, though, proved to be a miserable one for their fans as the Robins finished bottom of the pile and conceded 100 goals... a record for the Premier League.

• **Swindon won the Fourth Division title in 1985/86 with a then Football League best 102 points, a total which remains a record for the bottom tier.**

• On 22nd January 2008 Swindon Town set an unwanted record when they became the first club to miss all four of their penalties in an FA Cup shoot-out. Their opponents, Barnet, scored two to win the third round replay.

> HONOURS
> *Second Division champions 1996*
> *Division 4 champions 1986*
> *League Cup 1969*

IS THAT A FACT?
In 1936 Swansea set a Football League record for the longest distance travelled in consecutive matches when they travelled to Newcastle on Easter Saturday just a day after visiting Plymouth!

JOHN TERRY

JOHN TERRY

Born: Barking, 7th December 1980
Position: Defender
Club career:
1998- Chelsea 310 (19)
2000 Nottingham Forest (loan) 6 (0)
International record:
2003- England 65 (6)

• Chelsea captain since 2004, Terry is the most successful skipper in the club's history. To date he has won three Premiership titles, four FA Cups and two League Cups although he missed out on the biggest prize of all, the Champions League, when he slipped and put his penalty wide in the shoot-out against Manchester

United in the 2008 final in Moscow.
• A superb tackler who reads the game extremely well, Terry was voted PFA Player of the Year in 2005 after leading the Blues to the first of their back-to-back Premiership titles. With a total of 38 goals for the club in all competitions, he is the highest-scoring defender in Chelsea history.
• After making his England debut against Serbia & Montenegro in 2003, Terry went on to represent his country at Euro 2004 and the 2006 World Cup, where he was the only England player to be selected for the all-star FIFA squad at the end of the tournament. In May 2007 he became the first player to score in a full international at the new Wembley when he netted with a header in his side's 1-1 draw with Brazil.

• He was first appointed England captain by Steve McClaren in 2006 and retained the role under Fabio Capello. However, in February 2010 Terry was sensationally stripped of the armband following newspaper revelations about his private life. There was even speculation that he might be left out of the squad for the World Cup in South Africa, but in the event Terry was selected and played in all four of England's games at the finals.

CARLOS TEVEZ

Born: Buenos Aires, 5th February 1984
Position: Striker
Club career:
2001-04 Boca Juniors 75 (26)
2004-06 Corinthians 47 (31)
2006-07 West Ham United 26 (7)
2007-09 Manchester United 63 (19)
2009- Manchester City 35 (23)
International record:
2004- Argentina 56 (11)

Despite seeing his side just miss out on Champions League qualification, Manchester City striker Carlos Tevez enjoyed a tremendous first season at Eastlands in 2009/10. His total of 23 Premier League goals made him the division's fourth highest scorer and was the best return by a City player in the top flight since club legend Francis Lee hit 33 in 1971/72.
• Tevez began his career with Boca Juniors with whom he won the Copa Libertadores in 2003. He moved on to Brazilian side Corinthians the following year, and in 2005 became the first non-Brazilian for nearly 30 years to be named as the league's best player.
• He joined West Ham in 2006, but his first season in England was dogged by his controversial association with Media Sports Investments, a company that 'owned' Tevez and his fellow Argentine Javier Mascherano in breach of Premier League regulations.
• After scoring the goal that saved West Ham from relegation on the last day of the 2006/07 season, Tevez moved to Manchester United on a two-year deal. Despite winning two league titles and the Champions League during his time at Old Trafford,

JT: Chelsea's most successful skipper ever

Carlos Tevez: was once sent off for impersonating a chicken! (See Goal Celebrations, page 91)

• Throw ins were replaced by kick ins from the touchline in the Diadora League (now the Ryman League) during the 1994/95 season, but the experiment was abandoned at the end of the campaign.

TORQUAY UNITED

Year founded: 1898
Ground: Plainmoor (6,104)
Previous name: Torquay, Torquay Town
Nickname: The Gulls
Biggest win: 9-0 v Swindon (1952)
Heaviest defeat: 2-10 v Fulham (1931) and v Luton (1933)
Colours: Yellow shirts with navy blue trim, yellow shorts, yellow socks

Founded as Torquay in 1898 by old boys of two local colleges, the club merged with Ellacombe FC to become Torquay Town in 1910. After a further merger, with Babbacombe FC in 1921, the club adopted their present name.

• **The Gulls returned to the Football League after a two-year absence in 2009 following a 2-0 defeat of Cambridge United in the Conference play-off final at Wembley. The club had spent the previous 80 years in the bottom two divisions of the league, narrowly missing out on promotion to the old Second Division on goal average in both 1957 and 1968.**

• Torquay's leading scorer is Sammy Collins who banged in 204 league goals, including a club record eight hat-tricks, between 1948-58. His best season was in 1955/56 when he found the net 40 times to set another record for the Devon outfit.

• **On 3rd January 1977 Torquay defender Pat Kruse scored the fastest ever own goal in English football history, netting at the wrong end against Cambridge United after just six seconds!**

• Torquay's oldest player is goalkeeper Neville Southall, the most-capped Welsh international of all time, who was aged 41 and 135 days when he made his last apperance for The Gulls in January 2000.

• **Torquay's most famous fan is Helen Chamberlain, longserving presenter of Sky TV's *Soccer AM*.**

United boss Sir Alex Ferguson chose not to retain Tevez's services, and in the summer of 2009 he crossed the Manchester divide in a deal worth £25.5 million to MSI.

• A lively striker who never gives defenders a moment's peace, Tevez made his debut for Argentina in a World Cup qualifier against Ecuador in March 2004. Later that year he won a gold medal and the Golden Boot at the Athens Olympics.

• **At the 2010 World Cup in South Africa Tevez took his excellent club form into the finals, scoring one of the goals of the tournament with a fierce shot from the edge of the box against Mexico in the first knock-out round.**

THROW INS

Danny Brooks, a 28-year-old PE teacher from Halifax, holds the world record for the longest ever throw. Taking advantage of his training as a gymnast, he used a forward hand spring technique to hurl the ball 49.78 metres in December 2009.

• **Perhaps the most famous of all long throw specialists is Stoke's Rory Delap. Since the Potters gained promotion to the Premier League in 2008 his enormous throws, fired in with a flat trajectory, have caused huge problems for Stoke's opponents and led to a number of vital goals for the team.**

• The most bizarre goal from a throw in came in a derby between Birmingham City and Aston Villa in 2002. Villa defender Olaf Mellberg threw the ball back to goalkeeper Peter Enckelman and it dribbled under his foot and into the net. Despite Villa's protests, referee David Elleray ruled that the goal should stand because Enckelman had made contact with the ball.

Fernando Torres: Liverpool's record signing

FERNANDO TORRES

Born: Madrid, 20th March 1984
Position: Striker
Club career:
2001-07 Atletico Madrid 214 (82)
2007- Liverpool 79 (56)
International record:
2003- Spain 80 (24)

In the 2007/08 campaign Liverpool striker Fernando Torres enjoyed the most prolific debut season ever of a foreign player in English football, scoring 24 league goals to beat the old record set by Manchester United's Dutch marksman Ruud van Nistelrooy six years earlier.

• Torres began his career with local club Atletico Madrid, where his goalscoring feats earned him the nickname 'El Nino' (The Kid) and the skipper's armband. Aged just 19 at the time, he was the youngest captain in Atletico's history.

• In 2007 Torres signed for Liverpool for a club record £20 million (plus Luis Garcia, who moved in the opposite direction). He was an instant hit at Anfield, becoming the first Liverpool player since 1948 to hit hat-tricks in consecutive home matches when he notched trebles against Middlesbrough and West Ham

and, later in the season, scoring in eight successive home games to equal a record set by Reds legend Roger Hunt way back in 1962.

• Torres carried on his goalscoring form into Euro 2008, hitting the winning goal in the final in Vienna as Spain beat Germany to claim their first trophy for 44 years. To cap a

truly memorable year for the Kop icon he was named third in the World Footballer of the Year poll behind Cristiano Ronaldo and Lionel Messi.

• Despite playing well below par and failing to score a single goal, Torres ended the 2010 World Cup in South Africa by picking up a winners' medal. However, his poor form saw him relegated to the subs' bench and he only made a brief appearance in the final.

TOP 10

SPANISH PLAYERS IN ENGLISH FOOTBALL

1. Fernando Torres (Liverpool, 2007-)
2. Cesc Fabregas (Arsenal, 2003-)
3. Xavi Alonso (Liverpool, 2004-09)
4. Mikel Arteta (Everton, 2005-)
5. Pepe Reina (Liverpool, 2005-)
6. Ivan Campo (Bolton Wanderers 2002-08, Ipswich Town 2008-09)
7. Nayim (Tottenham Hotspur, 1988-1993)
8. Gaizka Mendieta (Middlesborough, 2003-08)
9. Albert Ferrer (Chelsea, 1998-2003)
10. Alvaro Arbeloa (Liverpool, 2007-09)

JOHN TOSHACK

Born: Cardiff, 22nd March 1949
Managerial career:
1978-84 Swansea City
1984-85 Sporting Lisbon
1985-89 Real Sociedad
1989-90 Real Madrid
1991-94 Real Sociedad
1994 Wales
1995-97 Deportivo de la Coruna
1997-99 Besiktas
1999 Real Madrid
2000-01 St Etienne
2001-02 Real Sociedad
2002-03 Catania
2004 Real Murcia
2004- Wales

John Toshack began his second spell as Wales manager in 2004, although his first crack at the job in 1994 was nothing to get excited about... he lasted 41 days!

• Toshack made his managerial reputation with Swansea City, whom he led from the Fourth to the old First Division in just four seasons between 1978-81. No club before or since has made a quicker ascent to the top flight from the basement division.

• He went on to manage clubs in Portugal, Spain, Turkey, France and Italy, winning the league title with Real Madrid in 1990 and the Turkish Cup with Besiktas in 1998. In 2004 Toshack became Wales manager for the second time, succeeding Mark Hughes, but he has struggled to recreate his club success at international level.

• A tall striker who won 40 caps for Wales in his playing career, Toshack formed a deadly attacking partnership with Kevin Keegan after joining Liverpool from Cardiff City for £110,000 in 1970. He won three league titles and two UEFA Cups with the Reds before becoming player/ manager of Swansea in 1978.

TOTTENHAM HOTSPUR

Year founded: 1882
Ground: White Hart Lane (36,310)
Previous name: Hotspur FC
Nickname: Spurs
Biggest win: 13-2 v Crewe (1960)
Heaviest defeat: 0-8 v Cologne (1995)
Colours: White shirts with blue trim, navy blue shorts, white socks

The club was founded as Hotspur FC in 1882 by a group of local cricketers, most of whom were former pupils of Tottenham Grammar School. Three years later the club decided to add the prefix 'Tottenham'.

• Tottenham were members of the Southern League when they won the FA Cup for the first time in 1901, defeating Sheffield United 3-1 in a replay at Burnden Park. Spurs' victory meant they were the first (and, so far, only) non-league club to win the cup since the formation of the Football League in 1888.

• In 1961 Tottenham created history when they became the first club in the 20th century to win the fabled League and Cup Double. Their title success was based on a storming start to the season, Bill Nicholson's side winning their first 11 games to set a top-flight record which has not been matched since. By the end of the campaign, the north Londoners had won 31 of their 42 league matches to create another record for the top tier.

• As Arsenal fans like to point out, Tottenham have failed to win the League since those 'Glory, Glory' days of skipper Danny Blanchflower, Dave Mackay and Cliff Jones. Spurs, though, have continued to enjoy cup success, and their total of eight victories in the FA Cup is only surpassed by the Gunners and Manchester United. Remarkably, five of those triumphs came in years ending in a '1', giving rise to the legend that these seasons were particularly lucky for Spurs.

• Tottenham have also enjoyed much success in the League Cup, winning the competition four times... a record which puts them joint third on the all-time honours list behind Liverpool and Aston Villa. The last of these triumphs, in 2008

following a 2-1 defeat of holders Chelsea in the final, saw Tottenham became the first club to win the League Cup at the new Wembley.

• Spurs have a decent record in Europe, too. In 1963 they thrashed Atletico Madrid 5-1 in the final of the European Cup-Winners' Cup, the legendary Jimmy Greaves grabbing a brace, to become the first British club to win a European trophy. Then, in 1972, Tottenham defeated Wolves 3-2 on aggregate in the first ever UEFA Cup final and the first European final to feature two English clubs. A third European triumph followed in 1984 when Tottenham beat Anderlecht in the first UEFA Cup final to be settled by penalties.

• Ace marksman Jimmy Greaves holds two goalscoring records for Tottenham. His total of 220 league goals between 1961-70 is a club best, as is his impressive tally of 37 league goals in 1962/63. Clive Allen, though, struck an incredible total of 49 goals in all competitions in 1986/87, including a record 12 in the League Cup.

• Stalwart defender Steve Perryman is the club's longest serving player, pulling on the famous white shirt in 655 league games between 1969-86.

• Tottenham's record buy is skilful Croatian midfielder Luka Modric, who cost £16.5 million when he moved to White Hart Lane from Dynamo Zagreb in 2008. In the same year Spurs

received a club record £30.75 million from Manchester United for Bulgarian striker Dimitar Berbatov.

• Tottenham's first title success was in 1950/51 when Arthur Rowe's stylish 'Push and Run' team topped the table just one year after winning the Second Division championship. In the years since only Ipswich Town (in 1961 and 1962) have managed to claim the top two titles in consecutive seasons.

• In 2000 Spurs' Ledley King scored the fastest ever goal in Premiership history, netting after just 9.7 seconds against Bradford City at Valley Parade.

• Spurs' incredible 9-1 trouncing of Wigan on 22nd November 2009 was only the second time a club had scored nine goals in a Premier League game. Jermain Defoe's five-goal haul in the same match also equalled the Premiership individual scoring record.

• Among the many famous faces who follow Spurs are actress Patsy Kensit, author Salman Rushdie and veteran TV presenter Bruce Forsyth.

HONOURS
Division 1 champions 1951, 1961
Division 2 champions 1920, 1950
FA Cup 1901, 1921, 1961, 1962, 1967, 1981, 1982, 1991
League Cup 1971, 1973, 1999, 2008
Double 1961
European Cup Winners' Cup 1963
UEFA Cup 1972, 1984

Spurs are traditionally succesful when the year ends in a '1'

TRANMERE ROVERS

Year founded: 1884
Ground: Prenton Park (16,789)
Previous name: Belmont FC
Nickname: Rovers
Biggest win: 13-0 v Oswestry United (1914)
Heaviest defeat: 1-9 v Tottenham (1953)
Colours: White shirts with blue trim, white shorts, white socks with blue trim.

The club was founded as Belmont FC in 1884 by members of two local cricket clubs, changing its name to Tranmere Rovers the following year. In 1921 Rovers joined the Football League for the first time as members of the newly-created Third Division (North).

• **The club enjoyed their greatest ever moment in 2000 when they played Leicester City in the League Cup final at Wembley. Despite performing well on the day, Rovers lost 2-1.**

• Rovers' best ever league victory, 13-4 against Oldham on Boxing Day 1935, set a record for the highest-scoring Football League match which remains to this day. Robert 'Bunny' Bell scored nine goals in the match, a record for the old Third Division (North).

• **Tranmere Rovers were the first club of the legendary goalscorer 'Dixie' Dean, who made his debut for the club aged 16 and 355 days in 1924. For many years Dean was Rovers' youngest ever player, but his record was eventually broken by Iain Hume in 2000.**

• Former manager John Aldridge is the club's most decorated international, winning 30 of his 69 Republic of Ireland caps while at Prenton Park. Aldridge's total of 176 goals in all competitions for the club in the 1990s put him just four goals behind Tranmere's top scorer, Ian Muir.

• **In 1964 Tranmere conceded the fastest ever goal in Football League history, Bradford Park Avenue's Jim Fryatt netting against them after just four seconds. Understandably perhaps, Rovers never recovered from that early shock, going down to a 4-2 defeat.**

> HONOURS
> **Division 3 (North) champions 1938**
> **Football League Trophy 1990**
> **Welsh Cup 1935**

TRANSFERS

The world's most expensive player is Portuguese winger Cristiano Ronaldo, who moved from Manchester United to Real Madrid in the summer of 2009 for a staggering £80 million. This beat the £56 million Real had paid AC Milan for Brazilian playmaker Kaka just a few weeks earlier. Prior to these two deals the transfer record had not been broken since 2001, when Zinedine Zidane moved from Juventus to Real Madrid for £46 million.

• **The biggest transfer deal involving a British club saw Manchester City pay Real Madrid £32.5 million for Brazilian star Robinho in August 2008.**

• The first player to be transferred for a four-figure fee in England was Alf Common, who moved from Sunderland to Middlesbrough in 1905. In 1966 World Cup winner Alan Ball became the first six-figure footballer when he joined Everton from Blackpool, while Trevor Francis broke the £1 million barrier when Nottingham Forest manager Brian Clough gave Birmingham City an eye-watering cheque for £1,150,000 in 1979.

• **At the opposite end of the scale, Ian Wright joined Crystal Palace from lowly Greenwich Borough for a set of weights in 1985. Even more bizarrely, Norwegian striker Kenneth Kristensen moved from Vindbjart to Floey in 2002 for his weight in fresh shrimp!**

GIOVANNI TRAPATTONI

Born: Milan, 17th March 1939
Managerial record:
1976 AC Milan
1976-86 Juventus
1986-91 Inter Milan
1991-94 Juventus
1994-95 Bayern Munich
1995-96 Cagliari
1996-98 Bayern Munich
1998-2000 Fiorentina
2000-04 Italy
2004-05 Benfica
2005-06 Stuttgart
2006-08 Red Bull Salzburg
2008- Republic of Ireland

Republic of Ireland manager Giovanni Trapattoni is one of the most successful coaches in the history of the game, being one of just two managers to have won league titles in four countries (Italy, Germany, Portugal and Austria).

• **Formerly a tough-tackling defender**

Ronaldo joins Real madrid for £80 million, a world record transfer

IS THAT A FACT?

Between 1946-55 Tranmere's Harold Bell appeared in an incredible 401 consecutive league games, a run unmatched by any other Football League player. Bell went on to make a club record 595 appearances before hanging up his boots in 1964.

with AC Milan and Italy, Trapattoni became manager of Juventus in 1976 and, over the next ten years, led the Old Lady to no fewer than six Serie A titles. He also guided Juve to triumphs in all three European trophies, and remains the only manager to have achieved this feat with the same club.

• In 2000 Trapattoni was appointed manager of Italy, but his four-year spell in charge of the Azzurri was a disappointing one. He returned to club football, winning league titles with Benfica and Red Bull Salzburg, before taking the Republic of Ireland job in 2008. The following year his dream of taking the Irish to the World Cup in South Africa was dashed by a hugely controversial goal by France's William Gallas in a play-off in Paris.

TV AND RADIO

The first ever live radio broadcast of a football match was on 22nd January 1927 when the BBC covered the First Division encounter between Arsenal and Sheffield United at Highbury. *The Radio Times* printed a pitch marked into numbered squares, which the commentators used to describe where the ball was at any given moment (which some suggest gave rise to the phrase 'back to square one').

• The 1937 FA Cup final between Sunderland and Preston was the first to be televised, although only parts of the match were shown by the BBC. The following year's final between Preston and Huddersfield was the first to be screened live and in full, although the audience was only around 10,000 as so few people had TV sets at the time.

• The biggest British TV audience ever for a football match (and, indeed, the biggest

ever for any TV broadcast in this country) was 32.3 million for the 1966 World Cup final between England and West Germany. The viewing figures for the match, which was shown live by both BBC and ITV, were all the more remarkable as only 15 million households in the UK had TV sets. The biggest TV audience for an FA Cup final was in 1970 when 28.49 million people watched Chelsea beat Leeds 2-1 in a midweek replay.

• A record cumulative TV audience of 26.4 billion watched the 2002 World Cup finals, including a record 1.3 billion for the final between Brazil and Germany.

• The 2009 TV deal between Sky and the Premiership was the biggest in the history of the game. Under the terms of the deal Sky paid £1.62 billion over three years to show 115 live games per season. By 2013 TV companies will have ploughed more than £8 billion into the English game since the formation of the Premier League in 1992.

FC TWENTE

Year founded: 1965
Ground: The Grolsch Fortress (24,000)
Nickname: The Tukkers
Colours: Red shirts, red shorts, red socks

Reigning Dutch champions FC Twente were founded in 1965 following the merger of two local professional clubs, Sportclub Enschede and Enschedese Boys.

• **The Tukkers, as they are known after the Dutch name for the people from the Twente region, reached the UEFA Cup final in 1975 but failed to live up the occasion, going down limply 5-1 on aggregate to Borussia Monchengladbach.**

• In 2008 Twente appointed former England manager Steve McClaren as their new boss. Reviled by the English

In the absence of an umbrella, Steve McLaren grabs the nearest thing to hand!

press after his failure to lead the nation to the Euro 2008 finals, McClaren went some way to restoring his battered reputation when he guided Twente to second place in the league behind champions AZ Alkmaar in his first season in Holland.

• **The following year McClaren went one better, leading Twente to their first ever league title. Shortly afterwards, though, he resigned from the post to become the manager of 2009 German champions Wolfsburg.**

> HONOURS
> *Dutch League champions 2010*
> *Dutch Cup 1977, 2001*

UEFA

UEFA, the Union of European Football Associations, was founded in 1954 at a meeting in Basel during the Swiss World Cup. Holding power over all the national FAs in Europe, it is the largest and most influential of the six continental confederations of FIFA.

• **UEFA competitions include the Champions League (first won as the European Cup by Real Madrid), the Europa League (formerly the UEFA Cup) and the UEFA Super Cup.**

Current UEFA President Michel Platini, a former captain of France, is the sixth man to fill the role. The longest-serving UEFA President was Sweden's Lennart Johansson, who did the job for 17 years between 1990-2007.

• **Controversial UEFA decisions in the past include the introduction of penalty kicks to decide drawn European ties (from 1970) and the ban on English clubs competing in European competitions for five years from 1985 after the Heysel tragedy.**

URUGUAY

First international: Uruguay 2 Argentina 3, 1901
Most capped player: Rodolfo Rodriguez, 79 caps (1976-86)
Leading goalscorer: Hector Scarone, 31 goals (1917-30)
First World Cup appearance: Uruguay 1 Peru 0, 1930
Biggest win: Uruguay 9 Bolivia 0, 1927
Heaviest defeat: Uruguay 0 Argentina 6, 1902
Colours: Sky blue shirts, black shorts, black socks

In 1930 Uruguay became the first winners of the World Cup, beating arch-rivals Argentina 4-2 in the final on home soil in Montevideo. The match was a repeat of the Olympic final of 1928, which Uruguay had also won.

• **In 1950 Uruguay won the World Cup for a second time, defeating hosts Brazil 2-1 in 'the final' (it was actually the last and decisive match in a four-team final group). The match was watched by a massive crowd of 199,589 in the**

Maracana stadium in Rio de Janeiro, the largest ever to attend a football match anywhere in the world.
• **At the 2010 World Cup in South Africa**

Despite being two-time winners of the World Cup, Diego Forlan's Uruguay were the surprise package in 2010

Uruguay finished fourth, their best showing since Mexico in 1970. However, the South Americans' campaign will mostly be remembered for a blatant handball on the line by striker Luis Suarez, which denied their opponents Ghana a certain winning goal in the teams' quarter-final clash.

• **In terms of population, Uruguay is the easily the smallest nation ever to win the World Cup.**
• Uruguay and Argentina have played more international matches against each other than any other pair of countries in the world, a total of 162 games since 1901.
• **Along with Argentina, Uruguay are the most successful team in the history of the Copa America. Winners of the inaugural tournament in 1916, Uruguay have won the competition a total of 14 times.**

HONOURS
World Cup 1930, 1950
Copa America 1916, 1917, 1920, 1923, 1924, 1926, 1935, 1942, 1956, 1959, 1967, 1983, 1987, 1995
World Cup record
1930 Winners
1934 Did not enter
1938 Did not enter
1950 Winners
1954 Fourth place
1958 Did not qualify
1962 Round 1

1966 Quarter-finals
1970 Fourth place
1974 Round 1
1978 Did not qualify
1982 Did not qualify
1986 Round 2
1990 Round 2
1994 Did not qualify
1998 Did not qualify
2002 Round 1
2006 Did not qualify
2010 Fourth place

MARCO VAN BASTEN

Born: Utrecht, Holland, 31st October 1964
Position: Striker
Club career:
1982-87 Ajax 133 (128)
1987-93 AC Milan 147 (90)
International record:
1983-92 Holland 58 (24)

The greatest goalscorer of his generation, Marco Van Basten is one of just three men to have won the European Footballer of the Year award three times (after Johan Cruyff and Michel Platini).

• **With his first club, Ajax, van Basten won a European Cup-Winners' Cup medal in 1987 and the European Golden Boot in 1986, after scoring 37 goals in just 26 league matches. He then moved to AC Milan, joining fellow Dutch internationals Ruud Gullit and Frank Rijkaard, where he won three league titles and two European Cups before an ankle injury ended his career at the age of 29.**

• Van Basten starred for Holland as they won the European championships in 1988, top scoring in the tournament with five goals, including a brilliant hat-trick against England (the only player in the last 50 years to achieve

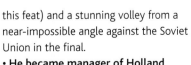

this feat) and a stunning volley from a near-impossible angle against the Soviet Union in the final.

• **He became manager of Holland in 2004, leading the Dutch to the knock-out stages of both the 2006 World Cup and Euro 2008. He resigned** after the latter tournament to become manager of Ajax but left the job after just one season when the Amsterdam club failed to qualify for the Champions League.

TOP 10

GOALSCORERS FOR HOLLAND

1. Patrick Kluivert (1994-2004) 40 goals
2. Dennis Bergkamp (1990-2000) 37 goals
3. Abe Lenstra (1940-59) 33 goals
   Johan Cruyff (1966-77) 33 goals
   Ruud van Nistelrooy (1998-2008) 33 goals
6. Beb Bakhuys (1928-37) 28 goals
7. Kick Smit (1935-46) 26 goals
8. Marco van Basten (1983-92) 24 goals
9. Leen Vente (1933-40) 19 goals
   Wesley Sneijder (2003-) 19 goals
   Robin van Persie (2005-) 19 goals

ROBIN VAN PERSIE

Born: Rotterdam, Holland, 6th August 1983
Position: Striker
Club career:
2001-04 Feyenoord 59 (15)
2004- Arsenal 131 (48)
International record:
2005- Holland 51 (19)

The son of two artists, Arsenal striker Robin van Persie began his career with his local side, Feyenoord, making his first-team debut aged 17 in 2001 and winning the Dutch league's Best Young Talent award at the end of his first season. A UEFA Cup winner the following year, he moved to north London in 2004 for a £2.75 million fee.

• In his first season with the Gunners, Van Persie fired his new club to the FA Cup final with two goals in the semi-final defeat of Blackburn Rovers. A month later he collected his first, and so far only, medal in English football when Arsenal defeated Manchester United on penalties in the final.

• A clean striker of the ball, especially on his preferred left side, Van Persie made

Arsenal's Van Persie savours a goal against arch rivals Spurs

his international debut for Holland in a World Cup qualifier against Romania in 2005.

EDWIN VAN DER SAR

Born: Voorhout, Holland, 29th October 1970
Position: Goalkeeper
Club career:
1990-99 Ajax 226 (1)
1999-2001 Juventus 66
2001-05 Fulham 127
2005- Manchester United 153
International record:
1995-2008 Holland 130

Manchester United goalkeeper Edwin van der Sar holds the British record for clean sheets, keeping the ball out of his net for 14 Premiership matches and a total of

1,311 minutes during United's 2008/09 title-winning season.

• Van der Sar began his career with Ajax, with whom he won four league titles and the Champions League in 1995. He moved to Juventus in 1999, becoming the first non-Italian to keep goal for the Serie A side, before joining Fulham two years later.

• In 2005 Van der Sar signed for Manchester United, with whom he has since won three Premiership titles and the Champions League in 2008, his save from Nicolas Anelka in the penalty shoot-out against Chelsea in Moscow clinching the trophy for the Reds.

• Van der Sar is the most capped Dutch international ever, playing 130 times for his country between 1995-2008. Along with French defender Lilian Thuram he holds the record for the highest number of appearances (16) at the European Championships.

PATRICK VIEIRA

Born: Dakar, Senegal,
23rd June 1976
Position: Midfielder
Club career:
1993-95 Cannes 49 (2)
1995-96 AC Milan 2 (0)
1996-2005 Arsenal 279 (29)
2005-06 Juventus 31 (5)
2006-10 Inter Milan 67 (6)
2010 Manchester City 13 (1)
International record:
1997-2009 France 107 (6)

One of the greatest players in Arsenal's history, Patrick Vieira joined the Gunners from AC Milan in September 1996 for a bargain £3.5 million.

• The Senegal-born midfielder had a stellar career at Highbury, winning the Double in his first season at the club, another Double in 2002 and, in 2003/04, skippering the Gunners as they claimed the Premiership title without losing a single match. His last act as an Arsenal player was to score the winning penalty in the 2005 FA Cup final shoot-out against Manchester United.

• Vieira left north London that summer, joining Juventus in a £13.7 million deal. He won the league championship in his one season with the club, before moving to Inter Milan with whom he won three more Serie A titles in 2007, 2008 and 2009. In 2010 he made a surprise move back to the Premier League, joining Manchester City in the January transfer window.

• Tall, strong and mobile, Vieira made his debut for France in 1997. The following year he helped his country win the World Cup for the first time and was rewarded with the Legion d'honneur, France's highest decoration. In 2000 he was a key member of the French side that won the European Championships and in 2006 he came close to winning the World Cup again but had to settle for a runners-up medal after France lost on penalties in the final to Italy.

• Although acclaimed as one of the best midfield players of his generation, Vieira has often been criticised for his poor disciplinary record. He was sent off eight times in league games while with Arsenal, a figure only matched in the Premier League era by Duncan Ferguson and Richard Dunne.

Spain star David Villa after signing for Barcelona

DAVID VILLA

Born: Tuilla, Spain, 3rd December 1981
Position: Striker
Club career:
1999-2001 Sporting Gijon B 65 (25)
2001-03 Sporting Gijon 80 (38)
2003-05 Zaragoza 73 (32)
2005-10 Valencia 160 (108)
2010- Barcelona
International record:
2005- Spain 65 (43)

One of the most dangerous strikers in world football, Spain's David Villa was the top scorer at Euro 2008 with four goals – a haul which helped his country win the championships in Austria and Switzerland. Two years later he was joint top scorer at the World Cup in South Africa, his five goals contributing hugely to Spain's first ever triumph in the competition.

• Fast, clever and a cool finisher inside the penalty box, Villa has scored goals at an impressive rate since his early years with Sporting Gijon and Zaragoza. He came to prominence, though, with Valencia with whom he found the net an incredible 108 times in five seasons before signing for Barcelona for around £30 million in May 2010.

• Villa made his international debut against San Marino in 2005 and is now his country's second-highest scorer ever behind the man he eventually replaced in the Spanish line-up, Raul. His partnership with Fernando Torres has been central to Spain's success in recent years, with the stats showing that Villa is easily the more prolific of the pair.

• In February 2009 Villa became the first Spanish player ever to score in six consecutive internationals when he hit the target in a 2-0 defeat of England in February 2009. In the period 2005-09, meanwhile, he was the deadliest striker in the world, scoring a staggering 156 goals for club and country.

WALES

First international:
Scotland 4
Wales 0, 1876
Most capped player:
Neville Southall, 92 caps (1982-98)
Leading goalscorer:
Ian Rush, 28 goals (1980-96)
First World Cup appearance: Wales 1 Hungary 1, 1958
Biggest win: Wales 11 Ireland 0, 1888
Heaviest defeat: Scotland 9 Wales 0, 1878
Colours: Red shirts, white shorts, red and white socks

Wales are the least successful of the four British national sides, having qualified for just two major international tournaments in their history.

• **Their finest hour came in 1958 when a Welsh side including such great names as John Charles, Ivor Allchurch and Jack Kelsey qualified for the World Cup** finals in Sweden after beating Israel in a two-legged play-off. After drawing all three of their group matches, Wales then beat Hungary in a play-off to reach the quarter-finals where they lost 1-0 to eventual winners Brazil.

• In 1976 Wales made their best ever showing in the European Championships, reaching the quarter-finals before going down 3-1 on aggregate to Yugoslavia. Since then Wales supporters have had little to cheer, despite the efforts of the likes of Mark Hughes, Ryan Giggs and all-time leading scorer Ian Rush.

• **Wales winger Billy Meredith is the oldest international in the history of British football. He was aged 45 years and 229 days when he won the last of his 48 caps against England in 1920, a quarter of a century after making his international debut.**

• Wales have the third best record in the British Home Championships with seven outright wins and five shared victories. Their best decade was the 1930s when they won the championship three times.

WORLD CUP RECORD
1930-38 Did not enter
1950-54 Did not qualify
1958 Quarter-finals
1962-2010 Did not qualify

WALSALL

Year founded: 1888
Ground: Banks' Stadium (11,300)
Previous name: Walsall Town Swifts
Nickname: The Saddlers
Biggest win: 10-0 v Darwen (1899)
Heaviest defeat: 0-12 v Small Heath (1892) and v Darwen (1896)
Colours: Red shirts with black trim, red shorts, red socks

The club was founded in 1888 as Walsall Town Swifts, following an amalgamation of Walsall Swifts and Walsall Town. Founder members of the Second Division in 1892, the club changed to its present name three years later.

• **Walsall have never played in the top flight but they have a history of producing cup shocks, the most famous coming back in 1933 when they sensationally beat eventual league champions Arsenal 2-0 in the FA Cup.**

• Two players share the distinction of being Walsall's all-time leading scorer: Tony Richards, who notched 184 league goals for the club between 1954-

Even the ball boys look cheesed off about the form of the Welsh football team

63, and his strike partner Colin Taylor, who banged in exactly the same number in three spells with the Saddlers between 1958-73.

• **Colin Harrison is the club's longest-serving player, making a record 467 league appearances between 1964-82.**

• Striker Alan Buckley, who went on to manage the club, is Walsall's record signing, costing £175,000 when he joined the Saddlers from Midlands neighbours Birmingham City in June 1979. No other Football League club's most expensive purchase goes back as many years, and with the credit crunch biting there's every chance that it's a record Walsall won't be breaking any time soon..

> **HONOURS**
> *Division 4 champions 1960*
> *League Two champions 2007*

WATFORD

Year founded: 1881
Ground: Vicarage Road (17,000)
Previous name: Watford Rovers, West Herts
Nickname: The Hornets
Biggest win: 10-1 v Lowestoft Town (1926)
Heaviest defeat: 0-10 v Wolves (1912)
Colours: Yellow shirts with red and black stripe, black shorts, yellow socks

Founded as Watford Rovers in 1881, the club changed its name to West Herts in 1893. Five years later, following a merger with Watford St Mary's, the club became Watford FC.

• **The club's history was fairly nondescript until pop star Elton John became chairman in 1976 and invested a large part of his personal wealth in the team. With future England manager Graham Taylor at the helm, the Hornets went on to enjoy a golden era, rising from the Fourth to the First Division in just five years and reaching the FA Cup final in 1984. In the late 1990s Taylor returned to the club and worked his magic again, guiding the Hornets to two successive promotions and a brief taste of life in the Premiership.**

• After finishing second in the old First Division in 1983, Watford made their one

Watford take on Chelsea in the FA Cup

foray into Europe the following season, reaching the third round of the UEFA Cup before losing to Sparta Prague.

• **Luther Blissett, one of the star players of that period, is the club's record appearance maker. In three spells at Vicarage Road the energetic striker notched up 415 league appearances and scored 148 league goals (also a club record).**

• In January 2007 Watford received a club record £9.65 million when they sold skilful winger Ashley Young to Aston Villa. A few months later the Hornets splashed £3.25 million of this cash on West Brom's Nathan Ellington, their most expensive ever signing.

> **HONOURS**
> *Division 3 champions 1969*
> *Second Division champions 1998*
> *Division 4 champions 1978*

GEORGE WEAH

Born: Monrovia, Liberia, 1st October 1966
Position: Striker
Club career:
1984-85 Bongrange Company 2 (1)
1985-86 Mighty Barolle 10 (7)
1986-87 Invincible Eleven 23 (24)
1987-88 Tonerre Yaounde 18 (15)
1988-92 Monaco 102 (47)
1992-95 Paris St Germain 96 (32)
1995-2000 AC Milan 114 (46)
2000 Chelsea 11 (4)
2000 Manchester City 7 (1)
2000-01 Marseille 19 (5)
2001-03 Al-Jazira 8 (13)
International record:
1988-2002 Liberia 60 (22)

The greatest ever player to emerge from Africa, George Weah pulled off a unique treble in 1995 when he was voted FIFA World Player of the Year, European Player of the Year and African Player of the Year all in the space of a month.

• **Weah began his career with clubs in his native Liberia and Cameroon, but made his name playing under Arsene Wenger at Monaco. He won the French Cup with the south of France outfit, before moving to Paris St Germain with whom he won the French title in 1994. The following year Weah joined AC Milan, helping the Italian giants win the Serie A title in both 1996 and 1999.**

• On loan at Chelsea in 2000 he appeared in the last FA Cup final at the old Wembley, finishing on the winning side as the Blues beat Aston Villa 1-0. He later had a short spell at Manchester City before ending his career with Abu Dhabi club Al-Jazira.

• **A national icon in Liberia, Weah stood for the presidency of his country in 2005 but lost out in the second round of voting to Ellen Johnson-Sirleaf, the first woman ever to be elected president of an**

> **IS THAT A FACT?**
> George Weah is the only World Player of the Year never to have played at the World Cup finals. He tried everything to get Liberia there, even paying for his team-mates' boots and kit and coaching the side himself, but all to no avail.

African nation. The signs are that he may stand again in 2011, although at the time of writing no formal announcement had been made.

WEMBLEY STADIUM

Built at a cost of £798 million, the new Wembley Stadium is the most expensive sporting venue ever. With a capacity of 90,000 it is also the second largest in Europe and the largest in the world to have every seat under cover.

• **The stadium's most spectacular feature is a 315m-wide arch, the world's longest unsupported roof structure. Wembley also boasts a staggering 2,618 toilets, more than any other venue in the world.**

• Originally scheduled to open in 2003, the stadium was not completed until 2007 due to a variety of financial and legal difficulties. The first professional match was played at the new venue on 17th March 2007 when England under-21s met their Italian counterparts, with the first goal arriving after just 28 seconds when Giampaolo Pazzini struck for the visitors. Half an hour later, David Bentley became the first Englishman to score at the new stadium.

• The Wembley pitch has been relaid ten times since the stadium opened in 2007 and has attracted a lot of criticism during that time, Chelsea captain John Terry declaring it "the worst we've played on all year" after the Blues beat Portsmouth in the 2010 FA Cup final. Nonetheless, his team-mate Didier Drogba seems very much at home at Wembley, having scored a record six goals in club games at the new stadium, including strikes in three FA Cup finals.

• The first Wembley Stadium was opened in 1923, having been constructed in just 300 days at a cost of £750,000. The first match played at the venue was the 1923 FA Cup final between Bolton and West Ham, although the kick-off was delayed for nearly an hour when thousands of fans spilled onto the pitch because of overcrowding in the stands.

• **The last game played at the old Wembley was the World Cup qualifier between England and Germany on 7th October 2000. It proved to be a sad send off to the original 'home of English football' as Germany won 1-0, Dietmar Hamman scoring the last ever goal under the Twin Towers.**

• Arsenal and England defender Tony

Adams played a record 60 games at Wembley between 1987-2000, a total boosted by the fact that the Gunners used the stadium for their home games in the Champions League in the 1990s.

ARSENE WENGER

Born: Strasbourg, France, 22nd October 1949
Managerial career:
1984-87 Nancy
1987-94 Monaco
1995-96 Nagoya Grampus Eight
1996- Arsenal

Arsenal boss Arsene Wenger is the most successful manager in the Gunners' history, having won the Premiership title three times and the FA Cup on four occasions – although it's now five years since he last held a trophy aloft.

• **After a modest playing career which included a stint with his local club Strasbourg, Wenger cut his managerial teeth with Nancy before moving to Monaco in 1987. He won the league title in his first season there, with a team including English stars Glenn**

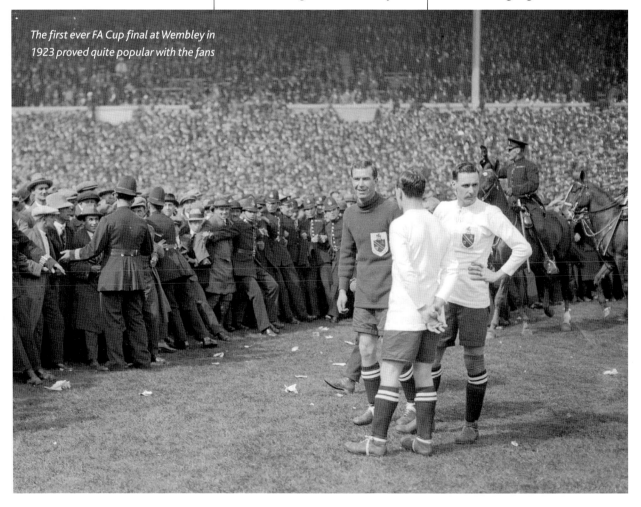

The first ever FA Cup final at Wembley in 1923 proved quite popular with the fans

Hoddle and Mark Hateley, and the French Cup in 1991.

• Following a year in Japan with Nagoya Grampus Eight, Wenger arrived in north London in September 1996. In his first full season at Highbury he became the first non-British manager to win the Double, and he repeated this accomplishment in 2002.

• His greatest achievement, though, came in 2004 when his Arsenal side won the title after going through the entire Premiership season undefeated. Wenger's 'Invincibles', as they were dubbed, were hailed as the greatest team in English football history, not only for their record 49-game unbeaten run but also for their fluid attacking style of play which made the most of exceptional talents like Thierry Henry, Dennis Bergkamp and Patrick Vieira.

• Despite all his domestic triumphs Wenger has found success in Europe elusive. In 2000 his Gunners side lost on penalties to Galatasaray

Arsene Wenger has transformed 'boring boring Arsenal' into one of the Premier League's most exciting teams... shame he didn't see any of it!

in the UEFA Cup final and, even more painfully, his team narrowly lost to Barcelona in the 2006 Champions League final in Paris.

WEST BROMWICH ALBION

Year founded: 1878
Ground: The Hawthorns (26,500)
Previous name: West Bromwich Strollers
Nickname: The Baggies
Biggest win: 12-0 v Darwen (1892)
Heaviest defeat: 3-10 v Stoke City (1937)
Colours: Navy blue-and- white-striped shirts, white shorts, white socks

Founded as West Bromwich Strollers in 1878 by workers at the local Salter's Spring Works, the club adopted the suffix 'Albion' two years later and were founder members of the Football League in 1888.

• **The Baggies were the first current club to lose two consecutive FA Cup finals, going down to Blackburn Rovers in 1886 and Aston Villa the following year. In 1888, though, West Brom recorded the first of their five triumphs in the cup, beating favourites Preston 2-1 in the final.**

• In 1931 West Brom became the first and only club to win promotion and the FA Cup in the same season. The Baggies came close to repeating this particular double in 2008, when they topped the Championship but were beaten in the FA Cup semi-finals by eventual winners Portsmouth.

• **West Brom claimed their only league title in 1920, in the first post-First World War season. The 60 points they amassed that season and the 104 goals they scored were both records at the time.**

• In 1966 West Brom won the last League Cup final to be played over two

legs, overcoming West Ham 5-3 on aggregate. The next year they appeared in the first one-off final at Wembley, but surprisingly lost 3-2 to Third Division QPR after leading 2-0 at half-time.

• **The Baggies, though, returned to Wembley the following season and beat Everton 1-0 in the FA Cup final. West Brom's winning goal was scored in extra-time by club legend Jeff Astle, who in the process became one of just 12 players to have scored in every round of the competition. Astle also found the target in his side's 2-1 defeat by Manchester City in the 1970 League Cup final to become the first player to score in both domestic cup finals at Wembley.**

• In 1892 West Brom thrashed Darwen 12-0 to record their biggest ever win. The score set a record for the top flight which has never been beaten, although Nottingham Forest equalled it in 1909. The Baggies' worst ever defeat was a 10-3 mauling against Stoke City in 1937.

• **Cult hero Tony 'Bomber' Brown is West Brom's record scorer with 218 league goals to his name. The attacking midfielder is also the club's longest-serving player, turning out in 574 league games between 1963-80.**

• In the 2004/05 season West Brom became the first club to avoid relegation from the Premiership after propping up the table at Christmas. However, the Baggies went down the following season and have since become something of a yo-yo club, making their most recent return to the top flight in 2010 under Italian manager Roberto di Matteo.

• **The club's record purchase is Spanish midfielder Borja Valero, who joined the Baggies from Mallorca for £4.7 million in 2008. In the same year the club's bank balance was boosted by a record £8.5 million when gangly defender Curtis Davies joined local rivals Aston Villa.**

• Among the famous faces who regularly attend matches at the Hawthorns are comedians Lenny Henry and Frank Skinner, and ITV football presenter Adrian Childs.

HONOURS
Division 1 champions 1920
Division 2 champions 1902, 1911
Championship champions 2008
FA Cup 1888, 1892, 1931, 1954, 1968
League Cup 1966

Bobby Moore lifts the FA Cup to send the Hammers home happy in 1964

TOP 10

DOUBLE FIGURE TOP FLIGHT VICTORIES

1. West Bromwich Albion 12 Darwen 0, 1892
   Nottingham Forest 12 Leicester Fosse 0, 190
3. Aston Villa 12 Accrington 2, 1892
4. Sheffield United 11 Cardiff City 2, 1926
5. Preston North End 10 Stoke City 0, 1889
   Aston Villa 10 Sheffield Wednesday 0, 1912
7. Newton Heath 10 Wolverhampton Wanderers 1, 1892
   Fulham 10 Ipswich Town 1, 1963
9. Stoke City 10 West Bromwich Albion 3, 1937
10. Tottenham Hotspur 10 Everton 4, 1958

WEST HAM UNITED

Year founded: 1895
Ground: Upton Park (35,303)
Previous name: Thames Ironworks
Nickname: The Hammers
Biggest win: 10-0 v Bury (1983)
Heaviest defeat: 2-8 v Blackburn (1963)
Colours: Claret shirts with blue trim, white shorts, white socks

The club was founded in 1895 as Thames Ironworks by shipyard workers employed by a company of the same name. In 1900 the club was disbanded but immediately reformed under its present name.

• **The biggest and best supported club in east London, West Ham have a proud tradition in the FA Cup. In 1923 they reached the first final to be played at the original Wembley stadium, losing 2-0 to Bolton Wanderers.**

• The Hammers experienced a more enjoyable Wembley 'first' in 1965 when they became the first English side to win a European trophy on home soil, defeating Munich 1860 2-0 in the final of the Cup-Winners' Cup.

• **The following year West Ham were the only club to provide three members – Bobby Moore, Geoff Hurst and Martin Peters – of England's World Cup-winning team. Between them Hurst and Peters scored all four of England's goals in the final against West Germany while Moore, as captain, collected the trophy. The Hammers trio's remarkable contribution to the victory is commemorated by a statue near Upton Park.**

• Striker Vic Watson holds three significant goalscoring records for the club. He is West Ham's leading scorer, with an impressive 298 goals league between 1920-35, including a record 42 goals in the 1929/30 season. In the same campaign Watson hit a record six goals in a match, a feat later equalled by Geoff Hurst in an 8-0 drubbing of Sunderland in 1968.

• **No West Ham player has turned out more often for the club than former manager Billy Bonds. Between 1967-88 'Bonzo', as he was dubbed by fans and team-mates alike, appeared in 663 league games.**

• In 1980 West Ham became the last club from outside the top flight to win the FA Cup. The Hammers, then residing in the old Second Division, beat favourites Arsenal 1-0 thanks to a rare headed goal by Trevor Brooking. That was the last of their three FA Cup triumphs, although they were unfortunate to lose the 2006 final to Liverpool on penalties after an exciting 3-3 draw.

• The legendary Bobby Moore is the club's most capped international. He played 108 times for England to set a record that has since only been passed by Peter Shilton and David Beckham.

• In their long and distinguished history West Ham have had just 13 managers, fewer than any other major English club. The longest serving of the dozen was Syd King, who held the reins for 31 years from 1901-32.

• **On Boxing Day 2006 Teddy Sheringham became the oldest player ever to score in the Premier League when he netted for West Ham against Portsmouth aged 40 years and 266 days. Four days later he made his last appearance for the Hammers at Manchester City, stretching his own record as the oldest outfield player in the league's history.**

• The Hammers made their record signing in 2007, shelling out £7.5 million for Liverpool striker Craig Bellamy. The club's record sale came in 2000, when Rio Ferdinand joined Leeds United in an £18 million deal which, at the time, made him the world's most expensive defender.

HONOURS
Division 2 champions 1958, 1981
FA Cup 1964, 1975, 1980
European Cup Winners' Cup 1965

WIGAN ATHLETIC

Year founded: 1932
Ground: JJB Stadium (25,138)
Nickname: The Latics
Biggest win: 7-1 v Scarborough (1997)
Heaviest defeat: 1-9 v Tottenham Hotspur (2009)
Colours: Blue shirts, with white trim, blue shorts, white socks

The club was founded at a public meeting at the Queen's Hotel in 1932 as successors to Wigan Borough, who the previous year had become the first ever club to resign from the Football League.

• After 34 failed attempts, including a bizarre application to join the Scottish Second Division in 1972, Wigan were finally elected to the old Fourth Division in 1978 in place of Southport. The Latics' fortunes, though, only really changed for the better in 1995 when local millionaire and owner of JJB Sports Dave Whelan bought the club and announced his intention to bring Premier League football to the rugby-mad town within ten years.

• Remarkably, Whelan's dream was fulfilled exactly a decade later when Wigan clinched promotion to the Premiership with a 3-1 home win over Reading. Since then, the Latics have confounded the sceptics by retaining their top-flight status despite regularly being among the pre-season favourites for the drop.

• In 2006 Wigan played in a major cup final for the first time in their history when they took on Manchester United in the Carling Cup final at the Millennium Stadium in Cardiff. However, the Latics went home empty-handed after losing 4-0.

• In November 2009 Wigan were hammered 9-1 at Tottenham, only the second time in Premier League history that a side had conceded nine goals. The eight goals the Latics let in after the break was also a record for a Premiership half.

• The club's record goalscorer is Andy Liddell, who hit 70 league goals between 1998-2003. Graeme Jones scored a season's best 33 goals in 1996/97 when Wigan were crowned champions of the Third Division (now League Two).

• No player has pulled on Wigan's blue-and-white stripes more often than Kevin Langley, who made 317 league appearances in two spells at the club between 1981-94.

• Wigan have never got beyond the quarter-finals of the FA Cup but in 1934, while a member of the Northern Premier League, they trounced Carlisle United 6-1 at Brunton Park... the biggest ever win by a non-league club over a league club in the competition's history.

• In June 2009 Wigan received a club record £16 million when they sold Ecuadorian winger Antonio Valencia to Manchester United. Earlier that year they had spent £6 million on their most expensive purchase, Newcastle's Charles N'Zogbia.

• For many years the Latics' most famous fan was thought to be Mikhail Gorbachev, former president of the Soviet Union. While it's true that 'Gorby' attended a friendly match between Wigan and Metallist Kharkov at Springfield Road in 1970 as part of the visitors' delegation, reports of his passion for the Latics are now known to have been concocted by the club's former commercial manager as a publicity stunt.

HONOURS
Second Division champions 2003
Third Division champions 1997
Football League Trophy 1985, 1999

WOLVERHAMPTON WANDERERS

Year founded: 1877
Ground: Molineux (29,195)
Previous name: St Luke's
Nickname: Wolves
Biggest win: 14-0 v Cresswell's Brewery
Heaviest defeat: 1-10 v Newton Heath
Colours: Gold shirts, black shorts, gold socks

Founded as St Luke's by pupils at a local school of that name in 1877, the club adopted its present name after merging with Blakenhall Wanderers

Premier League Wigan were only elected to the Football League in 1978

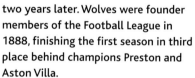
Wolves won the league title three times in the 1950s

two years later. Wolves were founder members of the Football League in 1888, finishing the first season in third place behind champions Preston and Aston Villa.

• The Black Country club enjoyed their heyday in the 1950s under manager Stan Cullis, a pioneer of long ball 'kick and rush' tactics. After a number of near misses, Wolves were crowned league champions for the first time in their history in 1954 and won two more titles later in the decade to cement their reputation as the top English club of the era.

• When Wolves won a number of high profile friendlies against foreign opposition in the 1950s in some of the first ever televised matches they were hailed as 'champions of the world' by the national press, a claim which helped inspire the creation of the European Cup. In 1958 Wolves became only the second English team to compete in the competition, following in the footsteps of trailblazers Manchester United.

• The skipper of that great Wolves team, centre half Billy Wright, is the club's most capped international. Between 1946-59 he won a then record 105 caps for England, captaining his country in 90 of those games.

• Steve Bull is Wolves' record scorer with an incredible haul of 250 league goals between 1986-99. His impressive total of 306 goals in all competitions included a record 18 hat-tricks for the club.

• Stalwart defender Derek Parkin has pulled on the famous gold shirt more often than any other player, making 501 appearances in the league between 1967-82.

• In 1972 Wolves reached the final of the UEFA Cup, losing 3-2 on aggregate to Tottenham in the first ever European final between two English clubs. Two years later the club won the League Cup for the first time, beating Manchester City 2-1 in the final, and in 1980 they repeated that success thanks to a single goal by Andy Gray in the final against Nottingham Forest.

• In August 1999 Wolves sold Robbie Keane to Coventry City for a club record £6 million, the fee also being a then British record for a teenager. In June 2009 newly-promoted Wolves spent a club record £6.5 million on Reading striker Kevin Doyle, and they splashed out the same amount a year later on Burnley's Steven Fletcher.

• In December 2006 Wolves became the first club to score 7,000 league goals, although they have since fallen behind Manchester United in the all-time goalscoring stakes.

• Wolves' most famous fan is veteran singer Robert Plant, formerly the front man of rock legends Led Zeppelin.

HONOURS
Division 1 champions 1954, 1958, 1959
Division 2 champions 1932, 1977
Championship champions 2009
Division 3 (North) champions 1924
Division 3 champions 1989
Division 4 champions 1988
FA Cup 1893, 1908, 1949, 1960
League Cup 1974, 1980
Football League Trophy 1988

IS THAT A FACT?
Wolves were the first team in the country to win all four divisions of the Football League, completing the 'full house' when they captured the Fourth and Third Division titles in consecutive seasons in the late 1980s.

Everton take on Arsenal in the 2010 Women's FA Cup final

WOMEN'S FOOTBALL

The first recorded women's football match took place between the north and south of England at Crouch End, London in 1895. The north won the game 7-1.

• **The Women's FA was founded in 1969 and the first Women's FA Cup final took place two years later, Southampton beating Stewart and Thistle 4-1. The Saints went on to win the cup another seven times in the next ten years, but the most successful side in the competition are Arsenal with ten victories.**

• The Women's Premier League was formed in 1992. Again Arsenal have the best record in the competition with a total of 12 league titles to their name including seven on the trot between 2004-10.

• **The first British international women's match took place in 1972 when England beat Scotland 3-2. In 2005 England recorded their biggest ever win, thrashing Hungary 13-0.**

Their worst defeat was in 2000 when Norway won 8-0. Current well-known players in the England team include goalkeeper Rachel Brown, captain Fara Williams, winger Rachel Yankey and striker Kelly Smith.

• Since it was first competed for in China in 1991 there have been five Women's World Cup tournaments. Germany are the only country to win the competition twice, in 2003 and 2007, and were also runners-up in 1995 to Norway.

• **The top scorer in the tournament is Germany striker Birgit Prinz with a total of 14 goals. In 2003 Prinz was offered the chance to join Italian men's side Perugia, but declined. Had she accepted, she would have been the first ever woman to play in a professional men's league.**

• Germany also hold the record for the biggest win in the tournament, thrashing Argentina 11-0 in 2007.

• **Two players, Kristine Lilly of the USA and Bente Nordby of Norway,** have played in all five editions of the Women's World Cup.

WORLD CLUB CUP

A competition contested between the champion clubs of all six continental confederations of FIFA, the World Club Cup was first played in Brazil in 2000 but has only been an annual tournament since 2005 when it replaced the old Intercontinental Cup.

• **Manchester United's participation in the first World Club Cup led to the Red Devils pulling out of the FA Cup in 2000, a tournament they had won in the previous season. United's decision attracted a lot of criticism at the time, not least from many of their own fans.**

• Brazilian clubs have the best record in the competition, having won three of the six finals. Corinthians set the ball rolling in 2000 and have been followed onto the winners' rostrum by Sao Paulo in 2005 and Internacional in 2006.

• After AC Milan won the 2007 edition, Manchester United became the first British winners of the tournament when a goal by Wayne Rooney saw off Ecuadorian side Quito in the 2008 final in Yokohama. Barcelona won the title in 2009 after beating Estudiantes 2-1 in the final.

WORLD CUP

The most successful country in the history of the World Cup are Brazil, who have won the competition a record five times. Italy are Europe's leading nation with four wins, closely followed by three-time winners Germany. South American neighbours Argentina and Uruguay have both won the competition twice, the Uruguayans emerging victorious when the pair met in the first ever World Cup final in Montevideo in 1930. The only other countries to claim the trophy are England, France and Spain, the first two countries taking advantage of their host nation status to win the competition in 1966 and 1998 respectively, while the Spanish triumphed in South Africa in 2010.

• Including both Japan and South Korea, who were joint hosts for the 2002 edition, the World Cup has been held in 15 different countries. The first nation to stage the tournament twice was Mexico (in 1970 and 1986), while Italy (1934 and 1990), France (1938 and 1998) and Germany (1974 and 2006) have also welcomed the world to the planet's biggest football festival on two occasions each.

• As well as their unique quintet of World Cup victories, Brazil hold a host of lesser records in the competition. The South Americans are the only country to have played at all 19 tournaments, and along with Germany have played in a record seven finals. Brazil, though, are out in front when it comes to total wins (67) and total goals scored (210, including more than a few 25-yard screamers into the top corner from the likes of Rivelino, Zico and Kaka!).

• However, Hungary hold the record for the most goals scored in a single tournament, banging in 27 in just five games at the 1954 finals in Switzerland. Even this incredible tally, though, was not quite sufficient for the 'Magical Magyars' to lift the trophy as they went down to a 3-2 defeat in the final against West Germany, a team they had previously beaten 8-3 earlier in the tournament.

• Hungary also hold the record for the biggest ever victory at the finals, demolishing El Salvador 10-1 in 1982. That, though, was a desperately close encounter compared to the biggest win in qualifying, Australia's 31-0 annihilation of American Samoa in 2001, a game in which Aussie striker Archie Thompson helped himself to a record 13 goals.

• The legendary Pele is the only player in World Cup history to have been presented with three winners' medals. The Brazilian superstar enjoyed his first success in 1958 when he scored twice in a 5-2 rout of hosts Sweden in the final, and was a winner again four years later in Chile despite hobbling out of the tournament with a torn leg muscle in the second match. He then made it a hat-trick in 1970, setting a sparkling Brazil side on the road to an emphatic 4-1 victory against Italy in the final with a trademark bullet header.

The World Cup final is the most-watched event on the planet

Gooaaalll!! Iniesta scores the goal that wins the 2010 World Cup final...

• The leading overall scorer in the World Cup is another famous Brazilian, Ronaldo, who notched 15 goals in total at three tournaments between 1998-2006, including both goals in his side's 2-0 defeat of Germany in the 2002 final.

• **England's Geoff Hurst had previously gone one better in 1966, scoring a hat-trick as the hosts beat West Germany 4-2 in the final at Wembley. His second goal, which gave England a decisive 3-2 lead in extra-time, was the most controversial in World Cup history and German fans still argue to this day that his shot bounced on the line after striking the crossbar, rather than over it. Naturally, England fans generally agree with the eagle-eyed Russian linesman who awarded the goal...**

• Just two players have appeared at a record five World Cups: Germany's midfield playmaker Lothar Matthaus (1982-98) and Mexican goalkeeper Antonio Carbajal (1950-66). Matthaus, though, holds the record for games played, making 25 appearances for his country.

• **Germany are the most successful side in World Cup shoot-outs, winning all four of their penalty duels including one in 1990 when they beat Bobby Robson's plucky England side in the semi-finals before going on to lift the trophy.**

• England may have endured some bitter disappointments at the tournament (including two more shoot-out defeats against Argentina in 1998 and Portugal

in 2006) but the most unfortunate country in World Cup history are arch rivals Scotland, who have made eight appearances at the finals without once advancing to the knock-out stages.

• **The youngest player to appear at the finals is Norman Whiteside, who was just 17 years and 41 days when he made his World Cup debut for Northern Ireland against Yugoslavia at the 1982 tournament in Spain. The competition's oldest player, meanwhile, is Cameroon's Roger Milla, who was aged 42 years and 39 days when he played against Russia in 1994. It was hardly a day to remember for the swivel-hipped striker, though, as Russia won 6-1 with a record five goals coming from the boot of Oleg Salenko.**

• Just two men have won the competition as both a player and a coach: Brazil's Mario Zagallo (in 1958, 1962 and 1970) and Germany's Franz Beckenbauer (in 1974 and 1990).

• **Switzerland went a record 551 minutes without conceding a goal at the 2006 and 2010 World Cups, their fortress-like defence finally being breached by Chile's Mark Gonzalez in a 1-0 defeat in Port Elizabeth, South Africa.**

• In their opening game at the 2010 World Cup Spain went down 1-0 to Switzerland. However, the Spanish recovered to win their group and went on to claim the trophy, to become the first country to lift the World Cup after losing their first match. Spain also set a

new record for the fewest goals scored by the tournament winner after finding the net just eight times in their seven games in South Africa.

• **Honduras made history in the 2010 World Cup when they became the first nation to select three brothers in their squad. Jerry Palacios, who plays up front for Chinese side Hangzhou Greentown, was called up to replace the injured Julio Cesar de Leon. He joined brothers Johnny, a defender who plays for Honduran side Olimpia, and all-action midfielder Wilson, who plays in the English Premiership for Tottenham Hotspur.**

WORLD CUP FINALS
1930 Uruguay 4 Argentina 2 (Uruguay)
1934 Italy 2 Czechoslovakia 1 (Italy)
1938 Italy 4 Hungary 2 (France)
1950 Uruguay 2 Brazil 1 (Brazil)
1954 West Germany 3 Hungary 2 (Switzerland)
1958 Brazil 5 Sweden 2 (Sweden)
1962 Brazil 3 Czechoslovakia 1 (Chile)
1966 England 4 West Germany 2 (England)
1970 Brazil 4 Italy 1 (Mexico)
1974 West Germany 2 Holland 1 (West Germany)

... and Spain lift the most coveted trophy in the game of football for the first time in their history

1978 Argentina 3 Holland 1
(Argentina)
1982 Italy 3 West Germany 1
(Spain)
1986 Argentina 3 West Germany 2
(Mexico)
1990 West Germany 1 Argentina 0
(Italy)
1994 Brazil 0• Italy 0
(USA)
1998 France 3 Brazil 0
(France)
2002 Brazil 2 Germany 0
(Japan/South Korea)
2006 Italy 1• France 1
(Germany)
2010 Spain 1 Holland 0
(South Africa)
• Won on penalties

WORLD CUP GOLDEN BALL

The Golden Ball is awarded to the best player at the World Cup following a poll of members of the global media. The first winner was Italian striker Paolo Rossi, whose six goals at the 1982 World Cup helped the Azzurri win that year's tournament in Spain.

• Rossi was followed in 1986 by another World Cup winner, Argentina captain Diego Maradona, but since then only one player has claimed the Golden Ball and a winners' medal at the same tournament, Brazilian striker Romario in 1994.

• The only goalkeeper to win the award to date is Germany's Oliver Kahn in 2002. The most controversial winner, meanwhile, was France's mercurial midfielder Zinedine Zidane, who was named as the outstanding performer at

TOP 10

SCORERS AT A SINGLE WORLD CUP

1. Just Fontaine (France 1958)   13
2. Sandor Kocsis (Hungary 1954)   11
3. Gerd Muller (West Germany
   1970)   10
4. Eusebio (Portugal 1966)   9
   Ademir Menezes (Brazil 1950)   9
6. Guillermo Stabile (Argentina
   1930)   8
   Ronaldo (Brazil 2002)   8
8. Leonidas da Silva (Brazil 1938) 7
   Jairzinho (Brazil 1970)   7
   Grzegorz Lato (Poland 1974)   7

the 2006 World Cup before the final – a game which ended in disgrace for Zidane after he was sent off for headbutting Italian defender Marco Materazzi.

WORLD CUP GOLDEN BALL WINNERS
1982 Paolo Rossi (Italy)
1986 Diego Maradona (Argentina)
1990 Salvatore Schillaci (Italy)
1994 Romario (Brazil)
1998 Ronaldo (Brazil)
2002 Oliver Kahn (Germany)
2006 Zinedine Zidane (France)
2010 Diego Forlan (Uruguay)

WORLD CUP GOLDEN BOOT

Now officially known as the 'Adidas Golden Shoe', the Golden Boot is awarded to the player who scores most goals in a World Cup finals tournament. The first winner was Guillermo Stabile, whose eight goals helped Argentina reach the final in 1930.

• French striker Just Fontaine scored a record 13 goals at the 1958 tournament in Sweden. At the other end of the scale, nobody managed more than four goals at the 1962 World Cup in Chile, so the award was shared between six players.

• Surprisingly, it wasn't until 1978 that the Golden Boot was won outright by a player, Argentina's Mario Kempes, whose country also won the tournament. Since then only Italy's Paolo Rossi in 1982 and Brazil's Ronaldo in 2002 have won both the Golden Boot and a World Cup winners' medal in the same year.

• The only English player to win the Golden Boot is Gary Lineker, whose six goals in 1986 helped the Three Lions reach the quarter-finals in Mexico.

• At the 2010 World Cup in South Africa Germany's Thomas Muller was one of four players to top the scoring charts with five goals, but FIFA's new rules gave him the Golden Boot because he had more assists than his three rivals for the award, David Villa, Wesley Sneijder and Diego Forlan.

WORLD FOOTBALLER OF THE YEAR

The FIFA World Footballer of the Year was first awarded in 1991 when it was won by Lothar Matthaus of Germany. The award is voted for by coaches and, since 2004, captains of international teams who

nominate their top players in 1-2-3 order.

• Two players, Brazilian striker Ronaldo and France's midfield maestro Zinedine Zidane, have won the award a record three times. Ronaldo picked up the award in 1996, 1997 and 2002, while Zidane was honoured in 1998, 2000 and 2003.

• Brazilian players have won the award a record eight times. No English player has ever won the award, although David Beckham was a runner-up in both 1999 and 2001.

• The oldest winner of the World Footballer of the Year award was 33-year-old Fabio Cannavaro in 2006. The youngest winner was Ronaldo, who was just 20 when he first won the award in 1996.

• Readers of World Soccer magazine have voted for their own World Footballer of the Year since 1982, when Italy's Paolo Rossi topped the poll. The only player to win the award three times is Ronaldo (in 1996, 1997 and 2002) while the only English player to head the list was Michael Owen in 2001.

Messi shows off the 2009 award

BILLY WRIGHT

Born: Ironbridge,
6th February 1924
Died: 3rd September 1994
Position: Defender
Club career:
1946-59 Wolverhampton
Wanderers 490 (13)
International record:
1946-59 England 105 (3)

The first footballer in the world to play 100 times for his country, Billy Wright reached the landmark when he turned out for England against Scotland in 1959. Of his 105 international appearances, 90 were as captain – a record matched by Bobby Moore in 1973 but never beaten

– and a record 70 came in consecutive matches.

• **As an imposing central defender with his one club, Wolves, Wright enjoyed huge success, skippering the Black Country side to three league titles in 1954, 1958**

Billy Wright captained England an incredible 90 times

and 1959 and to victory in the FA Cup in 1949.

• Still the fifth highest-capped England player ever, Wright captained his country at three World Cups in the 1950s but never came close to lifting the trophy. He was also in the England team that was twice humiliated by Hungary, losing 6-3 in 1953 and 7-1 the following year.

• **Wright tried his hand at management with Arsenal in the 1960s, before becoming a top TV executive. His wife, Jo, was a member of the Beverley Sisters singing group.**

WYCOMBE WANDERERS

Year founded: 1887
Ground: Adams Park (10,284)
Nickname: The Chairboys
Biggest win: 15-1 v Witney Town (1955)
Heaviest defeat: 0-8 v Reading (1899)
Colours: Dark-and-light-blue-quartered shirts, dark blue shorts, light blue socks

Wycombe Wanderers were founded in 1887 by a group of young furniture-makers (hence the club's nickname, The Chairboys) but had to wait until 1993 before earning promotion to the Football League.

• **Under then manager Martin O'Neill the club went up to the Second Division (now League One) in their first season, beating Preston in the play-off final.**

• In 2001 The Chairboys caused a sensation by reaching the semi-finals of the FA Cup where they lost 2-1 to eventual winners Liverpool at Villa Park.

• **The club's most capped international is defender Mark Rogers, who played seven times for Canada between 2000-03.**

• In 1956, while still a non-league team, Wycombe became the first British club to play a touring Ugandan team, beating their barefoot visitors 10-1 at their old Loakes Park ground.

> HONOURS
> **Conference champions 1993**
> **FA Amateur Cup 1931**

Lev Yashin

LEV YASHIN

Born: Moscow, 22nd October 1929
Died: 20th March 1990
Position: Goalkeeper
Club career:
1950-71 Dynamo Moscow 326
International record:
1954-67 Soviet Union 74

The legendary Lev Yashin is the only goalkeeper ever to have been voted European Footballer of the Year, winning the award in 1963. A superbly athletic figure between the posts known as the 'Black Panther' (a reference to his all-black kit), he is considered by many to be the best keeper of all time.

• **With club side Dynamo Moscow Yashin won five domestic championships, and he also helped the Soviet Union win the first ever European Championships in 1960 as well as the Olympic Gold in 1956. In 1967 Yashin became the only footballer to be awarded the ultimate honour of the Soviet state, the Order of Lenin.**

• Yashin, who also doubled as an ice hockey goalkeeper early in his career, saved more than 150 penalties. He once said, "The joy of seeing Yuri Gagarin flying in space is only superseded by the joy of saving a good penalty."

• **In 1994 FIFA established the Lev Yashin Award for the best goalkeeper at the World Cup. Four years later he was the only goalkeeper to be voted into the FIFA World Team of the 20th Century.**

(Nearly) last but definitely not least – the brilliant Zinedine Zidane

ZINEDINE ZIDANE

Born: Marseille, France,
23rd June 1972
Position: Midfielder
Club career:
1988-92 Cannes 61 (6)
1992-96 Bordeaux 139 (28)
1996-2001 Juventus 151 (24)
2001-06 Real Madrid 155 (37)
International record:
1994-2006 France 108 (31)

World Player of the Year in 1998, 2000 and 2003, brilliant French midfielder Zinedine Zidane is one of just two players (with Brazilian striker Ronaldo) to win the coveted award three times

• The extravagantly gifted Zidane started out with Cannes and Bordeaux before gaining worldwide attention with Juventus, with whom he won the Serie A title in 1997 and 1998. After five years with the Italian giants he moved to Real Madrid for a then world record fee of £46 million in 2001, and the following year scored a spectacular volleyed winner for his new club in the Champions League final against Bayer Leverkusen.

• Although of Algerian descent, Zidane chose to play for his native France and he became a hero to his fellow countrymen at the 1998 World Cup when he headed two goals in his side's surprisingly comfortable 3-0 defeat of favourites Brazil in the final in Paris. Two years later 'Zizou',

as he was known to his team-mates, was voted player of the tournament as France beat Italy in the final of the European Championships.

• Zidane came out of international retirement to help a struggling French team qualify for the 2006 World Cup. However, his magnificent career ended on a sour note when he was sent off in the final for headbutting Italian defender Marco Materazzi in the chest after his opponent had made derogatory comments about Zidane's family. Nonetheless, Zidane's sublime performances in the finals ensured that he was awarded the Golden Ball as the outstanding player of the tournament.

DINO ZOFF

Born: Mariano del Fruilli, Italy
28th February 1942
Position: Goalkeeper
Club career:
1961-63 Udinese 38
1963-67 Mantova 130
1967-72 Napoli 143
1972-83 Juventus 330
International record:
1968-83 Italy 112

One of just four players to make more than 100 appearances for Italy, Dino Zoff holds the world record for international clean sheets. Between September 1972 and June 1974 he went 1,142 minutes

without conceding a goal, a run which included 12 consecutive games.

• Zoff started his career at hometown club Udinese and played for Mantova and Napoli before enjoying great success with Juventus. During an 11-year stay with the Turin giants he helped Juve win six Serie A titles and the UEFA Cup.

• In 1982, at the age of 40, he became the oldest man ever to win the World Cup when Italy beat West Germany 3-1 in the final. As captain of the side Zoff was only the second goalkeeper (after compatriot Giampiero Combi in 1934) to skipper his country to World Cup glory.

• After a spell managing Juventus, Zoff was appointed coach of the Italian national team in 1998. He led Italy to the final of Euro 2000, but resigned a few days after their 2-1 defeat to France. He later managed Lazio and Fiorentina.

IS THAT A FACT?
Zinedine Zidane is one of just five men to have been dismissed in a World Cup final, along with Dutch defender Joh Heitinga (2010), fellow countryman Marcel Desailly (1998) and Argentines Pedro Monzon and Gustavo Abel Dezotti (1990).